Fairness, Responsibility, and Welfare

Fairness, Responsibility, and Welfare

Marc Fleurbaey

OXFORD
UNIVERSITY PRESS

Great Clarendon Street, Oxford OX2 6DP

Oxford University Press is a department of the University of Oxford.
It furthers the University's objective of excellence in research, scholarship,
and education by publishing worldwide. Oxford is a registered trade mark of
Oxford University Press in the UK and in certain other countries

British Library Cataloguing in Publication Data
Data available

Library of Congress Cataloging in Publication Data
Data available

ISBN 978–0–19–921591–1 (Hbk)
ISBN 978–0–19–965359–1 (Pbk)

Printed and bound by
CPI Group (UK) Ltd, Croydon, CRO 4YY

Contents

Preface to the paperback edition

The first edition of this book has been well received by economists and philosophers and it was particularly rewarding that it inspired Dan Hausman and John Roemer to write papers about the approach developed in it (D. Hausman, "Equality of Autonomy", *Ethics,* 119: 742-56, July 2009; J. Roemer, "On Several Approaches to Equality of Opportunity", *Economics and Philosophy*, forthcoming). We may not agree on everything, but the search for a satisfactory approach goes on, and progress is certainly being made in the mutual understanding of the various theories currently available (see my, "Equal opportunity, reward, and respect for preferences: reply to Roemer", *Economics and Philosophy*, forthcoming).

Since the first edition of this book has been published, two points which are cautiously made in the book have been confirmed by later research. First, as suggested in Section 9.5, the conflict between the principle of compensation and the various principles of reward is connected to a conflict between the ex post perspective that focuses on inequalities within responsibility classes and the ex ante perspective that focuses on the opportunities offered to circumstance classes. In M. Fleurbaey, V. Peragine, "Ex Ante Versus Ex Post Equality of Opportunity" (*Economica*, forthcoming), it is shown that the reward principles studied in this book can be derived from principles of ex ante compensation, all of which are incompatible with the (ex post) principle of compensation.

Second, as suggested in Section 10.4, respecting individual preferences has far-reaching implications for interpersonal comparisons. If one wants to respect the mutual comparisons made by individuals sharing the same preferences, ordinal preferences provide sufficient information for interpersonal comparisons and non-ordinal aspects of subjective well-being are not relevant for the evaluation and comparison of individual well-being in the context of social justice. There is, therefore, a direct implication from respecting preferences to holding individuals responsible for their utility. This point is developed in, "The Importance of What People Care About" (*Politics, Philosophy and Economics*, forthcoming).

Respecting preferences, which was once viewed as a main difficulty for social choice theory, may turn out to be a cornerstone of the development of an egalitarian theory of justice that accommodates and combines fairness, responsibility, and welfare considerations in an appealing way.

M.F., March 2012

Preface

This book emerges from a long story of collaborations and interactions and I am afraid I have lost track of all the direct and indirect help I am indebted for. First, I would like to thank the coauthors of the papers which have provided a good part of the material of this book, Walter Bossert, Dirk Van de gaer, and especially François Maniquet who collaborated on a handbook chapter on compensation and responsibility which formed an early backbone of, and an inducement into, this text. I thank him for his encouragements to develop this project.

John Roemer initially attracted me to this topic during a visit at U.C. Davis, and has always been a great source of inspiration. His comments on this project have been very encouraging. The first chapters were written while I was on sabbatical leave at Nuffield College, Oxford, and I am very grateful to Tony Atkinson and Kevin Roberts for their kind hospitality. During this period, a reading group on hypothetical insurance provided an excellent challenge to understand the attraction of Dworkin's theory, and Chapter 6 has been profoundly influenced by the discussions in this group, in particular with Paula Casal, Tom Christiano, Matthew Clayton, Jerry Cohen and Andrew Williams. At the last stages of preparation of the manuscript, a Lachmann Fellowship at the LSE provided not only an excellent environment to focus on the last chapters, but also the opportunity to benefit from a doctoral seminar on the manuscript, and I am very grateful to the attendants for their comments and their patience with the obscurities of the text. A lecture series at the Norwegian School of Economics provided the last round of valuable comments and I am very grateful to Alexander Cappelen and Bertil Tungodden for their kind invitation, and to the attendants for their reactions. I am also grateful to my colleagues at the University of Pau and at CERSES for their support.

In addition, several persons have made detailed and extremely helpful comments on all or extensive parts of the manuscript: Kristof Bosmans, Juan de Dios Moreno-Ternero, Giacomo Valletta, Dirk Van de gaer, Alex Voorhoeve. I have also benefited from comments on the book or on the related papers by Richard Arneson, François Bourguignon, Ian Carter, Michael Corrado, Valentino Dardanoni, Frédéric Gaspart, Louis Gevers, Paul Gomberg, Peter Hammond, Serge Kolm, Larry Kranich, Julian Lamont, Philippe Mongin, Hervé Moulin, Ruwen Ogien, Martin O'Neill, Erwin Ooghe, Michael Otsuka, Eugenio Peluso, Vito Peragine, Patrick Pharo, Anne Phillips, Mozaffar Qizilbash, Eric Rakowski,

Maurice Salles, Patrick Savidan, Erik Schokkaert, Amartya Sen, Yves Sprumont, Kotaro Suzumura, Koichi Tadenuma, William Thomson, Alain Trannoy, Bertil Tungodden, Peter Vallentyne, Philippe Van Parijs, Dan Wikler, Jo Wolff, and from discussions with Liz Anderson, Claude d'Aspremont, Kenneth Arrow, Harry Brighouse, David Copp, Keith Dowding, Ronald Dworkin, Francisco Ferreira, Wulf Gaertner, Robert Gary-Bobo, Nicolas Gravel, Dan Hausman, Carmen Herrero, Matthias Hild, Iñigo Iturbe-Ormaetxe, Roland-Iwan Luttens, Jorge Nieto, Emmanuel Picavet, Arthur Ripstein, Ingrid Robeyns, Tim Scanlon, Sam Scheffler, Hillel Steiner, Robert Sugden, Robert Van der Veen, Antonio Villar, and Naoki Yoshihara. Alice Obrecht has gone beyond her duty by chasing not only the errors of style but also the ambiguities in content, which has been a great assistance. Sarah Caro, Carol Bestley and Mike Nugent at Oxford University Press have made the preparation of this book a remarkably pleasant process thanks to their competence, enthusiasm and kindness. Last but not least, Christine and Hélène's affectionate company has been a constant reminder of the value of unconditional support in life – an inspiration for this book.

M.F.

Introduction

Why responsibility?

This book is about the distributive implications of the idea that individuals are or should be held responsible, to some degree, for their achievements. The concept of responsibility has been surprisingly absent from important strands of normative thinking in political philosophy and welfare economics alike for a long time and has only become prominent in recent developments.

One may feel some immediate resistance against giving responsibility a conspicuous role. Ill-intentioned ideologues may indeed misuse the notion in order to hastily justify inequalities and unfairly chastise the "undeserving poor."[1] On the other hand, when one tries to imagine a theory of distributive justice in which individuals would have no responsibility whatsoever, or a society in which personal responsibility would not have any role in shaping people's lives, one soon faces difficulties. The distribution of commodities through the market, for instance, leaves it to individual responsibility what particular combinations of goods and services people will eventually consume. The freedom to choose the quantity of one's working hours automatically entails that differential earnings will follow from choices for which one is personally responsible. Responsibility is a necessary consequence of any substantial amount of freedom and is therefore part and parcel of any free society.

The earnings example, however, also shows that public policy can alter the way in which personal responsibility relates to unequal achievements. With different tax schedules, individual choices of working hours and earnings will have different consequences in terms of inequalities in disposable income. An interesting set of issues emerges here. How do personal responsibility and public redistribution interact, and what guidelines for redistribution can follow from a normative reflection on the meaning of responsibility and the requirements of freedom? This is the topic of this book.

This intuitive necessity of taking account of responsibility has now been recognized in many theories of justice. The recent era of responsibility-sensitive egalitarianism starts with Rawls' theory of justice, which focuses on the distribution of rights and resources (primary goods) on the ground that autonomous moral agents must assume responsibility for their personal conceptions of the

---

[1] For an impressive list of examples of this sort, see Barry (2005).

good life and the personal goals and ambitions that are inspired by such conceptions.[2] Roughly speaking, the general scheme is that once rights and resources are equally allotted to all individuals, the differences in well-being that follow from different views of the good life and from the subsequent different uses of the rights and resources are down to individuals' responsibility. This departure from the long-lasting welfarist tradition linked to utilitarianism has been further defended by Dworkin, who pushed the theory ahead by tackling the difficult issue of personal talents and handicaps that call for compensatory transfers and question a simplistic notion of equality of resources.[3] Dworkin proposed to consider such personal characteristics as internal resources, extending the notion of resources accordingly, and he moreover defended the idea of a hypothetical insurance market as an appropriate device embodying the notion of equality of extended resources. In the hypothetical insurance market, individuals would be placed behind a veil of ignorance hiding their personal characteristics and would be able to take insurance against ending up with unfavorable traits. A good resource-egalitarian policy, in practice, would then have to approximate the result of this hypothetical market, with taxes and transfers playing the role of insurance premiums and indemnities.

Arneson and Cohen have since proposed to turn resource-egalitarianism into opportunity-egalitarianism, arguing that it is not appropriate in general simply to provide individuals with resources and to hold them responsible for their goals and their use of the resources. They argue that individuals should be held responsible only for characteristics and decisions that are fully within their control, and that this responsibility line may cut across internal resources and preferences in complex ways.[4] For instance, particular preferences inculcated by education may be harder to satisfy than other preferences in a particular economic environment and may reduce opportunities for welfare in a way that cannot be attributed, so they say, to individual responsibility. Originating from a different perspective, Sen's theory of capabilities and functionings actually comes very close to a similar proposal.[5]

It is an important task for economists to examine how these considerations can be accommodated in welfare economics and in the analysis of public policies of redistribution. In this endeavor economists, hopefully, are not simply confined to the passive role of applying theories of justice, and their analysis might possibly shed light on conceptual problems that have remained unsolved or have simply been ignored by philosophers. Beyond its focus on responsibility, then, this book is also an attempt at a dialogue between economics and philosophy and is motivated by the conviction that such a dialogue can produce results that cannot be achieved when each discipline works in isolation.

The purpose of this book is twofold. The main objective here is to develop a theory of the distributive implications of holding individuals partly respon-

---

[2] See in particular Rawls (1971, 1982, 1993, 2001).

[3] See Dworkin (1981a,b), reprinted with further discussions and extensions in Dworkin (2000).

[4] See in particular Arneson (1989, 1990a), Cohen (1989, 1993).

[5] See, e.g., Sen (1985, 1992, 1993).

sible for their situation. This requires defining a framework in which issues of freedom and responsibility can be conceptualized. The theory will display an array of reasonable criteria for the evaluation of social situations and redistributive policies. In these developments we will go from basic principles to concrete evaluations of welfare policies, via a rigorous line of reasoning which formulates precise requirements embodying ethical principles, identifies criteria which satisfy such requirements, and puts the criteria to work in the evaluation of policies. The criteria developed here can be viewed, in a sense, as extensions and refinements of the traditional social welfare functions which one finds in welfare economics. The traditional functions are not precise enough, or not adequately structured, in order to satisfy the ethical requirements which constitute the topic of this book. Our objective here will be to see how welfare economics can adapt to the new developments in ethical thinking.

A second goal of the book is to suggest that some principles and some lines of thought are more attractive than others, and ultimately to propose a variant of the egalitarian theories of justice which have been listed above. The risk of misusing the concept of responsibility that has been evoked above must be taken seriously, and most responsibility-sensitive theories of justice underestimate this risk by adopting a certain conception of responsibility which lends itself too easily to problematic and controversial applications. It will be argued here that the concept of responsibility can be handled in a better way in order to obtain a theory of justice which, hopefully, is immune to the main controversies about the proper scope of personal responsibility.

The first goal will occupy most of the book. The concepts developed here will touch upon many classic and recent issues of welfare economics and political philosophy, and there are cases in which bringing the question of responsibility to the fore helps to understand and settle certain puzzles which were not transparently connected to it. A flavor of the themes of this book and a hint at their relevance to well-known pending issues can be given by looking at a few examples of the problems addressed here. Let us first pick a few problems from economics, and then a few from philosophy.

Responsibility and economics

Income redistribution. An important topic in public economics is the redistribution of income through taxation. The theory of optimal taxation[6] has conspicuously focused on cases when the population has exactly the same tastes for consumption and leisure and is heterogeneous only in the dimension of skills that determine unequal market wages. A main topic of study has been the relation between the degree of inequality aversion of the government and the formula of the tax schedule. The assumption of identical tastes is relaxed mostly in studies which confine themselves to the study of efficiency considerations. The

---

[6] Mirrlees (1971) is the seminal reference. For more recent sources, see in particular Atkinson (1995) and Boadway and Keen (2004).

reason for keeping such an unrealistic assumption in most redistribution studies can be traced to two problems. One is the difficulty of studying incentive constraints when economic agents are heterogeneous in several dimensions. The mere determination of the set of feasible allocations becomes somewhat nightmarish in what are called "multidimensional screening" problems.[7] The second problem blocking the incorporation of heterogeneous preferences into taxation theory is the difficulty of formulating a precise social objective when individuals differ in tastes. Social welfare functions can be more easily parameterized when all individuals have the same preferences which can be represented by a unique utility function. With heterogeneous preferences, the problem of choosing different utility functions representing those preferences is much trickier and welfare economics is traditionally quite embarrassed with defining a precise social welfare function in this case. Moreover, there is a normative asymmetry between tastes and skills. Presumably, income inequalities coming from taste differences should not be viewed in the same fashion as inequalities due to skill differences. As already argued above, choice of working hours should be left free, and therefore it does not call for the same distributive concern as unequal earning potential.[8] Additional complexity is due to the fact that differences in earning potential can also sometimes be due to choices of specialization in education which do not raise the same distributional concern as inequalities in learning ability or social background for which the individuals are clearly not responsible. Conversely, the taste for leisure is partly linked to the menu of jobs to which agents have access in view of their qualifications, and it is no wonder that, for similar wage rates, people tend to volunteer less for overtime work in dangerous and unpleasant jobs than in pleasant jobs. In this book these issues will be addressed and it will be shown how taste heterogeneity can be incorporated into a social objective under various assumptions about personal responsibility for tastes, labor quantity and skill level. It will also be examined how such social objectives can be used for concrete policy evaluation.

No-envy and unequal skills. The conjunction of unequal skills and different preferences over leisure and consumption has also been an early source of concern in the theory of fair allocation, which has emerged independently of the main stream of public economics.[9] The main concept of equity in the first developments of this theory was the criterion of no-envy. An allocation is envy-free when no agent prefers another's bundle (of consumption and leisure) to his own. Pazner and Schmeidler (1974) noted that, in a production economy where *hardworking unskilled* agents coexist with *lazy talented* agents, it may be impossible to find an envy-free and Pareto-efficient allocation, because efficiency requires the talented to work more, but then, out of laziness, they envy the unskilled if

---

[7] A synthetic analysis is made by Rochet and Stole (2003).

[8] Boadway et al. (2002) represents a nice attempt to tackle these issues with standard weighted utilitarian social welfare functions. They examine the span of possible weights for different utility functions. The analysis presented in this book can be viewed as offering a way to obtain more precise social criteria and therefore more precise policy conclusions.

[9] The seminal reference is Kolm (1972). A recent survey can be found in Moulin and Thomson (1997).

they do not receive enough consumption, and when they do, the unskilled envy them. The literature[10] then focused on two special allocations that retain some flavor of the no-envy criterion. One, called the "wealth-fair" solution, consists in applying the no-envy test not to consumption and leisure but to consumption and earnings. The policy that distributes unearned income equally and lets people retain their earnings satisfies this criterion, by giving exactly the same opportunities for consumption and earnings to everybody. This is clearly unsatisfactory, as it does not perform any correction of inequalities due to skills. The other, called the "full-income-fair" solution, equalizes the maximum potential income that agents can have by working maximum time. The idea of adding the value of leisure to ordinary income in order to compute full income is widespread in applied works on the measurement of living standards.[11] This is, however, a questionable idea. As noted by Dworkin (1981b), equality of full incomes entails a "slavery of the talented" since the skilled agents then have a smaller budget set than the unskilled, and will typically be forced to work in order to pay their taxes. In this book we will study a variety of alternative solutions which are preferable to these two, and also more faithful to the original no-envy test.

Needs. While tastes and preferences are given a prominent role, needs are almost absent from welfare economics. This leads analysts to puzzling conclusions in some cases. Champsaur and Laroque (1981) study allocations that are envy-free and Pareto-efficient in large exchange economies (i.e., economies with no production). They show that when the diverse preferences of the population are sufficiently connected (roughly, this means that one can put agents on a line such that any pair of neighbors have almost the same preferences), then all envy-free and Pareto-efficient allocations give the same income to all agents. In their interpretation, this precludes giving additional income to a disabled person unless his preferences are disconnected from the rest of the population, such as paralytics who are the only persons to desire wheel-chairs. In order to reach such a conclusion, one must consider that individual characteristics of tastes and needs are lumped together in effective "preferences" and cannot be disentangled. We will see in this book how identifying a need parameter in people's preferences can yield different conclusions, since even a disabled person who has the same market demand as another person can receive a special income allowance if the need parameter can be observed. A variant of the no-envy criterion can still be useful for the calibration of this allowance, as we will see.

Another example is provided by Yaari and Bar-Hillel's (1984) questionnaire survey of opinions about distributive justice. They observe a striking difference in the pattern of answers when respondents are confronted with a distribution of fruits to individuals with different metabolism for the assimilation of vitamins from different fruits and when they are confronted with a distribution of fruits to individuals with different willingness to pay for various fruits, reflecting taste differences. In the former case, the respondents try to achieve equality of

---

[10] In particular Varian (1974, 1975).
[11] See, e.g., Nordhaus and Tobin (1973), and, more recently, OECD (2005).

outcomes across the population, whereas in the latter they give answers compatible with utilitarianism (give more of a fruit to those who enjoy it more) and also with an egalitarian auction (incomes being equalized, give more of a fruit to those who pay more for it) – the authors do not try to sort out which of these two solutions is really inspiring the answers. This paper is famous for questioning the welfarist approach to distributive justice and for suggesting that there is no single acceptable social criterion that is valid in all contexts. But the approach set out in this book gives us a simple explanation for this pattern of answers. If one considers that people are responsible for their tastes, or in other words, free to choose according to their tastes, whereas they are not held responsible for their metabolism, then a single social criterion can espouse our intuitions in the two contexts. For instance, consider the criterion that seeks equality of the hypothetical well-being that each individual would achieve if the characteristics for which he is responsible were at the average value. This criterion will play an important role in this book. When individuals differ only in their metabolism (for which they are not responsible), this criterion seeks equality of achieved well-being. When they differ in their willingness-to-pay and are responsible for it, then equality of incomes in a competitive auction is fine, since every individual would then achieve the same level of well-being if he had the average preferences.

Freedom. Following Sen's (1988) insistence on the importance of freedom, an important literature has emerged that studies the measurement of individual freedom on the one hand, and the distribution of opportunities on the other hand, in two related branches. Much of this literature firmly rejects welfarism and is attracted toward evaluating and comparing opportunity sets in terms of the number of options or the volume of the sets. A lot of it adopts an abstract framework which does not lend itself easily to applications.[12] Measuring the value of opportunity sets in an abstract setting appears particularly difficult because the concrete elements that determine the relative value of different dimensions of freedom are absent from the framework. The approach adopted in this book deliberately focuses on economic models which are more directly relevant to application issues. In particular, we will see how the value of an opportunity set can be assessed when there is sufficient information about how this set contributes to people's well-being in various precise circumstances. In the literature on the measurement of individual freedom, there is some work that examines how the value of a menu can be assessed from the point of view of a list of potential preferences that an individual could have.[13] This approach has had little application to the social question of distributing opportunities to a population of individuals. Although the question will be approached here from a different angle, this book will propose various ways of measuring the value of opportunity sets in concrete settings, which will be directly connected to the idea of referring to hypothetical preferences.

---

[12] Surveys of this literature can be found in Peragine (1999), Barbera, Bossert and Pattanaik (2004).

[13] See in particular Nehring and Puppe (1999).

Responsibility and philosophy

Let us now turn to problems that have occupied philosophers in related areas.

Reward and desert. Two very influential definitions of equality of opportunity are the following:

> We should ... compensate only for those welfare deficits which are not in some way traceable to the individual's choices. (Cohen 1989, p. 914).

> Distributive justice does not recommend any intervention by society to correct inequalities that arise through the voluntary choice or fault of those who end up with less, so long as it is proper to hold the individuals responsible for the voluntary choice or faulty behavior that gives rise to the inequalities. (Arneson 1990a, p. 176)

These important sentences have attracted a lot of attention, especially regarding the way they delineate the sphere of responsibility in relation to choice. What has been less closely examined by philosophers is the negative formulation they are based upon. These sentences do not simply say that unfair inequalities, i.e., those for which individuals are not responsible, should be corrected. They say that redistribution should stop at the border of individual responsibility. This is at least the clear meaning of Cohen's sentence. Arneson's is more ambiguous, and a grammatically correct interpretation of it would be that distributive justice does not say anything about inequalities arising from responsible choice. But this cautious interpretation is not the most natural one.

As it will be explained at length in the first chapters of this book, a contribution of economic analysis to this issue has been to disentangle the two separate ethical principles contained in such sentences. There is total logical independence (and even substantial tension) between the "compensation" principle saying that inequalities not due to responsibility should be eliminated and the particular "reward" principle saying that inequalities due to responsibility should be left untouched. As we will see, the compensation principle can be combined with a variety of alternative reward principles.

The philosophical literature has remained vague on this issue, except in relation to the danger of a laissez-faire policy that could leave an individual in dire straits whenever his situation can be traced to his responsible choice. Arneson, considering this problem, has adopted a modified version of responsibility-sensitive egalitarianism in which social priorities would take account of desert and responsibility but might still monitor the achieved level of welfare in order to avoid disproportionate penalties for those who poorly exercise their responsibility.[14] A main topic of this book will be the discussion of various reward principles that can be adopted in the context of responsibility-sensitive egalitarianism. The compensation principle itself has been the topic of other controversies which will be also scrutinized here, such as Hurley's (2003) alleged

---

[14]See in particular Arneson (1999a, 2000a).

discovery of an "egalitarian fallacy." According to her, it is wrong to believe that neutralizing the effect of factors for which individuals are not responsible entails some kind of equality, because the benchmark position from which these factors have an effect need not be egalitarian.

Brute luck and option luck. Examples of disproportionate penalty typically involve risky behavior, such as a motorbiker who has an accident without wearing a helmet. Such examples evoke Dworkin's famous distinction between "brute luck" (for which individuals are not responsible) and "option luck" (for which they are, because they have voluntarily submitted to a particular risk). This distinction has been criticized as hard to define in precise terms, and may be flawed.[15] For instance, individuals who find lottery tickets in the street and collect them may then end up with unequal prizes. Is that a matter of option luck, because they had the option not to collect the tickets? That is a strange conclusion, since collecting the tickets was obviously the rational thing to do in this case. Dworkin readily acknowledged that the distinction is fuzzy in practice, but we will examine the theoretical underpinnings of such a distinction. A priori, it does not make much sense to attribute responsibility to individuals for random events over which they have no control whatsoever, so the notion of option luck is, at a basic level, quite suspect. But we will see that, nonetheless, it is possible to make sense of standard uses of this notion by reference to a particular social criterion that will be studied in this book.

Hypothetical insurance. Dworkin's version of responsibility-sensitive egalitarianism gives an important role to the no-envy criterion introduced above. Instead of applying this criterion simply to ordinary consumption, Dworkin (1981b) applies it to extended resources, i.e., external resources plus internal parameters for which individuals are not responsible. This is clever because it naturally pushes in the direction of compensation of inequalities of internal resources by counteracting transfers in external resources. The problem well identified by Dworkin is that an envy-free allocation fails to exist in general because individuals who disagree about the value of their internal resources may have envy in one direction or the other for all possible levels of transfers. Think for instance of a painter who would like to have musical talents and a musician who regrets not having painting talents. They will tend to envy each other, and any transfer between them will increase the envy of the donor. The solution Dworkin proposes for this puzzle is to apply the no-envy test in a hypothetical insurance market in which individuals could, behind a veil of ignorance, insure against bad lots of internal resources. The no-envy test is then simply satisfied by giving them equal endowments to buy insurance in this market. The problem with this solution is that it radically alters the nature of the solution. In particular, in cases when an envy-free allocation was feasible in the simple application of the no-envy test to extended resources, the result of the hypothetical insurance can be very different.[16] Such a discrepancy proves that the hypothetical insurance is not a refinement or an extension of the no-envy test

---

[15] See, e.g., Lippert-Rasmussen (2001), Otsuka (2002), Dowding (2008).

[16] See Roemer (1985, 2002a), Fleurbaey (2002).

applied to extended resources.

Dworkin's solution, therefore, is not a clever adaptation of his initial idea, but a radical move that betrays his own initial vision. In this book we will see how, from the same starting point, a different direction could have been taken that is more faithful to the initial idea, and indeed yields more intuitively appealing solutions (e.g., giving extended resources of equal value to those with identical preferences). The solution is not to apply the no-envy test to a radically different setting such as insurance behind a veil of ignorance, but to weaken the requirements of the no-envy test so as to find feasible criteria. It turns out that this logical analysis of the no-envy criterion is closely connected to the analysis of compensation and reward principles introduced in the previous point. We will also analyze why the hypothetical insurance mechanism is not acceptable for responsibility-sensitive egalitarians, not only because of its strange consequences mentioned above, but also because of its basic underpinnings.

The indexing dilemma. Some responsibility-sensitive egalitarian theories, such as Rawls', Cohen's and Sen's, advocate measuring advantage in at least partly objective terms. Rawls' notion of "primary goods" makes his the most objectivist of these approaches, and it has been attacked[17] as being trapped in a dilemma that also affects the other theories. In all these theories, an index must aggregate the various dimensions of advantage for each individual, so that individuals can be compared, in particular in order to determine who are the worst-off. If the index espouses people's preferences, then, it is alleged, it is an index of utility and the approach falls back into welfarism. Moreover, this solution seems to blur the Rawlsian distinction between resources for which individuals are not responsible and subjective ambitions and goals for which, as autonomous moral agents, they are. The alternative horn of the dilemma is to impose a uniform index to all individuals, independently of their own preferences, but this index necessarily involves a special view on the relative importance of the various dimensions of advantage, and this seems akin to imposing a perfectionist view of the good. This is another position which these theories definitely want to avoid. Here we will show that this dilemma has been greatly exaggerated, and that it is possible to combine respect for individual preferences with a substantial degree of non-welfarism and of personal responsibility for one's preferences.

There are many other topics from the philosophical literature that will be touched upon here. For instance, Van Parijs' (1995) undominated diversity criterion will be critically examined, refined, and compared to other criteria. His plea for the highest possible basic income will receive support, although from a somewhat different line of thought. The role of desert in Roemer's (1998) and Arneson's (2000a) theories will also be discussed.

---

[17]In particular by Arrow (1973), Kolm (1972), Arneson (1990b).

Is responsibility-sensitive egalitarianism half-libertarian or half-utilitarian?

As announced above, an important theme in this book is the selection of an appropriate reward principle for the apportionment of personal outcomes to personal responsibility. Remaining agnostic on the reward principle is not a possibility, if only because this would condemn responsibility-sensitive egalitarianism to impotence on many practical issues, since the choice of particular policies will often necessarily embody special responses to this problem. In fact, the concept of responsibility itself suggests one or maybe two plausible reward principles. One is the "liberal" reward principle, according to which no further redistribution should be performed beyond what is required by the compensation principle. The quotations of Arneson and Cohen above were clearly in this vein. This may be called liberal because the absence of intervention may be viewed as a hallmark of neutrality toward different ways of exercising responsibility. One can also connect this reward principle to libertarianism, in particular because it implies that laissez-faire is the best policy (in absence of market failures) in the hypothetical situation in which all individuals enjoy equal circumstances and are fully responsible for their differences. As a result, responsibility-sensitive egalitarianism then appears as a middle way between outcome egalitarianism and libertarianism.

This approach is more or less explicitly suggested by most of the philosophical literature.[18] An alternative reward principle, originating in the economic literature, locates responsibility-sensitive egalitarianism between outcome egalitarianism and sum-utilitarianism. It is based on the idea that insofar as individuals are responsible for their differences, the social criterion may have no aversion to inequality, which, for traditional social welfare functions, means that one can simply maximize the sum total of individual well-being levels, as in the so-called "utilitarian" social welfare function. This alternative reward principle then legitimizes redistribution above and beyond what is required by the compensation principle in order to enhance the total outcome of individuals similarly situated with respect to circumstances. We will call this the "utilitarian" reward principle, by reference to its focus on the sum of well-beings.[19]

The economic literature on equality of opportunities has actually developed in two directions reflecting this divide. In one direction of research, Roemer and Van de gaer[20] have proposed combinations of the maximin and the utilitarian social welfare functions with the idea that a high aversion to inequality can be applied along the dimension of circumstances whereas a zero aversion to inequality is acceptable along the dimension of responsibility. This line of analysis

---

[18] An exception is Voorhoeve (2005). Arneson's (1999a, 2000a) recent views are also heading toward a more complex scheme, which will be discussed later in the book.

[19] This should not be confused with the utilitarian theory of responsibility, which advocates legal penalties determined according to their global consequences for society (including deterrence effects).

[20] See Roemer (1993, 1998) and Van de gaer (1993).

thus embraces the utilitarian reward principle briefly described above.[21] The liberal reward principle has been adopted by another branch of the literature.[22] Bossert and Fleurbaey have studied the idea of compensating inequalities due to circumstances only, while leaving other inequalities untouched.[23] Their framework was a simple model in which money can be used to make transfers and redistribution can be made with full information of individuals' characteristics. Fleurbaey and Maniquet have studied the case in which individuals work with unequal productivity and may have different preferences about consumption and leisure.[24] Many other contributions have enriched this approach with a variety of solutions and concepts.[25]

Whether responsibility-sensitive egalitarianism leans toward libertarianism or utilitarianism should be an important matter of debate for philosophers and economists because this has considerable consequences over the orientation of public policies. The two approaches are perhaps acceptable in different contexts, but if it is the case, it is urgent to determine which contexts are appropriate for each approach. A central message of this book is that this divide, which seems to have gone largely unnoticed in the philosophical literature, should attract much more attention.

In the early developments of the economic literature on equal opportunities, an important difference between the two branches, in addition to the difference in reward principles, was the following. The social welfare functions proposed by the utilitarian branch made it possible to rank all allocations in any context, so that they could be used in the evaluation of any kind of social policy.[26] In contrast, the liberal branch started by studying the special context in which the redistributive authority has full information about individuals' characteristics and can redistribute resources on the basis of this information. This is what is called the first-best context, as opposed to the second-best context in which lack of information about individuals makes it harder for the authorities to redistribute appropriately.[27] One problem for the liberal branch was then to extend its first-best allocation rules, which simply selected the best allocations under full information, into fine-grained rankings of all allocations, similar to social welfare functions, so as to be able to address more realistic policy issues.

---

[21] Further contributions to this approach include Bossert, Fleurbaey and Van de gaer (1999), Goux and Maurin (2002), Hild and Voorhoeve (2004), Mariotti (2003), Ooghe and Lauwers (2003), Ooghe, Schokkaert and Van de gaer (2003), Schokkaert et al. (2004), Peragine (2002, 2004), Roemer (2002b).

[22] This presentation is a reconstruction. None of the initial publications makes a case for adopting a particular reward principle as opposed to the other.

[23] See Bossert (1995), Fleurbaey (1994, 1995a,b,c,d), and Bossert and Fleurbaey (1996).

[24] See in particular Fleurbaey and Maniquet (1996, 1999).

[25] See in particular Cappelen and Tungodden (2002, 2003, 2006a,b, 2007a,b,c), Fleurbaey and Maniquet (2005), Gaspart (1996, 1998), Iturbe-Ormaetxe (1997), Iturbe-Ormaetxe and Nieto (1996), Kolm (1996a, 2004a,b), Maniquet (1998, 2004), Moulin (1994), Sprumont (1997) and Tungodden (2005).

[26] See, e.g., Roemer (1998), Roemer et al. (2003).

[27] As an example of second-best context, think of income tax, when the government cannot distinguish between a high-skilled individual who works part time and a low-skilled individual working full time, when their total earnings are equal.

This extension has since then been made,[28] and will be presented and further refined below. As a result, we now have a variety of operational social criteria, for each of the two branches and for any context of application. It makes it possible to compare the implications of the various relevant ethical principles with substantial precision.

Outline of the book

The book starts by examining the simple context in which there is a well-defined process determining individual well-being as a function of personal characteristics and money. These characteristics are fixed and are separated into circumstances (for which individuals are not responsible) and responsibility characteristics. Redistribution operates through transfers of money. This very simple framework is quite useful in order to analyze the basic structure of solutions in a simple way, and many of the concepts and qualitative results obtained with it carry over to the more complex settings studied in the sequel. It is the topic of the first two chapters.

Among the complexities introduced later on, from Chapter 3 to 5, are incentive issues, arising when imperfect information about individual characteristics and choices constrains redistributive policies, and multidimensional redistribution involving several goods, as in certain forms of in-kind transfers. The link between incentives and responsibility is quite interesting to analyze because, as one may guess, incentive constraints typically force public policies, to some extent, to let individual agents bear the consequences of their choices, which is akin to implementing liberal responsibility principles.[29]

The problem of redistributing income when unequal earnings are jointly due to unequal skills and different amounts of work combines both kinds of additional complexity (incentives and multidimensionality). Indeed, incentive effects obviously matter in the influence of taxation over the labor supply, and the presence of labor and consumption make for a multidimensional set of external resources, even though labor is not as directly transferable as money. This particular setting is given a rather detailed scrutiny in Chapters 4 and 5, due to its practical importance and central place in redistributive policies. Income redistribution is also a key topic in public economics, and incorporating fairness notions in the definition of social objectives makes it possible to obtain more precise conclusions about optimal policies than with general unspecified social welfare functions.

Chapter 6 is devoted to the difficult context of risky behavior. Individuals are typically not responsible for being lucky or unlucky, but they may expose themselves to various degrees of risk, and it is not a simple matter to determine

---

[28] In particular in Bossert et al. (1999) and Fleurbaey and Maniquet (2005, 2006, 2007, 2008).

[29] One may even suspect that popular support for responsibility-sensitive policies is grounded in pragmatic incentive concerns more than normative considerations about fairness. Interesting opinion polls about the principles of responsibility-sensitive egalitarianism are analyzed in Schokkaert and Devooght (1998, 2003). See also Gaertner and Schwettmann (2007).

the fair allocation of insurance in this context. Dworkin has proposed a famous but contentious distinction between brute luck (for which individuals are not responsible) and option luck (for which they are), and this chapter examines whether one can make sense of it. It turns out that the concepts developed in the first chapters are quite useful for shedding light on this issue.

Chapter 7 examines a particular variant of the incentive problem that has to do with the possibility for individuals to regret their past decisions and to request help in order to alleviate their regret. In a hard-hearted version of responsibility-sensitive egalitarianism their plight does not call for any particular concern, but it can be argued that individuals who change their mind need not bear the consequences of their past decisions for all their lives. This chapter studies the normative reasons for policies giving special help, a "fresh start," to such regretful people, and the practical possibilities and constraints due to the possibility for them to misrepresent their preferences and to express feigned regret just in order to be eligible for help.

These first chapters focus on the liberal approach to reward, which is closer to the commonsense understanding of the distributive implications of responsibility and also closer to philosophical formulations of the ideal of equality of resources or opportunities. The utilitarian approach to reward, epitomized in social welfare functions combining the maximin and the sum criteria such as Roemer's function, is the topic of Chapter 8. A description of the various options available in this approach and of the underlying ethical issues is followed by a comparison with the solutions put forth by the liberal approach.

The criteria studied in all these chapters take a global perspective on social evaluation, but one is sometimes interested in a partial aspect of distributions, such as the degree of inequality (of opportunities, for instance), or the degree of social mobility (from one generation to another). Such notions are examined in Chapter 9, with a variety of approaches and indices being scrutinized.

As this outline makes clear, the bulk of the book is about analyses coming from economics, and a central goal here is to make this material available in a synthetic, convenient way for economists, and in an accessible form to philosophers as well. The hope is in particular that some insights obtained in economic analysis may be helpful to the formulation of philosophical theories of justice and may even provide new concepts and additional topics for philosophical questioning. Meanwhile, in the direction of economists, the hope is also to make the recent theories of justice and the notion of responsibility more familiar and more easily applicable in the discussion of public policies.

The first chapters of the book mostly take for granted that there is a certain given definition of the sphere of personal responsibility, and work out the *implications* of this separation between "responsibility" and "circumstances." It is indeed valuable to develop a conceptual apparatus that is flexible enough to apply various conceptions of the responsibility sphere. Some discussions on the philosophical issue of defining the scope of personal responsibility appear in various chapters, especially Chapters 3, 6 and 7, but a complete examination of this issue is postponed to the last chapter. In this perspective, the last chapter examines the opposition between Rawls and Dworkin's view that individuals should assume responsibility for their goals and preferences and Arneson and Cohen's view that individuals should only be held responsible for variables under their genuine control. It also examines how the value of freedom is connected to personal responsibility. It proposes a variant of responsibility-sensitive egalitarianism (dubbed "equality of autonomy") which accommodates responsibility and freedom concerns in a different way from opportunity theories, and, building on the concepts developed in the first chapters, suggests how to construct a criterion for interpersonal comparisons and the evaluation of social situations.

A reader's guide

Making material that contains formal analysis accessible to a wide readership is always a challenge, and the method adopted in this book is similar to the widely celebrated separation of formal and non-formal chapters in Sen (1970). The separation is made here in sections. A section containing substantial mathematical modelling is marked by a star *, and the text is organized so that a reader skipping the formal sections would not miss any important concept or experience gaps in the reading. Formalism is not totally absent from the non-formal sections, due to the need of enough structure for the presentation of some concepts, but a special effort has been made to keep it to the minimum necessary.

The separation of formal sections from the main text entails some repetitions for the mathematically oriented reader, who will find the general explanations and motivations separated from the formal definitions and results. But hopefully the disruption is limited, and the proximity of formal sections to their non-formal counterparts makes this acceptable.

In the formal and non-formal parts alike, the text introduces conditions (axioms) that embody the various fairness principles studied in this book. By searching their name (e.g., *Equal Well-Being for Equal Responsibility*) in the index one can immediately locate their definition.

*General mathematical conventions

The main mathematical conventions and notations, in this book, are as follows.

The set of real (resp., non-negative, positive) numbers is $\mathbb{R}$ (resp., $\mathbb{R}_+$, $\mathbb{R}_{++}$). Vector inequalities are denoted $\geq, >, \gg$, and set inclusion is denoted $\subseteq, \subsetneq$.

For any set N, $|N|$ denotes its cardinality; Π_N denotes the set of permutations over N (i.e., bijections from N to N).

An ordering is a binary relation that is reflexive and transitive.

The symbol $\geq_{\mathrm{lex}}$ denotes the leximin (lexicographic maximin) ordering applied to vectors of real numbers. Namely, $x \geq_{\mathrm{lex}} x'$ if the lowest component of x is greater than the lowest component of x', or they are equal and the second lowest component of x is greater than the second lowest component of x', and so on.

Chapter 1

Defining fairness

1.1 Introduction

The aim of this chapter is to decipher some fairness requirements inspired by the responsibility-sensitive egalitarian ideal. It starts with a simple example in which a "natural" solution offers itself as almost self-evident, but will show that this solution actually involves two different ethical principles. One is the compensation principle, and the other is the liberal reward principle. These two principles are not precise distributive requirements; as will be discussed, they are embodied in a variety of specific conditions which are in some ways interrelated but in other ways quite different. The chapter discusses the foundations of such principles and conditions as well as the logical links between the conditions in a simple framework. It also extends the analysis to more general situations in which no natural solution is immediately apparent.

The framework of analysis for this chapter and the next is the simplest context possible. In this special context it is assumed that individuals have personal characteristics which are fixed and that a clear distinction separates characteristics for which they are responsible and characteristics for which they are not responsible. The assumption that characteristics are fixed is made so that no incentive issue arises in relation to a possible influence of redistribution over personal characteristics (this topic will be dealt with in a later chapter). As far as the separation of responsibility characteristics from other characteristics is concerned, its basis need not be elucidated here. It may be a separation between internal resources and preferences, as in Dworkin's view, or between circumstantial and controlled characteristics, as in Arneson and Cohen's definition of responsibility. We will focus here not on this problem, which will be addressed at the end of the book, but on the *distributive consequences* of attributing responsibility to individuals for some of their personal traits. It is useful at this point to fix some terminology. The characteristics for which individual are responsible will generally be called "responsibility characteristics," while those for which they are *not* responsible will generally be called "circumstances." In examples, of course, some more precise denominations will be used.

A second simplifying feature of the context under consideration here is that individuals' achievements are measured by a one-dimensional index of well-being, so that there is no problem in comparing and ranking them. This particular simplification will be retained throughout the bulk of the book, although it will soon appear that it plays little role in the construction of social criteria pertaining to the liberal approach to responsibility and reward. In the last chapter this issue will be examined in more detail.

A third simplifying feature is that we assume here that individual well-being is fully determined by personal characteristics (coming in the two categories mentioned above) and by a one-dimensional external transfer of a resource called "money." Moreover we will assume that individual well-being always increases with money, a rather standard assumption in Western-style economics and political philosophy alike, although, after due reflection, it is probably false for a morally sophisticated notion of well-being. It is nonetheless a useful simplification because it removes any complication arising from individual heterogeneous preferences over external resources, and makes Pareto efficiency an easy matter. The case of multidimensional resources is tackled later on. Satiation phenomena, due for instance to the emollient effects of affluence, will also be briefly examined in another chapter.

A fourth simplifying feature is that money is available in a given quantity that the government can distribute at will. It is not a cake the size of which depends on the incentive effects of redistribution, as in the context of production studied in Chapters 4 and 5.

A fifth and last (but not least) simplification comes from the assumption that we are in a "first-best" context, i.e., that the government has full knowledge of every individual's characteristics, so that redistribution can be fine-tuned in order to promote any conceivable and consistent ethical goal. This seems a very unrealistic assumption and it will be relaxed later on. The usefulness of this assumption comes from the fact that, first, there are special contexts in which this assumption is satisfied or almost so, and above all, the notions developed in this special setting are quite useful to study more complex cases and can be extended without much difficulty.[1]

1.2   *Model and notations

The population is $N = \{1, ..., n\}$, and every individual $i \in N$ is endowed with two kinds of characteristics: y_i, for which she is not responsible (circumstances), and z_i, for which she is. A profile of characteristics is $(y_N, z_N) = ((y_1, ..., y_n), (z_1, ..., z_n))$. The sets from which y_i and z_i are drawn, denoted Y and Z respectively, are assumed to have at least two elements. In some cases

---

[1]Philosophers, who typically take account of incentive issues even when they talk about "ideal" theory (Rawls 2001, p. 13), may be disconcerted by this first step of the analysis. Hopefully this book will make them more familiar with the standard economic methodology which has been quite successful in producing a good understanding of redistributive issues.

further assumptions on their structure will be introduced.

Individual i's well-being is denoted u_i and is determined by a function u which is the same for all individuals:

$$u_i = u(x_i, y_i, z_i),$$

where $x_i \in X \subseteq \mathbb{R}$ is the quantity of money transfer to which individual i is submitted. When $x_i < 0$, the transfer is a tax. The function u is assumed to be continuous and increasing in x_i over X.

An economy is denoted $e = ((y_N, z_N), \Omega)$, where Ω is an aggregate endowment. An allocation is denoted $x_N = (x_1, \ldots, x_n) \in X^N$. More generally, for any subpopulation $G \subseteq N$, the notation x_G stands for $(x_i)_{i \in G}$. The set of feasible allocations is

$$F(e) = \left\{ x_N \in X^N \mid \sum_{i \in N} x_i = \Omega \right\}.$$

As u is increasing in x_i, all allocations in $F(e)$ are Pareto efficient. This considerably simplifies the analysis.

This model is very similar to the model of allocation of indivisible goods, in which y is a transferable but indivisible resource and x is a transferable and divisible good.[2] What is studied here can be interpreted as a situation in which the indivisibles have already been distributed and it only remains to allocate the divisible good.[3]

Two general concepts of solutions will be useful here. Let $\mathcal{D}$ be the domain of economies $e = ((y_N, z_N), \Omega)$ under consideration and $\mathcal{P}$ be the corresponding domain of profiles $e_p = (y_N, z_N)$. An *allocation rule* is a correspondence S such that for all $e \in \mathcal{D}$, $S(e) \subseteq F(e)$. The set $S(e)$ is the subset of allocations selected by S. This chapter and the next one will focus on allocation rules, but starting in Chapter 3 we will also be interested in social ordering functions. A *social ordering function* is a mapping R such that for all $e_p \in \mathcal{P}$, $R(e_p)$ is a complete ordering over X^N. The expression $x_N R(e_p) x'_N$ will mean that x_N is weakly preferred to x'_N, and $P(e_p)$ and $I(e_p)$ will denote the corresponding strict preference and indifference relations, respectively.

Two special cases will be of particular interest. The "distribution" case is when x_i has to be non-negative: $X = \mathbb{R}_+$. The "TU" (transferable utility) case is when the well-being function is quasi-linear in x,

$$u_i = x_i + v(y_i, z_i)$$

and x_i is not bounded below:[4] $X = \mathbb{R}$.

The distribution case is relevant to situations in which the government has a fixed budget that can be used in order to provide targeted help to particular

---

[2] See Svensson (1983), Alkan et al. (1991).

[3] Another related model, studied by Moreno-Ternero and Roemer (2006), is the particular case with y only and no z, in which the responsibility issue vanishes.

[4] More realistically, one could impose that $x_i + v(y_i, z_i)$ is bounded below (for instance by zero). We will not study this variant.

categories of people, such as disabled individuals, victims of a natural disaster, families with different needs. The TU case is especially relevant to situations in which individual well-being is itself monetary. For instance, think of the idea of equalizing opportunities for income, in a case when individual labor supply is totally inelastic. Or, relatedly, think of equalizing opportunities for utility when utility depends only on disposable income and not on leisure, and when individuals are deemed responsible for their utility function so that the public policy disregards utilities (out of neutrality toward utility functions) and focuses on disposable income. But the most realistic applications of the TU case are offered by the federalism problem of organizing budget transfers between administrative units (local governments, sectorial administrations, social security agencies, etc.) which are partly responsible for their budget situation. For instance, they may be responsible for their management performance or their policy but not for the tax base in their jurisdiction or the demographic characteristics of the population they take care of.[5]

1.3 An example

Let us start our examination of the simple context described in the introduction of this chapter by one of the simplest examples that pertain to this context.

Example 1.1 *Assume that individual well-being depends only on two things, money and dedication to personal well-being. The degree of dedication is a personal trait that makes individuals use the quantity of money at their disposal in a more or less profitable way, in terms of well-being.[6] Over a whole life, a high degree of dedication transforms a modest amount of money into many occasions of personal enjoyment and accomplishment, whereas a low degree dampens well-being.*

Now, money is received from two sources. At the beginning of their adult lives, individuals receive a personal bequest coming from their family and at the same time are submitted to a transfer (tax or grant). The combination of these two operations determines their disposable wealth, and they then pursue their life plans and obtain a certain level of well-being. For simplicity we suppose that well-being is proportional to disposable wealth and to the degree of dedication. In other words, we have something like the following formula, for every individual:

$$well\text{-}being = (bequest \pm transfer) \times dedication.$$

---

[5]See esp. Cappelen and Tungodden (2007b). A related application, dealing with health insurance and risk selection, is made in Schokkaert et al. (1998), Schokkaert and Van de Voorde (2004, 2007).

[6]Dedication to one's well-being is chosen here instead of the more usual notion of "effort" for two reasons. First, it can be assumed that well-being is monotonically increasing in dedication, whereas effort may have an adverse effect when it is very high. Second, it is hopefully more transparent that this variable need not elicit a moral judgment. Being little dedicated to one's own well-being may be blamable or praiseworthy depending on what else one is dedicated to.

Let us illustrate the situation by looking at the distribution of well-being that is obtained in the case when the government does not perform any transfer. Imagine that there are four categories of people, an individual falling into one category or another depending on whether his bequest is low or high, and whether his dedication is low or high. We may then obtain a situation as depicted in Table 1.1. The figures in the table cells measure well-being achievements.

Table 1.1: Laissez-faire policy

	low dedication (= 1)	high dedication (= 3)
low bequest (= 1)	1	3
high bequest (= 3)	3	9

Is this situation acceptable? If we consider that individuals are not responsible for the level of bequest they receive, certainly there is a problem with this distribution. Having a low bequest clearly hinders one's well-being prospects. The fact that a lower bequest can sometimes be counterbalanced in this particular case by a higher dedication does not suffice to alleviate the problem.

What should be done, once the possibility of government transfer is brought into the picture? If individuals are no more responsible for their level of dedication than their level of bequest, then presumably responsibility-sensitive egalitarianism boils down to simple egalitarianism and equality of well-being is the desirable goal. For illustration and further reference, Table 1.2 describes the corresponding policy.[7]

Table 1.2: Egalitarian policy

	low dedication (= 1)	high dedication (= 3)
low bequest (= 1)	3 (transfer= +2)	3 (transfer= 0)
high bequest (= 3)	3 (transfer= 0)	3 (transfer= −2)

Now let us consider that, contrary to the above assumption, individuals are in fact to be held responsible for their level of dedication (but not for their level of bequest). We will however retain here the assumption that the level of dedication is a fixed characteristic and will not be influenced by any incentive effects of redistribution. The case in which individuals are responsible for some of their traits (dedication) but not for the others (bequest) is the interesting one for us here. We want to neutralize the inequalities due to unequal bequests.

---

[7] For simplicity of computation it is assumed that the four categories of individuals make subgroups of equal size and that a policy is feasible when the sum of per capita transfers indicated in the table is not greater than zero.

How should that be done? In this particular example, there is a "natural policy" that presents itself immediately as an appealing option. It consists in equalizing the wealth that is at the disposal of individuals after transfer. This policy is illustrated in Table 1.3.

Table 1.3: Natural policy

	low dedication (= 1)	high dedication (= 3)
low bequest (= 1)	2 (transfer= +1)	6 (transfer= +1)
high bequest (= 3)	2 (transfer= −1)	6 (transfer= −1)

Over the entire population, this policy equalizes exactly what individuals are not responsible for, namely, their wealth (made of bequest and transfers). In the table every individual has a disposable wealth equal to 2.

1.4   The reward problem

One may observe, however, that the natural policy is not the only one that neutralizes the inequalities due to differential bequest. For instance, the egalitarian policy described above also achieves a situation in which a greater bequest does not enable an individual to obtain a greater level of well-being. Tables 1.4 and 1.5 show two other examples of policies which perform the same neutralizing operation but apportion final well-being to dedication in a different way.

Table 1.4: Pro-dedication policy

	low dedication (= 1)	high dedication (= 3)
low bequest (= 1)	0 (transfer= −1)	12 (transfer= +3)
high bequest (= 3)	0 (transfer= −3)	12 (transfer= +1)

Table 1.5: Anti-dedication policy

	low dedication (= 1)	high dedication (= 3)
low bequest (= 1)	4 (transfer= +3)	0 (transfer= −1)
high bequest (= 3)	4 (transfer= +1)	0 (transfer= −3)

These examples show that a literal reading of the idea that inequalities for which individuals are not responsible should be suppressed leaves it quite indeterminate what precise redistribution should be done. *Compensation* for unequal circumstances cannot be the only goal of social policy; it must be supplemented by a *reward principle* telling us whether and how redistribution should be sensitive to responsibility characteristics as well and, eventually, how final well-being should relate to responsibility characteristics.

Why does the natural policy appear more "natural" than the others? It may be because it equalizes across *all* individuals the determining factor of their well-being for which they are not responsible, namely, their disposable wealth. It thereby puts all individuals on a par with respect to the dimensions for which they are not responsible. In contrast, under the pro-dedication policy, the individuals with low dedication are stripped of their wealth, whereas the anti-dedication policy does the same to individuals with high dedication. The resulting inequalities in disposable wealth across individuals are obviously inequalities for which they are not directly responsible. However, individuals may be considered to be indirectly responsible, since the transfer they are submitted to is related to their responsibility characteristic. These policies make individuals responsible not only for their level of dedication but also for the ensuing penalty or subsidy that is attached to this characteristic.

The relevant difference between the natural policy and the pro and anti-dedication policies is, then, that the former neutralizes bequest inequalities and does not perform any further redistribution, whereas the latter apparently convey the additional goal of rewarding or penalizing dedication. The natural policy appears to take a neutral stance regarding dedication since it gives the same treatment to individuals who differ only with respect to their level of dedication. Whether this neutral stance is justified or not will be discussed below. What matters at this point is only that there are different possibilities regarding the reward problem that arise even in the simplest setting.

1.5 Compensation, neutrality and no-envy

In Example 1.1, the natural policy achieves a simple equality of disposable wealth across all individuals and disposable wealth is the combination of personal characteristics and money transfers for which individuals are not responsible. But it is not always the case that such simple equality is achievable.

A first difficulty arises when differential circumstances across individuals are so overwhelming or when the government's taxing ability or budget is so meager that transfer possibilities are exhausted before equality is realized. In this case the next best option after equality seems to be the application of the maximin criterion to individuals' disposable wealth.

A second, more serious, difficulty arises when there is no composite object like disposable wealth that synthesizes personal circumstances and transfers and is well-defined independently of responsibility characteristics. This may be illustrated with a different example.

Example 1.2 *In this variant of Example 1.1, individuals receive their bequest late in their life, so that their level of dedication has no effect on what bequest brings to well-being. Government transfers, on the other hand, are still performed at the beginning of adult life (with correct foresight on the amounts of*

bequest that individuals are bound to receive later). Since there is no bequest to
tax at the time of making transfers, the transfers are made out of a fixed bud-
get, and we assume that bequests are not taxed even later on. In other words,
well-being is now produced in the following way:

$$well\text{-}being = (transfer \times dedication) + bequest,$$

where transfer is always non-negative.

With the formula of Example 1.1,

$$well\text{-}being = (bequest \pm transfer) \times dedication,$$

the term (bequest $\pm$ transfer) is the obvious focus of equalization because it is
one-dimensional. In contrast, in Example 1.2, transfer and bequest cannot be
similarly synthesized. With a greater dedication, a given amount of transfer is
more powerful for the compensation of bequest inequalities. In other words, the
pair (bequest, transfer) cannot be equalized across individuals in an unambiguous way, and for different individuals with different levels of dedication, the two
components of this pair do not have the same relative importance. Transfer is
relatively more important for individuals with a high level of dedication.

The economic theory of fairness suggests a solution. One extension of the
idea of equality to multidimensional goods, when individuals have heterogeneous
preferences over those goods, is the no-envy test.[8] Here it would mean that
no individual should be better-off with another's combination of bequest and
transfer than with his own. In this comparison it is assumed that the individual
always refers to his own level of dedication and is asking the question: "With
my own level of dedication, would I be better-off with someone else's bequest
and transfer?" The no-envy test is satisfied when the answer is negative for
every individual. In the general case, the no-envy test, seeking equality of the
combinations of circumstances and money across individuals, is captured by
the question: "With my own responsibility characteristics, would I be better-off
with someone else's circumstances and money?"

As will be illustrated in detail in the next chapter, the no-envy test is unfortunately too stringent in many cases, so that it fails to provide a workable
solution in general. This does not, however, impugn its ethical value and it is
worth understanding its properties and implications. In fact, most of the concepts of the first six chapters of this book are direct emanations of the no-envy
test. Let us therefore pause here and examine the ethical underpinnings of the
no-envy test, so as to justify paying so much attention to it. The computation
of the test itself can be illustrated as follows. Let us consider three individuals with characteristics and transfers shown in Table 1.6. Their well-being is
computed according to the formula of Example 1.2.

---

[8] See Arnsperger (1994) for a synthetic discussion of this concept in relation to theories of
justice.

Table 1.6: Example

	Ann	Bob	Chris
bequest	1	2	1
transfer	+2	+1	+1
dedication	2	2	1
well-being	5	4	2

The application of the envy test to Ann, for instance, amounts to computing hypothetical well-being in the counterfactual cases in Table 1.7, and checking that the resulting figures are not greater than Ann's actual well-being (five units).

Table 1.7: Envy test

	Ann with Bob's bequest and transfer	Ann with Chris' bequest and transfer
bequest	2	1
transfer	+1	+1
dedication	2	2
well-being	4	3

Why is this kind of computation ethically relevant? As it has just been said, this is an extension of the idea of equality to a multidimensional context, and this can be explained as follows:

1. When there is only *one* good, like money, and individuals are responsible for how they benefit from it, responsibility-sensitive equality is obviously achieved by distributing this good equally.[9] In a sense, the natural policy in Example 1.1 is doing just that, when the quantity *bequest ± transfer* is viewed as a one-good allotment.

2. When there are *several* goods and the individuals have *identical* preferences, equality is achieved by giving them bundles which they unanimously consider equivalent. In Example 1.1, when bequest and transfer are viewed as different goods, individuals have identical preferences (they all care about the aggregate *bequest ± transfer*) and the natural policy gives them equivalent bundles.

3. When individuals have *heterogeneous* preferences (as in Example 1.2 where they value bequest and transfer differently), such unanimity about the equivalence of bundles can no longer be achieved, but a similar unanimity can be obtained, namely, when everyone considers that his own bundle is at least as good as all the others. This is precisely the no-envy test.

---

[9] This is true under the liberal approach to the reward problem. The utilitarian approach to responsibility-sensitive egalitarianism would give more money to those with greater marginal utility.

Therefore, there is a direct and natural link between the simple equality of money in the one-dimensional context and the no-envy test in the multidimensional context.[10]

Another way to illustrate the connection between no-envy and responsibility-sensitive egalitarianism is that, when an envy-free allocation is realized, the distribution of bundles could be achieved by offering the same menu of bundles to all individuals (i.e., a menu containing at least the bundles actually consumed in this allocation) and letting them choose their bundle freely in this menu.[11] This is because no-envy means that everyone considers her bundle to be at least as good as the others, so that, in a menu containing all these bundles, everyone would accept to pick her own bundle.[12]

We can now make an observation that does not depend on how well-being is related to bequest, transfer and dedication and is therefore valid for Examples 1.1, 1.2 and beyond. Consider what happens when the no-envy test is applied to two individuals with the same level of dedication, such as Ann and Bob in the above tables. We already know that, because they have identical preferences over bequest and transfer, they will obtain equivalent bundles. But in fact, they have the same dedication and will end up with the same level of well-being. The no-envy test, for two individuals with identical levels of dedication, requires equality of well-being. This can be directly related to the compensation idea that no inequality of well-being should persist among individuals with identical responsibility characteristics.

Let us turn to what happens when the no-envy test is applied to two individuals with the same level of bequest, such as Ann and Chris in Table 1.6. Their cross-comparison of bequest and transfer then boils down to a comparison of transfers *simpliciter*, since they already have equal bequests, and what one obtains from the no-envy test is just a requirement of equality of transfers. Again, this is an observation that extends beyond these particular examples. The general idea is that, under application of the no-envy test, two individuals with identical circumstances should be given the same treatment by redistributive policy. This idea can be related to the neutral stance observed in the natural policy and the corresponding idea of "neutral" or "liberal" reward.

The fact that compensation and liberal reward implications can be derived from the no-envy test is interesting and suggests that they both come from a

---

[10]More on the ethical virtues of the envy test can be found in Varian (1975), Arnsperger (1994), Clayton and Williams (1999).

[11]This is emphasized by Kolm (1996b).

[12]As explained in Section 2.3 below, satisfying the no-envy test is, in the simple framework of this chapter (in which well-being depends on money, circumstances and responsibility characteristics), equivalent to achieving a competitive equilibrium in a hypothetical market in which individuals would have equal budgets and could exchange not only money but also their circumstances. Circumstances are not tradable in reality, but if they were, it would be an attractive solution to let individuals buy them freely with equal purchasing power. Therefore the no-envy concept, which is logically equivalent to this configuration, is equally attractive. Note that such hypothetical market is very different from Dworkin's hypothetical insurance market, because in the former individuals do accept to buy their actual circumstances with certainty, whereas in the latter they only accept the risk of ending up with them.

similar source of inspiration. Nonetheless, they appear logically quite distinct. The compensation and liberal reward ideas are moreover broad principles which can be turned into various specific requirements about the distribution of resources. They are examined in more detail in the next two sections.

1.6   Analyzing compensation

The general idea of compensation is that inequalities due to differential circumstances for which individuals are not responsible are illegitimate and should be suppressed, or at least that priority[13] should be given to those who are worse-off than others because of differential circumstances for which they are not responsible. Before discussing the ethical pros and cons for the general principle of compensation, it is useful to examine the various specific conditions which emanate from it. This will provide a more concrete view of the content and implications of this principle.

A first condition, which has already been invoked and may be the most immediate expression of the principle, is:

Equal Well-Being for Equal Responsibility: Two individuals with identical responsibility characteristics should have the same level of well-being.

We have seen above that it is a direct consequence of the no-envy test, but it obviously stands by itself. Notice that this condition does not say anything about individuals with different responsibility characteristics, no matter how close they are, and is therefore rather weak. On the other hand, it is quite strong since it imposes equality for every kind of responsibility characteristics, and this may be hard to achieve in some cases. One may then prefer:

Maximin Well-Being for Equal Responsibility: The allocation of resources between two individuals with identical responsibility characteristics should be such that it is impossible to redistribute among them and increase the level of well-being of the worse-off.

The constraints may be such that actually one wants to settle for even weaker versions of the compensation principle, such as the following one. It applies the above condition only in the special case when all individuals have the same responsibility characteristics. For simplicity, we focus on equality rather than maximin formulation.

Equal Well-Being for Uniform Responsibility: If all individuals have identical responsibility characteristics, they should all have the same level of well-being.

---

[13]Philosophers, after Parfit (1995), oppose egalitarianism – seeking equality for its own sake – and prioritarianism – giving priority to the worse-off without a direct concern for inequalities. In this book the words "equality" and "priority" are used without implying endorsement of either approach (an egalitarian will effectively give priority to the worse-off as a way to reduce inequalities, a prioritarian will effectively seek equality out of concern for the worse-off).

One may wonder about the relevance of such a condition, in view of the fact that it invokes a quite unrealistic counterfactual situation. The purpose of such a condition is to test the ethical soundness of general allocation rules which determine supposedly appropriate distributions of resources and well-being for all conceivable contexts. When a general allocation rule fails to satisfy this weak version of the compensation principle in this special context, one may generally conclude that its record in terms of compensation is bad overall, including in more realistic contexts.[14]

Another standard formulation of the compensation principle, which has also been used above several times, refers to the neutralization of the inequalities due to unequal circumstances for which individuals are not responsible. This can be more precisely expressed as in the following condition.

Circumstance Neutralization: At the selected allocation it should be possible to express individual well-being as a function of responsibility characteristics only.

Although rigorous, this formulation may cause some confusion. Admittedly, there is a causal mechanism which determines individual well-being as a function of personal characteristics (circumstances and responsibility) and transfer. This mechanism cannot be altered but the purpose of public policy can be to allocate resources so that the influence of circumstances over well-being, in this causal mechanism, is exactly counterbalanced by appropriate transfers. Once this is done, there is a possible description of the distribution of well-being in the population which describes well-being as a function of responsibility characteristics only, leaving it implicit that the effects of circumstances and transfers are cancelled out in the real mechanism. For instance, with the natural policy in Example 1.1, one observes that well-being ends up being equal to dedication multiplied by 2, for all individuals.[15]

Now, observe that *Equal Well-Being for Equal Responsibility* and *Circumstance Neutralization* are logically equivalent. The latter implies the former, because when individual well-being is described as a function of responsibility characteristics only, two individuals with identical responsibility characteristics cannot but have the same level of well-being. Conversely, when all pairs of individuals with identical responsibility characteristics have equal well-being (within each pair), then well-being can indeed be expressed as a function of such characteristics only, since there is no other remaining source of inequality. Knowing the well-being of an individual is then sufficient to know the (equal) well-being of all those who share the same responsibility characteristics, and this gives us the function that is referred to in *Circumstance Neutralization*.

---

[14]For instance, we will see in Chapter 6 that Dworkin's hypothetical insurance does not even satisfy this weak requirement.

[15]The pro-dedication policy produces a different function, for which well-being can be described as equal to (dedication − 1) × 6. Even the egalitarian policy achieves a similar outcome, but in a degenerate way since one then has well-being equal to (dedication × 0) + 3, the role of dedication being nullified as well.

Hurley (2003) objects that there is an "egalitarian fallacy" in the idea that neutralizing the effects of circumstances has egalitarian implications. According to her, one could just as well take an arbitrary unequal distribution as the reference point and neutralize all the effects of circumstances that would cause a departure from this reference point. Neutralization would then be achieved without entailing equality. For instance, assume that in the *reference* situation Ann and Bob have the same bequest and same dedication but Ann is taxed to the benefit of Bob so that her well-being is lower. If the *actual* situation features bequest inequalities between these two individuals, a transfer from the richly endowed to the other can neutralize the impact of bequest differences and restore the distribution of well-being of the reference situation. As Hurley observes, the outcome of this policy is not egalitarian even though it does neutralize the impact of bequest inequalities.

What this reasoning overlooks is that the positions in the reference point should then be taken to be part of individuals' circumstances in addition to bequests. In the final unequal outcome of the example, individual well-being cannot be expressed as a function of responsibility characteristics only, but as a function of responsibility characteristics *and* position in the reference point. Clearly, the influence of one's *circumstantial* position in the reference point over one's well-being is not neutralized in this case. A full neutralization of circumstances does have egalitarian implications and requires individuals with the same responsibility characteristics to have the same well-being.

Another type of condition is also related to the compensation principle, but in a slightly less transparent way. This kind of condition considers changes in the population profile of circumstances, and requires the effect of such changes over the distribution of well-being to be sufficiently uniform across individuals. The idea is that there should be some solidarity among individuals in order to share the bad or good luck of changes in circumstances affecting some of them. This idea can be related in particular to Rawls' famous proposal "to regard the distribution of natural talents as a common asset and to share in the benefits of this distribution whatever it turns out to be" (1971, p. 101). The formulation of the solidarity idea can take the following form, among several other possibilities.

Circumstance Solidarity: A change in individuals' circumstances should never simultaneously make some individuals' well-being increase and some others' decrease.

Equal Well-Being for Equal Responsibility is actually a logical consequence of *Circumstance Solidarity* when one assumes that the allocation rule also satisfies the following basic anonymity condition. It says that when one permutes individuals' characteristics, one may as well permute the transfers they are submitted to – reflecting the idea that transfers depend on relevant characteristics and not on individuals' names.

Anonymity: If an allocation is selected, the allocation in which some transfers are permuted across individuals is also selected for the profile such that individual characteristics are similarly permuted.

The deduction of *Equal Well-Being for Equal Responsibility* from *Circumstance Solidarity* and *Anonymity* is straightforward. Consider two individuals with identical responsibility characteristics but possibly different circumstances (such as Ann and Bob). Consider a counterfactual situation in which their circumstances are permuted (e.g., "Ann with Bob's bequest" and "Bob with Ann's bequest" as in Table 1.8).

Table 1.8: Illustration of the reasoning

	Ann	Bob	Ann with Bob's bequest	Bob with Ann's bequest
bequest	1	2	2	1
dedication	2	2	2	2

By *Circumstance Solidarity* it cannot be the case that one would be better-off and the other worse-off as a result. Now, since they have identical responsibility characteristics, permuting their circumstances is equivalent to permuting all their characteristics, as is apparent in the table. *Anonymity* then implies that it is acceptable to permute their well-being levels in this context. If their well-being levels were initially unequal, it would then be the case that one is better-off and the other is worse-off after the permutation, but that was precluded by *Circumstance Solidarity*. Therefore the only possibility is that their initial levels of well-being are equal, as it would indeed be requested by *Equal Well-Being for Equal Responsibility*.

These are various conditions which give flesh to the principle of compensation. The list is not exhaustive and a few other related conditions will appear later on.

The principle of compensation is a basic tenet of responsibility-sensitive egalitarianism, and does not need much argument in its favor in the abstract. But its formulation in terms of some of the strongest conditions above may appear questionable in certain contexts. Here is an example.[16]

Example 1.3 *Assume that individual well-being depends on money, bodily function and lifestyle preferences. Assume also that individuals are not held responsible for their bodily function but are held responsible for their lifestyle preferences. Well-being is determined as follows:*

$$well\text{-}being = transfer + (body \times preference)$$

where "body" measures the degree of bodily function and "preference" is a parameter measuring the importance of "body" in well-being.

In this example, the requirement of *Equal Well-Being for Equal Responsibility* would require a given deficit in bodily function to be compensated differently as a function of individual preference. Individuals who do not give a great importance to this deficit would receive a small compensation whereas those

---

[16] This is inspired by Van Parijs (1997).

who give an extraordinary importance to it (e.g., because they have athletic ambitions) would need an extraordinary compensation. This may look rather implausible. It might be more reasonable, in such a context, to reduce the application of the compensation principle to certain values of the responsibility characteristics, the idea being that one should have compensation at least for some "reasonable preferences," but not necessarily for all idiosyncratic views about the importance of bodily function.

Such a criticism of the compensation principle, in fact, merely points to a possible conflict between this principle and the idea that redistributive policies need not cater to the special wants created by responsibility characteristics. This idea is analyzed in the next section, and the conflict will be examined in detail in Chapter 2.

1.7   Analyzing neutrality

The description of the principle of compensation in the first two sentences of the previous section ("inequalities due to differential circumstances for which individuals are not responsible are illegitimate;" "priority should be given to those who are worse-off than others because of differential circumstances for which they are not responsible") comes strikingly close to a mere repetition of the canonical statement of responsibility-sensitive egalitarianism. Does that mean that the compensation principle is the only ethical implication of responsibility-sensitive egalitarianism, which then appears as characteristically underspecified as a guide to redistributive policies?

This has been argued by some authors,[17] but this restrictive understanding of responsibility-sensitive egalitarianism does not seem to take account of the usual implications of the notion of responsibility. The commonsense notion of personal responsibility implies that, when someone is responsible for his own plight, others are relieved from any duty to help. The phrase "this is your responsibility" usually means that the speaker will not intervene no matter how the responsible agent behaves. The idea of personal responsibility, when it is understood in terms of *self-reliance* or in terms of *private sphere*, does have clear implications about the reward problem.

The philosophical literature also provides a variety of statements that imply something rather precise about the reward problem. When Rawls and Dworkin argue that welfare should be replaced by resources as the focus of redistribution because individuals should assume responsibility for their preferences and ambitions, they indeed mean that no redistribution should be based on differences in ambitions. Dworkin makes a distinction between "endowment-insensitivity" and "ambition-sensitivity" which is quite close to the distinction between compensation and liberal reward.[18] Barry similarly distinguishes a "principle of

---

[17]See, e.g., Vandenbroucke (2001), Hild and Voorhoeve (2004).

[18] "The requirements of equality (...) pull in opposite directions. On the one hand we must, on pain of violating equality, allow the distribution of resources to be (...) ambition-sensitive (...) so that, for example, those who choose to invest rather than consume, or to consume less

compensation" and a "principle of responsibility."[19] And in the introduction we have quoted Cohen's and Arneson's pronouncements against any form of redistribution that would go beyond redressing differences in circumstances.[20]

One must admit, however, that the idea of responsibility alone cannot motivate the liberal reward principle. Consider the case of criminal responsibility. One would not say that the fact that crime is punished clashes with the idea that the criminals are responsible. Simply, criminal responsibility is associated with a perfectionist attitude toward responsibility characteristics (obeying the law is considered better than trespassing). It is only when responsibility is supplemented with a requirement of neutrality with respect to responsibility characteristics that a liberal kind of reward can appear legitimate. Moreover, it must be a rather strong kind of neutrality. A public policy can be neutral to different degrees. Neutrality of *judgment* means that the policy does not rely on any positive or negative evaluation of the object under consideration, such as a behavior or a personal trait. Neutrality of *aim* or *intent* means that the policy does not directly seek to reward or punish the object, although it may affect it indirectly in the pursuit of other aims. Neutrality as *no-intervention* means that the policy does not involve any reaction when the object appears or disappears.[21]

Neutrality as no-intervention is the vehicle of the liberal reward principle. Neutrality of judgment and neutrality of aim, by contrast, are compatible with policies which do not implement a liberal reward. For instance, the pro-dedication policy introduced in Example 1.1 may be based on a social criterion that is neutral in these two senses. Indeed, suppose that, above and beyond compensation for unequal bequests, the objective is to maximize the sum of well-beings, in a utilitarian fashion. This objective does not involve a condemnation of low levels of dedication, nor does it lead to seek punishment of low levels, but

---

expensively rather than more (...) must be permitted to retain the gains that flow from these decisions in an equal auction followed by free trade. But on the other hand, we must not allow the distribution of resources at any moment to be endowment-sensitive, that is, to be affected by differences in ability of the sort that produce income differences in a laissez-faire economy among people with the same ambitions." (1981b, p. 311)

[19] The former "says that the institutions of a society should operate in such a way as to counteract the effects of good and bad fortune," the latter "that social arrangements should be such that people finish up with the outcomes of their voluntary acts." (1991, p. 142)

[20] There may be a difference between Arneson and Cohen, though. Cohen (1989) clearly advocates not giving additional *resources* to those who are in control of their expensive tastes. Arneson, in contrast, defines equality of opportunity for welfare in more general terms. His theory leaves it possible to select the opportunity set according to various moral values. This may imply subsidizing expensive tastes, even when they are controlled, if doing so creates an opportunity set of a better quality. For instance, if the opportunity set is designed so as to maximize expected welfare, where expected welfare is defined with respect to certain probabilities to have certain preferences and to make certain choices (as in Vallentyne 2002), it is unlikely that the optimal set will provide equal resources to people with different goals, even when they are in control of their goals.

[21] To this list one may add neutrality of *effect*, which means that the policy provides equal prospects for success to individuals with or without the trait under consideration. This one is of a quite different kind and relates to the neutralization idea underlying the principle of compensation.

it can nonetheless justify the pro-dedication policy which taxes low dedication and subsidizes high dedication, because total well-being over the boxes of Table 1.4 is 24 with this policy, instead of 16 with the natural policy (Table 1.3), and this represents a difference in total well-being over the population if the boxes correspond to subgroups of equal sizes.

A very simple and direct way to formulate the idea of neutrality as no-intervention is in the following independence condition.

Independence of Responsibility Characteristics: The allocation of money should be independent of individuals' responsibility characteristics.

This condition means that individuals may change their responsibility characteristics without being submitted to adjustments in the amount of transfer.[22]

A related way to formulate the neutrality idea refers to the comparison of treatment between individuals with the same circumstances but possibly different responsibility characteristics. The following condition says that they should be submitted to the same redistributive treatment.

Equal Treatment for Equal Circumstances: Two individuals with identical circumstances should be submitted to the same transfer.

These two conditions express the same idea in slightly different ways, the counterfactual way and the comparative way.[23] They are in fact logically related. Consider indeed the following condition which, like Anonymity, expresses a basic impartiality requirement.

Equal Treatment of Equals: Two individuals with identical characteristics should be submitted to the same transfer.

It is then quite easy to see that *Independence of Responsibility Characteristics* and *Equal Treatment of Equals* imply *Equal Resources for Equal Circumstances*. Take two individuals with identical circumstances. If they also had identical responsibility characteristics, *Equal Treatment of Equals* would apply and require them to be submitted to the same transfer. Under *Independence of Responsibility Characteristics*, this equality of transfer is in fact required whatever their responsibility characteristics.

Just like *Equal Well-Being for Equal Responsibility* can be weakened into *Equal Well-Being for Uniform Responsibility*, it is possible to weaken *Equal Resource for Equal Circumstances* by restricting its application to uniform profiles of circumstances.

Equal Treatment for Uniform Circumstances: When all individuals have identical circumstances, they should all be submitted to the same transfer.

---

[22] In the framework of this chapter, individual characteristics are fixed. It is nonetheless meaningful to require the allocation rule to behave well in counterfactual situations involving such changes.

[23] Hurley (2003) usefully insists on this distinction.

This is a very intuitive requirement, because when circumstances are identical in the whole population, the compensation problem vanishes.

Let us now turn to a critical discussion of neutrality as embodied in the above conditions. Both *Independence of Responsibility Characteristics* and *Equal Treatment for Equal Circumstances* are absolutely compelling when transfers must be performed before individuals' responsibility characteristics have been determined or observed by the government. It is only when responsibility characteristics are known at the time of transfers that *Independence of Responsibility Characteristics* can be relaxed. Even then, it often appears natural to stick to it. A transfer policy that is sensitive to responsibility characteristics is like a race in which the length of track allotted to racers is not necessarily equal but depends on their performance during the race itself – a possible but rather contrived device.

Independence of Responsibility Characteristics is less acceptable when responsibility characteristics affect individual preferences over resources in such a way that Pareto-efficiency requires taking account of them in the allocation of resources. This problem, however, is absent in the framework adopted in this chapter because money is one-dimensional and all allocations which do not waste resources are Pareto-efficient.

More importantly, *Equal Treatment for Equal Circumstances* can be criticized for failing to take account of the possible interplay between circumstances and responsibility characteristics. Bad circumstances may not only reduce well-being but also alter the influence of responsibility characteristics over well-being. Both consequences should be dealt with through compensation, yet *Equal Treatment for Equal Circumstances* precludes dealing with the latter. This can be illustrated with another variant of Examples 1.1 and 1.2.

Example 1.4 *Individuals receive their bequest early in their life. Government transfers, on the other hand, are now performed at the end of adult life, so that they do not interfere with dedication. In other words, well-being is now produced in the following way:*

$$well\text{-}being = transfer + (bequest \times dedication),$$

where transfer may be positive or negative.

In this example, a low bequest dampens the positive impact of dedication. Consider the example of a neutral policy in Table 1.9.

Table 1.9: A neutral policy

	low dedication ($= 1$)	high dedication ($= 3$)
low bequest ($= 1$)	3 (transfer$= +2$)	5 (transfer$= +2$)
high bequest ($= 3$)	1 (transfer$= -2$)	7 (transfer$= -2$)

This policy fails to perform full compensation among the high-dedication sub-population, because its neglects the full impact of a low bequest for such individuals. In reverse fashion, it overcompensates among the individuals with low dedication.

Examples 1.2 and 1.4 manifestly point to a conflict between the compensation principle and the liberal reward principle. This conflict will be one of the topics of the next chapter, and we will come back then to the relative attractiveness of the various conditions related to these two principles.

The liberal reward principle may also be questioned when it implies condoning large *ex post* inequalities. The natural policy in Example 1.1, for instance, produces a distribution of well-being with some individuals having three times as much well-being as others. These figures have little meaning in this abstract example, but in real-life applications it is clear that this kind of policy can yield large inequalities. One may consider that responsibility does not justify such inequalities. It may also happen that the low-dedication individuals fall below a minimum threshold of subsistence or decency, and it is certainly sensible to think that responsibility does not trump the right of all individuals to be guaranteed the minimum. This is all the more so as, in practice, one can never be sure that the attribution of responsibility is correct given the real conditions in which individuals live. In a nutshell, the appeal to responsibility in general and to neutrality and the liberal reward principle in particular should not eliminate concerns for *ex post* inequalities and poverty. These issues are taken up in more detail in Chapter 10.

It is also possible to formulate a more radical criticism against the idea of neutrality as no-intervention itself. Some authors[24] have argued that a no-intervention policy, in front of responsible agents, is not a salient option in any respect. Institutions shape individuals' opportunities in many ways, it is said, and no intervention is not really even an option. One should simply evaluate individuals' opportunities so that they best satisfy some satisfaction or efficiency principle. In other words, this criticism holds that a sound consequentialist criterion does not care about the degree of redistribution or intervention and focuses instead on the value of outcomes and opportunities offered to individuals. An alternative formulation of this criticism is that the principle of liberal reward gives an illegitimate importance to respecting the natural relation between well-being and responsibility characteristics. If in some contexts this relation is naturally almost flat – well-being depends little on responsibility characteristics – whereas in others it is very steep – a case of high productivity of responsibility characteristics – it seems odd, the objection goes, to prefer flatness in one case and steepness in the other, as if natural contingencies shaped our moral principles.

This criticism is too extreme. It points toward a consistent and interesting view, with possible applications that will be the topic of Chapter 8, but it fails to see the appeal of neutrality and its requirements for redistribution.

---

[24]See, e.g., Vandenbroucke (2001), Vallentyne (2002), Hild and Voorhoeve (2004). See also Fleurbaey (1995b, 2001) on this point.

The idea of responsibility is closely associated with the idea that individuals can be left alone. In this perspective, the degree of redistribution, as well as the reactiveness of redistribution to responsibility characteristics, are important features of an allocation and cannot a priori be ignored and considered to be irrelevant for social evaluation. Under the narrowly consequentialist perspective described above, it is for instance impossible to understand the salience of the natural policy in Example 1.1. It is only under the banner of neutrality that one can identify reasonable criteria and policies which limit the scope of redistribution to the neutralization of circumstances and do not use redistribution as a tool for other purposes. It is in this approach only that responsibility-sensitive egalitarianism can find a place between egalitarianism and libertarianism. Observe indeed that if individuals are responsible for all their characteristics, they trivially have identical circumstances and *Equal Treatment for Uniform Circumstances* recommends equality of transfer, which means zero transfer when the sum of transfers has to be zero. This libertarian conclusion is obtained on the basis of the liberal reward principle.

Chapters 8 and 10 contain further discussions of the pros and cons of the various reward principles.

1.8   *Fairness conditions

This section briefly provides the mathematical formulation of the main conditions defined above, introduces a few others and analyzes their logical links. Let us start with the basic conditions. Let $x_{\pi(N)}$ denote the permuted vector $\left(x_{\pi(i)}\right)_{i \in N}$.

Anonymity: $\forall e = ((y_N, z_N), \Omega) \in \mathcal{D}, \forall x_N \in S(e), \forall \pi \in \Pi_N,$

$$x_{\pi(N)} \in S(y_{\pi(N)}, z_{\pi(N)}).$$

Equal Treatment of Equals: $\forall e \in \mathcal{D}, \forall x_N \in S(e), \forall i, j \in N$ such that $y_i = y_j$ and $z_i = z_j,$

$$x_i = x_j.$$

Equal Treatment of Equals is implied by *Anonymity* when the allocation rule is single-valued.

In this section we focus on the TU case, which is simpler than the distribution case, in particular because it entails the following property:

$$\forall y, y' \in Y, \forall z \in Z, \forall x \in X, \exists x' \in X, \ u(x', y', z) \geq u(x, y, z).$$

That is, it is always possible to compensate inequalities by transfers. This is not generally true in the distribution case, which is examined in the next section. Another feature of the TU case is that, since utilities are quasi-linear, the average well-being does not depend on the allocation of resources and is computed as:

$$\bar{v}(e) = \frac{\Omega}{n} + \frac{1}{n} \sum_{i \in N} v(y_i, z_i).$$

The no-envy condition is written as follows.

No-Envy: $\forall e \in \mathcal{D}$, $\forall x_N \in S(e)$, $\forall i, j \in N$,

$$x_i + v\left(y_i, z_i\right) \geq x_j + v\left(y_j, z_i\right).$$

We now turn to the compensation conditions.

Equal Well-Being for Equal Responsibility: $\forall e \in \mathcal{D}$, $\forall x_N \in S(e)$, $\forall i, j \in N$ such that $z_i = z_j$,

$$u_i = u_j.$$

Equal Well-Being for Uniform Responsibility: $\forall e \in \mathcal{D}$, $\forall x_N \in S(e)$, if $\forall i, j \in N$, $z_i = z_j$, then

$$\forall i, j \in N, \ u_i = u_j.$$

We also introduce a condition that is even weaker and applies the equality requirement only when the uniform z takes particular values (possibly just one).

Equal Well-Being for Reference Responsibility: $\exists \tilde{z} \in Z$, $\forall e \in \mathcal{D}$, $\forall x_N \in S(e)$, if $\forall i \in N$, $z_i = \tilde{z}$, then

$$\forall i, j \in N, \ u_i = u_j.$$

Circumstance Solidarity: $\forall e = \left((y_N, z_N), \Omega\right)$, $e' = \left((y'_N, z_N), \Omega\right) \in \mathcal{D}$, $\forall x_N \in S(e)$, $\forall x'_N \in S(e')$,

$$\forall i \ \in \ N, \ x_i + v(y_i, z_i) \geq x'_i + v(y'_i, z_i) \text{ or}$$
$$\forall i \ \in \ N, \ x_i + v(y_i, z_i) \leq x'_i + v(y'_i, z_i).$$

Some variants of *Circumstance Solidarity* have been considered for the TU case. For instance, one can strengthen it, relying on the argument that there is no reason to make some agents benefit unequally from variations in the profile.

Additive Circumstance Solidarity: $\forall e = \left((y_N, z_N), \Omega\right)$, $e' = \left((y'_N, z_N), \Omega\right) \in \mathcal{D}$, $\forall x_N \in S(e)$, $\forall x'_N \in S(e')$,

$$\forall i, j \in N, \ x_i + v(y_i, z_i) - (x'_i + v(y'_i, z_i)) = x_j + v(y_j, z_j) - (x'_j + v(y'_j, z_j)).$$

At the opposite, a weaker version of the *Circumstance Solidarity* axiom applies only when mean utility is unchanged.

Weak Circumstance Solidarity: $\forall e = ((y_N, z_N), \Omega),\; e' = ((y'_N, z_N), \Omega) \in \mathcal{D},\; \forall x_N \in S(e),\; \forall x'_N \in S(e'),$

$$\bar{v}(e) = \bar{v}(e') \Rightarrow \forall i \in N,\; x_i + v(y_i, z_i) = x'_i + v(y'_i, z_i).$$

There is an interesting formal duality between compensation axioms relating z_i to u_i and neutrality (liberal reward) axioms relating y_i to x_i. This is rather transparent for the equality axioms. The dual counterparts of the Equal Well-Being axioms are the following Equal Treatment conditions.

Equal Treatment for Equal Circumstances: $\forall e \in \mathcal{D},\; \forall x_N \in S(e),\; \forall i, j \in N$ such that $y_i = y_j$,

$$x_i = x_j.$$

Equal Treatment for Uniform Circumstances: $\forall e \in \mathcal{D},\; \forall x_N \in S(e),$ if $\forall i, j \in N,\; y_i = y_j$, then

$$\forall i, j \in N,\; x_i = x_j.$$

Equal Treatment for Reference Circumstances: $\exists \tilde{y} \in Y,\; \forall e \in \mathcal{D},\; \forall x_N \in S(e),$ if $\forall i \in N,\; y_i = \tilde{y}$, then

$$\forall i, j \in N,\; x_i = x_j.$$

Circumstance Solidarity says that all utilities should move in the same direction when y_N changes. Dually, *Independence of Responsibility Characteristics* says that all x_i should move in the same direction when z_N changes, and since the sum of x_i does not change, they must all keep the same value. One can check that this axiom is actually the joint dual of the three axioms of solidarity listed above.

Independence of Responsibility Characteristics: $\forall e = ((y_N, z_N), \Omega),\; e' = ((y_N, z'_N), \Omega) \in \mathcal{D},$

$$S(e) = S(e').$$

Another interesting condition is the following. It compares two kinds of circumstances by computing the well-being obtained with them at all levels of money and with all responsibility characteristics (as observed in the population). A kind of circumstance that is consistently dominated in such comparison should then receive at least as much money as the other.

Acknowledged Handicap: $\forall e \in \mathcal{D},\; \forall i, j \in N,$

$$[\forall k \in N,\; v(y_i, z_k) \leq v(y_j, z_k)] \Rightarrow [\forall x_N \in S(e),\; x_i \geq x_j].$$

It sounds like a compensation requirement[25] but this is quite misleading. In fact, the *Acknowledged Handicap* condition logically implies *Equal Treatment for Equal Circumstances*. It is satisfied by the policy which submits everyone to the same transfer, and this is certainly not the hallmark of compensation.[26]

There is a dual condition, on the compensation side, which is worth introducing. It says that when z_i yields a better outcome than z_j for all circumstances, then agent i deserves a better outcome. This reads as follows:

Acknowledged Merit: $\forall e \in \mathcal{D}, \forall i, j \in N,$

$$[\forall k \in N, \ v(y_k, z_i) \geq v(y_k, z_j)] \Rightarrow [\forall x_N \in S(e), \ u_i \geq u_j].$$

This axiom sounds like a reward axiom, but it is really about compensation, since it means that i deserves a better outcome than j *independently of their differential circumstances*.

A few other conditions are worth mentioning. The first one says that two individuals with identical circumstances may receive different amounts of money, but not on different sides of the threshold formed by the per capita amount of money.

Fair Treatment for Equal Circumstances: $\forall e \in \mathcal{D}, \forall x_N \in S(e), \forall i, j \in N$ such that $y_i = y_j$,

$$\left(x_i - \frac{\Omega}{n}\right)\left(x_j - \frac{\Omega}{n}\right) \geq 0.$$

Its dual requires that two agents with the same function should be similarly ranked with respect to average well-being.

Fair Ranking for Equal Responsibility: $\forall e \in \mathcal{D}, \forall x_N \in S(e), \forall i, j \in N$ such that $z_i = z_j$,

$$(u_i - \bar{v}(e))(u_j - \bar{v}(e)) \geq 0.$$

The last condition below refers to the hypothetical situation in which all agents would have the same responsibility characteristics as agent i. In that case, it would be natural to apply *Equal Well-Being for Uniform Responsibility*, and agent i would obtain some quantity of money, denoted $m_i(y_N, z_i, \Omega)$ since it is a function of y_N and z_i. This quantity is easily computed in the TU case,

$$m_i(y_N, z_i, \Omega) = -v(y_i, z_i) + \frac{1}{n}\sum_{j=1}^{n} v(y_j, z_i) + \frac{\Omega}{n},$$

---

[25] It bears some similarity with Sen's (1973) Weak Equity Axiom, which says that when an individual has a lower utility than another at all levels of income, he should not be given less income.

[26] Obviously, one could strengthen *Acknowledged Handicap* and require a strictly greater transfer for individuals whose circumstances systematically yield strictly lower well-being. This would push it a little in the direction of compensation. But the degree of compensation could be arbitrarily low, and therefore the intuition that makes us think of such a condition as related to the compensation principle is probably just an illusion.

and may serve as a benchmark to which the actual amount x_i distributed by S can be compared. It would be nice in particular if one could have $x_i \geq m_i(y_N, z_i, \Omega)$ for all $i \in N$, since then no one could complain that his evaluation of his circumstances y_i is not properly taken into account. This is, however, hard to achieve in general and Moulin (1994) proposes to use $m_i(y_N, z_i, \Omega)$ as an upper bound in case it cannot operate as a lower bound.[27]

Egalitarian Bound: $\forall e = ((y_N, z_N), \Omega) \in \mathcal{D}, \forall x_N \in S(e)$,

$$\forall i \in N, \ x_i \geq m_i(y_N, z_i, \Omega) \text{ or } \forall i \in N, \ x_i \leq m_i(y_N, z_i, \Omega).$$

This list of conditions is not exhaustive and the literature contains several others, but these are sufficient to obtain some insights in the structure of the basic issues.

We can now examine the logical relations between the axioms. Proposition 1.1 also summarizes the classification of the axioms in terms of compensation and reward. In particular, the positions of *Acknowledged Handicap* and *Egalitarian Bound* in the logical implications is quite helpful to get a better understanding of their ethical content.

Table 1.10: Logical links between axioms

Compensation					Liberal Reward
(Weak) Circumst. Solidarity $\Downarrow^{(1)}$					Independ. of Resp. Charact. $\Downarrow^{(2)}$
Equal WB for Equal Resp. $\Downarrow$	$\Leftarrow$ Ackn. Merit	$\Leftarrow$	No-Envy$^{(3)}$ $\Rightarrow$	Ackn. Hand. $\Rightarrow$	Equal Treatm. for Equal Circ. $\Downarrow$
Fair Ranking for Equal Resp. $\Downarrow$			$\Downarrow$		Fair Treatm. for Equal Circ. $\Downarrow$
Equal WB for Unif. Resp. $\Downarrow$		$\Leftarrow$	Egalit. Bound $\Rightarrow$		Equal Treatm. for Unif. Circ. $\Downarrow$
Equal WB for Ref. Resp.					Equal Treatm. for Ref. Circ.

$^{(1)}$Assuming that S satisfies Anonymity.
$^{(2)}$Assuming that S satisfies Equal Treatment of Equals.
$^{(3)}$Considered on the subdomain where it can be satisfied.

---

[27]This is somewhat questionable as the following situation may occur. Suppose some individual i has an extraordinary bad assessment of his own circumstances y_i, so that $m_i(y_N, z_i, \Omega)$ is extremely high. If this implies that the bound must be used as an upper bound, then everyone should receive less than the bound, including those who have a modest evaluation of their circumstances and would not require much money for compensation. It is nonetheless quite interesting to introduce this axiom in view of its relation with the others, and also because it is satisfied by some important solutions in the TU case.

Proposition 1.1 *Table 1.10 describes the logical implications between the axioms.*

Proof. A proof is provided only for the less obvious implications.
(1) No-Envy implies Acknowledged Merit. Consider $i, j \in N$ such that for all $k \in N$,

$$v(y_k, z_i) \geq v(y_k, z_j).$$

No-Envy requires

$$x_i + v(y_i, z_i) \geq x_j + v(y_j, z_i)$$

and we have $v(y_j, z_i) \geq v(y_j, z_j)$, so that

$$u_i = x_i + v(y_i, z_i) \geq x_j + v(y_j, z_j) = u_j.$$

(2) No-Envy implies Egalitarian Bound. No-Envy means that for all $i, j \in N$, $x_i + v(y_i, z_i) \geq x_j + v(y_j, z_i)$. Taking the means of this inequality over all j, one obtains

$$u_i \geq \frac{1}{n} \sum_{j=1}^{n} v(y_j, z_i) + \frac{\Omega}{n}.$$

Recalling that

$$m_i(y_N, z_i, \Omega) = -v(y_i, z_i) + \frac{1}{n} \sum_{j=1}^{n} v(y_j, z_i) + \frac{\Omega}{n},$$

this is equivalent to $x_i \geq m_i(y_N, z_i, \Omega)$. Notice that under No-Envy, $m_i(y_N, z_i, \Omega)$ is always a *lower* bound. ∎

1.9 *The distribution case

The distribution case is slightly more complicated because the fact that x_i cannot be negative, together with a greater variety of possible forms for the utility function u, constrains the compensation of inequalities. In particular, *Equal Well-Being for Equal Responsibility* cannot be satisfied in general, so that only a maximin variant makes sense.

Maximin Well-Being for Equal Responsibility: $\forall e \in \mathcal{D}, \forall x_N \in S(e), \forall i, j \in N$ such that $z_i = z_j$,

$$u_i = u_j \text{ or } [u_i < u_j \text{ and } x_j = 0].$$

Similar alterations have to be made for the cases of "uniform" and "reference" responsibility, as well as for *Acknowledged Merit* and *Fair Ranking for Equal Responsibility*. The definition of *Circumstance Solidarity* is affected as follows. In this case, it makes sense to apply the solidarity requirement only to agents who receive money, because the other agents (who obtain no money because presumably their circumstances are fabulous) will have their well-being depend only on the change in their own circumstances, independently of changes in the whole profile. More precisely, when most agents are made weakly worse-off by the change, one can tolerate that some agents gain if they have no money after the change, and when most agents are made weakly better-off, some agents may lose if they have no money before the change.

Circumstance Solidarity: $\forall e = ((y_N, z_N), \Omega), \ e' = ((y'_N, z_N), \Omega) \in \mathcal{D},$
$\forall x_N \in S(e), \ \forall x'_N \in S(e'),$

$$\forall i \ \in \ N \text{ such that } x'_i > 0, \ u(x_i, y_i, z_i) \geq u(x'_i, y'_i, z_i) \text{ or}$$
$$\forall i \ \in \ N \text{ such that } x_i > 0, \ u(x_i, y_i, z_i) \leq u(x'_i, y'_i, z_i).$$

The neutrality axioms are less affected. Acknowledged Handicap now reads:

Acknowledged Handicap: $\forall e \in \mathcal{D}, \ \forall i, j \in N,$

$$[\forall x \in \mathbb{R}_+, \forall k \in N, \ u(x, y_i, z_k) \leq u(x, y_j, z_k)] \Rightarrow [\forall x_N \in S(e), \ x_i \geq x_j].$$

With these adaptations, the logical relationships of Proposition 1.1 are preserved, with one restriction (namely, the implication from *Fair (Maximin) Ranking for Equal Responsibility* to *Maximin Well-Being for Uniform Responsibility* holds only when well-being can be equalized in the economy with the uniform profile).[28]

1.10   Conclusion

This chapter has introduced the main concepts of fairness related to the idea of the neutralization of circumstances ("compensation principle") and to the idea of responsibility which has been interpreted in terms of neutrality as no-intervention ("liberal reward principle"). The compensation principle can be expressed in conditions of equality or maximin of well-being for individuals with identical responsibility characteristics, or of solidarity in well-being with respect to changes of circumstances. The liberal reward principle can be expressed in conditions of equality of resources for individuals with identical circumstances, or of independence of resources with respect to changes in responsibility characteristics. Many of these conditions are intimately linked to, sometimes directly derived from, the no-envy condition, which therefore embodies the two principles to a substantial extent.

Once these various conditions have been introduced, it remains to examine how they shape a fair distribution of resources. This is the topic of the next chapter.

---

[28] See Fleurbaey and Maniquet (2004) for details.

Chapter 2

Distributing fairly

2.1 Introduction

This chapter pursues the analysis of responsibility principles undertaken in the first chapter, retaining the same simple framework with fixed individual characteristics and money transfers in the first-best context. In the first chapter, some precise fairness requirements have been obtained and interpreted in the light of various principles, in particular the compensation principle and the liberal reward principle.

It remains to see how these requirements can be fulfilled concretely. In particular the natural policy that offered itself as a salient solution in Example 1.1 and was proven to pass the no-envy test and therefore most of the other requirements, is not available in other cases, such as Examples 1.2 and 1.4. In this chapter it is shown how this problem is due to a basic conflict between the principle of compensation and the principle of liberal reward in cases when responsibility characteristics interfere with the relative importance of circumstances and transfers in the determination of well-being. In such a situation, the liberal reward principle, which essentially advocates ignoring responsibility characteristics, clashes with the compensation principle, which obviously requires paying attention to the impact of circumstances and transfers.

This dilemma offers three options as far as distributive policies are concerned. One option is to go back to the core idea of the no-envy test and to see how it can be reformulated in a weakened form. This amounts to accepting that both the compensation principle and the liberal reward principle will be satisfied in a modest way. The two other options give full precedence to one principle over the other, without however totally relinquishing the latter. They produce two interesting families of solutions. As it turns out, the solutions connected to the liberal reward principle are rather common in actual policy decisions, while the solutions linked to the compensation principle are somewhat less simple and therefore less widespread, although they might deserve more popularity, as will be argued below.

41

2.2   Impossibilities and incompatibilities

As briefly mentioned in the previous chapter, the no-envy test is too demanding when it is applied to circumstances and external resources instead of external resources only. The most obvious example of an impossibility is when each one of two individuals considers that the other has better circumstances. Then both request more resources than the other, and it is impossible to satisfy them simultaneously.

But the problem remains even when both agree about how to rank their circumstances. The key issue is the relative importance they assign to circumstances and resources in the determination of their own well-being. As an illustration, let us consider again Example 1.4, in which well-being was determined by the formula

$$\text{well-being} = \text{transfer} + (\text{bequest} \times \text{dedication}).$$

Let us see if one can achieve a distribution of resources such that the no-envy test can be satisfied, i.e., such that every individual is at least as well-off, according to his own dedication level, as with another's combination of transfer and bequest. The distribution of characteristics in the population is assumed to be as in Example 1.1, and the situation without redistribution is shown in Table 2.1 in order to make things clear.

Table 2.1: Laissez-faire policy

	low dedication (= 1)	high dedication (= 3)
low bequest (= 1)	1	3
high bequest (= 3)	3	9

In order to guarantee that an individual (say, i) with low bequest and low dedication does not envy an individual (say, j) with high values for both, this individual must receive at least two units of transfer more. This is indeed required in order to have

$$\text{transfer}_i + \underbrace{1}_{i\text{'s beq.}} \times \underbrace{1}_{i\text{'s dedic.}} \geq \text{transfer}_j + \underbrace{3}_{j\text{'s beq.}} \times \underbrace{1}_{i\text{'s dedic.}}.$$

Conversely, if one wants j not to envy i, the extra transfer received by i must not exceed six units, as shown from the following computation.

$$\text{transfer}_j + \underbrace{3}_{j\text{'s beq.}} \times \underbrace{3}_{j\text{'s dedic.}} \geq \text{transfer}_i + \underbrace{1}_{i\text{'s beq.}} \times \underbrace{3}_{j\text{'s dedic.}}.$$

In the case of these two individuals, the extra transfer for i must be between two and six units in order to guarantee mutual no-envy among them. This is a positive result. Now let us turn to two individuals of the other boxes of the table. Let individual k have a low bequest and a high dedication. He will not envy another individual l with high bequest and a low dedication only if he obtains an extra transfer of at least six units:

$$\text{transfer}_k + \underbrace{1}_{k\text{'s beq.}} \times \underbrace{3}_{k\text{'s dedic.}} \geq \text{transfer}_l + \underbrace{3}_{l\text{'s beq.}} \times \underbrace{3}_{k\text{'s dedic.}} .$$

But l, in order not to envy k, should not pay an extra transfer of more than two units, as shown by the following inequality:

$$\text{transfer}_l + \underbrace{3}_{l\text{'s beq.}} \times \underbrace{1}_{l\text{'s dedic.}} \geq \text{transfer}_k + \underbrace{1}_{k\text{'s beq.}} \times \underbrace{1}_{l\text{'s dedic.}} .$$

For instance, if k gets four units of transfer more than l, then each of them will envy the other, and modifying the gap in transfers will only increase the degree of envy of one of them. The reason for this difficulty is simple. The individual with low bequest happens to be the one who thinks that this justifies a big compensatory transfer, whereas the individual with high bequest has the opposite opinion and therefore cannot stand being much less well treated than the other.

This simple example suggests a conclusion which indeed has a wide validity: it is easy to achieve no-envy among individuals for which the circumstances and the responsibility characteristics are positively correlated, in the sense that those with more favorable circumstances also have responsibility characteristics which enhance the impact of circumstances on well-being;[1] it is more difficult, and generally impossible, to achieve no-envy among individuals with inverse correlation, i.e., when those with unfavorable circumstances are also those whose responsibility characteristics increase the impact of circumstances on well-being.

The difficulty with no-envy in the case of inverse correlation, as described above, can be analyzed as a clash between the two principles of compensation and liberal reward which have been shown in the previous chapter to be jointly encapsulated in the no-envy test.

Let us focus on two precise requirements linked to these two principles, namely, *Equal Well-Being for Equal Responsibility* and *Equal Treatment for Equal Circumstances*. Recall that each of these two conditions is a direct logical consequence of the no-envy test. Applied to Example 1.4, the first condition requires that among the low-dedication subpopulation, those with low bequest should receive an extra transfer of two units. Likewise, it also requires, for the high-dedication subpopulation, that those with low bequest receive an extra transfer of six units. Now, the second condition, *Equal Treatment for Equal Circumstances*, would want the extra transfer obtained by those with low bequest to be the same independently of their dedication. This is in outright contradiction with what was imposed by *Equal Well-Being for Equal Responsibility*.

This clash is not special to this particular pair of conditions. Other combinations of conditions representing the two principles can be shown to entail similar

---

[1] See Piketty (1994).

incompatibilities. The conflict between the two principles is actually very intuitive. The principle of liberal reward advocates a distribution of resources that
is somehow insensitive to responsibility characteristics. But responsibility characteristics may alter the need for extra resources for those who are endowed with
poor circumstances, so that a full compensation within each subclass of individuals with identical responsibility characteristics may require a greater sensitivity
to such characteristics than allowed for by the liberal reward principle.

2.3   *The compensation-neutrality trade-off

The formal framework is the same as in the previous chapter and we first focus on
the TU case. Let us illustrate how demanding the no-envy test is in this context.
One can represent the preferences of individuals by indifference "curves" in the
(x, y) space (see Fig. 2.1). The specificity of the TU case is that any given
individual's curves are all parallel to each other, horizontally.

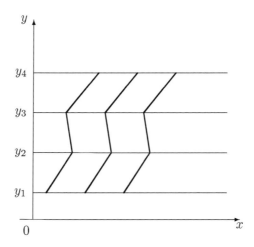

Figure 2.1: Individual preferences over (x, y)

Consider two individuals, i and j. An envy-free allocation between them
is impossible if their indifference curves are as in Fig. 2.2. Moreover, even
if a favorable configuration is observed for every pair of individuals, it may
nonetheless be impossible to achieve no-envy over all agents because no-envy
for third agents may impose constraints on the resource gap between given pairs
of agents. The following proposition shows, for the TU case, how demanding it
is to achieve no-envy.

Proposition 2.1 *Let* $e = ((y_N, z_N), \Omega) \in \mathcal{D}$. *There exists an envy-free allocation if and only if, for every permutation* $\sigma \in \Pi_N$,

$$\sum_{i \in N} v(y_i, z_i) \geq \sum_{i \in N} v(y_{\sigma(i)}, z_i).$$

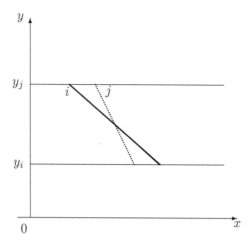

Figure 2.2: Impossibility of no-envy between i and j

Proof. Only if. Let x_N be an envy-free allocation and pick any $\sigma \in \Pi_N$. By no-envy, for all $i \in N$,

$$x_i + v(y_i, z_i) \geq x_{\sigma(i)} + v(y_{\sigma(i)}, z_i).$$

Summing over all $i \in N$, one obtains

$$\sum_{i \in N} [x_i + v(y_i, z_i)] \geq \sum_{i \in N} \left[x_{\sigma(i)} + v(y_{\sigma(i)}, z_i)\right].$$

Eliminating $\sum_{i \in N} x_i = \sum_{i \in N} x_{\sigma(i)}$ yields the desired result.

If. This is the duality theorem for the optimal assignment problem (see Alkan et al. 1991, p. 1028; Gale 1960, in Th. 5.5, p. 156, gives a direct proof of it for the special case of integers). ∎

This proposition shows that no-envy is achievable only if there is a perfect fit between circumstances and responsibility characteristics. If one considers *No-Envy* as an axiom to be satisfied by an allocation rule over the whole domain of profiles $(y_N, z_N) \in Y^N \times Z^N$, this proposition can be read as an impossibility, because possibility is obtained only under the requirement that

$$\sum_{i \in N} v(y_i, z_i) = \sum_{i \in N} v(y_{\sigma(i)}, z_i)$$

for all $\sigma \in \Pi_N$ and all $(y_N, z_N) \in Y^N \times Z^N$. This is equivalent to requiring v to be additively separable, i.e., there must exist two functions f, g such that $v(y, z) = f(y) + g(z)$ for all $(y, z) \in Y \times Z$.

The link between no-envy and the competitive equilibrium with equal wealth, in this context, is stated in the following proposition (due to Svensson 1983). Recall that with perfectly divisible goods, the egalitarian competitive equilibrium is a more restrictive concept than no-envy, in the sense that the set of envy-free and efficient allocations strictly includes the set of egalitarian competitive equilibria. Here the two sets coincide.

Proposition 2.2 *An allocation $x_N \in F(e)$ is envy-free if and only if it is a hypothetical competitive equilibrium with equal wealth, i.e., there is a price function $q(y)$ defined for every $y \in \{y_i \mid i \in N\}$ such that for all $i \in N$, (x_i, y_i) maximizes $x + v(y, z_i)$ subject to $x \in \mathbb{R}$, $y \in \{y_j \mid j \in N\}$, and $x + q(y) \leq (1/n) \sum_{j \in N} q(y_j) + (\Omega/n)$.*

Proof. If. Let $I = (1/n) \sum_{j \in N} q(y_j) + (\Omega/n)$. If x is an egalitarian competitive equilibrium, then for all $i \in N$, $x_i + q(y_i) = I$, by monotonicity of preferences. Since i maximizes in his budget, his satisfaction with (x_i, y_i) is at least as great as with $(I - q(y_j), y_j)$. In other words, for all $i, j \in N$,

$$x_i + v(y_i, z_i) \geq I - q(y_j) + v(y_j, z_i) = x_j + v(y_j, z_i).$$

Only if. Let x_N be an envy-free allocation. Pick a number I and let $q(y_i) = I - x_i$, for all $i \in N$. By construction, $I = (1/n) \sum_{j \in N} q(y_j) + (\Omega/n)$. By no-envy, one has, for all $i, j \in N$,

$$x_i + v(y_i, z_i) \geq x_j + v(y_j, z_i) = I - q(y_j) + v(y_j, z_i),$$

which shows that (x_i, y_i) maximizes $x + v(y, z_i)$ subject to $x \in \mathbb{R}$, $y \in \{y_j \mid j \in N\}$, and $x + q(y) \leq I$. ∎

We now turn to the conflict between compensation and liberal reward which underlies the above difficulty. Table 2.2 reproduces the configuration of axioms from Proposition 1.1 and highlights some axioms which play a role in the next proposition.

Table 2.2: Logical links between axioms

Compensation				Liberal Reward
(Weak) Circumst. Solidarity				**Independ. of Resp. Charact.**
⇓				⇓
Equal WB for Equal Resp. ⇐	**Ackn. Merit**	⇐ No-Envy ⇒	**Ackn. Hand.**	⇒ Equal Treatm. for Equal Circ.
⇓				⇓
Fair Ranking for Equal Resp.		⇓		Fair Treatm. for Equal Circ.
⇓				⇓
Equal WB for Unif. Resp.		⇐ **Egalit. Bound** ⇒		Equal Treatm. for Unif. Circ.
⇓				⇓
Equal WB for Ref. Resp.				Equal Treatm. for Ref. Circ.

A key incompatibility in the proposition below is between *Fair Ranking for Equal Responsibility* and *Fair Treatment for Equal Circumstances.*

Proposition 2.3 *The following combinations of axioms are compatible:*
(1) Circumstance Solidarity, Acknowledged Merit *and* Egalitarian Bound;
(2) Equal Well-Being for Reference Responsibility *and* Independence of Responsibility Characteristics;
(3) Equal Well-Being for Uniform Responsibility *and* Acknowledged Handicap;
(4) Acknowledged Handicap *and* Independence of Responsibility Characteristics.
In the general case (i.e., when no restriction is assumed for v), all the combinations of axioms for which the compatibility cannot be deduced from the above and the logical implications of Table 2.2 are incompatible.[2]
If v is additively separable, i.e., $v(y, z) = f(y) + g(z)$, then all axioms are compatible and are satisfied by the "natural" allocation rule:

$$x_i = -f(y_i) + \frac{1}{n} \sum_{j \in N} f(y_j) + \frac{\Omega}{n}.$$

Proof. (1) *Circumstance Solidarity, Acknowledged Merit* and *Egalitarian Bound* are jointly satisfied by the Average Egalitarian-Equivalence rule defined by:

$$x_i = -v(y_i, z_i) + \frac{1}{n} \sum_{j \in N} v(y_j, z_i) + c,$$

where c is adjusted for every profile so as to obtain $\sum_{i \in N} x_i = \Omega$.
(2) *Equal Well-Being for Reference Responsibility* and *Independence of Responsibility Characteristics* are jointly satisfied by the Conditional Equality rule defined by:

$$x_i = -v(y_i, \tilde{z}) + c,$$

where $\tilde{z}$ is a fixed reference value and c is adjusted so as to obtain $\sum_{i \in N} x_i = \Omega$.
(3) *Equal Well-Being for Uniform Responsibility* and *Acknowledged Handicap* are jointly satisfied by the Φ-Conditional Equality rule defined by:

$$x_i = -v(y_i, \Phi(z_N)) + c,$$

where $\Phi : Z^N \to Z$ is such that for all z_N, there is j such that $\Phi(z_N) = z_j$, and c is adjusted so as to obtain $\sum_{i \in N} x_i = \Omega$.
(4) *Acknowledged Handicap* and *Independence of Responsibility Characteristics* are jointly satisfied by the "no-compensation" rule $x_i = \Omega/n$ for all $i \in N$.[3]

---

[2] For instance, *Equal Well-Being for Equal Responsibility* and *Equal Treatment for Uniform Circumstances* are compatible because the former is weaker than *Circumstance Solidarity* and the latter is weaker than *Egalitarian Bound*, two compatible axioms. In contrast, *Fair Ranking for Equal Responsibility* and *Fair Treatment for Equal Circumstances* are incompatible.

[3] A strict version of *Acknowledged Handicap* (SAH, requiring $x_i > x_j$ whenever $v(y_i, z_k) < v(y_j, z_k)$ for all $k \in N$) is incompatible with *Independence of Responsibility Characteristics* (IRC). Consider the example of point (5) of the proof, but with a population $N = \{1, 3\}$. SAH requires $x_1 < x_3$. Now consider a change in z_N such that the profile is now as in population $\{2, 4\}$. With this new profile, SAH requires $x_1 > x_3$. This contradicts IRC.

(5) *Fair Ranking for Equal Responsibility* (FRER) and *Fair Treatment for Equal Circumstances* (FTEC) are incompatible. Take an economy with a function $v((y^a, y^b), (z^a, z^b)) = y^a z^a + y^b z^b$, $\Omega = 0$, and four agents with a profile described in Table 2.3.

Table 2.3: Profile

i	y_i^a	y_i^b	z_i^a	z_i^b
1	1	2	1	2
2	1	2	2	1
3	2	1	1	2
4	2	1	2	1

One computes $\bar{v}(e) = 4.5$. FRER then requires

$$\begin{cases} (x_1 + 0.5)(x_3 - 0.5) \geq 0 \\ (x_2 - 0.5)(x_4 + 0.5) \geq 0, \end{cases}$$

while FTEC requires

$$\begin{cases} x_1 x_2 \geq 0 \\ x_3 x_4 \geq 0. \end{cases}$$

Try $x_1 \geq 0$. This implies $x_3 \geq 0.5$, and $x_4 \geq 0$ (from $x_3 x_4 \geq 0$), and therefore $x_2 \geq 0.5$. This makes it impossible to achieve $x_1 + x_2 + x_3 + x_4 = 0$.

Try $x_1 < 0$. This implies $x_2 \leq 0$, and therefore $x_4 \leq -0.5$, and therefore $x_3 \leq 0$. Same contradiction.

(6) *Egalitarian Bound* (EB) and *Fair Treatment for Equal Circumstances* (FTEC) are incompatible. Pursue with the same example. One has $m_i(y_N, z_i, \Omega) = 4.5$ for all $i \in N$. Since this is also the value of $\bar{v}(e)$, EB imposes that $x_i + v(y_i, z_i) = 4.5$ for all $i \in N$. This is obtained with $x_1 = x_4 = -0.5$, $x_2 = x_3 = 0.5$. This contradicts the requirements of FTEC (e.g., $x_1 x_2 \geq 0$).

(7) *Equal Well-Being for Uniform Responsibility* (EWUR) and *Independence of Responsibility Characteristics* (IRC) are incompatible. Let v and y, y', z, z' be such that

$$v(y', z) - v(y, z) \neq v(y', z') - v(y, z').$$

Consider an economy e with two agents 1 and 2 with profile, respectively, $(y, z), (y', z)$. By EWUR, one must have $x_1 + v(y, z) = x_2 + v(y', z)$. Consider another economy e' with two agents and a new profile $(y, z'), (y', z')$. By EWUR again, one must have $x_1' + v(y, z') = x_2' + v(y', z')$. And by IRC, one must have $x_1' = x_1$ and $x_2' = x_2$, which is impossible. ∎

For the additively separable case, this proposition mentions the allocation rule corresponding to the "natural policy" exemplified in Chapter 1. This natural allocation rule makes every agent's well-being equal to the average contribution of y_N (and Ω) plus the individual contribution of z_i:

$$u_i = \frac{\Omega}{n} + \frac{1}{n} \sum_{j \in N} f(y_j) + g(z_i).$$

Some of the above incompatibilities are obtained whenever the function v is not additively separable. This is the case in particular for *Equal Well-Being for Equal Responsibility* and *Equal Treatment for Equal Circumstances* (but not for *Fair Ranking for Equal Responsibility* and *Fair Treatment for Equal Circumstances*). Let v and y, y', z, z' be such that

$$v(y', z) - v(y, z) \neq v(y', z') - v(y, z').$$

Consider an economy with four agents 1 through 4, with profile $((y, z), (y, z'), (y', z), (y', z'))$. By *Equal Well-Being for Equal Responsibility*, one must have

$$x_1 + v(y, z) = x_3 + v(y', z),$$
$$x_2 + v(y, z') = x_4 + v(y', z').$$

By *Equal Treatment for Equal Circumstances*, one must have $x_1 = x_2$ and $x_3 = x_4$. This is impossible. Since the additively separable case can be considered very special, this means that the conflict between the principle of compensation and the principle of liberal reward is serious.

Let us now briefly turn to the distribution case (i.e., a more general function $u = u(x, y, z)$ and the constraint $x \geq 0$). What decides of the conflict between the two principles in this case is the following separability condition: for all $x, x' \geq 0$, $i, j, k, l \in N$ (not necessarily different),

$$u(x, y_i, z_k) \geq u(x', y_j, z_k) \Leftrightarrow u(x, y_i, z_l) \geq u(x', y_j, z_l).$$

In other words, there is no conflict if the pair (x, y) is separable and one can write

$$u(x, y, z) = f(\varphi(x, y), z)$$

where f is increasing in its first argument. This corresponds to a situation in which all indifference curves in the (x, y) space (recall Fig. 2.1) are identical across individuals. In this case, the allocation rule which applies the maximin criterion to the distribution $(\varphi(x_i, y_i))_{i \in N}$ satisfies all of the axioms (except No-Envy, which is achieved only under perfect equality of $\varphi(x_i, y_i)$).

In the non-separable case, the incompatibilities depicted in Proposition 2.3 remain true. The compatibilities are also valid, with the exception that *Egalitarian Bound* is no longer compatible in general with *Circumstance Solidarity*.

2.4 Weakening no-envy

The conflict between compensation and liberal reward can trigger a search for solutions in three directions. Two of them consist in sticking to one of the two principles and accepting to satisfy only weak conditions reflecting the other one. These dual options will be developed in the next sections. Here we focus on the idea that, since no-envy nicely encapsulates both principles, one could simply try to satisfy as much of it as possible.

There are various ways to understand the phrase "as much as possible" with respect to the satisfaction of no-envy. One possibility is to measure the number of envy occurrences, i.e., the number of pairs of individuals such that one envies the other, and try to minimize this number (Feldman and Kirman 1974). This is not satisfactory, however, since the number of envy occurrences can be minimized by very asymmetric allocations in which one agent obtains all the available resources and is envied by all the others. The concern for symmetry can be captured by the criterion that for every individual, the number of those who envy him should be equal to the number of those he envies (Daniel 1975). But this criterion itself is too exclusive and fails to discriminate between an envy-free allocation and another in which everybody envies everybody. One can combine the two criteria by first focusing on the allocations satisfying the criterion of equality between numbers envied and numbers envying, for every individual, and then selecting among them those with the lowest number of envy occurrences (Fleurbaey 1994). A difficulty is that there do not always exist allocations satisfying the equality criterion.

In fact, the general idea underlying these first criteria is to examine the graph of envy relations with a double concern for symmetry and for minimizing the number of relations. In Fig. 2.3, five graphs are represented for a population of four individuals. In case (a), individual 1 is envied by all the others; in case (b), individual 1 envies all the others; in case (c), a cycle of envy occurs; in case (d), an envy relation has been reversed in comparison to case (c); in case (e), this envy relation has been deleted.

Although the number of envy relations is smaller in (a) and (b) than in (c), and the same in (d) as in (c), one should probably prefer (c) out of a concern for symmetry. Although (e) is not symmetric, it may not be worse than (c), because it has a strictly smaller graph of envy relations. This is a difficult case

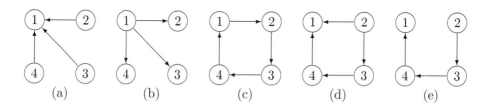

Figure 2.3: Envy graphs

since balancedness in (c) makes it look more equal than (e), but one must be careful to avoid the intuitive illusion that arrows form a transitive "better-off than" relation. In (e), there is no-envy between agents 1 and 2, and this is the relevant test of equality. The arrows from 2 to 1 via 3 and 4 do not mean that 2 is worse-off than 1. It is true that between two agents, reciprocal envy appears better than a one-way envy relation. But this does not necessarily extend to cycles of envy among more agents. Therefore it is not unreasonable to consider that removing a non-reciprocal envy relation between two agents is always a good thing (given that the only information is the envy graph, a limitation that will be discussed below).

Defining a more precise preference order on envy graphs is a complex matter. Suzumura (1983) proposes a very natural ranking that applies the reverse leximin criterion to the vector of individual envy indices, where an individual envy index is simply the number of other agents this individual envies (i.e., the number of outgoing arrows in the graph). The reverse leximin criterion prefers a vector to another if its greatest component is smaller, or if the greatest components are equal in the two vectors but the second greatest component is smaller, and so on. It corresponds to the application of the standard leximin criterion (which prefers a vector if its lowest component is greater, or in case of equality if its second lowest component is greater, and so on) to the opposite vectors.

Envious Count criterion: To every individual, assign the number of individuals he envies. Then apply the reverse leximin criterion to the list of these numbers.

This criterion, as shown in the next section, satisfies *Equal Well-Being for Equal Responsibility* on an interesting range of cases. However, this criterion is not concerned with symmetry and puts graph (a) from Fig. 2.3 at the top of the five graphs (at a tie with (e)), which appears questionable. It is possible to define refinements which incorporate a concern for symmetry, but they do not satisfy *Equal Well-Being for Equal Responsibility* (or *Equal Treatment for Equal Circumstances*) on a large domain, as shown in the next section. It appears that envy graphs provide insufficient information.

Let us now introduce a criterion which uses more information. Van Parijs (1990, 1995), inspired by Ackerman (1980), has proposed a criterion of "Undominated Diversity" which consists in seeking a situation in which there is no pair of individuals such that everybody would prefer to have one individual's bundle of external resources and circumstances rather than the other's. The idea is that when everybody considers, say, Ann's bundle to be better than Bob's, there is a clear sense in which Bob is worse off. Therefore such a dominance configuration should be avoided.

This criterion is too weak and too strong at the same time. It is weak because it sometimes selects a large set of allocations. In particular, when envy-free allocations exist it generally accepts many other allocations plagued with envy. For instance, imagine a three-agent population in which:

- 1 considers 2's circumstances to be equivalent to his, but, for all feasible allocations, always considers himself (and 2) to be better-off than 3;

- 2 considers 3's circumstances to be equivalent to his, but, for all feasible allocations, always considers himself (and 3) to be better-off than 1;

- 3 considers 1's circumstances to be equivalent to his, but, for all feasible allocations, always considers himself (and 1) to be better-off than 2.

In this example, all feasible allocations are acceptable for Undominated Diversity, even though the equal-split allocation is the only envy-free allocation!

But this criterion may also happen to be empty, which reveals that it can also be too restrictive. In fact, the underlying idea is again to rank graphs of envy relations. But instead of simply counting the arrows between individuals, the idea is to assign a number to every envy relation, which is equal to the number of individuals who share the envious' preferences. For instance, suppose i envies j, and there are three other individuals who, with their own responsibility characteristics, would be better-off with j's bundle of external resources and circumstances than with i's. Then the envy arrow from i to j is assigned a value of four. When i does not envy j, no arrow is drawn even if there are some other individuals who would be better-off with j's bundle than with i's. The absence of an arrow is equivalent to a value of zero. In summary, for every ordered pair (i, j), this procedure gives us a number, equal to zero if i does not envy j, and equal to a positive integer between one and the population size otherwise. "Undominated Diversity" is simply the rather special requirement that no pair should have a number with the maximal value (population size). It is much more sensible to apply the reverse leximin criterion to the list of these numbers. Let us call this the "Diversity" criterion, since it both extends and refines Van Parijs' criterion, and takes account of the diversity of preferences in the population.

Diversity criterion: To every pair of individuals (i, j), assign the value zero if i does not envy j, and a value equal to the total number of individuals who would be better-off with j's bundle than with i's otherwise. Then apply the reverse leximin criterion to the list of these numbers.

An envy-free allocation corresponds to a list containing only null figures, and will be selected whenever it exists. Similarly, if there exist allocations satisfying the undominated diversity criterion, the selected allocations will be drawn from this subset. An interesting feature of the Diversity criterion (already present in Undominated Diversity) is that it satisfies *Equal Treatment for Equal Circumstances.*

In spite of this, the Diversity criterion can still be criticized for being too crude. It ranks allocations on the basis of rather poor information, namely, the graphs of envy relations simply augmented with the numbers of similar rankings. Allocations are made of distributions of resources, which provide a much finer scale for the measurement of envy situations. It is quite unjustifiable to ignore this information and simply focus on zero-one markers of the presence or absence of envy relations. In particular, the above criteria are indifferent between any pair of allocations with the same (augmented) graph, even if one allocation may have much less inequality, i.e., a smaller degree of envy, than the other. They may also prefer an allocation with fewer relations of envy but with a very high degree of envy in these relations over another allocation with more envy occurrences but which is in fact much closer to an envy-free situation.

Here is an alternative approach. For every allocation and for every pair of individuals (i, j), compute the number t_{ij} as the lowest amount of external

resources such that giving this to i in addition to what he receives in this allocation would prevent him from envying j. If i already does not envy j, this
number is typically negative, meaning that one can diminish i's resources without making him envy j. And one always has $t_{ii} = 0$. Let t_{ij} be called the degree
of i's envy toward j. Fleurbaey (1994), inspired by Diamantaras and Thomson
(1990), proposed to retain the greatest t_{ij} for every i (ignoring t_{ii}) as a measure
of his greatest degree of envy (or smallest degree of non-envy if it is negative),
and to apply the reverse leximin criterion to the vector of these numbers. This
is a rather natural solution, but, as noticed in Fleurbaey (1994), it fails to satisfy *Equal Well-Being for Equal Responsibility* and *Equal Treatment for Equal
Circumstances*.

Two other options appear more attractive and will be highlighted here. The
first is similar to the above but incorporates t_{ii} in the computation of the greatest
degree of envy, so that this number is always non-negative and is equal to the
minimal increment in resources which would make i non-envious. Moreover,
the criterion applies the summation operation to these numbers rather than
the reverse leximin. The second solution computes, for every individual, the
greatest degree of envy among those who might envy him, which corresponds
to the minimal deduction in i's resources which would prevent him from being
envied. It then applies the summation operator to these numbers. In both cases,
the social objective is to minimize the value of these sums. The first is focused
on the degree of envy from the standpoint of the envious, while the second takes
the viewpoint of those who are envied.

Envious Intensity: Minimize the sum over all i of the maximum of t_{ij} over
all j.

Envied Intensity: Minimize the sum over all j of the maximum of t_{ij} over
all i.

Intuitively, Envious Intensity computes the total amount of money that
should be distributed to the population in order to make them "non-envious,"
in the special sense that when an individual receives his share of this money he
compares himself to the others' *pre-distribution* situations. Similarly, Envied
Intensity computes the total amount of money that should be taken from the
population so that none of them is "envied" any more, in a similar sense (the
envious comparing their pre-tax situation to the post-tax situation of the envied). Both criteria seek minimize this total amount, which is a natural way
to get as close as possible to an envy-free situation (in which both amounts are
null).

These two rankings have interesting properties. Both select all the envy-
free allocations when they exist. In addition, the former satisfies *Equal Treatment for Equal Circumstances*, while the latter, on a suitable domain, satisfies
Equal Well-Being for Equal Responsibility. Moreover, both of them satisfy *Equal
Treatment for Uniform Circumstances* and *Equal Well-Being for Uniform Responsibility*.

2.5   *No-envy rankings

We first provide a formal definition of the solutions introduced in the previous section, and then examine the properties they satisfy. As above, we focus on the TU case to begin with. The first relies on the number of agents a given agent envies, which is denoted as follows:

$$n_i(x_N) = |\{j \in N \mid x_i + v(y_i, z_i) < x_j + v(y_j, z_i)\}|.$$

Recall from the introduction that $\geq_{\text{lex}}$ denotes the leximin ordering.

Envious Count criterion (S_{EsC}): $\forall e \in \mathcal{D}, \forall x_N \in F(e)$, $x_N \in S_{EsC}(e)$ if and only if $\forall x'_N \in F(e)$,

$$- (n_i(x_N))_{i \in N} \geq_{\text{lex}} - (n_i(x'_N))_{i \in N}.$$

One can define a dual criterion to this one, which relies on the number of agents by whom a given agent is envied:

$$n'_i(x_N) = |\{j \in N \mid x_i + v(y_i, z_j) > x_j + v(y_j, z_j)\}|.$$

Envied Count criterion (S_{EdC}): $\forall e \in \mathcal{D}, \forall x_N \in F(e)$, $x_N \in S_{EdC}(e)$ if and only if $\forall x'_N \in F(e)$,

$$- (n'_i(x_N))_{i \in N} \geq_{\text{lex}} - (n'_i(x'_N))_{i \in N}.$$

Before introducing the formal definitions of the other criteria, let us briefly discuss the possibility to refine these rankings in order to take account of the symmetry of envy graphs. A concern for balance can be incorporated by measuring individual situations with respect to envy in terms of an index that depends on n_i *and* on n'_i. Let

$$d_i(x_N) = D(n_i(x_N), n'_i(x_N))$$

for a function D the properties of which are discussed below. One can apply the reverse leximin criterion to such indices. The properties of the criterion will then depend on how D ranks various (n_i, n'_i) vectors. Figure 2.4 shows iso-curves for the D function in the (n_i, n'_i) space. Panels (1) and (2) illustrate the two extreme cases of the Envious Count and Envied Count criteria:
(1) $D(n_i, n'_i) = n_i$;
(2) $D(n_i, n'_i) = n'_i$.
Panels (3) and (4) correspond to cases in which a concern for balance is introduced:
(3) $D(n_i, n'_i) = 2 \max \{n_i, n'_i\} + \min \{n_i, n'_i\}$.
(4) $D(n_i, n'_i) = 2 \max \{n_i, n'_i\} - \min \{n_i, n'_i\} = \max \{n_i, n'_i\} + |n_i - n'_i|$.
As far as the envy graphs of Fig. 2.3 are concerned, formula (3) puts (e) above (c) whereas formula (4), displaying a greater concern for balance, puts (c) above (e). Panel (5) depicts the extreme case in which only symmetry (Daniel's 1975

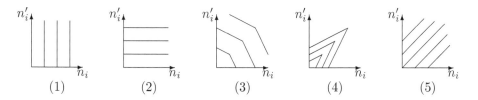

Figure 2.4: Iso-curves of D

concept of balanced allocations) matters:

(5) $D(n_i, n_i') = |n_i - n_i'|$.

The properties of such criteria will not be further explored here, because rankings based only on envy graphs suffer from intrinsic limitations which are described below.

The Diversity criterion is as follows, and can also be given a dual counterpart. For any allocation x_N, any pair of agents (i, j), let

$$n_{ij}(x_N) = \begin{cases} 0 \text{ if } i \text{ does not envy } j, \\ |\{k \in N \mid x_j + v(y_j, z_k) > x_i + v(y_i, z_k)\}| \text{ otherwise,} \end{cases}$$

$$n_{ij}'(x_N) = \begin{cases} 0 \text{ if } i \text{ does not envy } j, \\ |\{k \in N \mid u_j - v(y_k, z_j) > u_i - v(y_k, z_i)\}| \text{ otherwise.} \end{cases}$$

Diversity criterion (S_D): $\forall e \in \mathcal{D}, \forall x_N \in F(e)$, $x_N \in S_D(e)$ if and only if $\forall x_N' \in F(e)$,

$$- (n_{ij}(x_N))_{i,j \in N} \geq_{\text{lex}} - (n_{ij}(x_N'))_{i,j \in N}.$$

Compensation Diversity criterion (R_{CD}): $\forall e \in \mathcal{D}, \forall x_N \in F(e)$, $x_N \in S_{CD}(e)$ if and only if $\forall x_N' \in F(e)$,

$$- \left(n_{ij}'(x_N)\right)_{i,j \in N} \geq_{\text{lex}} - \left(n_{ij}'(x_N')\right)_{i,j \in N}.$$

In the definition of $n_{ij}'(x_N)$, the expression $u_j - v(y_k, z_j) > u_i - v(y_k, z_i)$ can be understood as follows. Agent i with u_i would be just as well-off with

$$\underbrace{u_i - v(y_k, z_i)}_{\hat{x}_{ik}} + v(y_k, z_i) = u_i.$$

A similar computation is made for agent j:

$$\underbrace{u_j - v(y_k, z_j)}_{\hat{x}_{jk}} + v(y_k, z_j) = u_j.$$

Now, if both agents had circumstances y_k, the ideal distribution of x among them would be egalitarian. If the current situation u_i, u_j were equivalent to such egalitarian situation with y_k for both agents, one should then have $\hat{x}_{ik} = \hat{x}_{jk}$. The Compensation Diversity criterion focuses on the number of y_k such that inequality in one direction is observed.[4]

Finally, we turn to the two Envy Intensity criteria. For any allocation $x_N \in F(e)$, any pair of agents $i, j \in N$, let

$$t_{ij}(x_N) = x_j + v(y_j, z_i) - x_i - v(y_i, z_i).$$

One has $t_{ij}(x_N) > 0$ if and only if i envies j, and $t_{ii}(x_N) \equiv 0$.

Envious Intensity (S_{EsI}): $\forall e \in \mathcal{D}, \forall x_N \in F(e)$, $x_N \in S_{EsI}(e)$ if and only if $\forall x'_N \in F(e)$,

$$\sum_{i \in N} \max_{j \in N} t_{ij}(x_N) \leq \sum_{i \in N} \max_{j \in N} t_{ij}(x'_N).$$

Envied Intensity (S_{EdI}): $\forall e \in \mathcal{D}, \forall x_N \in F(e)$, $x_N \in S_{EdI}(e)$ if and only if $\forall x'_N \in F(e)$,

$$\sum_{j \in N} \max_{i \in N} t_{ij}(x_N) \leq \sum_{j \in N} \max_{i \in N} t_{ij}(x'_N).$$

One can check that these allocation rules, which are obviously based on rankings of allocations, are never empty in the whole domain. The following proposition lists the main properties satisfied by them.

Proposition 2.4 *The six allocation rules (Envious Count, Envied Count, Diversity, Compensation Diversity, Envious Intensity, Envied Intensity) exactly select the subset of envy-free allocations whenever it is non-empty. Table 2.4 displays their pattern of axiom satisfaction.*

Table 2.4: Axioms satisfied by solutions

	S_{EsC}	S_{EdC}	S_{CD} S_{EdI}	S_D S_{EsI}
Circumstance Solidarity				
Acknowledged. Merit			✓	
Eq. W-B for Eq. Respons.	✓		✓	
Eq. W-B for Un. Respons.	✓	✓	✓	✓
Indep. of Resp. Charac.				
Acknowledged Handicap				✓
Eq. Transf. for Eq. Circums.		✓		✓
Eq. Transf. for Un. Circums.	✓	✓	✓	✓

Proof. The proof is only provided for Envious Count, Diversity and Envious Intensity. The proof for the dual criteria has similar structure.

---

[4]Observe the dual reference to the envious and the envied in these two criteria. When i envies j, this is recorded by Diversity by taking $z_k = z_i$, i.e., the preferences of the envious. In contrast, this is recorded by Compensation Diversity by taking $y_k = y_j$, i.e., the circumstances of the envied agent.

Envious Count. (1) An envy-free allocation is such that $(n_i(x_N))_{i \in N} = 0$, and this dominates any $-(n_i(x'_N))_{i \in N} < 0$ for the leximin criterion. Therefore the subset of envy-free allocations is selected whenever it is non-empty.

(2) It satisfies *Equal Treatment for Uniform Circumstances* because, when $y_i = y_j$ for all $i, j \in N$, the only envy-free allocation is $x_i = \Omega/n$ for all $i \in N$ and is the only one to be selected.

(3) It satisfies *Equal Well-Being for Equal Responsibility*. Consider two agents $i, j \in N$ such that $z_i = z_j$ and an allocation x_N such that $u_i > u_j$. Let x'_N be such that $x'_i = x_i - (u_i - u_j)$ and $x'_k = x_k$ for all $k \neq i$. Then $n_i(x'_N) = n_j(x'_N) = n_j(x_N) - 1$, while $n_k(x'_N) \leq n_k(x_N)$ for all $k \neq i, j$. Since $n_j(x_N) > n_i(x_N)$, the vector $(n_i(x'_N), n_j(x'_N))$ is better for the reverse leximin than $(n_i(x_N), n_j(x_N))$, and since $n_k(x'_N) \leq n_k(x_N)$ for all $k \neq i, j$, the whole vector $(n_k(x'_N))_{k \in N}$ is better than $(n_k(x_N))_{k \in N}$. The allocation x'_N is not in $F(e)$, but the allocation

$$x''_N = x'_N - \frac{1}{n} \sum_{i \in N} x'_i + \frac{\Omega}{n}$$

is, and is such that $n_k(x''_N) = n_k(x'_N)$ for all $k \in N$.

(4) *Acknowledged Merit* is not satisfied. Consider the four-agent economy in which $\Omega = 0$ and

$$(v(y_i, z_j))_{\substack{i=1,\dots,4 \\ j=1,\dots,4}} = \begin{pmatrix} 10 & 10 & 10 & 10 \\ 10 & 2 & 1 & 1 \\ 8 & 8 & 5 & 2 \\ 4 & 4 & 2 & 5 \end{pmatrix}.$$

The best allocation for Envious Count is $x_N = (-4, 5, -2, 1)$, entailing $u_N = (6, 7, 3, 6)$ and $n_N(x_N) = (1, 0, 2, 0)$. One observes that $u_1 < u_2$ in spite of $v(y_k, z_1) \geq v(y_k, z_2)$ for all $k \in N$.

(5) Satisfaction of *Equal Well-Being for Equal Responsibility* implies, by Proposition 2.3, that *Equal Treatment for Equal Circumstances* is not satisfied.

Diversity. (1) An envy-free allocation is such that $(n_{ij}(x_N))_{i,j \in N} = 0$, and this dominates any $-(n_{ij}(x'_N))_{i,j \in N} < 0$ for the leximin criterion. Therefore the subset of envy-free allocations is selected whenever it is non-empty.

(2) By a similar argument as in point (2) above, this implies that Diversity satisfies *Equal Well-Being for Uniform Responsibility*.

(3) That it satisfies *Acknowledged Handicap* is a consequence of the fact that $n_{ij}(x_N) = n$ if $x_i < x_j$ while $v(y_i, z_k) \leq v(y_j, z_k)$ for all $k \in N$ and that, in the TU case, there always exist (undominated diversity) allocations x_N such that

$$\max (n_{ij}(x_N))_{i,j \in N} < n.$$

The latter fact, which is of independent interest, is proved as follows (this is inspired by Fleurbaey 1994, Prop. 10). Let

$$\Omega^* = (n-1) \max_{i,j,k \in N} (v(y_i, z_k) - v(y_j, z_k))$$

and $F^* = \left\{ x_N \in \mathbb{R}_+^N \mid \sum_{i \in N} x_i = \Omega^* \right\}$. For each $i \in N$, let

$$E_i = \{ x_N \in F^* \mid \forall j \in N, \exists k \in N, \ x_i + v(y_i, z_k) \geq x_j + v(y_j, z_k) \}.$$

The set E_i is closed. Now consider any allocation $x_N \in F^*$. There is $i \in N$ such that $x_i > 0$ and $x_N \in E_i$. Suppose otherwise. First imagine that $x_N \gg 0$. Then for all $i \in N$, there would be $j \in N$ such that $j \succ i$, where $\succ$ is the transitive and asymmetric relation defined by:

$$j \succ i \Leftrightarrow \forall k \in N, \ x_i + v(y_i, z_k) < x_j + v(y_j, z_k).$$

Since N is finite, this relation would then have a cycle, which is impossible. Therefore one must have $x_N \not\gg 0$, implying that there is $j \in N$ such that $x_j \geq \Omega^* / (n-1) > 0$. There is therefore j_1 such that $j_1 \succ j$, and this chain of preference can be pursued until one reaches some i with $x_i = 0$. By transitivity, $i \succ j$, meaning that for all $k \in N$,

$$x_i + v(y_i, z_k) > x_j + v(y_j, z_k),$$

or equivalently,

$$v(y_i, z_k) - v(y_j, z_k) > x_j - x_i \geq \frac{\Omega^*}{n-1},$$

contradicting the definition of Ω^*. This proves that for all $x_N \in F^*$, there is $i \in N$ such that $x_i > 0$ and $x_N \in E_i$. One can then apply the Knaster–Kuratowski–Mazurkiewicz lemma (Border 1985, 5.2) and conclude that there is $x_N \in F^*$ such that $x_N \in \bigcap_{i \in N} E_i$. This is equivalent to saying that for all $i, j \in N$, $n_{ij}(x_N) < n$. Let $x_i' = x_i - \frac{1}{n} \sum_{i \in N} x_i + \Omega/n$ for all $i \in N$. The allocation x_N' is such that $\sum_{i \in N} x_i' = \Omega$ and $(n_{ij}(x_N'))_{i,j \in N} = (n_{ij}(x_N))_{i,j \in N}$ and is thus as desired.

(4) That it satisfies *Acknowledged Handicap* in turn implies, by Proposition 2.3, that it does not satisfy *Equal Well-Being for Equal Responsibility*.

Envious Intensity. (1) The subset of envy-free allocations is selected whenever it is non-empty. For all $x_N \in F(e)$, all $i \in N$,

$$\max_{j \in N} t_{ij}(x_N) \geq t_{ii}(x_N) \equiv 0,$$

and $\max_{j \in N} t_{ij}(x_N) > 0$ if and only if i is envious, so that one has

$$\sum_{i \in N} \max_{j \in N} t_{ij}(x_N) = 0$$

if and only if x_N is envy-free.

(2) By the same argument as above, this implies that Diversity satisfies *Equal Well-Being for Uniform Responsibility*.

(3) With respect to *Acknowledged Handicap*, consider two agents i, j such that for all $k \in N$, $v(y_i, z_k) \geq v(y_j, z_k)$, and pick an allocation x_N minimizing

$\sum_{i \in N} \max_{j \in N} t_{ij}(x_N)$, with $x_i > x_j$. The fact that $x_i > x_j$ implies that $t_{ji}(x_N) > 0$ and that, for all $k \neq j$, $\max_{l \in N} t_{kl}(x_N) \geq t_{ki}(x_N) > t_{kj}(x_N)$. Take δ such that

$$0 < \delta < \frac{1}{n} \min_{k \in N} \left(\max_{l \in N} t_{kl}(x_N) - t_{kj}(x_N) \right).$$

Construct a new allocation such that $x'_k = x_k - \delta$ for all $k \neq j$, and $x'_j = x_j + (n-1)\delta$. One has $\max_{l \in N} t_{kl}(x'_N) = \max_{l \in N} t_{kl}(x_N)$ for all $k \neq j$, while $\max_{l \in N} t_{jl}(x'_N) < \max_{l \in N} t_{jl}(x_N)$. This contradicts the assumption that x_N minimizes $\sum_{i \in N} \max_{j \in N} t_{ij}(x_N)$.

(4) Satisfaction of *Acknowledged Handicap* in turn implies that it does not satisfy *Equal Well-Being for Equal Responsibility*. ∎

This proposition suggests that criteria that are only based on envy graphs are less satisfactory than criteria based on richer information, as far as the principles of compensation or liberal reward are concerned. Examination of the distribution case makes it even more striking, as witnessed in the following proposition. To keep things simple, attention is restricted to "reasonable" criteria that prefer an allocation with only one envy occurrence to any allocation with an asymmetric envy graph containing more than m envy occurrences, for m great enough. This restriction seems unquestionable when dealing with criteria that rely only on envy graphs.

Proposition 2.5 *In the distribution case, no allocation rule based on a reasonable ranking of envy graphs satisfies either* Equal Well-Being for Equal Responsibility *or* Equal Treatment for Equal Circumstances.

Proof. In the distribution case, two agents i, j can be in a situation in which no one envies the other when they have certain x_i^*, x_j^*, whereas at all other allocations at least one envies the other. In such a case, let us say that i and j are "locked" at (x_i^*, x_j^*). Let us illustrate how this can happen. Let $u(x, y_i, z_i) = u(x, y_j, z_i)$ for all x, and $u(x, y_j, z_j) < u(x, y_i, z_j)$ for all $x \neq x^*$ while $u(x^*, y_j, z_j) = u(x^*, y_i, z_j)$. Then i and j are locked at (x^*, x^*), since there is no envy at (x^*, x^*), whereas for x_i, x_j (with at least one different from x^*), i envies j if $x_i < x_j$ and j envies i if $x_i \geq x_j$.

Consider an n-agent population $\{1, ..., n\}$ where $z_1 = z_2$ and such that agents i and j, for all $i, j > 1$, are locked at $(1,1)$. Assume that $\Omega = n$, that for all $x_N \in F(e)$ agents $3, ..., n$ do not envy agent 1, and that $u_1 > u_2$ at allocation $(1, ..., 1)$, implying that 1 is envied by 2 at this allocation. Necessarily this is the only envy occurrence in this allocation. At any other allocation in $F(e)$, there will be at least $n-2$ envy occurrences, because at least one of the agents $i > 1$ will have a different x and this will create at least one envy occurrence between him and each one of the others.

Moreover, no allocation x_N in which 1 and 2 do not envy each other is such that $n_i(x_N) = n'_i(x_N)$ for all $i \in N$. Indeed, if 2 envies another agent, then 1 envies this other agent as well, but 1 is not envied by 2 in such an allocation, and is never envied by $3, ..., n$ in all allocations. In this case $n_1(x_N) > n'_1(x_N)$.

If 2 does not envy other agents, he must be envied by at least one agent $3, ..., n$ and $n_2(x_N) < n_2'(x_N)$.

Therefore, for n great enough, a reasonable criterion will prefer $(1, ..., 1)$ to any allocation in which 1 and 2 do not envy each other, and the corresponding allocation rule will violate *Equal Well-Being for Equal Responsibility*.

For *Equal Treatment for Equal Circumstances*, assume $y_1 = y_2$, and all pairs of agents $i, j > 1$ are similarly locked together. Then, for certain preferences, the allocation $(0, 1, ..., 1)$ has only one envy occurrence, namely 1 envying 2. The rest of the argument is as above. ∎

In contrast, the criteria involving richer information behave rather well in the distribution case. The results concerning the Diversity criterion are the same, provided one restricts attention to the subdomain $\mathcal{D}_1$ of economies satisfying, for all $i, j \in N$,

$$u\left(\frac{\Omega}{n-1}, y_i, z_i\right) \geq u(0, y_j, z_i).$$

For Compensation Diversity, the computation of the criterion itself is a little problematic in general, since it requires computing the value of $x_{ik}(x_N)$ satisfying

$$u_i = u(x_{ik}(x_N), y_k, z_i),$$

for $i, k \in N$. This equation may not have a solution if $u_i \neq u(x, y_k, z_i)$ for all $x \geq 0$. This problem is alleviated on the domain $\mathcal{D}_2$ such that for all $i, j \in N$,

$$u(0, y_i, z_i) = u(0, y_j, z_i)$$

and

$$u(\Omega, y_i, z_i) < \lim_{x \to +\infty} u(x, y_j, z_i).$$

On this domain the properties of Compensation Diversity are as in the above proposition.

Concerning envy intensity, in the distribution case one defines $t_{ij}(x_N)$ as the lowest $t \geq 0$ satisfying

$$u(x_i + t, y_i, z_i) \geq u(x_j, y_j, z_i).$$

There is a problem when for all t, $u(x_i+t, y_i, z_i) < u(x_j, y_j, z_i)$, and one therefore may restrict attention to the domain $\mathcal{D}_0$ such that for all $i, j \in N$,

$$\lim_{x \to +\infty} u(x, y_i, z_i) > u(\Omega, y_j, z_i).$$

The results concerning Envious Intensity are then the same as above for the intersection of $\mathcal{D}_0$ and $\mathcal{D}_1$.

As far as Envied Intensity is concerned, one must define the envy intensity number in a different way.[5] Let $d_{ij}(x_N)$ be the lowest value of d such that

$$u(x_i, y_i, z_i) \geq u(x_j - d, y_j, z_i).$$

---

[5] This notion appeared in Tadenuma and Thomson (1995).

This definition is indeterminate if $u(x_i, y_i, z_i) < u(0, y_j, z_i)$, or if $u(x_i, y_i, z_i) > u(x, y_j, z_i)$ for all $x \geq 0$. It is then convenient to restrict attention to the subdomain $\mathcal{D}_2$. On this subdomain the above results about Envied Intensity go through in the distribution case.

2.6 Conditional equality, egalitarian-equivalence

Among the envy criteria, some lean on the compensation principle, while the others lie on the side of the liberal reward principle. We now turn to solutions which side even more clearly with one principle.

The simplest solution to the problem of neutralizing the impact of unequal circumstances while letting responsibility play its role is to give individuals equal "access" to one good option, and consider that it is their fault if they fail to attain it. In fact the whole idea of defining a responsibility-sensitive form of egalitarianism is sometimes formulated in this way.[6] This type of solution can be called "Conditional Equality," and it consists in seeking equality between individuals in the counterfactual situation in which their responsibility characteristics take some "normal" or "reference" value which is considered to be equally accessible to all.

Conditional Equality: Define a reference value of responsibility characteristics and give priority (according to the leximin criterion) to individuals who, with their current resources and circumstances and this reference value of responsibility characteristics, would be the worst-off.

For instance, in the context of Example 1.4 where

$$\text{well-being} = \text{transfer} + (\text{bequest} \times \text{dedication}),$$

this solution seeks to equalize, across individuals, the hypothetical well-being computed as follows:

$$\text{hyp. well-being} = \text{transfer} + (\text{bequest} \times \text{reference dedication}).$$

Tables 2.5 and 2.6 show two numerical examples corresponding to two different values of reference dedication.

Table 2.5: Conditional Equality policy (reference dedication=1)

	low dedication ($=1$)	high dedication ($=3$)
low bequest ($=1$)	2 (transfer$= +1$)	4 (transfer$= +1$)
high bequest ($=3$)	2 (transfer$= -1$)	8 (transfer$= -1$)

---

[6] For instance, the distinction between option luck and brute luck is often made in terms of "having access to insurance."

Table 2.6: Conditional Equality policy (reference dedication = 3)

	low dedication (= 1)	high dedication (= 3)
low bequest (= 1)	4 (transfer= +3)	6 (transfer= +3)
high bequest (= 3)	0 (transfer= −3)	6 (transfer= −3)

We observe that taking a low value of reference dedication is favorable to the individuals with high bequest, whereas the reverse occurs with a high reference value. This observation has a general validity. The "higher" the reference value of responsibility characteristics, the more redistribution is made by Conditional Equality toward individuals with circumstances inducing a low marginal productivity of effort.

This solution is so simple that it is observed in many contexts. In France, for instance, it is applied in the compensation schemes between pension funds for different professions (where one wants to compensate for demographic differences but not for differences in management) and between regional electricity networks (where one wants to compensate for geographic and population density inequalities). Part of its simplicity comes from the fact that it ignores actual responsibility characteristics and is only concerned with what individuals could achieve with the reference responsibility characteristics. Since actual responsibility characteristics are often hard to observe, this is quite convenient.

This solution frankly embraces the liberal reward principle, satisfying *Independence of Responsibility Characteristics* and all the other requirements of the same inspiration. It does not totally ignore the compensation goal, however, since it satisfies *Equal Well-Being for Equal Responsibility* restricted to individuals whose responsibility characteristics correspond to the reference (first column in Table 2.5, second column in Table 2.6).[7]

It can nonetheless be criticized for failing to fully satisfy *Equal Well-Being for Equal Responsibility*, as illustrated in the tables. In many contexts, it appears more reasonable to give priority to the principle of compensation over the principle of liberal reward, and this suggests paying due attention to the solution that is "dual" to Conditional Equality (just like Envied Intensity is dual to Envious Intensity), namely, Egalitarian-Equivalence.[8] It is less simple than Conditional Equality but no less intuitive. It is inspired by the ideal situation in which all individuals have the same circumstances. In this situation, there is no need for compensatory transfers and equality of external resources is warranted. The goal of egalitarian-equivalence is to obtain a distribution of well-being that could occur in such a simple egalitarian situation.

---

[7]It satisfies *Equal Well-Being for Uniform Responsibility* when, as seems quite natural, the current value of the responsibility characteristics is retained as the norm when it is uniform over the whole population (this implies, however, some dependence of the reference value with respect to the population characteristics which entails that the solution no longer satisfies *Independence of Responsibility Characteristics*).

[8]The expression is borrowed from Pazner and Schmeidler (1978a).

Take a reference type of circumstances C and consider an arbitrary allocation A. For every individual, ask what amount of external resources would maintain the level of well-being she has in A if her circumstances were changed into C (and her responsibility characteristics unchanged). This amounts to computing that the current distribution of well-being could be obtained in the counterfactual situation where everyone's circumstances would be C, with another distribution of external resources A^*. Now we have just said that in such a counterfactual situation, the ideal allocation of external resources would be perfectly egalitarian. This is what the Egalitarian-Equivalent solution seeks to achieve, by giving priority to those who have the least resources in A^*.

Egalitarian-Equivalence: Define a reference type of circumstances and give priority (leximin) to individuals whose current level of well-being would be obtained with the least resources if their circumstances were of the reference type (and their responsibility characteristics unchanged).

In order to illustrate this, let us look again at Example 1.4 where

$$\text{well-being} = \text{transfer} + (\text{bequest} \times \text{dedication}).$$

This solution seeks to equalize, across individuals, the hypothetical transfer computed as follows:

$$\text{well-being} = \text{hyp. transfer} + (\text{reference bequest} \times \text{dedication}).$$

Numerical examples are provided in Tables 2.7 and 2.8 for different values of the reference bequest. The first one produces a distribution of well-being that could equivalently be obtained if bequests were uniformly low, with a transfer of $+2$ for everyone. The second yields a distribution of well-being that is equivalent to what one would observe if bequests were uniformly high, with a tax of -2 for everyone.[9]

Table 2.7: Egalitarian-Equivalence policy (reference bequest $= 1$)

	low dedication ($=1$)	high dedication ($=3$)
low bequest ($=1$)	3 (transfer$= +2$)	5 (transfer$= +2$)
high bequest ($=3$)	3 (transfer$= 0$)	5 (transfer$= -4$)

---

[9] The pattern of well-being corresponds in this case, for all classes of bequests, to the gain provided by dedication over the reference level of bequest. As a consequence, and this is again a general property of this solution, the more favorable the reference circumstances, the better an Egalitarian-Equivalence policy is for those who are able to exploit better circumstances well with their responsibility characteristics.

Table 2.8: Egalitarian-Equivalence policy (reference bequest $= 3$)

	low dedication ($= 1$)	high dedication ($= 3$)
low bequest ($= 1$)	1 (transfer$= 0$)	7 (transfer$= +4$)
high bequest ($= 3$)	1 (transfer$= -2$)	7 (transfer$= -2$)

This solution always gives priority to the worst-off among individuals with the same responsibility characteristics because their hypothetical transfers are necessary ranked like their levels of well-being, and therefore it satisfies *Equal Well-Being for Equal Responsibility*. Actually, in general it satisfies *Circumstance Solidarity*. On the side of liberal reward, it satisfies *Equal Treatment for Equal Circumstances* restricted to individuals whose circumstances correspond to the reference.[10]

Observe an interesting duality between Conditional Equality and Egalitarian-Equivalence. The former asks what level of well-being an individual would achieve with reference responsibility characteristics and his current combination of resources and circumstances; the latter asks what amount of resource an individual would need, with reference circumstances and his current responsibility characteristics, in order to achieve his current level of well-being.

If one is wary about implementing a policy inducing inequalities due to responsibility characteristics, it is safer to adopt an Egalitarian-Equivalence policy which performs better in terms of compensation, and moreover to adopt a reference type of circumstances which is not very sensitive to responsibility characteristics, in the sense that, with this type of circumstance, the level of well-being does not vary much with responsibility characteristics. This guarantees that the outcome inequalities that will eventually be obtained will not be very important (as in Table 2.7, compared to Table 2.8).

2.7 *Characterization results

We first define the two allocation rules, focusing once again on the TU case first.

Conditional Equality (S_{CE}): Let $\tilde{z} \in Z$ be the reference. $\forall e \in \mathcal{D}, \forall x_N \in S_{CE}(e), \forall i \in N$,

$$x_i = -v(y_i, \tilde{z}) + \frac{1}{n} \sum_{j \in N} v(y_j, \tilde{z}) + \frac{\Omega}{n}.$$

The aim for Conditional Equality is to obtain a situation in which $u(x_i, y_i, \tilde{z})$ has the same value for all $i \in N$.

---

[10]It satisfies *Equal Treatment for Uniform Circumstances* if the reference type of circumstances is chosen to coincide with the population's uniform type in this case (this, however, complicates the satisfaction of *Circumstance Solidarity*).

Egalitarian-Equivalence (S_{EE}): Let $\tilde{y} \in Y$ be the reference. $\forall e \in \mathcal{D}, \forall x_N \in S_{EE}(e), \forall i \in N$,

$$x_i = -v(y_i, z_i) + v(\tilde{y}, z_i) + \frac{1}{n} \sum_{j \in N} (v(y_j, z_j) - v(\tilde{y}, z_j)) + \frac{\Omega}{n}.$$

The aim for Egalitarian-Equivalence is to have: for all $i \in N$,

$$u_i = v(\tilde{y}, z_i) + \text{constant}.$$

These are actually families of allocation rules, which contain many specific solutions depending on how the reference value $\tilde{z}$ or $\tilde{y}$ is selected. We will focus here on three ways of selecting the reference.

1. Fixed reference: This consists in keeping the same value $\tilde{z}$ or $\tilde{y}$ for all economies $e \in \mathcal{D}$.

2. Average value: Let $\mathcal{D}'$ denote the domain such that one can always compute the mean of the quantities y_i and z_i over the whole population. Such average values can serve as the reference.

3. Balancing value: Let $\mathcal{D}''$ denote the domain such that there always is a unique solution $(\tilde{y}, \tilde{z})$ to the equations

$$\sum_{i \in N} v(\tilde{y}, z_i) = \sum_{i \in N} v(y_i, z_i),$$

$$\sum_{i \in N} v(y_i, \tilde{z}) = \sum_{i \in N} v(y_i, z_i).$$

These values can serve as the reference.

There is yet another way to proceed, which yields a different allocation rule. For every $i \in N$, compute the Egalitarian-Equivalence allocation for $\tilde{y} = y_i$. Then select the allocation that is the average of these n allocations. This gives agent i a well-being equal to

$$\frac{1}{n} \sum_{j \in N} v(y_j, z_i),$$

up to a constant term.[11] A similar computation can be done for the Conditional Equality allocation rule. This gives the following allocation rules.

Average Conditional Equality (S_{ACE}): $\forall e \in \mathcal{D}, \forall x_N \in S_{ACE}(e), \forall i \in N$,

$$x_i = -\frac{1}{n} \sum_{j \in N} v(y_i, z_j) + \frac{1}{n^2} \sum_{j,k \in N} v(y_j, z_k) + \frac{\Omega}{n}.$$

---

[11] All the solutions presented here refer to additive constants, and this is not arbitrary because it is implied by the axiomatic characterizations. An alternative, however, is to use multiplicative constants. See Bossert (1995), Iturbe-Ormaetxe (1997), Cappelen and Tungodden (2007a).

Average Egalitarian-Equivalence (S_{AEE}): $\forall e \in \mathcal{D}$, $\forall x_N \in S_{AEE}(e)$, $\forall i \in N$,

$$x_i = -v(y_i, z_i) + \frac{1}{n} \sum_{j \in N} v(y_j, z_i) + \frac{1}{n^2} \sum_{j,k \in N} (v(y_j, z_j) - v(y_k, z_j)) + \frac{\Omega}{n}.$$

Let us briefly summarize the properties satisfied by these various allocation rules.

Proposition 2.6 *Table 2.9 displays the axioms satisfied by the four kinds of solutions. The axioms are satisfied on the domains that were introduced in the definitions of the variants.*[12]

Table 2.9: Axioms satisfied by solutions

	S_{CE}	S_{ACE}	S_{EE}	S_{AEE}
Circ. Solidarity			✓ (fixed)	
Ackn. Merit			✓	✓
Eq. W-B for Eq. Resp.			✓	✓
Fair R. for Eq. Resp.	✓ (balancing)		✓	✓
Eq. W-B for Un. Resp.	✓ (balancing & average)	✓	✓	✓
Eq. W-B for Ref. Resp.	✓	✓	✓	✓
Indep. of Resp. Char.	✓ (fixed)			
Ackn. Handicap	✓	✓		
Eq. Treat. for Eq. Circ.	✓	✓		
Fair Treat. for Eq. Circ.	✓	✓	✓ (balancing)	
Eq. Treat. for Un. Circ.	✓	✓	✓ (balancing & average)	✓
Eq. Treat. for Ref. Circ.	✓	✓	✓	✓

The literature contains many characterizations of these various solutions. We restrict attention to characterizations involving the main axioms of compensation and liberal reward, and some of the results below are new.

First observe that Conditional Equality with a fixed reference is immediately characterized by the combination of *Independence of Responsibility Characteristics* and *Equal Well-Being for Reference Responsibility*, since the latter requires having

$$x_i + v(y_i, \tilde{z}) = x_j + v(y_j, \tilde{z})$$

for all $i, j \in N$ and for some reference $\tilde{z}$ when $z_N = (\tilde{z}, ..., \tilde{z})$, which is obtained by

$$x_i = -v(y_i, \tilde{z}) + \frac{1}{n} \sum_{j \in N} v(y_j, \tilde{z}) + \frac{\Omega}{n},$$

---

[12]There is a slight complication about the *Acknowledged Merit* and *Acknowledged Handicap* axioms. These axioms refer to unanimity over the values of y_i or z_i in the current profile, and violations of these axioms may occur when the reference values do not belong to these ranges of values. But these violations are pathological and are ignored here.

while the former axiom requires this allocation to be selected for all $e \in \mathcal{D}$. Dually, Egalitarian-Equivalence with a fixed reference is characterized by *Equal Treatment for Reference Circumstances* and *Additive Circumstance Solidarity* (Bossert and Fleurbaey 1996).

Similarly, on the subdomain of $\mathcal{D}''$ in which it satisfies *Circumstance Solidarity*,[13] Egalitarian-Equivalence with a balancing reference is immediately characterized by *Equal Treatment for Uniform Circumstances* and *Weak Circumstance Solidarity* (Iturbe-Ormaetxe 1997). Indeed, if $\tilde{y}$ is such that

$$\sum_{i \in N} v(\tilde{y}, z_i) = \sum_{i \in N} v(y_i, z_i),$$

then by *Weak Circumstance Solidarity*, u_i is the same in $e = ((y_N, z_N), \Omega)$ as in $e' = ((\tilde{y}, ..., \tilde{y}), z_N)$. In e', *Equal Treatment for Uniform Circumstances* requires $x_i = \Omega/n$ for all $i \in N$. This implies that in e, $u_i = v(\tilde{y}, z_i) + \Omega/n$ for all $i \in N$. Dually, Conditional Equality with a balancing reference is characterized by *Equal Well-Being for Uniform Circumstances* and a weakening of *Independence of Responsibility Characteristics* that applies only to changes of z_N which do not alter $\sum_{i \in N} v(y_i, z_i)$.

One can also observe that, when all combinations (y_i, z_j) are observed in the profile and there is $j \in N$ such that

$$\sum_{i \in N} v(y_j, z_i) = \sum_{i \in N} v(y_i, z_i),$$

then the allocation selected by S_{EE} with a balancing reference is the only one that satisfies *Equal Well-Being for Equal Responsibility* and *Fair Treatment for Equal Circumstances* (these axioms are defined for allocation rules rather than allocations but they directly bear on allocations). Let us briefly prove this fact (which inspires a characterization of this allocation rule for a domain with a continuum of agents in Sprumont 1997). *Equal Well-Being for Equal Responsibility* requires that, after redistribution, there is a function f such that for all $i \in N$, $u_i = f(z_i)$. By the feasibility constraint,

$$\sum_{i \in N} f(z_i) = \sum_{i \in N} v(y_i, z_i) + \Omega = \sum_{i \in N} v(y_j, z_i) + \Omega.$$

Suppose that $f(z_i) > v(y_j, z_i) + \Omega/n$ for some $i \in N$. Then, by feasibility, one must have $f(z_k) < v(y_j, z_k) + \Omega/n$ for some $k \in N$. Consider $i_1 \in N$ with $(y_{i_1}, z_{i_1}) = (y_j, z_i)$ and $i_2 \in N$ with $(y_{i_2}, z_{i_2}) = (y_j, z_k)$. Such agents exist by the assumption that all combinations (y_i, z_j) are observed in the profile. One has

$$x_{i_1} = f(z_i) - v(y_j, z_i) > \frac{\Omega}{n}$$

---

[13] Although this is not absolutely necessary, typically the equation $\sum_{i \in N} v(\tilde{y}, z_i) = \sum_{i \in N} v(y_i, z_i)$ has a unique solution when v is strictly monotonic in y (with respect to some order of Y). Then S_{EE} with balancing reference satisfies *Circumstance Solidarity*.

and

$$x_{i_2} = f(z_k) - v(y_j, z_k) < \frac{\Omega}{n},$$

which contradicts *Fair Treatment for Equal Circumstances*. Therefore one must have $f(z_i) = v(y_j, z_i) + \Omega/n$ for all $i \in N$, which proves the fact. There is a dual result for S_{CE} with balancing reference.

Let us now focus on the Equal Well-Being and Equal Treatment axioms. These axioms do not put any constraint on the allocation of resources for economies with heterogeneous profiles in which every individual is different from everybody else. It is, however, reasonable to require the allocation rule to behave in a certain consistent way across profiles. We will examine here the combination of such axioms with various consistency requirements. Since there is a perfect duality between results for Conditional Equality and Egalitarian-Equivalence allocation rules, we only deal with the latter.

The first proposition (due to Fleurbaey 1995d) characterizes Egalitarian-Equivalence with a fixed reference. It involves the standard consistency condition (e.g., Thomson 1988) that after resources have been distributed, considering a subpopulation in isolation would not lead to changing the allocation of resources among them.

Proposition 2.7 *On $\mathcal{D}$, the family of S_{EE} with a fixed reference coincides with the family of single-valued allocation rules satisfying* Equal Well-Being for Uniform Responsibility, Equal Treatment for Reference Circumstances *and the consistency condition requiring that for all $x_N \in S(e)$, all $G \subseteq N$, $x_G \in S((y_G, z_G), \frac{1}{|G|} \sum_{i \in G} x_i)$.*

Proof. First notice that *Equal Well-Being for Uniform Responsibility* and consistency imply *Equal Well-Being for Equal Responsibility*. Let $\tilde{y}$ be a reference value for which *Equal Treatment for Reference Circumstances* is satisfied. Consider $e = ((y_N, z_N), \Omega)$ and the corresponding allocation $x_N^* \in S_{EE}(e)$ such that, for some $\tilde{x}$ and for all $i \in N$:

$$x_i^* + v(y_i, z_i) = \tilde{x} + v(\tilde{y}, z_i).$$

Let

$$e' = ((y_N, (\tilde{y}, ..., \tilde{y})), (z_N, z_N), \Omega'),$$

where $\Omega' = \Omega + n\tilde{x}$. Let $(x_N, x_N') \in S(e')$ (with obvious notations about the concerned subgroups of the population). By *Equal Treatment for Reference Circumstances* and consistency, there is $\tilde{x}'$ such that $x_i' = x_j' = \tilde{x}'$ for all $i, j \in N$. By *Equal Well-Being for Equal Responsibility*, $u_i = u_i'$ for all $i \in N$. This implies that x_N satisfies, for all $i \in N$:

$$x_i + v(y_i, z_i) = \tilde{x}' + v(\tilde{y}, z_i).$$

By the feasibility constraint, one must therefore have $\tilde{x}' = \tilde{x}$ and $x_N = x_N^*$. By consistency, this implies $x_N^* \in S(e)$. ∎

The next propositions involve stronger fairness axioms and weaker consistency conditions.

Proposition 2.8 *On* $\mathcal{D}'$, S_{EE} *with average reference is the only single-valued allocation rule satisfying* Equal Well-Being for Equal Responsibility, Equal Treatment for Uniform Circumstances *and the consistency condition requiring that for all* $x_N \in S(e)$, *all* $G \subseteq N$, *if* $\frac{1}{|G|}\sum_{i \in G}(y_i, z_i) = \frac{1}{n}\sum_{i \in N}(y_i, z_i)$ *then* $x_G \in S((y_G, z_G), \frac{1}{|G|}\sum_{i \in G} x_i)$.

Proof. Let $e = ((y_N, z_N), \Omega)$ and the corresponding allocation $x_N^* \in S_{EE}(e)$ such that, for some $\tilde{x}$ and for all $i \in N$:

$$x_i^* + v(y_i, z_i) = \tilde{x} + v(\bar{y}, z_i),$$

where $\bar{y} = \frac{1}{n}\sum_{i \in N} y_i$. Let

$$e' = ((y_N, (\bar{y}, ..., \bar{y})), (z_N, z_N), \Omega'),$$

with $\Omega' = \Omega + n\tilde{x}$. Let $(x_N, x'_N) \in S(e')$. By *Equal Treatment for Uniform Circumstances* and consistency, there is $\tilde{x}'$ such that $x'_i = x'_j = \tilde{x}'$ for all $i, j \in N$. The rest of the proof is as above. ∎

Similarly, one shows that on $\mathcal{D}''$ S_{EE} with balancing reference is the only single-valued allocation rule satisfying the same fairness axioms and the different consistency condition that for all $x_N \in S(e)$, all $G \subseteq N$, if $\frac{1}{|G|}\sum_{i \in G} v(y_i, z_i) = \frac{1}{n}\sum_{i \in N} v(y_i, z_i)$ then $x_G \in S((y_G, z_G), \frac{1}{|G|}\sum_{i \in G} x_i)$.

The next proposition introduces another axiom of liberal reward. Let a subset of agents with a given value of z be called a "responsibility class" and let $\mathfrak{R}(N)$ denote the partition of N into responsibility classes. This axiom says that when all responsibility classes display the same distribution of circumstances (i.e., when y and z are statistically independent), each of these classes should receive the same amount of resources per capita. Let $dist(q_N)$ denote the statistical distribution of variable q over the population N (i.e., the frequencies of the various values of q).

Equal Treatment for Uniform Class Circumstances: $\forall e = ((y_N, z_N), \Omega)$
$\in \mathcal{D}$, if $\forall I \in \mathfrak{R}(N)$, $dist(y_I) = dist(y_N)$, then $\forall x_N \in S(e)$, $\forall I \in \mathfrak{R}(N)$, $\frac{1}{|I|}\sum_{i \in I} x_i = \frac{\Omega}{n}$.

This axiom is logically intermediate between *Equal Treatment for Equal Circumstances* and (under *Anonymity*) *Equal Treatment for Uniform Circumstances*. It is logically independent of *Fair Treatment for Equal Circumstances*. It is not in general satisfied by S_{EE} but is satisfied by S_{AEE}.[14]

When y and z are statistically independent, the combination of *Equal Treatment for Uniform Class Circumstances* with *Equal Well-Being for Equal Responsibility* completely determines the allocation, because transfers must take place only within responsibility classes, by the former axiom, and well-being

---

[14]There is a dual axiom which requires equal average well-being across circumstance classes when y and z are independent. The two axioms are compatible, they are both satisfied by S_{ACE} and S_{AEE}.

must be equalized within each responsibility class, by the latter axiom.[15] The following result is based on this observation and invokes a consistency condition which is logically weaker than the first two introduced above.

Proposition 2.9 *On* $\mathcal{D}$, S_{AEE} *is the only single-valued allocation rule satisfying* Equal Well-Being for Equal Responsibility, Equal Treatment for Uniform Class Circumstances *and the consistency condition that for all* $x_N \in S(e)$, *all* $G \subseteq N$, *if* $dist(y_G) = dist(y_N)$ *and* $dist(z_G) = dist(z_N)$, *then* $x_G \in S((y_G, z_G), \frac{1}{|G|} \sum_{i \in G} x_i)$.

Proof. Let $e = ((y_N, z_N), \Omega)$ and

$$e' = \left(\left(y_{\pi_1(N)}, ..., y_{\pi_n(N)} \right), (z_N, ..., z_N), \Omega' \right),$$

where

$$\Omega' = n\Omega + \sum_{j,k \in N} \left(v(y_j, z_j) - v(y_k, z_j) \right).$$

and $\pi_1, ..., \pi_n$ are n permutations of $\Pi(N)$ that rotate the agents of N on a circle, as in the following sequence: $(1, 2, 3, ...)$, $(2, 3, 4, ...)$, ..., $(n, 1, 2, ...)$. Let π_1 be the identity.

By Equal Treatment for Uniform Class Circumstances, every responsibility class in e' corresponding to a responsibility class of a agents in e gets $a\Omega'/n$ in $S(e')$, and by Equal Well-Being for Equal Responsibility, it distributes it so as to equalize well-being among its members. This defines $S(e')$ unambiguously. The uniform well-being in a responsibility class for z_i equals:

$$\frac{\Omega'}{n^2} + \frac{1}{n} \sum_{j \in N} v(y_j, z_i),$$

implying that an agent k with characteristics $(y_k, z_k) = (y_j, z_i)$ gets

$$x_k = -v(y_j, z_i) + \frac{\Omega'}{n^2} + \frac{1}{n} \sum_{l \in N} v(y_l, z_i).$$

Letting N' denotes the population of e', one observes that $dist(y_N) = dist(y_{N'})$ and $dist(z_N) = dist(z_{N'})$. Therefore, by consistency applied to the first n agents of e', one obtains that, for $x_N \in S(e)$, for all $i \in N$,

$$x_i = -v(y_i, z_i) + \frac{\Omega'}{n^2} + \frac{1}{n} \sum_{j \in N} v(y_j, z_i),$$

which corresponds to S_{AEE} after one replaces Ω' by its value. ∎

These results are summarized in Table 2.10 and single out these egalitarian-equivalent allocations rules as the maximally consistent solutions satisfying the considered combinations of "Equal Well-Being" and "Equal Treatment" axioms.

---

[15] This observation is due to Cappelen and Tungodden (2007a).

Table 2.10: Summary of characterizations

	Equal Well-Being for Equal Respons.	Equal Well-Being for Unif. Respons.
Equal Treatment for Unif. Class Circ.	S_{AEE}	
Equal Treatment for Unif. Circumst.	S_{EE} with average $\tilde{y}$, S_{EE} with balancing $\tilde{y}$	
Equal Treatment for Ref. Circumst.		S_{EE} with fixed $\tilde{y}$

Another kind of Egalitarian-Equivalence solution, which has not been studied in this section, takes an *extreme* value for reference, such as the least productive circumstances. As alluded to at the end of the previous section, this solution is worth considering if one wants to minimize *ex post* inequalities (see Cappelen and Tungodden 2002 and Tungodden 2005 for a defense of this solution).[16]

Finally, it may be worth stressing that all the solutions studied in this chapter coincide with the natural allocation rule presented in Proposition 2.3 when v is additively separable.

The distribution case is more complicated than the TU case because many equalities have to be rewritten in terms of the maximin criterion, but the outlook of the results is basically the same (see for instance Fleurbaey 1995d and Fleurbaey and Maniquet 2008).

2.8   Conclusion

This chapter has examined the conflict between the compensation principle and the liberal reward principle and has shown how, at the limit of compatibility between these two principles, one finds an array of solutions. Some of them are directly related to the core ideal of no-envy, others are more closely connected to one of the two principles. A rather beautiful duality between solutions embodying one principle and solutions embodying the other has emerged. It has been argued in particular that the Egalitarian-Equivalence solution, which is less intuitive than Conditional Equality but better as far as compensation is concerned, deserves to receive more attention.

There is one striking common point shared by all the solutions studied here. They are all purely ordinal, in the sense that the allocation of resources depends only on how, with their own responsibility characteristics, individuals would rank various combinations of resources and circumstances. The allocation does not depend at all on the particular values taken by well-being. To take an example, go back to Example 1.1 and imagine that the determination of well-being that was originally described by the formula

$$\text{well-being} = (\text{bequest} \pm \text{transfer}) \times \text{dedication},$$

---

[16] See also Cappelen and Tungodden (2007c) for characterizations of general families of egalitarian equivalent allocation rules.

is replaced by another formula:

$$\text{well-being} = (\text{bequest} \pm \text{transfer}) + (10 \times \text{dedication}),$$

such that the ranking of combinations (bequest ± transfer) is not affected (the more, the better). The natural policy is unanimously selected by all the solutions studied in this chapter in both cases, even though the distribution of well-being is quite different in the two cases.

This ordinal feature of the solutions is a consequence of the liberal reward principle. Consider one of the weakest requirements connected to this principle that has been invoked here, namely, Equal Treatment for Uniform Circumstances. This condition requires a uniform distribution of resources to all individuals, when they all have the same circumstances, independently of the differences in their well-being due to their different responsibility characteristics and of the particular way in which well-being is measured. It therefore already contains a substantial amount of ordinalism.

This observation reveals that, for the most part, the framework adopted in these first two chapters was unduly rich in information. In order to study the allocation rules examined here, it is not essential to know the well-being function and to measure well-being levels. One could proceed simply with individual rankings of combinations of resources and circumstances (as in much of the economic literature on these issues). The possibility to work with such rankings only is important[17] when it is considered, as in Rawls' theory, that well-being is essentially incommensurable across individuals with different goals in life. Such rankings are, however, more demanding in terms of information than ordinary preferences over external resources because they require comparisons over internal resources (circumstances) as well. There appears to be no alternative to invoking such extended preferences. In order to properly compensate individuals for differential circumstances, one obviously needs information about how they rank different circumstances.

---

[17]It has repeatedly been claimed in the theory of social choice, after Arrow's theorem (Arrow 1963), that ordinal non-comparable preferences do not give sufficient information to construct appealing social criteria. This is correct only if one adopts Arrow's axiom of independence of irrelevant alternatives – which says that the comparison of two alternatives should only depend on how individuals rank them, at the exclusion of any information about how they rank them with respect to other alternatives. Although social choice theorists have long held on to this axiom, it is controversial and is violated by many standard approaches (Bergson-Samuelson welfare economics, cost-benefit analysis, the theory of fair allocation). For a critical discussion, see, e.g., Fleurbaey (2007).

Chapter 3

Introduction to incentive issues

3.1 Introduction

The first two chapters have dealt with a simple if not simplistic framework. In particular it was assumed that (1) individual characteristics were fixed and observable; (2) transferable resources were one-dimensional, like money; (3) individual well-being was always increasing with money. In this chapter we relax each of these assumptions one by one and in particular provide an introduction to the difficult issue of incentives. This issue will be central in Chapters 5 and 7, devoted to income redistribution, and it is useful to examine the main tenets of this problem in a more abstract and general framework. The incentive issue is related to the dimensionality of external resources, since the difficulty to elicit individual preferences over circumstances may be partly alleviated when they are connected to preferences over external resources.

Analyzing the incentive problem will also give us the occasion to touch on conceptual issues having to do with the connection between responsibility and choice. It is natural to imagine that the incentive problem mostly comes from the fact that individuals make choices, and that holding them responsible for their choices will alleviate the difficulty for social policy of coping with the consequences of such choices. There is a grain of truth in this view, but things are more complex. First, incentive problems are more generally related to the difficulty of observing individual characteristics, which need not be only actions. For instance, compensating for unobservable handicaps raises incentive problems when individual declarations of handicaps are not trustworthy. Second, the view that individuals should be held responsible for their choices appears problematic when one tries to apply it in a rigorous framework where individual choices are modelled as variables that are determined by preferences and constraints shaped by redistributive policy. If individuals have chosen neither their preferences nor the constraints they face, how can they be held responsible for the choices that mechanically follow from them?

3.2   From allocation rules to social orderings

Tackling incentive issues requires abandoning the comfortable setting in which one can pick an allocation rule and enforce it with full knowledge of the population's profile of characteristics. Incentive constraints typically make it impossible to implement allocation rules perfectly, and this problem is particularly damaging for egalitarian rules. While laissez-faire is never hard to implement, achieving equality of standard of living is often rendered impossible or inefficient by the fact that individuals can adapt to the transfer policy and, pursuing their personal interest, hinder the achievement of social goals. For instance, equalizing income completely across individuals would dissociate disposable income from personal work and would induce many people to stay idle, thereby reducing the amount to share dramatically and creating a situation that may be worse for everyone than laissez-faire.

When one cannot reach the ideal allocation dictated by the chosen allocation rule, one has to settle for imperfect allocations, and allocation rules are of little help for this purpose. It is therefore more useful to have a full ranking of allocations, a *social ordering*, so that when the "first-best" is not attainable, one can at least go for a "second-best."

In this book incentive constraints are taken into account in the following framework, which has been crystallized by Mirrlees' (1971) seminal work on taxes. It is assumed that the agency in charge of redistribution has a full knowledge of the statistical distribution of characteristics in the population, but does not observe these characteristics perfectly at the individual level. Assuming that the distribution of characteristics is known is useful in order to forecast with accuracy the distribution of well-being (and its relation to personal characteristics) that follows from any possible policy. It is not possible to know what level of well-being a particular individual will enjoy, but for the purpose of social evaluation, it is enough to know that individuals of a certain type end up in a certain situation. If one is able to rank distributions of well-being, one can then rank policies according to their consequences over well-being and select the policy that yields the best social situation among those which are attainable.

We therefore need to formulate the criteria in terms of rankings rather than in terms of selected allocations. Fortunately, the definitions of the previous chapter were already, for most of them, cast in this language. We will focus here on Conditional Equality and Egalitarian-Equivalence because the Envy Intensity criteria are more involved and would require a lengthy study.

Conditional Equality: Define a reference value of responsibility characteristics and give priority (according to the leximin criterion) to individuals who, with their current resources and circumstances and this reference value of responsibility characteristics, would be the worst-off.

Egalitarian-Equivalence: Define a reference kind of circumstances and give priority (leximin) to individuals whose current level of well-being would be obtained with the least resources if their circumstances were of the reference kind (and their responsibility characteristics unchanged).

3.3 *Social ordering functions

We focus on the TU case for simplicity. The social ordering functions introduced above are formally defined as follows.

Conditional Equality (R_{CE}): Let $\tilde{z} \in Z$ be the reference. $\forall e_p = (y_N, z_N) \in \mathcal{P}$, $\forall x_N, x'_N \in X^N$, $x_N R_{CE}(e_p) x'_N$ if and only if

$$(x_i + v(y_i, \tilde{z}))_{i \in N} \geq_{\text{lex}} (x'_i + v(y_i, \tilde{z}))_{i \in N}.$$

Egalitarian-Equivalence (R_{EE}): Let $\tilde{y} \in Y$ be the reference. $\forall e_p = (y_N, z_N) \in \mathcal{P}$, $\forall x_N, x'_N \in X^N$, $x_N R_{EE}(e_p) x'_N$ if and only if

$$(x_i + v(y_i, z_i) - v(\tilde{y}, z_i))_{i \in N} \geq_{\text{lex}} (x'_i + v(y_i, z_i) - v(\tilde{y}, z_i))_{i \in N}.$$

An axiomatic analysis is possible for social ordering functions, and bears substantial similarity with the axiomatics of allocation rules. In particular, the equality axioms can be given the same names as above, since no confusion is possible and their inspiration is really the same. Note that the axioms, which now compare two allocations, include a part with inequality reduction and a part with a permutation.

Equal Well-Being for Equal Responsibility: $\forall e_p = (y_N, z_N) \in \mathcal{P}$, $\forall i, j \in N$ such that $z_i = z_j$, $\forall x_N, x'_N \in X^N$ such that $\forall k \neq i, j$, $x'_k = x_k$, if

$$x'_i + v(y_i, z_i) > x_i + v(y_i, z_i) > x_j + v(y_j, z_j) > x'_j + v(y_j, z_j),$$

then $x_N R(e_p) x'_N$; if

$$x'_i + v(y_i, z_i) = x_j + v(y_j, z_j) \text{ and } x'_j + v(y_j, z_j) = x_i + v(y_i, z_i),$$

then $x_N I(e_p) x'_N$.

Equal Treatment for Equal Circumstances: $\forall e_p = (y_N, z_N) \in \mathcal{P}$, $\forall i, j \in N$ such that $y_i = y_j$, $\forall x_N, x'_N \in X^N$ such that $\forall k \neq i, j$, $x'_k = x_k$, if

$$x'_i > x_i > x_j > x'_j,$$

then $x_N R(e_p) x'_N$; if

$$x'_i = x_j \text{ and } x'_j = x_i,$$

then $x_N I(e_p) x'_N$.

Similarly, one can write axioms referring to "Uniform" or "Reference" Responsibility or Circumstances. Now that we rank all allocations in X^N, we also introduce the Strong Pareto axiom, which takes a very simple form in this setting in which resources are one-dimensional.

Strong Pareto: $\forall e_p = (y_N, z_N) \in \mathcal{P}$, $\forall x_N, x'_N \in X^N$, $x_N > x'_N$ implies $x_N P(e_p) x'_N$.

For social ordering functions, the clash between compensation and liberal reward is no less real than for allocation rules. *Equal Well-Being for Equal Responsibility* and *Equal Treatment for Equal Circumstances* are compatible because they are formulated in terms of weak preference or indifference; as a result, the social ordering function which is indifferent between all allocations satisfies both. But under Strong Pareto, the inequality reduction part of any of these two axioms is incompatible with any of the two parts (inequality reduction or permutation) of the other axiom.[1] This can be seen from successive applications of these axioms to a four-agent economy with two values of y and two values of z, starting from an allocation as depicted in Fig. 3.1(a). Agents 1 and 2 (resp., 3 and 4) have the same y, while agents 1 and 4 (resp., 2 and 3) have the same z and therefore the same preferences over (x, y). In the initial allocation, agents 1 and 4 (resp., 2 and 3) have equivalent bundles. Successive changes in the allocation are presented for the case when the inequality reduction part of *Equal Well-Being for Equal Responsibility* is confronted to the permutation part of *Equal Treatment for Equal Circumstances*. In Fig. 3.1(b) one sees a new allocation obtained after permutation of x_1 and x_2 and of x_3 and x_4. In Fig. 3.1(c) a third allocation is shown, after inequality reduction between u_2 and u_3 and between u_1 and u_4. This third allocation is dominated by the initial allocation for Strong Pareto.

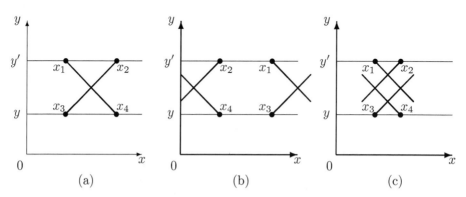

Figure 3.1: Incompatibility between compensation and liberal reward

With weaker versions of the axioms one can obtain characterizations of social ordering functions, as illustrated by the following proposition. We provide only

---

[1] The permutation parts of the two axoms are jointly satisfied by the $\sum_i x_i$ criterion, which also satisfies Strong Pareto.

one example of such a result; other characterizations can be developed along the same lines.[2] The consistency condition that was used previously is now replaced with an axiom of Separability saying that when an agent has the same x in two allocations, he can be ignored.

Separability: $\forall e_p = (y_N, z_N) \in \mathcal{P}$, $\forall x_N, x'_N \in X^N$, $\forall G \subseteq N$, $G \neq \varnothing$, if $\forall i \in N \setminus G$, $x_i = x'_i$, then

$$x_N \, R(e_p) \, x'_N \Leftrightarrow x_G \, R(y_G, z_G) \, x'_G.$$

Proposition 3.1 *If R satisfies Strong Pareto, Equal Well-Being for Uniform Responsibility, Equal Treatment for Reference Circumstances and Separability, then $R = R_{EE}$ with fixed $\tilde{y}$.*

Proof. (1) We first show that, for all $x_N, x'_N \in X^N$, all $i, j \in N$, if

$$
\begin{aligned}
x'_i + v(y_i, z_i) - v(\tilde{y}, z_i) &> x_i + v(y_i, z_i) - v(\tilde{y}, z_i) > \\
x_j + v(y_j, z_j) - v(\tilde{y}, z_j) &> x'_j + v(y_j, z_j) - v(\tilde{y}, z_j)
\end{aligned}
$$

while $x'_k = x_k$ for all $k \neq i, j$, then $x_N \, R(e_p) \, x'_N$.

Introduce two agents $a, b \notin N$ such that $y_a = y_b = \tilde{y}$, $z_a = z_i$ and $z_b = z_j$. Let $N^{ab} = N \cup \{a, b\}$ and $e_p^{ab} = (y_{N^{ab}}, z_{N^{ab}})$. Let x_a, x_b, x'_a, x'_b be such that

$$x_i + v(y_i, z_i) - v(\tilde{y}, z_i) > x_a = x'_b > x'_a = x_b > x_j + v(y_j, z_j) - v(\tilde{y}, z_j).$$

By *Equal Well-Being for Uniform Responsibility* and *Separability*,

$$(x'_{N \setminus \{i\}}, x_i, x_a, x'_b) \, R(e_p^{ab}) \, (x'_N, x'_a, x'_b),$$
$$(x'_{N \setminus \{i,j\}}, x_i, x_j, x_a, x_b) \, R(e_p^{ab}) \, (x'_{N \setminus \{i\}}, x_i, x_a, x'_b).$$

By *Equal Treatment for Reference Circumstances* and *Separability*,

$$(x'_{N \setminus \{i,j\}}, x_i, x_j, x'_a, x'_b) \, I(e_p^{ab}) \, (x'_{N \setminus \{i,j\}}, x_i, x_j, x_a, x_b).$$

By transitivity,

$$(x'_{N \setminus \{i,j\}}, x_i, x_j, x'_a, x'_b) \, R(e_p^{ab}) \, (x'_N, x'_a, x'_b).$$

Recall that $x'_{N \setminus \{i,j\}} = x_{N \setminus \{i,j\}}$. By *Separability*, $x_N \, R(e_p) \, x'_N$.[3]

---

[2] See Valletta (2007) for other characterizations of R_{EE}. In particular, he shows how to derive a strong inequality aversion from axioms which are much weaker in this respect than the equality axioms introduced here.

[3] Notice that we only used the inequality-reduction part of *Equal Well-Being for Uniform Responsibility* and the transposition part of *Equal Treatment for Reference Circumstances*. We could have done the opposite, i.e., use the transposition part of *Equal Well-Being for Uniform Responsibility* and the inequality-reduction part of *Equal Treatment for Reference Circumstances*.

(2) We then show that, for all $x_N, x'_N \in X^N$, all $i, j \in N$, if

$$
\begin{aligned}
x'_i + v(y_i, z_i) - v(\tilde{y}, z_i) &= x_j + v(y_j, z_j) - v(\tilde{y}, z_j), \\
x'_j + v(y_j, z_j) - v(\tilde{y}, z_j) &= x_i + v(y_i, z_i) - v(\tilde{y}, z_i),
\end{aligned}
$$

while $x'_k = x_k$ for all $k \neq i, j$, then $x_N \, I(e_p) \, x'_N$.

The proof is similar as step (1). One simply lets

$$
\begin{aligned}
x_a = x'_b &= x'_i + v(y_i, z_i) - v(\tilde{y}, z_i), \\
x'_a = x_b &= x'_j + v(y_j, z_j) - v(\tilde{y}, z_j).
\end{aligned}
$$

(3) The rest of the proof derives from standard characterizations of the leximin criterion (Hammond 1979). ∎

In the distribution case, similar results can be obtained.

We conclude this section with a remark on the Envied Intensity criterion. It cannot be directly used as a social ordering function ranking the whole set X^N, but it does rank $F(e)$ in a transparent way, and it is moreover related to an interesting social ordering function that we now introduce. Recall Proposition 2.2 which established an equivalence between no-envy and the egalitarian competitive equilibrium. Let $q(y)$ be a price function giving the price of y in a virtual market in which agents could buy bundles (x, y). The budget constraint for $i \in N$ on this market is such that a bundle (x, y_j) is affordable if

$$
x + q(y_j) = I_i,
$$

where I_i denotes i's personal wealth. Let e_i denote i's expenditure function:

$$
e_i(u_i, q) = \min \{ x + q(y_j) \mid (x, j) \in X \times N \text{ and } x + v(y_j, z_i) \geq u_i \}.
$$

This notion is illustrated in Fig. 3.2. Note that the price function $q(.)$ is represented on the inverse horizontal axis, so that a positive price is on the left of the vertical axis.

We now define the Egalitarian Walras social ordering function. Let Q be the set of price functions $q(.)$ such that $\sum_{i \in N} q(y_i) = 0$. The idea of the Egalitarian Walras social ordering function is to compare individual situations in terms of expenditure functions, for a price function $q(.)$ that is endogenously determined so as to make the situation of the worst-off look as good as possible.

Egalitarian Walras (R_{EW}): $\forall e_p = (y_N, z_N) \in \mathcal{P}, \forall x_N, x'_N \in X^N$,
  $x_N \, R_{EW}(e_p) \, x'_N$ if and only if

$$
\max_{q \in Q} \min_{i \in N} e_i(x_i + v(y_i, z_i), q) \geq \max_{q \in Q} \min_{i \in N} e_i(x'_i + v(y_i, z_i), q)
$$

This social ordering function is a direct adaptation to this model of a function introduced in Fleurbaey and Maniquet (2008) for the fair division context in order to rationalize the egalitarian competitive equilibrium.[4]

---

[4]It is easy to show that, in the model of indivisibles (i.e., when y is transferable), the Egalitarian Walrasian social ordering function defined here also rationalizes the egalitarian competitive equilibrium.

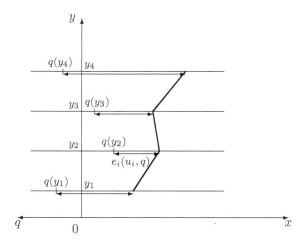

Figure 3.2: Computation of $e_i(u_i, q)$

The practical computation of

$$\max_{q \in Q} \min_{i \in N} e_i(x_i + v(y_i, z_i), q)$$

is easy and is illustrated in Fig. 3.3, where only two indifference curves are depicted for clarity. The value of this expression is simply the mean value of the horizontal thick segments. Indeed, this mean is equal to each of the arrow-delimited segments, because $\sum_{i \in N} q(y_i) = 0$. Observe that if $q \in Q$ is changed, this will necessarily decrease one of the $e_i(x_i + v(y_i, z_i), q)$ and thereby $\min_{i \in N} e_i(x_i + v(y_i, z_i), q)$. Therefore each of the arrow-delimited segments measures the greatest possible value of $\min_{i \in N} e_i(x_i + v(y_i, z_i), q)$ for $q \in Q$. The fact that a maximin criterion like R_{EW} is computed as the mean value of a list of numbers is the clue to the following proposition, which connects R_{EW} to Envied Intensity.

Proposition 3.2 For all $e = ((y_N, z_N), \Omega) \in \mathcal{D}$, all $x_N, x'_N \in F(e)$, one has $x_N \, R_{EW}(y_N, z_N) \, x'_N$ if and only if

$$\sum_{j \in N} \max_{i \in N} t_{ij}(x_N) \leq \sum_{j \in N} \max_{i \in N} t_{ij}(x'_N).$$

Proof. When i buys y_j, the lowest value of x such that $x + v(y_j, z_i) \geq u_i$ is

$$x = x_i + v(y_i, z_i) - v(y_j, z_i).$$

Therefore

$$e_i(x_i + v(y_i, z_i), q) = \min_{j \in N} \left(x_i + v(y_i, z_i) - v(y_j, z_i) + q(y_j) \right).$$

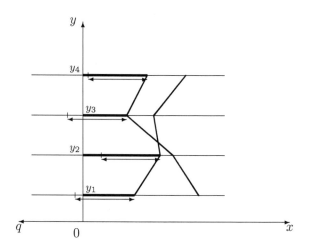

Figure 3.3: Computation of Egalitarian Walrasian

Recall that $t_{ij}(x_N) = x_j - (x_i + v(y_i, z_i) - v(y_j, z_i))$, so that

$$e_i(x_i + v(y_i, z_i), q) = \min_{j \in N} (x_j - t_{ij}(x_N) + q(y_j)).$$

One therefore has

$$
\begin{aligned}
\min_{i \in N} e_i(x_i + v(y_i, z_i), q) &= \min_{i,j \in N} (x_j - t_{ij}(x_N) + q(y_j)) \\
&= \min_{j \in N} \left(x_j + q(y_j) - \max_{i \in N} t_{ij}(x_N) \right)
\end{aligned}
$$

implying that for all $x_N \in F(e)$, $q \in Q$,

$$\min_{i \in N} e_i(x_i + v(y_i, z_i), q) \leq \frac{1}{n} \sum_{j \in N} \left(x_j + q(y_j) - \max_{i \in N} t_{ij}(x_N) \right).$$

Since $\sum_{j \in N} (x_j + q(y_j)) = \Omega$, this can be simplified into

$$\min_{i \in N} e_i(x_i + v(y_i, z_i), q) \leq \frac{\Omega}{n} - \frac{1}{n} \sum_{j \in N} \max_{i \in N} t_{ij}(x_N).$$

Now let, for all $j \in N$,

$$q(y_j) = \frac{\Omega}{n} - \left(x_j - \max_{i \in N} t_{ij}(x_N) \right) - \frac{1}{n} \sum_{k \in N} \max_{i \in N} t_{ik}(x_N).$$

By construction, $q \in Q$. Moreover, this formula implies that for all $j \in N$,

$$x_j + q(y_j) - \max_{i \in N} t_{ij}(x_N) = \frac{\Omega}{n} - \frac{1}{n} \sum_{k \in N} \max_{i \in N} t_{ik}(x_N),$$

and hence,

$$\min_{i \in N} e_i(x_i + v(y_i, z_i), q) = \min_{j \in N} \left(x_j + q(y_j) - \max_{i \in N} t_{ij}(x_N) \right)$$
$$= \frac{\Omega}{n} - \frac{1}{n} \sum_{k \in N} \max_{i \in N} t_{ik}(x_N).$$

Since we have seen above that this is an upper bound for $\min_{i \in N} e_i(x_i + v(y_i, z_i), q)$ when q varies, one actually has

$$\max_{q \in Q} \min_{i \in N} e_i(x_i + v(y_i, z_i), q) = \frac{\Omega}{n} - \frac{1}{n} \sum_{j \in N} \max_{i \in N} t_{ij}(x_N),$$

from which the equivalence stated in the proposition is immediate. ∎

This equivalence also holds in the distribution case provided Envied Intensity is redefined in terms of d_{ij} (see Section 2.5).[5]

3.4 Incentives

Incentive issues arise when individual characteristics are not perfectly observed or when they can be modified by individuals in a way that eludes observation. We retain here the assumption that there is a clear conceptual distinction between circumstances for which individuals are not held responsible and the other characteristics for which they are. It is tempting to assume that individuals control the latter and not the former, but this need not be the case. In Rawls' and Dworkin's theories, for instance, individuals are held responsible for their preferences even if they do not fully control them. Conversely, it may be sensible not to hold individuals responsible for circumstances they partly control, such as aspects of their physical condition. If one combines the various possibilities concerning individual's control over their characteristics with the multifarious possibilities concerning informational limitations of the "principal" (i.e., the agency in charge of devising the redistributive policy), one obtains an overwhelming multitude of cases to study. Another source of variety in these matters is that individual personal objectives need not be to maximize their well-being as measured by the social criterion that serves to select the policy.

---

[5] Regarding Envious Intensity, one can similarly establish an equivalence with the social ordering function that evaluates an allocation x_N by computing

$$\max_{q \in Q} \min_{i \in N} (x_i + q(y_i) - \max_{j \in N} t_{ij}(x_N)).$$

This amounts to measuring the agents' wealth $x_i + q(y_i)$ and deducting from it their maximal degree of envy. Again, this is based on the maximin criterion but this is less essential here and any inequality-averse social welfare function, instead of the min function, would yield an equivalent criterion in this case. One notices here that the duality between compensation and liberal reward is related to the duality of consumer theory. However, contrary to Egalitarian Walras, this social ordering function does not satisfy the weak Pareto principle and therefore appears less interesting.

Some individuals may maximize a different thing, and others may not maximize at all.

We will not explore all these possibilities. The modest purpose here is to gain a few insights about how incentive-compatible policies inspired by such criteria as Conditional Equality and Egalitarian-Equivalence can work and how different they are from the corresponding first-best policies studied in the previous chapter.

As far as the information of the principal is concerned, two important cases are worth examining in some detail. The first case is when circumstances are observable, such as a physical disability which may be ascertained by physicians, while responsibility characteristics are not observable. Let us call this the "observable circumstance" case. The second case is when the principal observes well-being for any amount of transfer, but not the underlying individual characteristics, as in the context of income taxation when pre-tax income is observed, and obviously post-tax income as well, whereas the underlying amounts of talent and effort are not observed. This will be called the "observable well-being" case in the sequel. Recall that the word "well-being" here is just the label for whatever outcome is deemed relevant.

Let us focus on the observable circumstance case first. Assume, to begin with, that all individual characteristics are fixed and cannot be modified by individuals. There is still the problem of unobservable responsibility characteristics, which individuals may misrepresent if this is in their interest. It appears, however, that Conditional Equality is not bothered at all by this incentive problem, since in the first-best context it does not need to observe responsibility characteristics at the individual level. Knowing the distribution of responsibility characteristics is the most one may possibly need in order to determine the reference value that serves in the computation of Conditional Equality, and this information is assumed to be available.

This observation has a deep meaning that must be emphasized. When responsibility characteristics are unobservable, redistribution can be made only as a function of individual circumstances and the final allocation will be largely independent of the profile of responsibility characteristics, since it can depend only on some general features of the distribution of such characteristics. Therefore incentive constraints almost force us to satisfy the axiom of Independence of Responsibility Characteristics, which was shown to be one of the strongest conditions embodying the principle of liberal reward. They certainly force us to satisfy the axiom of Equal Treatment for Equal Circumstances, since two individuals with identical circumstances are now indistinguishable. The fact that incentive constraints impose a substantial degree of liberal reward on the final allocation will be repeatedly observed in the sequel. This should not be surprising, since incentive considerations often come up when people are asked to explain why they endorse principles of responsibility and self-reliance. The possible confusion between pragmatic reasons for liberal reward (incentives) and ethical reasons (neutrality) must be disentangled and this analysis should help to put the principle of liberal reward in its proper – i.e., modest – place.

Egalitarian-Equivalence is not incentive-compatible, as can be expected after these remarks, because it caters to differences in responsibility characteristics in order to achieve full compensation. One can, however, use the corresponding social ordering in order to choose a feasible policy. In this context a feasible policy makes transfers as a function of individual circumstances only. What must be done, therefore, is determine who in each circumstance class (i.e., a subpopulation of individuals with identical circumstances) is the worst-off, compare them across classes, and give priority to the worst-off among them. Recall how Egalitarian-Equivalence measures the situation of an individual. It computes the amount of resources that the individual would need to achieve his current level of well-being if he enjoyed reference circumstances. The question is therefore to assess how this figure varies with responsibility characteristics, for any given kind of circumstances. Several possibilities arise. As an example, consider Example 1.4, where one had

$$\text{well-being} = \text{transfer} + (\text{bequest} \times \text{dedication}).$$

The computation made by Egalitarian-Equivalence is the equivalent transfer solution to

$$\text{current well-being} = \text{equivalent transfer} + (\text{reference bequest} \times \text{dedication}).$$

Simple algebra, substituting the first formula for well-being in the second, yields

$$\text{equivalent transfer} = \text{transfer} + (\text{bequest} - \text{reference bequest}) \times \text{dedication}.$$

One observes that this figure varies with dedication, which is the responsibility characteristics here, in a way that depends on the comparison between the individual's bequest and the reference bequest. In a "low-bequest" class, with bequest smaller than the reference, the worst-off will be those with high dedication. In a "high-bequest" class, the worst-off will, on the contrary, be those with low dedication. This implies that the "second-best" Egalitarian-Equivalence policy will give priority to the worst-off among two groups, the "deserving poor" (i.e., the low-bequest-high-dedication people) and the "undeserving rich" (i.e., the high-bequest-low-dedication people). These two categories of people will be the worst-off according to the Egalitarian-Equivalence measure, while the "undeserving poor" and the "deserving rich" will be left above the others by benefiting from the incentive constraints.

If the reference bequest were chosen below all observed levels, then this policy would cater to the low-dedication people of all classes. On the contrary, with a reference bequest greater than observed levels, the priority would be given to all the high-dedication people. It is noteworthy that, as one can check, the former case would then make the final allocation equivalent to a Conditional Equality policy with low reference dedication, while the latter case would be equivalent to the outcome of the Conditional Equality policy with high reference dedication. In other words, the incentive constraints tend to diminish the difference between the allocations obtained with Conditional Equality and Egalitarian-Equivalence. This is again a consequence of the imposition of liberal reward constraints due to incentives.

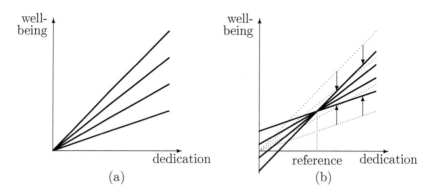

Figure 3.4: Conditional Equality, first-best = second-best

There is a simple graphical way of understanding these issues. Let us continue with this example but, as a variant to Example 1.4, let us now assume that dedication covers a continuum of values in the population. The laissez-faire situation is such that people with a given level of bequest are represented with a line, the slope of which is equal to their bequest. Four such classes are represented on Fig. 3.4, and the laissez-faire is represented in (a). For simplicity it is assumed that the four classes have the same number of individuals. The Conditional Equality policy is shown in (b), with a typical crossing of lines at the reference level of dedication. The transfer to which an individual is submitted can be visualized by the (vertical) difference between his position at the laissez-faire and his eventual position, as illustrated by a few arrows in the figure. One sees in (b) that people with the same bequest receive the same transfer.

The *first-best* Egalitarian-Equivalence policy is displayed in Fig. 3.5(a), for a reference level that corresponds to the third level of bequest in this population. After redistribution, all individuals are on a same line, the slope of which equals the reference bequest. Contrary to the Conditional Equality policy, this policy makes transfers that depend on the level of dedication (except for people with a bequest equal to the reference level). It is therefore not incentive-compatible when dedication is not observable.

When dedication is not observable, one has to look for a second-best policy which makes transfers only as a function of people's bequest. Each class of bequest will then keep its original line, up to some translation up or down. The configuration of the second-best policy for Egalitarian-Equivalence is shown in (b) for the same level of reference bequest as in (a). The reference line is tangent to all other lines, which encapsulates the requirement that the worst-off from all bequest classes are brought to the same level. One observes in (b) that the worst-off, as measured by the point of each line which touches the reference line, are indeed the deserving poor and the undeserving rich.

The two lower panels of the figure illustrate what happens for alternative reference levels. In (c) a lower level of reference (equal to the lowest level) is

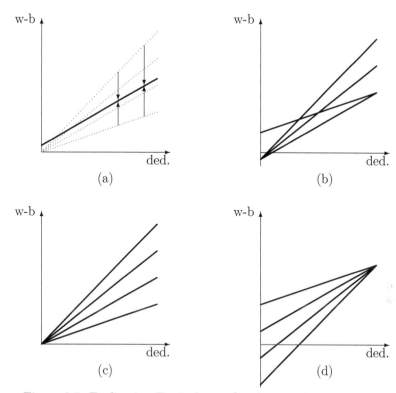

Figure 3.5: Egalitarian-Equivalence, first-best and second-best

adopted, and in (d) a high level (equal to the greatest level) is depicted. The policy chosen in (c) is equivalent to the laissez-faire in this particular example. This is specific to this example but it is important to note that a criterion that redistributes a lot in the first-best context (as in (a)) may end up redistributing little in the second-best context (as in (b)), and a reference that leads to more equality *ex post* in the first-best context (i.e., a lower reference bequest in this example) may redistribute less in the second-best (compare (c) to (d)).

Now modify the assumptions slightly and consider that individuals may change their characteristics. Then, the Conditional Equality and Egalitarian-Equivalence criteria may have a problem if the reference value depends on the distribution, for instance if it is the average value in the whole population. Because redistribution of resources may alter the choice of characteristics by individuals and thereby alter the mean value that serves as a reference. It then becomes difficult to compare the outcomes of policies producing different reference values. These criteria, as defined above, rank allocations for a given reference value, but are not designed to rank allocations with different reference values. Therefore it appears necessary to avoid relying on endogenous reference values with these criteria. It is possible, of course, to choose reference values depending on the distribution at some benchmark allocation.

When redistribution influences individual choices of responsibility characteristics, one typically still obtains a distribution of well-being which is, under Conditional Equality or Egalitarian-Equivalence policies, intermediate between the distribution under a laissez-faire policy and the distribution obtained under a well-being egalitarian policy. Redistribution may push responsibility characteristics in a direction that is favorable or unfavorable to well-being, depending on circumstances and on the sign of the "income effect" on responsibility characteristics. Consider for instance the situation in which a subsidy discourages effort (negative income effect). Redistribution will then discourage individual effort in the unfavorable circumstance classes which receive transfers but will also encourage effort in the favorable circumstances classes which pay taxes. The contrary would happen if the income effect were positive. In the observable circumstance case, therefore, redistribution does not have a dampening impact on effort across the board.[6]

The analysis of incentive issues when individuals can change their responsibility characteristics reveals a conceptual difficulty inherent in a certain view of responsibility. This issue will be discussed again in Chapter 10 but it is useful to briefly mention it here in order to clarify some features of the analysis in the next chapters. In some theories of equality of opportunity (Arneson, Cohen, Roemer), individuals are held responsible for their "genuine choices." The sphere of responsibility in such theories coincides with the scope of individual control. Such an approach actually corresponds more or less to the commonsense view on responsibility. Now, in economic models individual choice is generally depicted as the maximization of personal utility under constraints, and is therefore totally explained causally by individual preferences and constraints. If the individual is not held responsible for his given preferences and these constraints, how can he be held responsible for the choice that mechanically results from these exogenous data? This seems incompatible with the notion of "genuine choice."

More generally, consider a conception for which circumstances correspond exactly to the personal characteristics that are fixed and responsibility characteristics are those that are chosen by individuals. Then two individuals with the same circumstances, if they face the same transfer policy (and they should since their circumstances are identical), will necessarily choose the same responsibility characteristics, except in the case of ties or in the case of random choice.[7] Rational behavior in terms of maximization is not even necessary for this to

---

[6]In contrast, when individuals can control their circumstances, a compensation policy typically generates disincentives across the board. The incentive problem in this case is quite classical: It may sometimes be preferable to allow for some inequality so as to preserve incentives for people to maintain their circumstance characteristics (e.g., talent); it may also be acceptable to discourage individuals with low potential talent or low propensity to develop their talent, if transferring external resources to them is more efficient (under incentive constraints) than inducing them to achieve their potential. This is the kind of result that one usually obtains in public economics with egalitarian welfarist policies.

[7]The case of random choice is in fact similar, if one considers that the random factor that intervenes in the choice is not the agent's responsibility (it is certainly not "chosen" by the agent).

happen, since any non-maximizing deterministic method of choice will also lead to the same choice in the same circumstances. In general, then, one will obtain a perfect correlation between circumstances and responsibility characteristics, a rather counter-intuitive situation for the control view.

One might think of salvaging the concept of "genuine choice" by identifying it with non-causally determined free will. Interestingly, however, the best candidates for non-causally determined characteristics are fixed characteristics in a causal model. Indeed, all endogenous variables are causally influenced by other variables of the model and therefore cannot embody this kind of free will. Intuitively, when a decision variable reacts to external stimuli it is problematic for the control approach to hold the agent fully responsible for it. It makes more sense to hold him responsible for the underlying disposition that governs the agent's reactions to stimuli. This disposition is a fixed characteristic in the eyes of causal analysis. In conclusion, one should not be afraid of assigning responsibility to individuals for a fixed characteristic and this seems the most sensible way to proceed in economic models.

As a consequence, in the next chapters we will never assign full responsibility to individuals for a quantity they control, and instead we will sort individual *fixed* characteristics into circumstance characteristics and responsibility characteristics. For instance, individuals will not be held fully responsible for their working decisions, because they jointly result from their preferences (for which they will be held responsible) and their budget constraint (determined by the policy and by their productivity, a personal characteristic ranked among circumstances).[8] This is similar to what is done in Roemer's (1998) analysis. There, individuals are held responsible for their relative position in their circumstance class, and one can check that, typically, such a position is ultimately determined, in the model, by a fixed preference parameter.

Finally, let us examine the case of observable well-being. Instead of just trying to modify the distribution of well-being, under Conditional Equality or Egalitarian-Equivalence one tries to cater to the interests of those who, in a given subpopulation having a certain level of well-being, are the "truly" worst-off because they have unfavorable circumstances and favorable responsibility characteristics. By assumption it is impossible to give a different treatment to individuals with the same observed well-being, but the transfers will be calibrated so as to equalize the situations (as they are evaluated by the relevant criterion) of these "truly" worst-off across classes of well-being. This typically implies a redistribution policy that is, again, intermediate between laissez-faire and full equalization of well-being. To understand why one does not obtain full equality of well-being, consider the case of Conditional Equality and suppose that there is a sizeable class of individuals with the worst circumstances but a variety of responsibility characteristics and therefore a variety of levels of well-being. For the range of well-being levels that prevails in this class, the worst-off, as measured by Conditional Equality, are precisely the people from

---

[8] Incidentally, this is more in line with Rawls' and Dworkin's view that individuals must, as autonomous moral agents, assume responsibility for their preferences even if their preferences are not "chosen."

this class. But since the measure of their situation refers to a reference value of responsibility and not to their actual well-being, there is no need to redistribute among them. Therefore Conditional Equality will give the same transfer to all individuals whose well-being falls within the range obtained in the worst class of circumstances.

3.5   *Optimal compensation policies

We stick to the TU case for ease of exposition, assuming moreover that $\Omega = 0$, that y and z are ordered by a complete ordering denoted $\succeq$, and that $v(y, z)$ is increasing in its two arguments. We say that v is supermodular if $v(y, z) - v(y, z') \geq 0$ is non-decreasing in y, or equivalently $v(y, z) - v(y', z) \geq 0$ is non-decreasing in z, and submodular if non-increasing. The supermodular case is, intuitively, when effort pays more with greater talent, or equivalently a better talent is more profitable with more effort, whereas the submodular case is when hard work pays more in absence of talent, or equivalently talent matters less for those who work hard.[9]

We examine different problems in the following order: 1) the observable-circumstance case when individuals' characteristics (y_i, z_i) are fixed and z_i is not observable; 2) the same except that characteristics can be modified by the individuals; 3) the observable-well-being case when individuals' characteristics (y_i, z_i) are fixed. We do not study the observable-well-being case when some characteristics are chosen because in Chapter 5 we will extensively analyze a similar situation (namely, when income is observed and labor is chosen).

1. y_i is observed, z_i is not, (y_i, z_i) is fixed. An incentive-compatible redistributive policy is a function $x(y)$. Let $\mu(q)$ denote the mean of any given variable q over the population.

The first-best Conditional Equality policy

$$x(y) = -v(y_i, \tilde{z}) + \mu\left(v(y, \tilde{z})\right)$$

is incentive-compatible.

Let $x(y)$ be any policy and let us examine how individuals are ranked by the Egalitarian-Equivalence measure

$$x(y_i) + v(y_i, z_i) - v(\tilde{y}, z_i).$$

In a circumstance class $N_y = \{i \in N \mid y_i = y\}$ with $y \prec \tilde{y}$, the lowest value is obtained for $\max_{i \in N_y} z_i$ if v is supermodular, and for $\min_{i \in N_y} z_i$ if v is submodular. The reverse obtains for $y \succ \tilde{y}$. Consider the supermodular case first. According

---

[9] Supermodularity and submodularity imply that indifference curves in (x, y) space satisfy the single-crossing property, because the slope of an indifference curve between two adjacent values of y equals

$$-\frac{y - y'}{v(y, z) - v(y', z)}.$$

to the leximin criterion, one must equalize across classes N_y the situation of the worst-off of each class, i.e.

$$x(y) + v(y, \max_{i \in N_y} z_i) - v(\tilde{y}, \max_{i \in N_y} z_i) \quad \text{for } y \prec \tilde{y},$$

$$x(y) + v(y, \min_{i \in N_y} z_i) - v(\tilde{y}, \min_{i \in N_y} z_i) \quad \text{for } y \succeq \tilde{y}.$$

This defines the second-best Egalitarian-Equivalence policy: For some c computed so as to have $\sum_{i \in N} x(y_i) = 0$, one must have

$$x(y) = c - \left(v(y, \max_{i \in N_y} z_i) - v(\tilde{y}, \max_{i \in N_y} z_i) \right) \quad \text{for } y \prec \tilde{y},$$

$$x(y) = c - \left(v(y, \min_{i \in N_y} z_i) - v(\tilde{y}, \min_{i \in N_y} z_i) \right) \quad \text{for } y \succeq \tilde{y}.$$

In the submodular case, one obtains, for some c',

$$x(y) = c' - \left(v(y, \min_{i \in N_y} z_i) - v(\tilde{y}, \min_{i \in N_y} z_i) \right) \quad \text{for } y \prec \tilde{y},$$

$$x(y) = c' - \left(v(y, \max_{i \in N_y} z_i) - v(\tilde{y}, \max_{i \in N_y} z_i) \right) \quad \text{for } y \succeq \tilde{y}.$$

In summary, in the supermodular case, the Egalitarian-Equivalence policy gives priority to (and equalizes the situations of) the deserving poor and the undeserving rich, while in the submodular case it gives priority to the undeserving poor and the deserving rich.[10]

2. y_i is observed, z_i is not, (y_i, z_i) is modifiable. Since (y_i, z_i) fully describe an individual's characteristics, assuming rationality one must be able to describe individual behavior as the maximization of a common function $U(x_i, y_i, z_i)$. The general model is that i maximizes $U(x_i, y_i, z_i)$ by choosing (y_i, z_i) in a set T_i that may differ from one individual to another. The function $U(x_i, y_i, z_i)$, which represents people's subjective goals, may in general be different from the well-being function $u(x_i, y_i, z_i)$ which serves for social evaluation. But we will only consider cases in which the two functions are identical. Moreover, we will simply examine two illustrative examples. The first deals with a case of endogenous z. The second illustrates what happens when individuals can also waste their talent y.

Example 3.1 *Assume that*

$$U(x, y, z) = u(x, y, z) = (x + yz)(1 - z).$$

with y uniformly distributed on $[0, 1]$ (for a continuum of agents) and z chosen by individuals in the interval $[0, 1]$.

---

[10] Valletta (2007) pushes the analysis of Egalitarian-Equivalence further in a more specific model.

In this example, all individuals in the same class of y will choose the same z, so that Conditional Equality and Egalitarian-Equivalence will be able to achieve equality of their measure of individual situations with a policy $x(y)$. Individual maximization yields

$$z = \frac{y - x}{2y}$$

if this value lies in the interval $[0, 1]$ and 0 or 1 otherwise. Let $z(y)$ denote the value of z chosen by agents of class y.

The Conditional Equality policy with reference $\tilde{z}$ is $x(y) = c - y\tilde{z}$, where by feasibility one must have $c = \mu(y)\tilde{z}$. The Egalitarian-Equivalence policy is $x(y) = c' - (y - \tilde{y})z(y)$, feasibility requiring $c' = \mu((y - \tilde{y})z(y))$.

With Conditional Equality, one obtains

$$\frac{y - x(y)}{2y} = \frac{1 + \tilde{z}}{2} - \frac{\mu(y)\tilde{z}}{2y}.$$

Necessarily it is less than 1, and therefore one has

$$z(y) = \max\left\{0, \frac{1 + \tilde{z}}{2} - \frac{\mu(y)\tilde{z}}{2y}\right\}.$$

With Egalitarian-Equivalence, one computes

$$\frac{y - x(y)}{2y} = \frac{1}{2} - \frac{\mu((y - \tilde{y})z(y))}{2y} + \frac{(y - \tilde{y})z(y)}{2y}$$

Resolving in $z(y)$ the equation

$$z(y) = \frac{1}{2} - \frac{\mu((y - \tilde{y})z(y))}{2y} + \frac{(y - \tilde{y})z(y)}{2y},$$

one obtains

$$z(y) = \frac{y - \mu((y - \tilde{y})z(y))}{y + \tilde{y}}$$

if this quantity belongs to the interval $[0, 1]$ (otherwise the relevant bound applies).

Figure 3.6 shows the distribution of z as a function of y after redistribution, compared to before redistribution where $z = 1/2$ for everyone. The next figure (Fig. 3.7) shows the corresponding distributions of well-being. The reference values that have served for these computations are $\tilde{z} = \tilde{y} = 0.5$. Both figures also show the consequences of a policy designed to simply equalize well-being.

One sees that effort is reduced for the agents with low y, who benefit from redistribution, but is increased on the other side of the distribution of y. The two criteria reduce well-being inequality but not fully, because individuals are compensated for a lower y but not for the lower z that goes with it in this example. Interestingly, and somewhat surprisingly, the Egalitarian-Equivalence policy appears in some sense intermediate between laissez-faire and the Conditional Equality policy, while the latter appears intermediate between

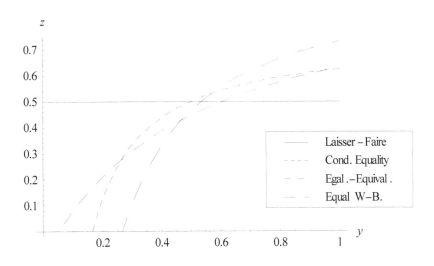

Figure 3.6: Responsibility characteristics as a function of circumstances (Example 3.1)

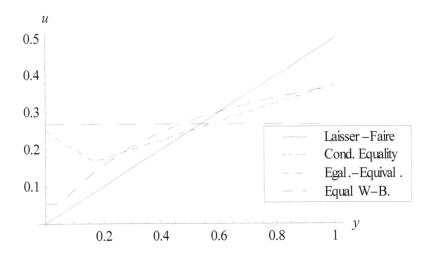

Figure 3.7: Well-being as a function of circumstances (Example 3.1)

Egalitarian-Equivalence and a policy equalizing well-being. This example is a little extreme because only y is compensated while z is perfectly correlated with y. This possibility was discussed in the previous section. But similar results would be obtained with a richer example in which agents differ in an additional fixed responsibility parameter so that one no longer has such perfect correlation.

Example 3.2 *Let y, z be real numbers, with $Y_i = [0, \bar{y}_i]$ and $Z_i = Z = \{P, L\}$, where $\bar{y}_i$ is i's (non-observable) potential talent, which he can spoil at will, and which is distributed over $[0, 1]$, and $P > L$ are a "productive" and a "leisurely" value of z which represent different uses of his talent which the individual may choose. Functions u and U are assumed to be:*

$$U(x, y, z) = u(x, y, z) = x + v(y, z),$$

where v is an increasing supermodular function such that $v(0, P) = v(0, L)$.

Let us briefly look at the first-best policies in this example. Efficiency requires $y_i = \bar{y}_i$ and $z_i = P$ for all $i \in N$. A Conditional Equality policy taking P as the reference would equalize $x_i + v(\bar{y}_i, P)$ across individuals and would therefore achieve perfect equality of well-being. Egalitarian-Equivalence taking $\tilde{y}$ as a reference would equalize $x_i + v(\bar{y}_i, P) - v(\tilde{y}, P)$ and would also end up in full equality.

Is this incentive-compatible? The problem for the principal is that $\bar{y}_i$ is not observable, only y_i is. Consider the egalitarian policy defined by

$$x(y) = c - v(y, P)$$

for some constant c. An individual i who has chosen $z_i = P$ and considers how to choose y_i faces the problem

$$\max_{0 \le y \le \bar{y}_i} x(y) + v(y, P) = c,$$

and is therefore indifferent between all values of y. An individual i who has chosen $z_i = L$ and considers how to choose y_i faces the problem

$$\max_{0 \le y \le \bar{y}_i} x(y) + v(y, L) = c + v(y, L) - v(y, P),$$

and will choose $y_i = 0$ because of supermodularity. Considering the choice between P and L, since the outcome is always c, indifference is obtained again. Full equality and efficiency is incentive-compatible, but only in a borderline way. It is perfectly possible for individuals to choose $y_i = 0$ and $z_i = L$.

Now consider a variant of this example such that the z_i characteristic is fixed (at either P or L). One can then check that the optimal policy, for Conditional Equality with $\tilde{z} = P$, is one of these two:

Policy 1: It equalizes $x(y) + v(y, L) = c$ across agents. For an agent i with $z_i = P$, the problem is to choose y_i so as to maximize $c - v(y, L) + v(y, P)$, which implies $y_i = \bar{y}_i$ by supermodularity. An agent with $z_i = L$ will be indifferent between all values of y_i and we will assume here that he chooses $y_i = \bar{y}_i$.

Policy 2: It equalizes $x(y) + v(y, P) = c'$ across agents. Now the P agents are indifferent, while the L agents choose $y_i = 0$. Again let us assume that indifferent agents choose $y_i = \bar{y}_i$.

With the first policy, the worst-off are those with the lowest

$$x(y) + v(y, P) = c - v(y, L) + v(y, P)$$

and they have $y_i = \bar{y}_i = 0$, so that $x(y_i) + v(y_i, P) = c$. With the second policy, the worst-off by definition have $x(y_i) + v(y_i, P) = c'$. The ranking of the two policies depends on $c \gtrless c'$. Feasibility implies that

$$
\begin{aligned}
c &= \mu\left(v\left(\bar{y}, L\right)\right), \\
c' &= p_L v(0, L) + (1 - p_L)\mu_P\left(v\left(\bar{y}, P\right)\right),
\end{aligned}
$$

where p_L is the proportion of L agents in the population and μ_P the mean over the P population. Which policy is best depends on the proportion of L agents and of the average value of the difference $v(y, P) - v(y, L)$. If the former is sufficiently small and the latter is sufficiently high, the second policy is better, even though it generates a waste of talent among all L agents.[11]

The Egalitarian-Equivalence criterion produces the same conclusions about the choice between these two policies, because, as one can check, the worst-off with the first policy are the P agents with $\bar{y} = 0$, for whom the equivalent resource equals $c - v(\tilde{y}, P)$, while the worst-off with the second policy are the P agents who all have an equivalent resource equal to $c' - v(\tilde{y}, P)$. (When $\tilde{y} = 0$, the L agents are also among the worst-off.)

In conclusion, this example shows that when disincentives affect the maintenance of talent, it can be optimal to discourage some agents to maintain their potential because it is more convenient, under incentive constraints, to give them money.

3. $v(y_i, z_i)$ **is observed,** (y_i, z_i) **is not,** (y_i, z_i) **is fixed.** A feasible policy is now a function $x(v(y, z))$. For Conditional Equality, an individual's situation is evaluated by

$$x(v(y, z)) + v(y, \tilde{z}).$$

The term $v(y, \tilde{z})$ is not observable, and one must determine who, in a given class of v level, are the worst-off. Let N_v denote this class of agents with $v(y, z) = v$. One then sees that the lowest value of $v(y, \tilde{z})$ is attained by the agents with the lowest value of y in N_v. The second-best policy is therefore such that, for some constant c,

$$x(v) = c - v(\min_{i \in N_v} y_i, \tilde{z}).$$

Egalitarian-Equivalence evaluates an individual situation by

$$x(v(y, z)) + v(y, z) - v(\tilde{y}, z).$$

---

[11] For Conditional Equality with $\tilde{z} = L$, in contrast, the first policy is always optimal.

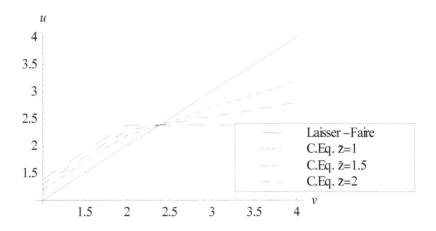

Figure 3.8: Well-being under Conditional Equality (Example 3.3)

The question is then to determine who, in the v class, has the greatest $v(\tilde{y}, z)$. The answer is $z = \max_{i \in N_v} z_i$. The second-best policy is therefore of the following kind, for some c' :

$$x(v) = c' - v + v(\tilde{y}, \max_{i \in N_v} z_i).$$

Let us examine the resulting distribution of well-being. Under the Conditional Equality policy, one has

$$x(v) + v = c + v - v(\min_{i \in N_v} y_i, \tilde{z}),$$

to be compared to the first-best formula $u_i = c^* + v(y_i, z_i) - v(y_i, \tilde{z})$. The above expression increases like v if $\min_{i \in N_v} y_i$ is a constant in v, and increases less than v if $\min_{i \in N_v} y_i$ is increasing in v. In the latter case, the slope is increasing in $\tilde{z}$ for a submodular function v, and decreasing in $\tilde{z}$ for a supermodular function. Under the Egalitarian-Equivalence policy, one has

$$x(v) + v = c' + v(\tilde{y}, \max_{i \in N_v} z_i),$$

to be compared to the first-best formula $u_i = c'^* + v(\tilde{y}, z_i)$. The above expression is constant in v if $\max_{i \in N_v} z_i$ is constant, and increasing when $\max_{i \in N_v} z_i$ in increasing in v. In the latter case, the slope increases with $\tilde{y}$ for a supermodular function v, and decreases with $\tilde{y}$ for a submodular function.

We illustrate these two policies in an example.

Example 3.3 *Assume that* (y, z) *is uniformly distributed over the unit square* $[1, 2]^2$ *(with a continuum of agents), and that* $v(y, z) = yz$ *(a supermodular function).*

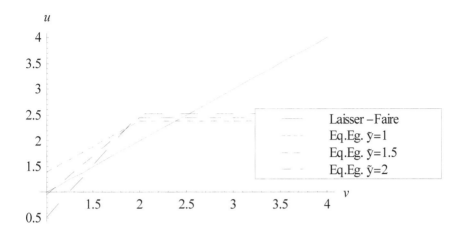

Figure 3.9: Well-being under Egalitarian-Equivalence (Example 3.3)

One computes

$$\min_{i \in N_v} y_i = \begin{cases} v/2 & \text{if } v \geq 2 \\ 1 & \text{if } v < 2, \end{cases}$$

$$\max_{i \in N_v} z_i = \begin{cases} 2 & \text{if } v \geq 2 \\ v & \text{if } v < 2. \end{cases}$$

The Conditional Equality policy is then such that

$$x(v) = \begin{cases} c - v\tilde{z}/2 & \text{if } v \geq 2 \\ c - \tilde{z} & \text{if } v < 2, \end{cases}$$

for $c = \tilde{z} \left(\ln 2 + .5\right)$. The Egalitarian-Equivalence policy is described by

$$x(v) = \begin{cases} c' - v + 2\tilde{y} & \text{if } v \geq 2 \\ c' - v + v\tilde{y} & \text{if } v < 2, \end{cases}$$

for $c' = 9/4 + \tilde{y}(2 \ln 2 - 13/4)$. Figure 3.8 illustrates the resulting distribution of well-being, as a function of well-being in the laissez-faire, i.e. v, for Conditional Equality when $\tilde{z}$ takes different values. Figure 3.9 shows the similar curves for Egalitarian-Equivalence, for various values of $\tilde{y}$.

One observes that the reference parameter has a greater impact on well-off individuals under Conditional Equality, whereas badly-off individuals are more concerned by the reference parameter under Egalitarian-Equivalence. An important observation here again is that Egalitarian-Equivalence is not always more egalitarian in outcomes than Conditional Equality.

3.6   Multiple goods and in-kind transfers

We have so far confined our attention to the case when transferable resources take the form of a single good, or alternatively, when prices are fixed so that money gives sufficient information about access to external resources. If one drops this simplifying assumption, there are some complications even in the first-best context of full information. In particular, Conditional Equality has to be refined if one wants to avoid a direct clash with Pareto-efficiency. Indeed, this criterion evaluates bundles of resources and circumstances with reference "preferences." As far as circumstances are concerned, this is not problematic when they are fixed characteristics of the individual. But it would be much more questionable not to respect individual preferences over external resources which can be reallocated between individuals.

Egalitarian-Equivalence, interestingly, does not have this problem because it refers to individual preferences in order to compute "equivalent resources," i.e., the resources which would yield the same well-being with reference circumstances. The only difficulty for Egalitarian-Equivalence is to define equivalent resources in a way that permits unequivocal ranking. A convenient way to do this is to rely on a family of nested budget sets, and to compute equivalent resources in terms of indirect utility, i.e., to seek the particular budget set in this family such that, with reference circumstances and being free to choose a bundle of resources in this set, the individual would be just as well-off as in his current situation. The comparison between individual situations is then made in terms of equivalent budget sets, and since they are nested there is no ambiguity about how to rank them.

Indirect utility can also be useful for addressing the above problem about Conditional Equality. Again, take a family of nested budget sets, and, for every individual, determine the budget set from this family that would give him the same well-being with his current characteristics (including circumstances). Since these budget sets are nested, again the greater the "corresponding budget" unambiguously is, the better-off the individual is. Now, Conditional Equality can be modified so that reference "preferences" are applied to the individual combinations of such corresponding budgets and circumstances. When an individual is better-off, this gives him a greater corresponding budget, and reference preferences have to agree that this is a better situation. In this way, the reference preferences always conform to individual preferences about external resources, although they do not generally agree with individual preferences about the combination of resources and circumstances. Incidentally, one is not forced to take the same family of budgets for every individual, and in particular it is possible to take a specific family for each kind of circumstances. This refinement of Conditional Equality in terms of budgets will appear particularly useful in the next chapter.

Multiplicity of goods also raises another kind of issue. It can indeed help to alleviate a particular kind of incentive problem. In the previous sections we have not examined the problem that occurs when none of the individuals' characteristics are observable, not even their well-being. When only one good is available for transfers, nothing can then be done in terms of compensation for bad circumstances. With multiple goods, the outlook is sometimes less grim. Suppose indeed that circumstances affect preferences over external resources. Then preferences over resources can be used in order to elicit information about individuals' circumstances. More specifically, this is a situation where in-kind transfers may be helpful, as described in Blackorby and Donaldson (1988). If a particular circumstance (say, a disability) increases the preference for a particular good (say, a wheelchair), then offering this good for free (up to some maximal amount) or at a highly subsidized price may be a way to provide compensation to those affected by this particular condition, without attracting the others.

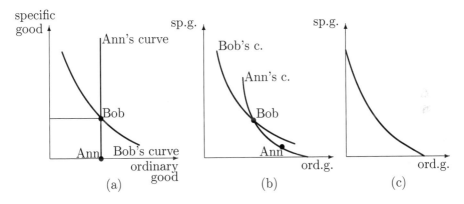

Figure 3.10: Second-best compensation with two goods

Blackorby and Donaldson focus on the particularly favorable case when the individuals who are not a target of compensation effectively do not like the good offered in-kind. In this case, a rationing scheme distributing this specific good for free only attracts those who should have it. But a similar reasoning also applies in the less favorable case when everybody likes all the goods but with different intensity of preferences (i.e., different marginal rates of substitution) depending on how bad their circumstances are. The optimal policy in the second-best context, however, no longer consists in rationing the specific good, and must be of a more complex kind. Assuming that there is no second-hand market for the specific good, the typical optimal policy will consist of selling the good at the producer price (marginal cost) for small quantities and then at a degressive price. Figure 3.10 illustrates, for a simple two-individual case, the difference between the case (a) when the advantaged individual (called Ann in the figure) is indifferent to the good, and the case (b) with different intensities. In both cases, we focus on the situation when the incentive constraint of the non-targeted agent is binding, i.e., the interesting situation where one cannot achieve full compensation because of incentive constraints. In (a), Ann has vertical indifference curves, and this is what makes rationing without charge optimal. In (b), optimality requires Ann to pay the marginal cost, while the targeted individual (Bob in the figure) will pay less. With a large number of individuals, the optimal budget line would, with a smoothly decreasing price, typically look like an indifference curve (c).

Another important issue, raised in De-Shalit and Wolff (2007), is the fact that certain types of in-kind transfers, or even certain changes in daily life environment provided by public goods, may be better than money transfers in enhancing the condition of disabled individuals. This may sometimes be a simple matter of efficiency. In addition, there may be special benefits in terms of social integration and of symbolic recognition of the diversity of human abilities. For instance, accessible buses might be preferable to taxi vouchers on all these counts. The possibility of performing compensation by public goods will not be studied further in this book but it should attract more research.

3.7   *Satiation

Let us now come back for simplicity to the assumption of a single transferable good, but consider the possibility of local and global satiation. We focus on the distribution case in this section, since there is no satiation in the TU case. Satiation raises a problem for compensation, because it may make it impossible to equalize well-being between two individuals with the same responsibility characteristics, if one has a maximum well-being below the level of the other. But this is not, in essence, very different from what happens when well-being is increasing but bounded.

A more specific issue is to respect the Pareto principle and avoid wasting resources on agents who have passed their satiation point. This is problematic for the Conditional Equality criterion, which relies on reference preferences instead of each agent's own preferences. Indeed, the function $u(x, y_i, \tilde{z})$ may have a different satiation pattern, with respect to x, than the function $u(x, y_i, z_i)$. The solution proposed in the previous section can be useful here as well. Instead of reasoning in terms of allocations of resources x_N let us consider allocations of budgets $(\{x \mid 0 \leq x \leq b_i\})_{i \in N}$.

Define the indirect utility function $V(b, y, z)$ as the maximum well-being attainable with a budget bounded by b:

$$V(b, y, z) = \max \{u(x, y, z) \mid 0 \leq x \leq b\}$$

This function is non-decreasing and continuous in b.

If one applies the leximin criterion to $V(b_i, y_i, \tilde{z})$, one does not always obtain an efficient criterion, because $V(b, y_i, \tilde{z})$ may have a plateau at values of b for which $V(b, y_i, z_i)$ is still increasing. A remedy to this is to define Conditional Equality as follows: First determine the subset of allocations which are optimal for the leximin criterion applied to $V(b_i, y_i, \tilde{z})$ and then, within this subset, apply the leximin criterion to b_i. This second step eliminates any possible inefficiency. Another advantage is that, for two agents i, j such that $y_i = y_j$, this necessarily implies $b_i = b_j$ at the optimal allocation (if this is efficient), which is well in line with the liberal reward principle underlying Conditional Equality.

It remains to prove that this solution always works out.

Proposition 3.3 *The Conditional Equality allocation rule thus defined always yields a non empty subset of Pareto efficient allocations.*

Proof. Let us define

$$
\begin{aligned}
U &= \left\{ (u(x_i, y_i, z_i))_{i \in N} \mid x_N \in F(e) \right\}, \\
B &= \left\{ b_N \in [0, \Omega]^N \mid \exists u_N \in U, \forall i \in N, V(b_i, y_i, z_i) = u_i \right\}.
\end{aligned}
$$

The set $F(e)$ is compact. By continuity of u in x, U is compact as well. By closedness of U and continuity of V in b, B is closed. As it is bounded by construction, B is also compact.

Maximizing $\min_i V(b_i, y_i, \tilde{z})$ over B selects a compact subset of B. By iteration, the leximin criterion applied to $(V(b_i, y_i, \tilde{z}))_{i \in N}$ selects a compact subset B^* of B. On this subset, the leximin applied to b_N again selects a compact subset B^{**}.

Let $b_N^{**} \in B^{**}$, and $u_N \in U$ be the corresponding utilities. Suppose there exists another $u_N' \in U$ such that $u_N' > u_N$. For i such that $u_i' > u_i$, one must have $b_i^{**} < \Omega$ because the level $V(\Omega, y_i, z_i)$ of utility for i cannot be surpassed with a feasible allocation. As V is non-decreasing in b, necessarily there is $b_N' \in B$ such that for all $i \in N$, $V(b_i', y_i, z_i) = u_i'$, and $b_N' > b_N^{**}$. But this contradicts the assumption $b_N^{**} \in B^{**}$, because b_N' must beat b_N^{**} either in the first or in the second step of the selection. ∎

3.8 Conclusion

This chapter was a modest introduction to a wide set of issues. The Conditional Equality and Egalitarian-Equivalence criteria appear sufficiently flexible to be adaptable to various contexts. We have seen that the second-best policies for these two criteria are typically closer to each other in the second-best context than in the first-best, because incentive constraints generally impose a dose of liberal reward. Indeed, under incentive constraints the Egalitarian-Equivalence criterion does not always induce policies which are more redistributive than Conditional Equality. As is customary to specialists of public economics, it therefore appears here again that intuitions derived from first-best analysis may be misleading in the second-best context.

Nevertheless, even if one must be cautious about any extension of observations made on first-best allocation rules to second-best policies, the analysis of the properties of the *social orderings* (as opposed to allocation rules) stands by itself and is valid independently of the content of the set of attainable allocations. For instance, the fact that Egalitarian-Equivalence always gives priority to the worst-off among individuals with the same responsibility characteristics, in accordance with the compensation principle, is worth retaining in its favor. The observation that incentive constraints sometimes hinder the full expression of such a priority does not make it irrelevant. It is, however, worth exploring every specific context of application in detail in order to see exactly how the properties of the criteria translate into concrete redistributive policies. In this perspective, the next two chapters study redistribution of earnings in some detail.

Pride of place has been given in this book to Conditional Equality and Egalitarian-Equivalence because of their simplicity and of the fact that they have attracted much attention so far. But the newer Envy Intensity criteria, on which little is known, should also be submitted to closer scrutiny in future research.

Chapter 4

Unequal skills

4.1 Introduction

The most immediate application of the conceptual apparatus developed in the previous chapters, and one of the most important for social justice in general, is the question of income redistribution. Individuals suffer from inequalities in earning potentials due to discrepancies in their innate ability and social background. But inequality can also be ascribed to different views about the use of one's time and the kind of jobs one likes, and one's freedom to make different choices in these matters should be accepted.

In this chapter, we postulate that individuals are not responsible at all for their earning possibilities, but are fully responsible for their preferences over consumption and leisure. (In this chapter, "consumption" will always refer to a one-dimensional quantity and will be identified with disposable income.) Although this responsibility cut is questionable – variants will be explored in the next chapter – it appears to be the most natural starting point. This viewpoint has been implicitly adopted in the early fairness literature which considered that the no-envy test should be applied to consumption-leisure bundles. Indeed, we have seen that the no-envy criterion is justified when one considers that individuals are not responsible for the bundles to be compared ("circumstances and money" in the previous chapters) but are responsible for the characteristics that determine how they rank such bundles (the "responsibility characteristics" of the previous chapters). Therefore, if one applies the no-envy test by asking people to compare their own consumption-leisure bundle to others' bundles with their own preferences, this means that one is implicitly considering that people are responsible for their preferences, but not for their consumption and leisure, and in particular not for their skill level (productivity, market wage rate) which determines how much leisure they must sacrifice in order to earn a given amount of money. Observe in particular that the no-envy test applied in this way implies that two individuals with the same amount of labor (and therefore of leisure) should have equal consumption levels, irrespective of their skill level. This clearly means that inequalities linked to skills differentials are not accepted in this approach.

Now, Pazner and Schmeidler (1974) noticed the following problem (see Table 4.1). Consider a two-agent economy. Ann earns two dollars per hour but never accepts to work an hour for less than five dollars. In other words, her willingness-to-pay (WTP) for an hour of leisure is five dollars. Barb earns twenty dollars per hour and always accepts working an hour for fifteen dollars.

Table 4.1: Example

	Earnings per hour (in $)	WTP for leisure (in $)
Ann	2	5
Barb	20	15

Efficiency recommends that Barb should work full time, and that Ann should not work unless all her earnings are transferred to Barb. Since the latter situation makes Ann obviously very envious, we can restrict attention to allocations in which she does not work. Total earnings in an eight-hour day, for these two individuals when Barb alone works, equal $8 \times 20 = 160$ dollars. If no redistribution is made between them, Ann envies Barb. Suppose fifty dollars are redistributed from Barb to Ann. Then Ann with $50 still envies Barb with $110, because she would accept to work for an extra forty dollars a day, and this is less than the consumption gap of sixty dollars between Barb and her. But Barb already envies Ann, because she does not want to work for less than $8 \times 15 = 120$ dollars a day of additional consumption, and would therefore rather go idle with $50 (or even zero) than work full time with $110. Any other redistribution will increase the envy of one of them. In summary, it is impossible to find an envy-free and efficient allocation in such a situation.

In this chapter we will show how this difficulty connects to the conflict between compensation and neutrality analyzed in Chapter 2, and how this suggests various solutions to this problem, based on sufficiently weak formulations of these two principles. The early fairness literature[1] has been content with considering only two extreme solutions, the "wealth-fair" allocation and the "full-income-fair" allocation. The wealth-fair approach applies the no-envy test to consumption-*earnings* bundles instead of consumption-*leisure* bundles. In other words, it requires each individual to compare her own combination of consumption and earnings to the others', examining whether she would prefer to consume and to earn as much as the others – with her own productivity. This makes it much harder for the unskilled to envy the skilled agents, since it is difficult for them to earn as much. As a consequence, this solution generates too little redistribution. In fact it is compatible with laissez-faire in an economy of wage-earners with no capital income. For instance, in the Ann–Barb example the allocation in which Barb alone works and keeps her earnings is wealth-fair, since Ann is unable to earn 160 dollars. When there is capital income it is sufficient for this approach to equalize capital income and let agents retain their earnings.

---

[1] In particular Varian (1974, 1975), Pazner and Schmeidler (1978b).

The full-income-fair allocation is quite different. It equalizes "full income" across individuals, which is defined as the net income they would have if they worked full time. In the Ann–Barb example, this is obtained by letting Barb work alone (out of efficiency) and transferring seventy-two dollars to Ann. Then Barb's full income equals $160 - 72 = 88$ dollars; Ann's full income equals $16 + 72 = 88$ dollars, too. This makes Ann non-envious, since the consumption gap between Barb and her is only equal to sixteen dollars, which is much less than the forty-dollar gap that would make her envious, but Barb is then very envious. This solution is very favorable to the unskilled and quite harsh on the skilled agents. As noticed by Dworkin,[2] this solution entails a "slavery of the talented" because they may be forced to work in order to pay their taxes.

It is worth pausing here in order to stress that the notion of full income, which is still fashionable in studies of living standards, should be definitively banned from welfare economics. It is deceptively attractive for the following reason. It is reasonable to evaluate consumers' standard of living by the market value of their consumption when they are considered responsible for their tastes. In such a situation, the no-envy test applied to consumption bundles is a reasonable evaluation device for the assessment of inequalities, and it is satisfied when all consumers have the same income, since everyone can then choose from the same menu. Moreover, for any fixed price vector, a higher income automatically guarantees a greater consumer satisfaction, so that this approach respects individual preferences (at least when prices do not vary). From this starting point it seems natural to incorporate leisure into the picture by adding the market value of leisure. After all, people freely choose their quantity of labor on the market just as they buy vegetables and soap (assuming away rationing constraints on the labor market). The mistake in this reasoning lies in the fact that people face different prices for their leisure. If they all had the same market wage rate, this reasoning would be fine. But when wage rates are unequal, full incomes are not the correct quantity that one should try to equalize across agents, because this unduly penalizes the talented, as it has been illustrated above. Moreover, when two individuals with the same preferences have different skill levels, the one with the greater full income need not be in the better position, which proves that full incomes do not correctly record preference satisfaction.

Figure 4.1 illustrates the budget sets that typically correspond to a wealth-fair allocation (a) and a full-income-fair allocation (b). In the former, the unskilled agent has a strictly smaller budget, while the situation is reversed in the latter. It is apparent that these two solutions lie at the extremes of a spectrum, and that one should hope to find more reasonable compromises. We will examine in this chapter various ways of devising fair allocations in this context.

In this chapter, we come back for a while to a first-best setting, i.e., we assume that the redistributing agency has all the information necessary to preserve full efficiency of the allocation while performing transfers between agents. The next chapter will examine what happens when a tax on earnings is the only available instrument for redistribution, in which case disincentives auto-

---

[2] See Dworkin (2000), p. 90.

consumption

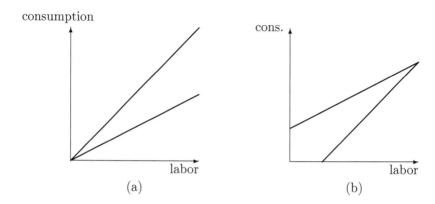

(a)   (b)

Figure 4.1: Wealth fairness and full-income fairness

matically plague any redistributive policy because of the wedge between gross earnings per hour and net income per hour.

4.2 *The model

The population is $N = \{1, ..., n\}$, and every individual $i \in N$ is endowed with two characteristics: a wage rate, identified with the agent's skill level $s_i \geq 0$, and u_i, a utility function over consumption and labor: $(c_i, \ell_i) \in \mathbb{R}_+ \times [0, 1]$. Let $X = \mathbb{R}_+ \times [0, 1]$. A profile of characteristics is $(s_N, u_N) = ((s_1, \ldots, s_n), (u_1, \ldots, u_n))$. The function u_i is assumed to be continuous, increasing in c_i, non-increasing in ℓ_i, and quasi-concave.

In this model an economy is simply described by the profile: $e = (s_N, u_N)$. An allocation is denoted $x_N = (x_1, \ldots, x_n)$, where $x_i = (c_i, \ell_i)$. The set of feasible allocations is denoted $F(e)$, and is defined by the condition $\sum_{i \in N} c_i \leq \sum_{i \in N} s_i \ell_i$. The literature contains studies of more complex economies with variable returns,[3] but for our purposes this simple technology with constant returns to scale is sufficient. Moreover, this is a pure labor economy, and capital income is introduced in a section of the next chapter.

We let $\mathcal{D}$ denote the domain of economies $e = (s_N, u_N)$ satisfying the above conditions. An *allocation rule* is a correspondence S such that for all $e = (s_N, u_N) \in \mathcal{D}$, $S(e) \subseteq F(e)$ is the subset of allocations selected by S. This chapter focuses on allocation rules since it deals with the first-best context. In the next, social ordering functions will be prominent. A *social ordering function* is a mapping R such that for all $e = (s_N, u_N) \in \mathcal{D}$, $R(e)$ is a complete ordering over X^N.

Allocation rules are required here to satisfy the following efficiency condition.

---

[3] See in particular Fleurbaey and Maniquet (1996, 1999), Gaspart (1998). A greater variety of technologies gives more power to some axioms, so that additional results are obtained, which will not be presented here.

Pareto Efficiency: $\forall e = (s_N, u_N) \in \mathcal{D}$, $\forall x_N \in S(e)$, $\forall x'_N \in F(e)$, if $\forall i \in N$, $u_i(x'_i) \geq u_i(x_i)$, then $\forall i \in N$, $u_i(x'_i) = u_i(x_i)$.

This model can be related to the model of the previous chapters in the following way. The circumstances (formerly y_i) are s_i, the responsibility characteristics (formerly z_i) are u_i, and the transferable resources (formerly x_i) are a two-dimensional bundle (c_i, q_i), where q_i denotes earnings: $q_i = s_i \ell_i$. Note that labor is not transferable, because it is heterogeneous across agents, but earnings are (within the bounds of s_i). The former general utility function $u(x_i, y_i, z_i)$ can be defined here as:

$$u((c_i, q_i), s_i, u_i) = u_i \left(c_i, \frac{q_i}{s_i} \right).$$

In this formula we see that the skill level affects preferences over transferable resources in a special way, and this is quite important for the analysis of this problem. In particular, there is no ambiguity about how to rank various skill levels on a scale of advantage.

An even more direct connection to the previous model can be established by noting that all Pareto-efficient allocations can be obtained by giving each i a lump-sum transfer t_i and letting her choose under the budget constraint $c_i \leq s_i \ell_i + t_i$. A Pareto-efficient allocation satisfies the constraint $\sum_{i \in N} t_i = 0$ and (in order to make sure that budget sets are not empty) for all $i \in N$, $t_i \geq -s_i$. One can then define the general utility function of the previous model as follows:

$$u(t_i, s_i, u_i) = \max \{ u_i(c, \ell) \mid c \leq s_i \ell + t_i \}.$$

Under this formulation, the current model is almost a special subcase of the distribution case of the previous model.

4.3 Compensation and neutrality

The difficulty of finding envy-free and efficient allocations when individuals are heterogeneous in skills and preferences is connected to the conflict between the compensation principle and the liberal reward principle. Recall that the former principle can be formulated by applying the no-envy test to individuals with identical responsibility characteristics, while, for the latter, one should apply the test to individuals with identical circumstances. This line of analysis gives us two sensible requirements:

Equal Well-Being for Equal Utility: Two individuals whose well-being depends on consumption and leisure in the same way should have the same level of well-being.

Equal Treatment for Equal Skills: Two individuals with identical skills should not suffer envy between themselves.

The first condition is a direct adaptation of *Equal Well-Being for Equal Responsibility* to the case in which individuals are responsible for their "utility function" which transforms consumption and leisure into (the appropriate measure of) well-being. The second is slightly more complicated than *Equal Treatment for Equal Circumstances*, because external resources are now multi-dimensional and include consumption and leisure. *Equal Treatment for Equal Circumstances* simply required "the same transfer," but this was just the simple application of the no-envy test to the case of a one-dimensional resource. Retaining the original no-envy test is the natural choice here. It is in fact also possible to reason here in terms of transfers (i.e., the difference between consumption and earnings) and to require two agents with equal skills to receive the same transfer. This is a possible variant of *Equal Treatment for Equal Skills*.

Let us look at a modified version of the Ann–Barb example, enriched with two new characters, Chris and Deb. Their earnings per hour and WTP for leisure are depicted in Table 4.2. Moreover, it is assumed that Ann and Deb have not only the same WTP for leisure but really the same utility function, and similarly for Barb and Chris.

Table 4.2: Example

	Earnings per hour (in $)	WTP for leisure (in $)
Ann	2	5
Barb	20	15
Chris	2	15
Deb	20	5

Pareto-efficiency requires Barb and Deb to work, because their hourly production exceeds the compensation they request in order to work an additional hour. It also requires that Ann and Chris should not work (unless they are forced to work to the benefit of someone else, but this will be excluded by the fairness conditions). *Equal Well-Being for Equal Utility* imposes that Ann and Deb should have the same utility, as well as Barb and Chris. In view of the fact that in each of these pairs only one of them works, this means that the consumption gap between the working and the idle must equal 40 dollars for Ann and Deb, and 120 dollars for Barb and Chris. Indeed, if Deb consumes 40 dollars more than Ann, this exactly compensates, in their common preferences, for the difference in leisure (eight hours). The same occurs for Barb and Chris if Barb consumes 120 dollars more than Chris. On the other hand, *Equal Treatment for Equal Skills* says that Ann and Chris, on one side, and Barb and Deb, on the other side, should have equal consumption. This is due to the fact that in each pair they have the same quantity of labor, and no-envy between two individuals working the same quantity can only be obtained if they have equal consumption. But if this is achieved, necessarily there will be the same consumption gap between (working) Deb and (idle) Ann and between (working) Barb and (idle) Chris, contradicting the above point that it should be 40 dollars for the former and 120 for the latter.

This shows that the difficulty of finding envy-free and efficient allocations in this setting can be traced, once again, to an internal conflict between no-envy among individuals with identical circumstances and no-envy among individuals with identical responsibility. This conflict, as in Chapter 2, opens the way to three different families of solutions: refinements of no-envy, conditional equality, egalitarian-equivalence. In the sequel we focus mainly on the last two, which have benefited from more scrutiny and are simpler for axiomatic analysis and applications. But some refinements of no-envy appear promising and are examined in a technical section.

4.4 *Axioms of fairness

In this section we briefly examine how the axioms of fairness have to be adapted to the current framework. The obvious cases are omitted.

No-Envy: $\forall e \in \mathcal{D},\ \forall x_N \in S(e),\ \forall i, j \in N$,

$$u_i(x_i) \geq u_i(x_j).$$

Let us first consider the compensation conditions.

Equal Well-Being for Equal Utility: $\forall e \in \mathcal{D},\ \forall x_N \in S(e),\ \forall i, j \in N$ such that $u_i = u_j$,

$$u_i(x_i) = u_j(x_j).$$

The "uniform" and "reference" variants of this axiom are straightforward.

Skill Solidarity: $\forall e = (s_N, u_N),\ e' = (s'_N, u_N) \in \mathcal{D},\ \forall x_N \in S(e),\ \forall x'_N \in S(e')$,

$$\forall i \in N,\ u_i(x_i) \geq u_i(x'_i) \text{ or}$$
$$\forall i \in N,\ u_i(x_i) \leq u_i(x'_i).$$

Acknowledged Merit: $\forall e \in \mathcal{D},\ \forall i, j \in N$,

$$[\forall x \in X,\ u_i(x) \geq u_j(x)] \Rightarrow [\forall x_N \in S(e),\ u_i(x_i) \geq u_j(x_j)].$$

We now turn to the neutrality (liberal reward) axioms.

Equal Treatment for Equal Skills: $\forall e \in \mathcal{D},\ \forall x_N \in S(e),\ \forall i, j \in N$ such that $s_i = s_j$,

$$u_i(x_i) \geq u_i(x_j).$$

A variant of this, which is logically stronger for Paretian allocation rules, requires equal monetary transfers:

Equal Transfer for Equal Skills: $\forall e \in \mathcal{D}$, $\forall x_N \in S(e)$, $\forall i, j \in N$ such that $s_i = s_j$,

$$c_i - s_i \ell_i = c_j - s_j \ell_j.$$

Again the "uniform" and "reference" variants of these axioms need not be written. *Independence of Responsibility Characteristics* is problematic here, because multidimensionality of resources makes it inefficient to let the allocation of resources be independent of individual preferences. This difficulty can be taken into account by restricting independence to changes of preferences which do not affect the efficiency of the selected allocation.

Paretian Independence of Utility: $\forall e = (s_N, u_N)$, $e' = (s_N, u'_N) \in \mathcal{D}$, $\forall x_N \in S(e)$, if x_N is Pareto-efficient in e', then $x_N \in S(e')$.

A logically weaker axiom restricts attention to changes of preferences which correspond to an improvement of the relative ranking of the selected allocation in the agents' eyes, as in Maskin Monotonicity (Maskin 1999). Let $uc(x_i)$ denote the upper contour set:

$$uc_i(x_i) = \{x \in X \mid u_i(x) \geq u_i(x_i)\}.$$

Independence of Improved Utility: $\forall e = (s_N, u_N)$, $e' = (s_N, u'_N) \in \mathcal{D}$, $\forall x_N \in S(e)$, if $\forall i \in N$, $uc'_i(x_i) \subseteq uc_i(x_i)$, then $x_N \in S(e')$.

Another way of tackling the difficulty consists in reasoning in terms of transfer $c_i - s_i \ell_i$ rather than in terms of bundles (c_i, ℓ_i). This is then compatible with Pareto-Efficiency.

Transfer Independence of Utility: $\forall e = (s_N, u_N)$, $e' = (s_N, u'_N) \in \mathcal{D}$, $\forall x_N \in S(e)$, $\exists x'_N \in S(e')$, $\forall i \in N$, $c_i - s_i \ell_i = c'_i - s_i \ell'_i$.

Acknowledged Handicap is not immediately adapted to this setting, but one possibility is again to think in terms of transfers and to say that an agent with lower skill should receive at least as great a transfer.

Acknowledged Handicap: $\forall e \in \mathcal{D}$, $\forall i, j \in N$,

$$[s_i \leq s_j] \Rightarrow [\forall x_N \in S(e), \; c_i - s_i \ell_i \geq c_j - s_j \ell_j].$$

The axiom of Fair Treatment for Equal Circumstances could be similarly adapted. For simplicity, we will ignore the Fair Treatment and Fair Ranking axioms here. *Egalitarian Bound* can still be defined, by reference to the level of utility $m(s_N, u_i)$ that i would obtain in the Pareto-efficient allocation that would equalize all utilities in the economy with profile $(s_N, (u_i, ..., u_i))$.

The counterpart of Proposition 1.1 reads as follows.

Proposition 4.1 *Table 4.3 describes the logical implications between the axioms.*

Table 4.3: Logical links between axioms

Compensation					Liberal Reward
					Paret. Indep. of Utility $\Downarrow$
Skill. Solidarity $\Downarrow^{(1)}$			Ackn. Hand. $\Downarrow$	Transfer Ind. of Utility $\Downarrow^{(2,3)}$ Equal Transfer for Eq. Skills $\searrow^{(3)}$	Indep. of Imp. Utility $\Downarrow^{(2)}$
Equal WB for Equal Ut.	Ackn. $\overset{\Leftarrow}{\text{Merit}}$	$\overset{\Leftarrow}{\Rightarrow}$ No-Envy			Equal Treatm. for Equal Skills
$\Downarrow$					$\Downarrow$
Equal WB for Unif. Ut.	$\overset{\Leftarrow}{\Rightarrow}$ Egalit. Bound		Eq. Transfer for Unif. Skills	$\Rightarrow^{(3)}$	Equal Treatm. for Unif. Skills
$\Downarrow$					$\Downarrow$
Equal WB for Ref. Ut.					Equal Treatm. for Ref. Skills

$^{(1)}$Assuming that S satisfies Anonymity.
$^{(2)}$Assuming that S satisfies Equal Treatment of Equals.
$^{(3)}$Assuming that S satisfies Pareto-Efficiency.

Proof. A proof is provided only for the implications that are not obvious and differ from those of Proposition 1.1.

(1) *Independence of Improved Utility* and *Equal Treatment of Equals* imply *Equal Treatment for Equal Skills*. Let $e = (s_N, u_N)$ and $i, j \in N$ be such that $s_i = s_j$, and consider an allocation x_N such that $u_i(x_i) < u_i(x_j)$. It is then easy to find u_0 such that

$$
\begin{aligned}
uc_0(x_j) &\subseteq uc_j(x_j) \cap \{x \in X \mid u_i(x) > u_i(x_i)\}, \\
uc_0(x_i) &= uc_i(x_i).
\end{aligned}
$$

By construction, $u_0(x_i) < u_0(x_j)$. If $x_N \in S(e)$, then by *Independence of Improved Utility*, $x_N \in S(e')$, where e' differs from e by replacing u_i and u_j by u_0. But *Equal Treatment of Equals* requires $u_0(x_i) = u_0(x_j)$, yielding a contradiction.

(2) *Equal Transfer for Equal Skills* and *Pareto-Efficiency* imply *Equal Treatment for Equal Skills*. By *Pareto-Efficiency*, two agents i, j such that $s_i = s_j$ must have bundles that they choose from budget lines of the same slope $s_i = s_j$. If they receive the same transfer $c_i - s_i \ell_i = c_j - s_j \ell_j$, this means that they have the same budget line, and therefore cannot envy each other.

(3) *Egalitarian Bound* implies *Equal Transfer for Uniform Skills*. When all agents have the same skill s and the same utility function, *Pareto-Efficiency* implies that equalizing their utility is obtained by the laissez-faire allocation in which everyone chooses the best bundle in the budget $c = s\ell$. When all agents

have the same skill s but possibly different utility functions, this utility level
defines $m_i(s_N, u_i)$ for every i. This still corresponds to the laissez-faire utility
levels in this economy, i.e., when every i chooses in the budget $c = s\ell$. Therefore
Egalitarian Bound requires selecting the laissez-faire allocation when all agents
have equal skills, which is also the requirement of *Equal Transfer for Uniform
Skills*. ■

Notice that *No-Envy* no longer implies *Egalitarian Bound*, as can be deduced
from the fact that *No-Envy* does not imply *Equal Transfer for Uniform Skills*.

In the context of production it is also interesting to mention the axiom of
Participation, which takes care of the "slavery" problem, by avoiding situations
in which an agent would rather opt out of the economy than participate in the
production process.

Participation: $\forall e = (s_N, u_N) \in \mathcal{D}$, $\forall x_N \in S(e)$,

$$\forall i \in N, \ u_i(x_i) \geq u_i(0,0).$$

4.5   Conditional-equality solutions

As we will now see, the wealth-fair and full-income-fair solutions are just two
extreme examples of Conditional Equality solutions. Consider first the general
family of solutions which consist in defining a transfer scheme for each possible profile of skills in the population. These are lump-sum transfers, which do
not depend on individual preferences and are therefore independent of people's
choices of labor once the transfers are made. This is the hallmark of a liberal reward kind of policy: Transfers are independent of responsibility characteristics.
In particular, two individuals with identical skills will obtain the same transfer,
and therefore the same budget set, guaranteeing the absence of envy between
them (*Equal Treatment for Equal Skills*).

Within this family of solutions, however, some are not acceptable because
they perform no compensation, such as the wealth-fair solution which performs
no transfer at all and simply follows a laissez-faire policy. There are even some
which perform transfers in the wrong direction. One should therefore, minimally,
be interested only in solutions which give greater transfers to individuals with
lower skills. This makes laissez-faire an extreme bound of the acceptable policies.

In order to find a reasonable calibration of transfers, it is natural to seek a
configuration of budget sets, for all the individuals, such that no budget set is
obviously better than another. In order to check that such a configuration is
obtained a benchmark preference over consumption and leisure can be used as
a yardstick for the comparison of budget sets. This reference preference relation
can be inspired from preferences observed in the population profile. Once a
reference preference is chosen, one may seek to compute the transfers that make
all the budget sets equivalent for the reference preference relation (two budget
sets are equivalent for a preference relation when they yield the same satisfaction, once the best bundle is chosen from each set). Figure 4.2 illustrates typical

configurations of budget lines which are equivalent for reference preferences, for the case of a population with three levels of skills.

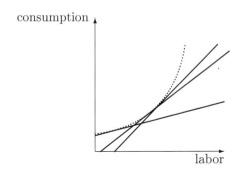

Figure 4.2: Conditional Equality solution

The advantage of choosing this way of calibrating transfers is that it incorporates a concern for compensation by guaranteeing that agents with similar preferences as the reference will obtain appropriate compensation for their different skills. In the case when all individuals have similar preferences, choosing the common preferences as the reference then makes it possible to satisfy *Equal Well-Being for Uniform Utility*. Any other method of calibration that does not refer to preferences in order to compare budgets will fail at the bar of the compensation principle.

The next figures show how the relative fate of individuals with different skill levels depends on the choice of reference preferences. In Fig. 4.3(a) one sees that when reference preferences are work-averse (i.e., with steep indifference curves), this is rather favorable to the skilled and unfavorable to the less skilled agents, with the wealth-fair allocation as the limit case. The reverse occurs with hardworking reference preferences, i.e., with flatter indifference curves as in panel (b). The extreme case of reference preferences which are indifferent to work (totally flat indifference curve) yields the full-income fair solution.

Figure 4.4 enables us to see that when substitutability between consumption and leisure is low for the reference preferences (i.e., corresponding to strongly curved indifference curves), this is favorable to the extremely low- and high-skilled and unfavorable to the middle-class. The case of indifference curves with a cusp, for the reference preferences, may yield a situation in which all the budget lines cross at one point. This particular configuration is advocated by Kolm (2004b), who insists on having the intersection occur for a specific quantity of labor, so that the situation can be described in terms of equal sharing of the product of this quantity of labor between all agents, each of them being free to keep the additional earnings obtained by working more.[4]

---

[4]This can also be described as a simple application of the idea of conditional equality to the context where individuals are responsible for their labor and their well-being is measured in terms of consumption: There is equality of the consumption that everyone would obtain

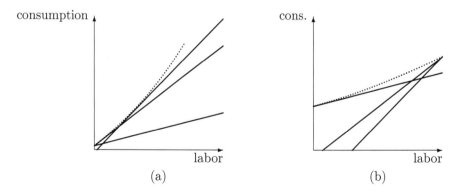

Figure 4.3: Conditional Equality solutions

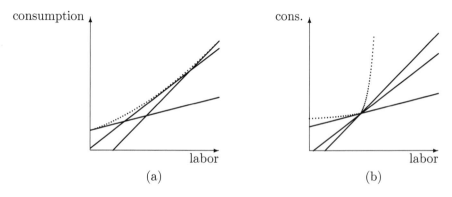

Figure 4.4: Conditional Equality solutions

With the situations obtained in these figures, it is possible for a high-skilled agent to envy a less skilled agent who has the same preferences. Some overcompensation is thus likely to occur, which is problematic in terms of incentives if agents can choose to work at a lower productivity than their potential. Moreover, one can even obtain a certain "slavery of the talented," since the budget lines of the high-skilled agents go below the origin, which may entail that some of them would rather opt out of the economy, i.e., have zero work and zero consumption, than face such unfavorable budget sets. A sobering result, which is easy to prove, is that in the whole family of Conditional Equality solutions, the only one that avoids any of these two problems completely is the wealth-fair solution. The proof goes like this. A Conditional Equality solution is defined by a transfer scheme which depends only on the profile of skills and not on the profile of preferences of the population. The sum of transfers must add up to zero, which means that if some agents receive a subsidy, others pay a tax. The

---

with the reference quantity of labor.

latter must therefore have a budget line which goes below the origin, and therefore below the budget line of the subsidized agents. Since, in these solutions, all budget lines are judged equivalent by the reference preferences, no budget line is entirely below another. This requires that transfers are greater for the less skilled agents. The agents who pay taxes are more skilled than those who are subsidized. Therefore, for agents who are sufficiently work-averse, it is better to be less skilled, and the skilled agents who work sufficiently little are worse-off than at the origin.

4.6 Egalitarian-equivalent solutions

In the model from the first chapters, the Egalitarian-Equivalence solution was defined by equalizing the hypothetical amount of external resources that would provide every individual with her current level of well-being if her circumstances were of the reference kind (and her responsibility characteristics unchanged). Applying this method to the current framework, we may ask every individual what hypothetical amount of (lump-sum) transfer would make her as happy as in the current situation if her skills were at a reference level. Then we try to equalize this amount across individuals.

Intuitively, this solution tries to mimic a situation in which all agents would have the same skills (at the reference level) and the same budget line for all, independently of their preferences. The individuals' real skills cannot be rendered equal, but the actual allocation can be made equivalent, in terms of well-being, to an ideal equal-skill situation.

Figure 4.5 illustrates the resulting configuration. In panel (a), all individual indifference curves are tangent to the same hypothetical budget line (the dotted line in the figure). This budget line is virtual and generally does not correspond to the agents' real budget line, since their actual consumption-leisure bundles (the dots on the indifference curves of the figure) may lie outside this line. The solid lines in panel (b) show possible real budget lines corresponding to agents receiving lump-sum transfers as a function of their characteristics (skills and preferences).

As can be seen from the figure, two agents with identical utility functions will necessarily obtain the same utility level in this configuration, which means that *Equal Well-Being for Equal Utility* will always be satisfied. Since this solution is good in terms of compensation, it is less good in terms of liberal reward. But, if the reference skill level is chosen so as to correspond to the observed level when all agents do have the same skill, *Equal Treatment for Uniform Skills* will also be satisfied because the selected allocation will then simply be a laissez-faire allocation in which every agent has the same budget thanks to the fact that all skills are equal. It is very natural to require the laissez-faire policy when all skills are identical, and it is worth stating this as a separate condition (which is logically stronger than *Equal Treatment for Uniform Skills*):

Laissez-Faire for Uniform Skills: When all skills are equal, laissez-faire is the best policy.

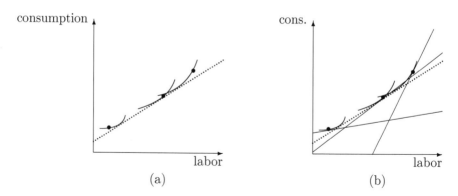

Figure 4.5: Egalitarian-Equivalence

How should the reference level be chosen in general? Let us first consider the family of straightforward methods which choose the reference level independently of population preferences. As can be guessed from Fig. 4.5(a), the greater the reference level, the more favorable the solution is toward the hardworking agents. The solution that is the most favorable to the work-averse agents is to pick zero as the reference level of skill. Choosing zero as the reference level for all kinds of populations is a rather extreme solution,[5] but this "Zero Egalitarian-Equivalence" solution, illustrated in Fig. 4.6(a), has interesting features.

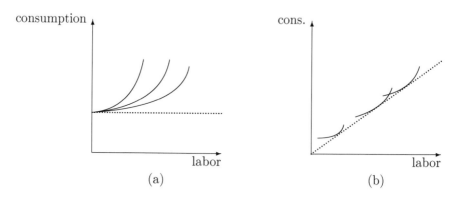

Figure 4.6: Zero and Wage Egalitarian-Equivalence

Zero Egalitarian-Equivalence: Equalize the counterfactual amount of transfer which, combined with a null wage rate, would make every individual as happy as in the current situation.

Among all the solutions which have a fixed reference level of skill, this is

---

[5]This solution was briefly mentioned in Kolm (1969), and then it seems to have been ignored for a long time.

the only one which guarantees that all non-working agents will consume the same amount. All solutions with a positive (fixed) reference level will treat them unequally, allowing the less work-averse to consume more than the more work-averse, as if the latter needed to be penalized for their laziness. This is rather questionable when none of them works anyway. A second feature is that, among all the solutions with a fixed reference level, this is the only one that avoids slavery of the talented. A positive (fixed) level of reference will always, for some configuration of skills and preferences, yield an allocation in which some skilled agents would rather opt out of the economy, i.e., are worse-off than with the zero-consumption-zero-labor bundle.

If one enlarges the analysis to solutions which allow the reference skill to depend on the skill profile of the population, these two features (identical consumption for the non-working, no slavery of the talented) are shared by all solutions which always pick a reference level of skill that is less than or equal to the lowest skill level of the population under consideration. The solution that exactly picks the lowest skill level as the reference, for every profile of skills, is particularly interesting, because in addition it satisfies *Laissez-Faire for Uniform Skills*, so that it is better than the Zero Egalitarian-Equivalence solution in terms of liberal reward. Let us call it "Min Egalitarian-Equivalence," for further reference.

Min Egalitarian-Equivalence: Equalize the counterfactual amount of transfer which, combined with the lowest skill of the current profile, would make every individual as happy as in the current situation.

If one enlarges again the analysis in order to consider solutions which allow the reference skill to depend also on the population preferences, there is another interesting solution which avoids slavery of the talented and satisfies *Laissez-Faire for Uniform Skills*. It consists in picking a reference skill so that the virtual budget line that is obtained contains the origin. In this way, the counterfactual ideally egalitarian situation that is mimicked is really like a true situation of zero transfer for all agents when they have equal skills. This is illustrated in Fig. 4.6(b). In addition, it has a nice property of *Skill Solidarity* that the Zero Egalitarian-Equivalence has but not the Min Egalitarian-Equivalence: When the profile of skills changes, either all individuals benefit from it, or they all suffer. This kind of solidarity with respect to changes of circumstances has been introduced in Chapter 1 and shown to express the compensation principle to an even higher degree than *Equal Well-Being for Equal Responsibility*. Therefore this third solution is particularly interesting. Let it be called "Wage Egalitarian-Equivalence," by reference to the fact that the ideal situation it refers to is a pure wage economy, with no unearned income.

Wage Egalitarian-Equivalence: Equalize the counterfactual wage rate (with no transfer) that would make every individual as happy as in the current situation.

Note, however, that, contrary to the other two solutions, this one does not guarantee that all non-working agents will have the same consumption. It turns out, unfortunately, that this property cannot be satisfied by a Pareto-efficient allocation rule in conjunction with *Skill Solidarity* and *Laissez-Faire for Uniform Skills*, because, as shown in Section 4.8, Wage Egalitarian-Equivalence is the only allocation rule satisfying these properties.

It is worth noting that in the infinitely rich family of Egalitarian-Equivalence solutions we have been able to single out three of them as particularly worthy of interest. The concrete framework of this analysis enabled us to select reference parameters on the basis of ethical principles.

The duality between Conditional Equality and Egalitarian-Equivalence should be mentioned once again. The former focuses on budget sets and makes sure that they are equivalent, in the sense that a reference preference would be indifferent between them. In particular, no budget line should be everywhere below another. The latter focuses on individual indifference curves and makes sure that they are equivalent, in the sense that they could be obtained by choosing from the same budget set. In particular, no indifference curve should be everywhere below another. No solution exists that would simultaneously avoid dominance among budget sets and among indifference curves.

4.7   *Refinements of no-envy

In this section we examine how Envy Intensity criteria work in the current framework.

Let $e = (s_N, u_N)$ be any given economy. Define a budget set determined by a skill s and a lump-sum transfer t as follows:

$$B(s,t) = \{(c, \ell) \in X \mid c \leq s\ell + t\} .$$

Let $u_i(B)$ denote the indirect utility derived from any compact subset $B \subseteq X$:

$$u_i(B) = \max \{u_i(x) \mid x \in B\} ,$$

and $uc_i(B)$ denote the corresponding upper contour set:

$$uc_i(B) = \{x \in X \mid u_i(x) \geq u_i(B)\} .$$

For an arbitrary closed set $A \subseteq X$ (which will typically be an upper contour set hereafter), let $ex(s, A)$ denote the expenditure function:

$$ex(s, A) = \min \{t \in \mathbb{R} \mid B(s,t) \cap A \neq \varnothing\} .$$

This definition of an expenditure function is not standard but will be convenient here.

For any allocation $x_N \in F(e)$, associated to lump-sum transfers t_N, any pair of agents $i, j \in N$, i envies j's budget if, in order to reach utility $u_i(B(s_j, t_j))$ with his own skill s_i, he would need a greater transfer than t_i, or equivalently if, in order to reach utility $u_i(x_i)$ with j's skill s_j, he would need a smaller transfer than t_j:

$$u_i\left(B(s_i,t_i)\right) < u_i\left(B(s_j,t_j)\right) \quad \Leftrightarrow \quad ex(s_i, uc_i(B(s_j,t_j))) > t_i$$
$$\Leftrightarrow \quad ex(s_j, uc_i(x_i)) < t_j.$$

Let

$$t_{ij}(x_N) = ex(s_i, uc_i(B(s_j,t_j))) - t_i,$$
$$d_{ij}(x_N) = t_j - ex(s_j, uc_i(x_i)).$$

Intuitively, $t_{ij}(x_N)$ is the increment that must be added to t_i so that i no longer envies j's budget, while $d_{ij}(x_N)$ is what should be deducted from t_j so that i no longer envies j's budget. One has $t_{ij}(x_N) > 0$ if and only if i envies j's budget, and $t_{ii}(x_N) \equiv 0$. The same holds for $d_{ij}(x_N)$.

Envious Intensity (S_{EsI}): $\forall e \in \mathcal{D}, \forall x_N \in F(e)$, $x_N \in S_{EsI}(e)$ if and only if x_N is Pareto-efficient and $\forall x'_N \in F(e)$ such that x'_N is Pareto-efficient,

$$\sum_{i \in N} \max_{j \in N} t_{ij}(x_N) \le \sum_{i \in N} \max_{j \in N} t_{ij}(x'_N).$$

Envied Intensity (S_{EdI}): $\forall e \in \mathcal{D}, \forall x_N \in F(e)$, $x_N \in S_{EdI}(e)$ if and only if x_N is Pareto-efficient and $\forall x'_N \in F(e)$ such that x'_N is Pareto-efficient,

$$\sum_{j \in N} \max_{i \in N} d_{ij}(x_N) \le \sum_{j \in N} \max_{i \in N} d_{ij}(x'_N).$$

In this special model there is an equivalent, simpler way of describing these two solutions. For any allocation, let $B^\cup(x_N)$ denote the union of the budget sets:

$$B^\cup(x_N) = \bigcup_{i \in N} B(s_i, t_i).$$

Note that

$$\max_{j \in N} t_{ij}(x_N) = ex(s_i, uc_i(B^\cup(x_N))) - t_i,$$

and since $\sum_{i \in N} t_i = 0$,

$$\sum_{i \in N} \max_{j \in N} t_{ij}(x_N) = \sum_{i \in N} ex(s_i, uc_i(B^\cup(x_N))).$$

In other words, the Envious Intensity criterion seeks to minimize the sum of transfers that the agents would need in order to obtain, with their own skills, the utility they would get from $B^\cup(x_N)$.

A dual configuration is obtained for Envied Intensity. Let $uc^\cup(x_N)$ denote the union of the upper contour sets:

$$uc^\cup(x_N) = \bigcup_{i \in N} uc_i(x_i).$$

One has

$$\max_{i \in N} d_{ij}(x_N) = t_j - ex(s_j, uc^{\cup}(x_N)),$$

$$\sum_{j \in N} \max_{i \in N} d_{ij}(x_N) = -\sum_{i \in N} ex(s_i, uc^{\cup}(x_N)),$$

so that the Envied Intensity criterion can be described as maximizing the sum of transfers that are needed in order to make all the budget sets (corresponding to the various levels of skills in s_N) tangent to $uc^{\cup}(x_N)$.

The following proposition gives some further information about the configuration of budget sets and indifference curves at optimal allocations.

Proposition 4.2 *If an allocation x_N is selected by Envious Intensity, then $\forall i \in N$, $\exists j \in N$,*

$$u_j(B(s_i, t_i)) = u_j(B^{\cup}(x_N)),$$

i.e., every budget is a best budget for some j. This implies that this allocation rule satisfies Equal Transfer for Equal Skills *and* Equal Well-Being for Uniform Utility.

Dually, if an allocation x_N is selected by Envied Intensity, then $\forall i \in N$, $\exists j \in N$,

$$ex(s_j, uc_i(x_i)) = ex(s_j, uc^{\cup}(x_N)),$$

i.e., every indifference curve is a worst indifference curve for some s_j (in the sense that it can be obtained with a budget not greater than for other curves). This implies that this allocation rule satisfies Equal Well-Being for Equal Utility *and* Equal Transfer for Uniform Skills *(i.e., Laissez-Faire for Uniform Skills).*

Proof. Consider a Pareto-efficient allocation x_N such that for some $i_0 \in N$ and for all $j \in N$,

$$u_j(B(s_{i_0}, t_{i_0})) < u_j(B^{\cup}(x_N)).$$

This means in particular that for all $i \in N$,

$$u_i(B^{\cup}(x_N)) = u_i(\bigcup_{j \neq i_0} B(s_j, t_j)).$$

Construct a new Pareto-efficient allocation x'_N by deducting $\varepsilon > 0$ from t_j for all $j \neq i_0$ and adding $(n-1)\varepsilon$ to t_{i_0}. If ε is small enough, one still has: for all $j \in N$,

$$u_j(B(s_{i_0}, t'_{i_0})) < u_j(B^{\cup}(x'_N)).$$

As a consequence, for all $i \in N$,

$$u_i(B^{\cup}(x'_N)) = u_i(\bigcup_{j \neq i_0} B(s_j, t'_j)),$$

and since by construction,

$$u_i(\bigcup_{j \neq i_0} B(s_j, t'_j)) < u_i(\bigcup_{j \neq i_0} B(s_j, t_j)),$$

one then has
$$u_i(B^{\cup}(x'_N)) < u_i(B^{\cup}(x_N)).$$

As a consequence, for all $i \in N$,
$$ex(s_i, uc_i(B^{\cup}(x'_N))) < ex(s_i, uc_i(B^{\cup}(x_N))),$$

so that x'_N is better than x_N for Envious Intensity. The allocation x_N could not be optimal for Envious Intensity.

It is straightforward that this implies *Equal Transfer for Equal Skills* and *Equal Well-Being for Uniform Utility*.

The proof for Envied Intensity is dually similar and is omitted. ∎

This proposition is illustrated in Fig. 4.7. In this figure every budget set touches the union of the upper contour sets, and every indifference curve touches the union of the budget sets. But such a graphical configuration corresponds to different realities with the two criteria. With Envious Intensity, the budget sets are the real budget sets of the agents, and the indifference curves are not the agents' actual curves (the indifference curve tangent to a budget line may be that of an agent with another skill level), but just the result of maximizing utility over the union of the budget sets, so that some of them are typically higher than the real curves at this allocation. These indifference curves only serve to check that no budget set is really too bad, and this is reminiscent of Conditional Equality, in which only one indifference curve is used for this purpose. Envious Intensity can be viewed as a variant of Conditional Equality in which all the agents' preferences are simultaneously used in order to compare the budget sets.

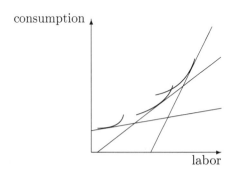

Figure 4.7: Envy Intensity criteria: typical configuration

With Envied Intensity, the figure must be read differently. The indifference curves are the actual curves at the allocation, and the budget lines are used only in order to check that no indifference curve is too high over the others. Again, this is similar to Egalitarian-Equivalence, with the twist that all the agents' skill levels are used simultaneously in order to produce a configuration in which all indifference curves are tangent to the same set.

Let it be clear that this graphical configuration does not characterize these solutions fully, it is only a necessary feature and the precise subset of optimal allocations is then selected by maximizing a particular quantity.

This description is rather appealing, but these solutions have a drawback described in the following proposition.

Proposition 4.3 *Neither allocation rule satisfies* Participation.[6]

Proof. Envious Intensity: Consider the two-agent economy with $s_N = (1, 3)$ and $u_N = (u_1, u_2)$ with $u_2(c, \ell) = c - 4\ell$ and u_1 such that

$$u_1(1, 0) = u_1(3, 1), \quad u_1(.7, 0) = u_1(2.75, 1),$$

and the marginal rate of substitution between c and ℓ is always greater than 1.

The only feasible allocation satisfying *Participation* is the null allocation $(x_1 = x_2 = 0)$. At this allocation one computes

$$\sum_{i \in N} ex(s_i, uc_i(B^{\cup}(x_N))) = 1.$$

Another efficient allocation is $x_1' = (1/4, 0)$, $x_2' = (0, 1/12)$. At this allocation one has

$$\sum_{i \in N} ex(s_i, uc_i(B^{\cup}(x_N'))) = .95 < 1.$$

This proves that the only allocation satisfying *Participation* is not optimal.

Envied Intensity: Consider the same economy as above, with the additional data about u_1 that

$$u_1(0, 0) = u_1(1.75, 1), \quad u_1(.25, 0) = u_1(2.25, 1),$$

and the marginal rate of substitution between c and ℓ is always greater than 1.

At the null allocation one computes

$$\sum_{i \in N} ex(s_i, uc^{\cup}(x_N)) = -1.25.$$

At the allocation $x_1' = (1/4, 0)$, $x_2' = (0, 1/12)$ one has

$$\sum_{i \in N} ex(s_i, uc^{\cup}(x_N)) = -1 > -1.25,$$

showing again that the only allocation satisfying *Participation* is not optimal. ∎

It was noted in Section 3.2 that Envied Intensity is related to a general social ordering function. This is also the case here, and let us simply make the

---

[6] The same result holds for the Diversity and Compensation Diversity criteria, which can easily be adapted to this model.

following observation. Take two arbitrary (not necessarily efficient) allocations $x_N, x'_N \in F(e)$ such that for all $i \in N$, $u_i(x_i) > u_i(x'_i)$. The lower frontier of $uc^\cup(x_N)$ is then everywhere above that of $uc^\cup(x'_N)$, so that

$$\sum_{i \in N} ex(s_i, uc^\cup(x_N)) > \sum_{i \in N} ex(s_i, uc^\cup(x'_N)).$$

As a consequence, if Envied Intensity is used in order to rank all allocations, one obtains a general criterion which satisfies the Weak Pareto principle, i.e., an allocation that is better for all agents is deemed better. The other envy criteria do not have this property and can only be used in order to rank efficient allocations, although it is possible to adapt them in order to rank second-best efficient allocations (when there are incentive constraints as in the next chapter).

4.8   *Characterizations

The results of Chapter 2 can be adapted in order to characterize the Conditional Equality and Egalitarian-Equivalence allocation rules, by relying on the identification of the current model with a special case of the distribution case of the previous model (this identification was explained at the end of Section 4.2). But there are additional results which make use of the special features of the current model, and these will be the topic of this section.

Let us first recall the definitions of the solutions discussed here.

Conditional Equality (S_{CE}): Let $\tilde{u}$ be the reference. $\forall e \in \mathcal{D}, \forall x_N \in S_{CE}(e)$, $\forall i, j \in N$,

$$\tilde{u}\left(B(s_i, t_i)\right) = \tilde{u}\left(B(s_j, t_j)\right).$$

Zero Egalitarian-Equivalence (S_{ZEE}): $\forall e \in \mathcal{D}, \forall x_N \in S_{ZEE}(e), \exists t \in \mathbb{R}$, $\forall i \in N$,

$$u_i(x_i) = u_i(B(0, t)).$$

Wage Egalitarian-Equivalence (S_{WEE}): $\forall e \in \mathcal{D}, \forall x_N \in S_{WEE}(e), \exists s \in \mathbb{R}_+, \forall i \in N$,

$$u_i(x_i) = u_i(B(s, 0)).$$

Min Egalitarian-Equivalence (S_{MEE}): $\forall e \in \mathcal{D}, \forall x_N \in S_{MEE}(e), \exists t \in \mathbb{R}$, $\forall i \in N$,

$$u_i(x_i) = u_i(B(\min_j s_j, t)).$$

Let us start with a result about Conditional Equality (due to Fleurbaey and Maniquet 1996) that does not involve a consistency condition. It uses an axiom of *Pareto Indifference* saying that if an allocation is selected, then all other feasible allocations which give the same level of well-being to each agent is also selected.

Pareto Indifference: $\forall e \in \mathcal{D}$, $\forall x_N \in S(e)$, $\forall x'_N \in F(e)$,

$$[\forall i \in N, \ u_i(x_i) = u_i(x'_i)] \Rightarrow x'_N \in S(e).$$

This result also refers to essentially single-valued allocation rules, namely, rules such that all selected allocations, for a given economy, give the same level of well-being to each agent: $\forall e \in \mathcal{D}$, $\forall x_N, x'_N \in S(e)$, $\forall i \in N$, $u_i(x_i) = u_i(x'_i)$.

Proposition 4.4 *On $\mathcal{D}$, the family of S_{CE} with a fixed reference coincides with the family of essentially single-valued rules satisfying* Pareto Efficiency, *Pareto* Indifference, *Equal Well-Being for Reference Utility and Independence of Improved Utility.*

Proof. Let S be an essentially single-valued rule satisfying these axioms, with $\tilde{u}$ as the reference utility for *Equal Well-Being for Reference Utility.* Let $e \in \mathcal{D}$ and $x_N^* \in S_{CE}(e)$.

Let $e' = (s_N, u'_N) \in \mathcal{D}$ be defined by: for all $i \in N$, $u'_i(c, \ell) = c - s_i \ell$. Take $x'_N \in S(e')$. Suppose that $x'_N \notin S_{CE}(e')$. Let $\tilde{e} = (s_N, (\tilde{u}, ..., \tilde{u}))$. Let $x''_N \in F(\tilde{e})$ be chosen so that for all $i \in N$,

$$\tilde{u}(x''_i) = \tilde{u}\left(B(s_i, c'_i - s_i \ell'_i)\right).$$

Necessarily, for all $i \in N$, $c''_i - s_i \ell''_i = c'_i - s_i \ell'_i$ so that $u'_i(x''_i) = u'_i(x'_i)$. By *Pareto Indifference,* $x''_N \in S(e')$. By *Independence of Improved Utility,* $x''_N \in S(\tilde{e})$. By construction, $x''_N \notin S_{CE}(\tilde{e})$, which contradicts *Equal Well-Being for Reference Utility.* This implies that $x'_N \in S_{CE}(e')$.

Given the profile of preferences in e', one has $S_{CE}(e) \subseteq S_{CE}(e')$, so that $x_N^* \in S_{CE}(e')$. Since $x'_N \in S_{CE}(e')$ and S_{CE} is essentially single-valued, this implies that for all $i \in N$, $u'_i(x_i^*) = u'_i(x'_i)$. By *Pareto Indifference,* $x_N^* \in S(e')$. By *Independence of Improved Utility,* $x_N^* \in S(e)$.

This shows that $S_{CE}(e) \subseteq S(e)$. By essential single-valuedness of S, one must actually have $S_{CE}(e) = S(e)$. ∎

Let us now turn to Zero Egalitarian-Equivalence (denoted S_{ZEE}), which has been defended above in particular by reference to *Skill Solidarity* and to the condition that non-working agents should have the same consumption (which is equivalent to saying that there should be no envy among them):

Equality among Idle: $\forall e \in \mathcal{D}$, $\forall x_N \in S(e)$, $\forall i, j \in N$,

$$\ell_i = \ell_j = 0 \Rightarrow c_i = c_j.$$

This axiom is clearly of liberal reward inspiration, and (for allocation rules satisfying *Pareto Indifference*) it implies *Equal Treatment for Reference Skill,* with a reference skill equal to zero.

The following proposition, due to Fleurbaey and Maniquet (1999), shows that these two properties (*Skill Solidarity, Equality among Idle*) essentially characterize this solution. An additional argument based on *Equal Well-Being for*

Equal Utility instead of *Skill Solidarity* is also provided in favor of the same solution. It is somewhat similar to Proposition 2.7 (with the complication here that we only consider self-sustained economies, with no exogenous endowment, so that the consistency condition is less restrictive).

Proposition 4.5 *On the subset of $\mathcal{D}$ of economies with at least three agents, S_{ZEE} is the only rule satisfying* Pareto Efficiency, Pareto Indifference, Skill Solidarity *and* Equality among Idle. *On $\mathcal{D}$, S_{ZEE} is the only essentially single-valued rule satisfying* Pareto Efficiency, Pareto Indifference, Equal Well-Being for Equal Utility, Equality among Idle *and the consistency condition that for all $x_N \in S(e)$, all $G \subseteq N$, if $\sum_{i \in G} c_i - s_i \ell_i = 0$ then $x_G \in S((s_G, u_G))$.*

Proof. First part. Let $e = (s_N, u_N)$ with $n \geq 3$, and $x_N^* \in S(e)$. Pick any agent i_0, and find a skill level s such that, in the economy e_0 where $s_{i_0}^0 = s$ and $s_i^0 = 0$ for all $i \neq i_0$, there is a Pareto-efficient allocation x_N^0 such that, for all $i \in N$, $u_i(x_i^0) = u_i(x_i^*)$. By *Skill Solidarity*, for every $x_N^{*0} \in S(e_0)$, for all $i \in N$, $u_i(x_i^{*0}) = u_i(x_i^*)$. By *Pareto Indifference*, $x_N^0 \in S(e_0)$.

In e_0, $s_i^0 = 0$ for all $i \neq i_0$, so there is a Pareto-efficient allocation $x_N'^0$ such that, for all $i \in N$, $u_i(x_i'^0) = u_i(x_i^0)$ and for all $i \neq i_0$, $\ell_i'^0 = 0$. By *Pareto Indifference*, $x_N'^0 \in S(e_0)$. By *Equality among Idle*, for all $i, j \neq i_0$, $c_i'^0 = c_j'^0$.

Since for all $i \in N$, $u_i(x_i) = u_i(x_i'^0)$, this means that there is t^0 such that for all $i \neq i_0$, $u_i(x_i) = u_i(B(0, t^0))$.

Now, i_0 was taken arbitrarily, and $n \geq 3$. By picking another i_1, one would find that $u_{i_0}(x_{i_0}) = u_{i_0}(B(0, t^0))$, too.

Second part. Let $e = (s_N, u_N)$ and $x_N^* \in S_{ZEE}(e)$ such that $u_i(x_i^*) = u_i(B(0, t^*))$ for all $i \in N$. Let $e' = (s_{N \cup M}, u_{N \cup M})$ be such that $|M| = n + 1$, $s_M = (0, ..., 0, s_0)$ and $u_M = (u_N, u_1)$, with s_0 chosen so that for any $x_{N \cup M}' \in S_{ZEE}(e')$, $u_i(x_i') = u_i(B(0, t^*))$ for all $i \in N \cup M$.

Let $x_{N \cup M}'^* \in S(e')$. By *Pareto Indifference* and *Pareto-Efficiency*, one can assume that $\ell_i'^* = 0$ for all i such that $s_i = 0$. By *Equality among Idle*, $c_i'^*$ is equal among all such agents to some t. But every $i \in N \cup M$ with $s_i > 0$ has a counterpart j with $u_j = u_i$ and $s_j = 0$. Therefore, by *Equal Well-Being for Equal Utility*, this implies that for all $i \in N \cup M$, $u_i(x_i'^*) = u_i(B(0, t))$. By *Pareto Efficiency*, necessarily $t = t^*$. By *Pareto Indifference*, $(x_N^*, x_M'^*) \in S(e')$. (Note that if for all $i \in N \cup M$, $u_i(x_i'^*) = u_i(B(0, t^*))$, necessarily there is no transfer between N and M in $x_{N \cup M}'^*$, so that $(x_N^*, x_M'^*) \in F(s_{N \cup M})$.) By consistency, $x_N^* \in S(e)$. This shows that $S_{ZEE}(e) \subseteq S(e)$. By essential single-valuedness, $S_{ZEE}(e) = S(e)$. ∎

We also obtain a characterization of the Wage Egalitarian-Equivalence rule (denoted S_{WEE}) with a similar argument when *Equality among Idle* is replaced by *Equal Transfer for Uniform Skills* (i.e., *Laissez-Faire for Uniform Skills*).

One part of the result below has a proof that works only for "discrete" economies. Let $\mathcal{D}^d$ denote the domain of discrete economies, i.e., such that utilities are defined only over discrete quantities of consumption (e.g., cents) and labor (e.g., seconds), and skills are measured in rational numbers (e.g., cents per second). We also need to introduce the standard replication invariance axiom. For any $e = (s_N, u_N)$ and any positive integer k, let

$$ke \;=\; (\underbrace{(s_N, ..., s_N)}_{k}, \underbrace{(u_N, ..., u_N)}_{k}),$$

$$kx_N \;=\; \underbrace{(x_N, ..., x_N)}_{k}.$$

Replication Invariance: $\forall e \in \mathcal{D}, \forall x_N \in S(e), \forall k \in \mathbb{N} \setminus \{0\}, kx_N \in S(ke)$.

Proposition 4.6 *On* $\mathcal{D}$, S_{WEE} *is the only rule satisfying* Pareto Efficiency, Pareto Indifference, Skill Solidarity *and* Equal Transfer for Uniform Skills. *On* $\mathcal{D}^d$, S_{WEE} *is the only essentially single-valued rule satisfying* Pareto Efficiency, Pareto Indifference, Equal Well-Being for Equal Utility, Equal Transfer for Uniform Skills, Replication Invariance *and the same consistency condition as in Proposition 4.5.*

Proof. First part. For every economy $e = (s_N, u_N)$, there is s such that, in $e' = ((s, ..., s), u_N)$ one can find an allocation $x'_N \in S_{WEE}(e')$ that is Pareto-indifferent to some allocation x^*_N that is efficient in e. In e', *Equal Transfer for Uniform Skills* requires $c'^*_i - s\ell'^*_i = 0$ for all $i \in N$, all $x'^*_N \in S(e')$. This implies $S(e') \subseteq S_{WEE}(e')$. By *Pareto Indifference*, $S(e') = S_{WEE}(e')$ and therefore $x'_N \in S(e')$. By *Skill Solidarity* and the fact that the utility levels $(u_i(x'_i))_{i \in N}$ are on the Pareto frontier in e, any $x_N \in S(e)$ is Pareto-indifferent to x'_N. This implies that $S(e) \subseteq S_{WEE}(e)$ and by *Pareto Indifference* again, $S(e) = S_{WEE}(e)$.

Second part. Let $e = (s_N, u_N)$ and $x^*_N \in S_{WEE}(e)$ such that $u_i(x^*_i) = u_i(B(s^*, 0))$ for all $i \in N$. Let $e' = (s_{N \cup M}, u_{N \cup M})$ be such that $|M| = n$, $s_M = (s^*, ..., s^*)$ and $u_M = u_N$. Let $x'^*_{N \cup M} \in S(e')$. By *Equal Well-Being for Equal Utility*, for all $i \in N$, $u_i(x'^*_i) = u_{i+n}(x'^*_{i+n})$.

Assume that $\sum_{i \in N} c'^*_i - s_i \ell'^*_i = 0$. Then $\sum_{i \in M} c'^*_i - s_i \ell'^*_i = 0$ and by consistency, $x'^*_M \in S(s_M, u_M)$. By *Equal Transfer for Uniform Skills*, one actually has $c'^*_i - s_i \ell'^*_i = 0$ for all $i \in M$. This implies that $x'^*_{N \cup M} \in S_{WEE}(e')$. By consistency, $x'^*_N \in S(e)$, and $x'^*_N \in S_{WEE}(e)$. By *Pareto Indifference*, $x^*_N \in S(e)$. This shows that $S_{WEE}(e) \subseteq S(e)$. By essential single-valuedness, $S_{WEE}(e) = S(e)$.

Now we prove that it is in fact impossible to have $\sum_{i \in N} c'^*_i - s_i \ell'^*_i \neq 0$. Suppose that it is the case. Since for all $i \in N$, $u_i(x'^*_i) = u_{i+n}(x'^*_{i+n})$, it is impossible to have $u_i(x'^*_i) \geq u_i(x^*_i)$ for all $i \in N$, or $u_i(x'^*_i) \leq u_i(x^*_i)$ for all $i \in N$. Note that for $i \in M$, $u_i(x'^*_i) \geq u_i(x^*_{i-n})$ if and only if $c'^*_i - s^* \ell'^*_i \geq 0$. Therefore there are $i, j \in M$, $c'^*_i - s^* \ell'^*_i < 0 < c'^*_j - s^* \ell'^*_j$. Since these are rational numbers, there are positive integers p, q such that

$$p\left(c'^*_i - s^* \ell'^*_i\right) + q\left(c'^*_j - s^* \ell'^*_j\right) = 0.$$

Let $k = \max\{p, q\}$ and consider ke'. By *Replication Invariance*, $kx'^*_{N \cup M} \in S(ke')$. By consistency,

$$(\underbrace{x'^*_i, ..., x'^*_i}_{p}, \underbrace{x'^*_j, ..., x'^*_j}_{q}) \in S((\underbrace{s^*, ..., s^*}_{p+q}), (\underbrace{u_i, ..., u_i}_{p}, \underbrace{u_j, ..., u_j}_{q})).$$

But this violates *Equal Transfer for Uniform Skills.* ∎

Zero Egalitarian-Equivalence and Wage Egalitarian-Equivalence are each singled out by *Equality among Idle* and *Laissez-Faire for Uniform Skills*, respectively. We have seen that these two properties are combined in Min Egalitarian-Equivalence (denoted S_{MEE}), which, necessarily, does not satisfy either *Skill Solidarity* or consistency. There are many other solutions which have the same profile, but on an interesting subset of economies, Min Egalitarian-Equivalence appears indeed as the natural solution in this perspective.

Let $\mathcal{D}^*$ be the subset of economies $e = (s_N, u_N)$ with a sufficient diversity of preferences and of preference-skill combinations so that:
(i) all combinations of skills and utility functions are observed: $\forall j, k \in N$, $\exists i \in N$, $(s_i, u_i) = (s_j, u_k)$;
(ii) there exist $j, k \in N$ such that: u_j and u_k satisfy the single-crossing property (every pair of indifference curves has at most one point of intersection); when offered a budget $B(s, t)$ with $t \geq 0$, they refuse to work if $s = \min_{i \in N} s_i$ but want to work if s equals the second smallest value of the components of s_N.

We now introduce a condition that is logically intermediate between *Equal Transfer for Equal Skills* and *Laissez-Faire for Uniform Skills*.

Equal Transfer for Some Skills: $\forall e = (s_N, u_N) \in \mathcal{D}$, $\forall x_N \in S(e)$, $\exists s \in \{s_i \mid i \in N\}$, $\forall i, j \in N$ such that $s_i = s_j = s$,

$$c_i - s_i \ell_i = c_j - s_j \ell_j.$$

The fact that Min Egalitarian-Equivalence satisfies this axiom, whereas Wage Egalitarian-Equivalence only satisfies the weaker *Laissez-Faire for Uniform Skills*, suggests that the former solution is more liberal than the latter. This will indeed be corroborated by the analysis of taxation made in the next chapter.

Proposition 4.7 *On $\mathcal{D}^*$, S_{MEE} is the only rule satisfying* Pareto Efficiency, Equal Well-Being for Equal Utility, Equality among Idle, Equal Transfer for Some Skills *and* Participation.

Proof. Let $x_N^* \in S(e)$, for $e = (s_N, u_N) \in \mathcal{D}^*$. Let s be such that all agents i with $s_i = s$ have the same transfer t^* (by *Equal Transfer for Some Skills*). By *Equal Well-Being for Equal Utility*, all agents with identical utility function have the same utility level. In particular every i has the same utility level as an agent j with $s_j = s$ and $u_j = u_i$. This implies that x_N^* is such that for all $i \in N$, $u_i(x_i^*) = u_i(B(s, t^*))$.

Assume that $s > \min_{i \in N} s_i$. By assumption (ii) and *Participation*, there are $j, k \in N$ who want to work in $B(s, t^*)$ (they are forced to if $t^* < 0$, and it holds by assumption (ii) if $t^* \geq 0$) so that their indifference curves at $u_j(B(s, t^*))$ and $u_k(B(s, t^*))$, which cross once, must have different intercepts. Moreover, these agents would not work for $\min_{i \in N} s_i$. By assumption (i), one can posit $s_j = s_k = \min_{i \in N} s_i$. Therefore by *Pareto Efficiency*, $\ell_j^* = \ell_k^* = 0$, so that c_j^*, c_k^*

correspond to the intercepts of the indifference curves. This implies $c_j^* \neq c_k^*$, which violates *Equality among Idle*. ∎

It may be worth emphasizing that without *Equality among Idle* or without *Participation*, the result would not hold (think of the solution that computes the Egalitarian-Equivalence with the highest reference skill compatible with either of these conditions). Finally, let us recall that *Participation* is satisfied not only by Min Egalitarian-Equivalence but also by the two other Egalitarian-Equivalence solutions studied above.

4.9   Conclusion

It is hoped that this chapter gives a sense of the progress made since the time when fairness analysis was focused on the two extreme and unappealing members of the family of Conditional Equality solutions. Several reasonable solutions have been presented here and, although none of them is ideal in the sense of satisfying all the appealing properties, each of them can be defended on serious grounds. In fact, only a sample of principles and solutions have been introduced here, and the literature offers other interesting ideas on this problem.[7]

If one wants to give priority to the compensation principle while retaining a concern for neutrality in rewards, the three Egalitarian-Equivalence solutions presented in this chapter and characterized in the last section appear as the most compelling solutions. And choosing between them is made easier by the comparison of their properties. If one wants a strong degree of compensation and is concerned about any differential treatment of the non-working on the basis of their preferences, Zero Egalitarian-Equivalence is the solution. If one feels compelled by *Laissez-Faire for Uniform Skills*, go for one of the other two, with a stronger degree of neutrality (especially toward the unskilled and the non-working) with Min Egalitarian-Equivalence and a stronger degree of compensation with Wage Egalitarian-Equivalence.

Additional pragmatic considerations may play a role. If one is wary about holding all people fully responsible for their preferences, and especially if one is afraid of being harsh against those who have high aversion to work, because, for instance, some of them may be housewives burdened with housework, or members of an alienated minority, then Zero Egalitarian-Equivalence is the best option because it is the most favorable to those people. Such issues obviously call for enriching the framework of analysis with additional features of real life, and some of these will be introduced in the next chapter.

---

[7]See in particular Fleurbaey and Maniquet (1996, 1999), Gaspart (1996, 1998), Kranich (1994), Luttens and Ooghe (2007), Maniquet (1998), Moulin and Roemer (1989).

Chapter 5

Income redistribution

5.1 Introduction

The previous chapter has focused on the situation in which fully efficient and fair allocations can be achieved by appropriate lump-sum transfers between individuals. This first-best context is worth studying in order to understand the fairness concepts well, and it serves as a benchmark in the analysis of more realistic situations. Here we turn to the "second-best" context in which redistribution is constrained by the fact that only (gross and net) income is observable, so that public authorities cannot distinguish between people working hard with low skill and people working little with a high wage rate. As one would like to redistribute from high-skilled individuals to low-skilled individuals, more or less independently of their preferences over leisure, failing to distinguish between them is a direct obstacle to achieving fairness.

In Chapter 3 we have already studied a similar situation, called the "observable well-being" case. The results of Chapter 3 could be imported here if we took disposable income as our measure of well-being. But this is not what we will do here, since we will consider, as in the previous chapter, that utility is the proper measure of well-being (for which individuals are partly responsible). A specific analysis is therefore necessary, and moreover we can take advantage of the specific features of the particular context of income taxation in order to reach more precise and more concrete conclusions.

In public economics, the study of income taxation for populations which are heterogeneous in preferences and in skills is traditionally considered difficult because it usually involves unspecified social objectives in the form of weighted utilitarian social welfare functions, and, in addition, the set of incentive-compatible allocations is hard to delineate. Our analysis removes the first difficulty by proposing precise social orderings.[1] Moreover, in this chapter we will bypass

---

[1] Stiglitz (1987) criticized the standard utilitarian approach in optimal taxation theory for making problematic interpersonal comparisons and for failing to adequately reflect the "widespread agreement that there ought to be redistribution from the more able to the less able" (p. 1019). The social orderings proposed in this book can be viewed as addressing this

the second difficulty by focusing on the comparison of arbitrary tax policies, an exercise which, contrary to the computation of the optimal tax, does not require knowing the limits of the feasible set. For lack of space, features of the optimal tax will not be discussed in detail, but some results can be found in Fleurbaey and Maniquet (2006, 2007).

The first sections of this chapter deal with the same simple context as in the previous chapter, namely, a wage economy in which earnings are the only source of income and individuals simply have preferences over consumption and leisure. The last three sections introduce additional complications which go in the direction of realistic application. Section 5.6 introduces capital income, which, depending on whether it comes from savings or inheritance may lead to various policy conclusions. Section 5.7 introduces individual preferences over various types of jobs, in addition to consumption and leisure. Section 5.8 introduces education, with the possibility for individuals to be partly responsible for their skills.

5.2   From allocation rules to social orderings

In order to be able to compare arbitrary allocations, one needs a criterion which ranks all allocations. In this section we examine how to adapt the concepts of the previous chapter in order to define full-fledged orderings.

Recall how Conditional Equality was defined in terms of making lump-sum transfers so that every individual's budget is deemed equivalent for reference preferences. Now, consider an arbitrary allocation obtained in an arbitrary way. It is still possible, considering a particular individual, to ask what lump-sum transfer would have given her the same satisfaction as in this allocation. This hypothetical lump-sum transfer associated with this individual's wage rate defines a hypothetical budget which can be evaluated with the reference preferences. In an optimal Conditional Equality allocation obtained with lump-sum transfers, all these individual hypothetical budget sets correspond to real budget sets, and they are all equivalent for the reference preferences. In an arbitrary allocation, they are generally not equivalent and therefore the aim is to identify the worst hypothetical budget. The comparison of two arbitrary allocations can then be made by asking the reference preferences to rank the two worst hypothetical budgets.[2] Let us christen this criterion in a definition.

Conditional Equality: Choose reference preferences and give priority (according to the leximin criterion) to individuals whose hypothetical budget (i.e., a budget with lump-sum transfer which would give them their current satisfaction) is the worst for the reference preferences.

When it is possible to achieve fully efficient allocations, the best allocation for this criterion is the Conditional Equality allocation defined in Section 4.5. This

criticism.

[2]A budget is better than another for given preferences if such preferences can be better satisfied when choice is made from this budget than from the other budget.

social ordering is therefore really an extension of the allocation rule defined in the previous chapter. Observe also that this criterion respects individual preferences over personal bundles for all arbitrary allocations. Indeed, a better bundle for an individual corresponds to a bigger hypothetical budget, and reference preferences always prefer bigger budgets as well.

The Egalitarian-Equivalence concepts are easily transformed into social orderings. It suffices to apply the leximin criterion to the quantity that is equalized in the optimal allocation.

Zero Egalitarian-Equivalence: For each individual, compute the counterfactual lump-sum transfer which, combined with a null wage rate, would make her as happy as in the current situation, and give priority (according to the leximin criterion) to individuals who are the worst-off in these terms.

Min Egalitarian-Equivalence: For each individual, compute the counterfactual lump-sum transfer that would make her as happy as in the current situation if her skills were the lowest of the current profile of the population, and give priority (according to the leximin criterion) to individuals who are the worst-off in these terms.

Wage Egalitarian-Equivalence: For each individual, compute the counterfactual wage rate (with no transfer) that would make her as happy as in the current situation, and give priority (according to the leximin criterion) to individuals who are the worst-off in these terms.

These three criteria respect individual preferences because the quantity that serves to measure individual situations is increasing with individual satisfaction.

Equipped with these criteria, we can rank arbitrary allocations.[3] In particular, it is possible to rank allocations which are obtained by an income tax which taxes and subsidizes individuals as a function of their earnings. From this ranking of allocations one then derives a ranking of tax policies, which allows one to evaluate tax reforms and to seek the optimal tax among those which are feasible.

Let us briefly illustrate how these criteria work. Consider Ann, whose wage rate is ten dollars per hour. She pays a twenty percent tax (at a flat rate) on all earnings, so that her net wage rate is eight dollars, but she also receives a

---

[3]Note that Zero and Wage Egalitarian-Equivalence do not rank all allocations, but only those such that every individual is at least as well-off as in the situation of zero consumption, zero work. For an individual who would prefer to be at this zero point than in her current situation, there is indeed no "counterfactual lump-sum transfer which, combined with a null wage rate, would make her as happy as in the current situation," and no "counterfactual wage rate (with no transfer) that would make her as happy as in the current situation," so that the criteria are not well defined for such an individual. This is not, however, a problematic limitation if we want to avoid the "slavery" problem and restrict attention, as we will do here, to tax policies such that those with no earnings are not taxed.

basic income of \$500 per month.[4] Given this budget constraint, she decides to work, say, forty hours a week. Assume that, in this situation, she feels as well off, given her preferences, as if she had:

(1) a basic income of \$260 per month and no tax on earnings – she would then work and consume a little more;

(2) a basic income of \$1,480 per month and no other income – she would then do some charity work and practice music;

(3) a basic income of \$570 and a six dollar hourly wage (assuming this is the market wage rate for unskilled work) – she would then work and consume less;

(4) no basic income and a twelve dollar hourly wage – she would then work even more than in (1).

Point (1) defines her hypothetical budget for Conditional Equality: a lump sum transfer of \$260 per month and a ten dollar hourly wage. Conditional Equality will examine how this hypothetical budget fares for the reference preferences (which may or may not differ from Ann's preferences). Points (2)–(4) give us the relevant figures, which can directly be compared with those of other individuals, for the Egalitarian-Equivalence criteria: \$1,480 per month for Zero Egalitarian-Equivalence, \$570 per month for Min Egalitarian-Equivalence, \$12 per hour for Wage Egalitarian-Equivalence. As we will see in Section 5.4, there fortunately are more convenient ways of comparing tax policies, which save us the work of computing such figures for each and every individual.

5.3   *Social ordering functions

The model is the same as in the previous chapter. Let us briefly provide the formal definitions of the social ordering functions that can be associated with allocation rules introduced there.

Conditional Equality (R_{CE}): Let $\tilde{u}$ be the reference. $\forall e = (s_N, u_N) \in \mathcal{D}, \forall x_N, x'_N \in X^N$, $x_N \, R_{CE}(e) \, x'_N$ if and only if

$$\left(\tilde{u} \left(B \left(s_i, \hat{t}_i \right) \right) \right)_{i \in N} \geq_{\text{lex}} \left(\tilde{u} \left(B \left(s_i, \hat{t}'_i \right) \right) \right)_{i \in N},$$

where $\hat{t}_i$ is defined by $u_i(x_i) = u_i(B(s_i, \hat{t}_i)).$[5]

Zero Egalitarian-Equivalence (R_{ZEE}): $\forall e = (s_N, u_N) \in \mathcal{D}, \forall x_N, x'_N \in X^N$ such that $\forall i \in N, u_i(x_i) \geq u_i(0,0), x_N \, R_{ZEE}(e) \, x'_N$ if and only if

$$\left(\hat{t}_i \right)_{i \in N} \geq_{\text{lex}} \left(\hat{t}'_i \right)_{i \in N},$$

where $\hat{t}_i$ is defined by $u_i(x_i) = u_i(B(0, \hat{t}_i)).$

---

[4]Equivalently, we could say that she does not get a basic income but her net annual tax equals twenty percent of her earnings minus \$6,000 (this yields a negative tax for low earnings). This would give her the same budget constraint.

[5]Equivalently, $\hat{t}_i = ex(s_i, uc_i(x_i))$. Simpler formulations are adopted in the text whenever possible. Recall that $B(s, t) = \{ (c, \ell) \in X \mid c \leq s\ell + t \}.$

Min Egalitarian-Equivalence (R_{MEE}): $\forall e = (s_N, u_N) \in \mathcal{D}, \forall x_N, x'_N \in X^N$, $x_N R_{MEE}(e) x'_N$ if and only if

$$\left(\hat{t}_i\right)_{i \in N} \geq_{\text{lex}} \left(\hat{t}_i\right)_{i \in N},$$

where $\hat{t}_i$ is defined by $u_i(x_i) = u_i(B(\min_{j \in N} s_j, \hat{t}_i))$.

Wage Egalitarian-Equivalence (R_{WEE}): $\forall e = (s_N, u_N) \in \mathcal{D}, \forall x_N, x'_N \in X^N$ such that $\forall i \in N$, $u_i(x_i) \geq u_i(0,0)$, $x_N R_{WEE}(e) x'_N$ if and only if

$$\left(\hat{s}_i\right)_{i \in N} \geq_{\text{lex}} \left(\hat{s}'_i\right)_{i \in N},$$

where $\hat{s}_i$ is defined by $u_i(x_i) = u_i(B(\hat{s}_i, 0))$.

Let us also provide the formal definition of Envied Intensity.

Envied Intensity (R_{EdI}): $\forall e = (s_N, u_N) \in \mathcal{D}, \forall x_N, x'_N \in X^N$, $x_N R_{EdI}(e) x'_N$ if and only if

$$\sum_{i \in N} ex(s_i, uc^\cup(x_N)) \geq \sum_{i \in N} ex(s_i, uc^\cup(x_N)).$$

The axiomatic characterizations of Sections 2.7 and 3.3 can be adapted rather easily in order to characterize Conditional Equality and Zero Egalitarian-Equivalence. Indeed, it suffices to note that any arbitrary allocation is Pareto-indifferent to an allocation obtained with lump-sum transfers (the sum of which may differ from zero). It is therefore sufficient to know how to rank such allocations in order to be able, by Pareto Indifference, to rank all allocations. Now, we have already noted in Section 4.2 that, when one restricts attention to allocations obtained with lump-sum transfers, this model is a special case of the distribution case of the model studied in the first three chapters. Let $LS(e)$ be the subset of X^N of allocations obtained with lump-sum transfers: $x_N \in LS(e)$ if and only if for all $i \in N$, there is $t_i \in \mathbb{R}$ such that

$$x_i \in \arg \max_{x \in B(s_i, t_i)} u_i(x).$$

Conditional Equality can then be characterized as the only social ordering function satisfying the following axioms:

Strong Pareto: $\forall e \in \mathcal{D}, \forall x_N, x'_N \in X^N$, if $(u_i(x_i))_{i \in N} \geq (u_i(x'_i))_{i \in N}$, then $x_N R(e) x'_N$; if $(u_i(x_i))_{i \in N} > (u_i(x'_i))_{i \in N}$, then $x_N P(e) x'_N$.

Equal Well-Being for Reference Utility: $\forall e = (s_N, u_N) \in \mathcal{D}$ such that $\forall i \in N$, $u_i = \tilde{u}$, $\forall x_N, x'_N \in X^N, \forall i, j \in N$ such that $\forall k \neq i, j$, $x'_k = x_k$,

$$\left[u_i(x'_i) > u_i(x_i) > u_j(x_j) > u_j(x'_j)\right] \implies x_N R(e) x'_N,$$
$$\left[u_i(x'_i) = u_j(x_j) \text{ and } u_j(x'_j) = u_i(x_i)\right] \implies x_N I(e) x'_N.$$

Equal Transfer for Uniform Skills: $\forall e = (s_N, u_N) \in \mathcal{D}$ such that $\forall i, j \in N$, $s_i = s_j$, $\forall x_N, x'_N \in LS(e)$ with corresponding t_N, t'_N, $\forall i, j \in N$ such that $\forall\, k \neq i, j$, $x'_k = x_k$,

$$\begin{aligned}
\left[t'_i > t_i > t_j > t'_j \right] &\Rightarrow x_N\, R(e)\, x'_N, \\
\left[t'_i = t_j \text{ and } t'_j = t_i \right] &\Rightarrow x_N\, I(e)\, x'_N.
\end{aligned}$$

Separability: $\forall e = (s_N, u_N) \in \mathcal{D}$, $\forall x_N, x'_N \in X^N$, $\forall G \subseteq N$, $G \neq \varnothing$, if $\forall i \in N \setminus G$, $x_i = x'_i$, then

$$x_N\, R(s_N, u_N)\, x'_N \Leftrightarrow x_G\, R(s_G, u_G)\, x'_G.$$

Similarly, Zero Egalitarian-Equivalence is characterized as the only social ordering function satisfying *Strong Pareto, Equal Well-Being for Uniform Utility, Equal Transfer for Reference Skill* (with $\tilde{s} = 0$) and *Separability*.[6] (The two middle axioms in this list are obvious variants of those defined above.) Recall from Section 4.8 that Zero Egalitarian-Equivalence, as an allocation rule, was characterized with a condition of *Equality among Idle*. Similarly here, *Equal Transfer for Reference Skill* can be replaced in the above list by a condition of equal transfer among agents who do not work at efficient allocations, i.e., agents such that $u_i(B(s_i, t_i)) = u_i(t_i, 0)$ for all $t_i \geq 0$.

Fleurbaey and Maniquet (2006) show that Wage Egalitarian-Equivalence is almost characterized by a similar list of axioms, in which *Equal Transfer for Reference Skill* is replaced by *Laissez-Faire for Uniform Skills*, which can be adapted to bear on social ordering functions instead of allocation rules.

Laissez-Faire for Uniform Skills: $\forall e = (s_N, u_N) \in \mathcal{D}$ such that $\forall i, j \in N$, $s_i = s_j$, $\forall x_N, x'_N \in F(e)$, if $\forall i \in N$, $x_i \in \arg\max_{x \in B(s_i, 0)} u_i(x)$, then $x_N\, R(e)\, x'_N$.

Proposition 5.1 *If the social ordering function R satisfies* Weak Pareto, Equal Well-Being for Uniform Utility, Laissez-Faire for Uniform Skills *and* Separability, *then for all $e = (s_N, u_N)$, all $x_N, x'_N \in X^N$, if*

$$\min_{i \in N} \hat{s}_i > \min_{i \in N} \hat{s}'_i,$$

where $\hat{s}_i$ is defined by $u_i(x_i) = u_i(B(\hat{s}_i, 0))$, then $x_N\, P(e)\, x'_N$.

Proof. (1) This is similar to the first part of the proof of Proposition 3.1, but with some modifications. We show that, for all $x_N, x'_N \in X^N$, all $i, j \in N$, if

$$\hat{s}'_i > \hat{s}_i > \hat{s}_j > \hat{s}'_j$$

while $x'_k = x_k$ for all $k \neq i, j$, then $x_N\, R(e)\, x'_N$.

---

[6]See Fleurbaey and Maniquet (2005) for a more detailed study of this kind of characterization.

Suppose not, i.e., $x'_N P(e) x_N$. Introduce two agents $a, b \notin N$ such that $s_a = s_b \in (\hat{s}_j, \hat{s}_i)$, $u_a = u_i$ and $u_b = u_j$. Let $N_{ab} = N \cup \{a, b\}$ and $e_{ab} = (s_{N_{ab}}, u_{N_{ab}})$. Let $(x_a, x_b), (x'_a, x'_b) \in F(s_{\{a,b\}})$ be such that

$$\hat{s}_i > \hat{s}_a > \hat{s}'_b = \hat{s}'_a = s_a > \hat{s}_b > \hat{s}_j$$

(where $\hat{s}_a$ is defined by $u_a(x_a) = u_a(B(\hat{s}_a, 0))$, and similarly for $\hat{s}_b, \hat{s}'_a, \hat{s}'_b$) and define allocations $x_{N_{ab}} = (x_N, x_a, x_b)$, $x'_{N_{ab}} = (x'_N, x_a, x_b)$. Note that $\hat{s}'_b = \hat{s}'_a = s_a$ and $(x'_a, x'_b) \in F(s_{\{a,b\}})$ implies that (x'_a, x'_b) is a laissez-faire allocation in the two-agent economy formed by a and b.

By *Separability*, $x'_{N_{ab}} R(e_{ab}) x_{N_{ab}}$. By *Equal Well-Being for Uniform Utility* and *Separability*,

$$(x'_{N \backslash \{i\}}, x_i, x_a, x'_b) R(e_{ab}) (x'_N, x'_a, x'_b),$$
$$(x'_{N \backslash \{i,j\}}, x_i, x_j, x_a, x_b) R(e_{ab}) (x'_{N \backslash \{i,j\}}, x_i, x_a, x'_b).$$

By *Laissez-Faire for Uniform Skills* and *Separability*,

$$(x'_{N \backslash \{i,j\}}, x_i, x_j, x'_a, x'_b) R(e_{ab}) (x'_{N \backslash \{i,j\}}, x_i, x_j, x_a, x_b).$$

By transitivity,

$$(x'_{N \backslash \{i,j\}}, x_i, x_j, x'_a, x'_b) R(e_{ab}) (x'_N, x'_a, x'_b).$$

Recall that $x'_{N \backslash \{i,j\}} = x_{N \backslash \{i,j\}}$. By *Separability*, $x_N R(e) x'_N$, a contradiction.

(2) Take any pair of allocations x_N, x'_N such that $\min_{i \in N} \hat{s}_i > \min_{i \in N} \hat{s}'_i$. Then one can find two allocations x^*_N, x'^*_N and an agent i_0 such that for all $j \neq i_0$,

$$\hat{s}'^*_{i_0} < \hat{s}^*_{i_0} < \hat{s}^*_j < \hat{s}'^*_j,$$

while for all $i \in N$, $u_i(x_i) > u_i(x^*_i)$ and $u_i(x'_i) < u_i(x'^*_i)$. By *Weak Pareto*, $x_N P(e) x^*_N$ and $x'^*_N P(e) x'_N$. By a repeated application of step (1) between i_0 and each $j \neq i_0$ (making i_0 climb from $\hat{s}'^*_{i_0}$ to $\hat{s}^*_{i_0}$ in $n-1$ steps), $x^*_N R(e) x'^*_N$. By transitivity, $x_N P(e) x'_N$. ∎

One does not obtain a full characterization of the leximin criterion in Wage Egalitarian-Equivalence because the axioms are too weak to impose social indifference to permutations of $\hat{s}_i$ across agents. It is actually hard to see why one should impose such indifference when the involved agents have different preferences and have skills that do not correspond to $\hat{s}_i$.

Observe that Zero and Wage Egalitarian-Equivalence criteria rank allocations in a way that is totally independent of the population profile of skills, because they evaluate individual situations solely by looking at indifference curves. This independence property is in fact a strong compensation property, which, combined with *Equal Treatment of Equals* (i.e., an Equality axiom like *Equal Well-Being for Equal Utility* but applied only to identical agents), can be shown to imply *Equal Well-Being for Equal Utility*.[7] In contrast, Min

---

[7] Take two agents with identical utility function. If they had the same skill level, they would be fully identical. Any social ordering function which is independent of the skill profile will treat them as identical agents.

Egalitarian-Equivalence and Envied Intensity only satisfy *Equal Well-Being for Equal Utility.*

Envied Intensity satisfies an interesting property that none of the other criteria studied in this section satisfies: If an allocation obtained with lump-sum transfers (i.e., from $LS(e)$) is such that no agent envies another's budget, then it is at least as good as any other allocation in the same feasibility class. Note that such an allocation is necessarily envy-free. No-envy over budget sets is more demanding than no-envy over bundles.[8]

Budget No-Envy: $\forall e = (s_N, u_N) \in \mathcal{D}, \forall x_N, x'_N \in LS(e)$ such that $\sum_{i \in N} t_i = \sum_{i \in N} t'_i$, if $\forall i, j \in N, u_i(x_i) \geq u_i(B(s_j, t_j))$, then $x_N R(e) x'_N$.

Combined with *Weak Pareto* and *Pareto Indifference,*[9] this axiom implies *Laissez-Faire for Uniform Skills.* But, like all no-envy conditions, Budget No-Envy is not just a liberal reward axiom. It also contains a good deal of compensation. In particular, combined with *Weak Pareto* and *Pareto Indifference*, it requires accepting the allocations which are Pareto-efficient and which equalize well-being in economies with uniform u_N. This is the compensation counterpart of *Laissez-Faire for Uniform Skills.*

Envied Intensity is not the only social ordering function satisfying this axiom, but it is interesting to note that it has valuable properties and deserves to be studied further.

5.4   Fair income tax

In this section we examine how to rank income tax policies on the basis of the allocations they generate. A tax policy is a function defining a transfer of income depending on the level of pre-tax income. This transfer can be a tax or a subsidy. The total amount of taxes collected, minus the total amount of subsidies paid, is the net tax receipt of the government, which can serve to fund government expenditures.

For our purposes, it is enough to consider a tax policy as defining a budget set for all agents. This budget set contains the combinations of earnings and disposable income (disposable income is called "consumption" here, for simplicity) among which individuals can choose, and is illustrated in Fig. 5.1. At earnings levels for which the budget curve is above the 45° line, the individual receives a subsidy equal to the vertical distance between the budget curve and the 45° line. When the budget curve is below the 45° line, the individual pays a tax equal to the vertical distance between the 45° line and the budget curve. For an individual with a certain level of skills, there is a maximum amount of money that she can earn (i.e., when working full time), and this defines a bound of the budget set. Obviously, an individual with higher skills has a greater maximum earnings level, and therefore a greater budget set.

---

[8] The idea of no-envy over opportunity sets can be found in Thomson (1994).

[9] For social ordering functions, *Weak Pareto* means $(u_i(x_i))_{i \in N} \gg (u_i(x'_i))_{i \in N} \Rightarrow x_N P(e) x'_N$; *Pareto Indifference* means $(u_i(x_i))_{i \in N} = (u_i(x'_i))_{i \in N} \Rightarrow x_N I(e) x'_N$.

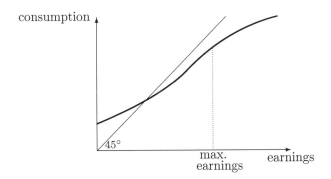

Figure 5.1: Budget set defined by a tax policy

The subsidy paid to individuals with no earnings can either be paid as a means-tested allowance, or as a basic income paid to all and added to the taxes (or deducted from the subsidies) of everyone. At this level of abstraction, there is no difference between a negative income tax and a universal grant. Here we will call it the "minimum income."

We will assume in this section that the population is large enough so that it is a good approximation to consider that, for every skill level earning a positive wage rate, there are individuals spread over the whole budget curve (up to the maximum earnings of individuals from this subpopulation). We will also assume that any given type of preferences over consumption and leisure is observed in all subpopulations of various skill levels. In view of the fact that a lower skill is associated with a smaller budget set, the latter assumption implies that, in a subpopulation with a given type of preferences, the worst-off according to these preferences are always those with the lowest skill level.

This observation is important because it has the following consequence: For any social criterion that satisfies the *compensation* principle and therefore gives priority to the worst-off in any subpopulation with a given type of preferences, *the worst-off of the whole population are among the individuals with the lowest skill.* For such a criterion, it is therefore enough to focus on this subpopulation in order to evaluate a tax policy. For simplicity, let us call this subpopulation the "unskilled."

Among the unskilled group, which is still heterogeneous in terms of preferences, different criteria (such as the various Egalitarian-Equivalence criteria) will identify the worst-off differently. Let us first consider the case in which the unskilled have a null productivity (a null wage rate on the market). All individuals in this category will receive the minimum income, and a tax policy is better for the worst-off among them if and only if it pays a greater minimum income. In this case, therefore, *the compensation principle implies that one should seek to maximize the minimum income.*

Let us now examine the case when the unskilled have a positive wage rate. In this case, depending on the tax and on the precise criterion one uses the worst-off among the unskilled can be either the idle, the hardworking, or those occupying a middle position. The three Egalitarian-Equivalence criteria introduced above provide an illustration of reasonable possibilities.

First, the Zero Egalitarian-Equivalence criterion always advocates *maximizing the minimum income.* By a different route, this concurs with Van Parijs' (1995) idea of setting the basic income at the highest possible level.[10]   The reason why we reach this conclusion with Zero Egalitarian-Equivalence is the following. Every individual who works is at least as well off as with the minimum income and no work, which is a possible point in his budget set. Therefore the counterfactual transfer with zero wage that serves to evaluate his situation is at least as great as the minimum income. By assumption, there are individuals over the whole budget curve, and therefore there are individuals who do not work and get the minimum income. For them, the "counterfactual transfer with zero wage that serves to evaluate their situation" is equal to their actual consumption, i.e., the minimum income. They are therefore deemed the worst-off by Zero Egalitarian-Equivalence. A tax is therefore better if and only if it features a greater minimum income.

The two other Egalitarian-Equivalence criteria do not support this conclusion. Min Egalitarian-Equivalence looks at the *smallest subsidy given to, or the greatest tax paid by, any unskilled individual,* and seeks to put it at the level that is the most favorable (i.e., to maximize it when it is a subsidy, to reduce it when it is a tax). The difference with Zero Egalitarian-Equivalence is that Min Egalitarian-Equivalence does not simply look at the subsidy obtained by the non-working, but considers the subsidies obtained by any unskilled individual. For this criterion, the worst-off individual of the whole population is the unskilled individual who, among all unskilled, receives the smallest subsidy (or pays the greatest tax).

This can be understood by looking at Fig. 5.2. In (a), one sees how Min Egalitarian-Equivalence evaluates the situation of a given individual by computing the hypothetical lump-sum transfer that would enable this individual to reach his current level of satisfaction. In (b), the unskilled's budget curve induced by the tax policy is represented in the same consumption-labor space. By assumption we have a large population spread over the whole curve (and their indifference curves touch the budget curve from above). The worst-off is therefore clearly the individual who receives the smallest subsidy.

With Wage Egalitarian-Equivalence, one obtains a different way of evaluating taxes. The worst-off individual, for this criterion, is the unskilled individual who has *the smallest subsidy, or the greatest tax, in proportion to her earnings.* It is therefore the smallest rate of subsidy granted to an unskilled individual that should be maximized for this criterion. Details about this computation are

---

[10] See also Van der Veen (2004) for an evaluation of the basic income in relation to the idea of equal opportunity.

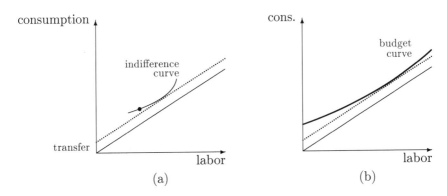

Figure 5.2: Min Egalitarian-Equivalence and income tax

given in the next section.

In summary, the three Egalitarian-Equivalence criteria introduced in Section 5.2 give us three simple ways of evaluating and comparing tax policies:

- the minimum income, for Zero Egalitarian-Equivalence;

- the smallest subsidy received (or the greater tax paid) by an unskilled individual, for Min Egalitarian-Equivalence;

- the smallest rate of subsidy received (or of tax paid) in proportion to earnings by an unskilled individual, for Wage Egalitarian-Equivalence.

Such criteria can easily be applied to the evaluation of policies. Figure 5.3 displays the budget set, with respect to earnings and net income, for a lone parent with two children, in the US before (1986) and after (2000) the Clinton reform of welfare which increased the Earned Income Tax Credit (EITC) and replaced the Aid to Families with Dependent Children (AFDC) with a Temporary Assistance for Needy Families (TANF). The full thick line for 2000 is the budget set resulting from the addition of food stamps, TANF and EITC. The dotted line depicts the 2000 budget after removal of TANF (which is temporary, and is limited to at most 60 months). The unskilled wage is around $10,000, which corresponds to the minimum wage for a full-time job. A segment of the 45° line is also represented. The 45° line depicts the budget line that would prevail under laissez-faire (since net income would then equal gross income).

Zero Egalitarian-Equivalence simply looks at the intercept of budget curves. It is apparent that for Zero Egalitarian-Equivalence the reform is bad, and the temporariness of TANF makes things even worse.

For Min Egalitarian-Equivalence, one has to seek the smallest subsidy received by someone earning less than $10,000. This can be visualized as the smallest vertical distance between a point of the budget curve and the segment of the 45° line that is drawn on the figure. A graphical way to make this evaluation is to take the 45° line segment which is drawn on the figure and slide

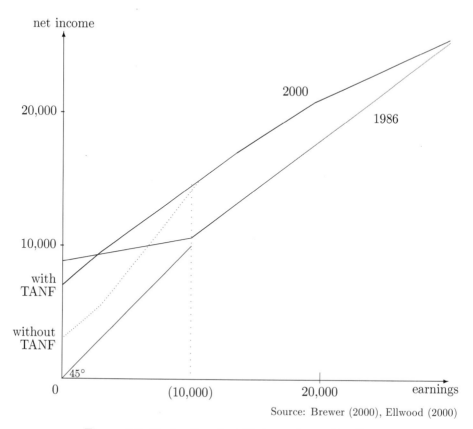

Source: Brewer (2000), Ellwood (2000)

Figure 5.3: Evaluating the Clinton reform of welfare

it upward, vertically, until it touches the budget curve to be evaluated. The higher the position of the 45° line segment when it touches the budget curve, the better. One sees on the figure that this criterion approves the reform, but a permanent variant of TANF would be better for it. Combined with a similar judgment by Zero Egalitarian-Equivalence, this suggests that the fact that TANF is temporary, contrary to the former AFDC, is problematic for social welfare.

For Wage Egalitarian-Equivalence, what matters is the rate of subsidy, not the total amount. Graphically, we are then interested in slopes, since the rate of subsidy at a point of the budget curve is equal to the difference between the slope of the line segment joining the origin to this point and the slope of the 45° line segment (which is equal to one). The technical underpinnings of the computation are provided in the next section, but the graphical evaluation is easy to make. One can take the 45° line segment again but, this time, one has to slide its right end up only (leaving the left end at the origin) until one touches the budget curve under evaluation. Again, the higher one goes before touching the budget curve with the segment, the better the tax function. As one can then see from the figure, this criterion also approves the reform, and even the temporariness of TANF does not affect social welfare for the Wage Egalitarian-Equivalence criterion.

In summary, the Zero Egalitarian-Equivalence criterion disapproves the reduction of the minimum income, especially when TANF reaches its time limit and is cancelled. The Min Egalitarian-Equivalence approves the increase in the subsidy given to the working poor, but still disapproves the temporariness of TANF which penalizes especially those with very low incomes. Only Wage Egalitarian-Equivalence is not against the temporariness of TANF, although it would accept a permanent variant of it.

This example only deals with the case of lone parents with two children. The above theoretical analysis was formulated for a population of individuals, and can easily be applied to a population of homogeneous households. When the whole population contains households of different sizes, the analysis can therefore be applied separately to each subpopulation of households of the same type (as done above for the subpopulation of lone parents with two children). The evaluation for the whole population, which involves a comparison of situations across households of different types, however, requires a specific analysis of households' needs which will not be undertaken here.

Conditional Equality also provides a similar way of evaluating taxes by determining who the worst-off are on the budget curve, but the computation is more complex and is explained in the next section. An important feature of Conditional Equality, linked to the fact that it does not satisfy the compensation principle to a great extent, is that in general it does not focus on the unskilled. One interesting case, though, is the full-income-fair criterion, i.e., Conditional Equality with reference preferences which are not averse to work. In the first-best context this criterion was rejected because it overcompensates and generates a "slavery of the talented." But here, incentive constraints protect the talented because they can always choose to earn less and pretend that they are unskilled. Therefore, the application of this criterion to income taxes cannot induce overcompensation, but presumably it will maximally compensate, in the family of Conditional Equality criteria. Indeed, it can be shown that this criterion evaluates income taxes like Min Egalitarian-Equivalence. Recall from Chapter 3 that incentive constraints tend to impose some degree of liberal reward in the feasible allocations, with the consequence that the difference between compensation and liberal reward criteria is blurred. The convergence here between a particular kind of Conditional Equality and a particular kind of Egalitarian-Equivalence is a good illustration of this phenomenon.

5.5 *Analyzing taxes

Recall that earnings are denoted $q_i = s_i \ell_i$. A tax function is denoted $\tau(q)$, and the budget constraint of agent i is, in consumption-labor and consumption-earnings respectively:

$$c_i = s_i \ell_i - \tau(s_i \ell_i) = q_i - \tau(q_i).$$

It is useful to define agent i's utility function over (c, q) associated with her utility function and her level of skill:

$$u_i^*(c, q) = u_i \left(c, \frac{q}{s_i} \right).$$

An allocation x_N is "incentive-compatible" if there is a tax function τ such that for all $i \in N$, x_i maximizes u_i under the budget constraint, or equivalently if for all $i, j \in N$, either $q_j > s_i$, or $q_j \leq s_i$ and $u_i^*(c_i, q_i) \geq u_i^*(c_j, q_j)$. We restrict attention to taxes such that the induced allocation satisfies the participation constraint, i.e., $\tau(0) \leq 0$. The minimum income is $-\tau(0)$.

Let $s_m = \min_{i \in N} s_i$ and $s_M = \max_{i \in N} s_i$. We no longer assume that the population is large and spread all over the budget curve, but one can still have situations in which the budget curve is everywhere occupied by the indifference curve of some agent. A tax τ is called "saturated" when for all $\bar{q} \in [0, s_M]$, the curve of equation $c = q - \tau(q)$ coincides over $[0, \bar{q}]$ with the envelope curve of agents with skill level $q \leq \bar{q}$ at the incentive-compatible allocation generated by τ.

As announced in the previous section, we have the following result (due to Fleurbaey and Maniquet 2006, 2007).

Proposition 5.2 *Let $\tau, \hat{\tau}$ be two saturated taxes. τ is preferred to $\hat{\tau}$:*

- *by Zero Egalitarian-Equivalence if $\tau(0) < \hat{\tau}(0)$;*

- *by Min Egalitarian-Equivalence if $\max_{q \leq s_m} \tau(q) < \max_{q \leq s_m} \hat{\tau}(q)$;*

- *by Wage Egalitarian-Equivalence (and assuming $\tau(0), \hat{\tau}(0) < 0$) if*

$$\max_{0 < q \leq s_m} \tau(q)/q < \max_{0 < q \leq s_m} \hat{\tau}(q)/q.$$

Proof. Consider a saturated tax function τ, with the induced allocation x_N. Note that, as preferences are monotonic, necessarily $q - \tau(q)$ is non-decreasing. (1) Zero Egalitarian-Equivalence: For all $i \in N$, $u_i(x_i) \geq u_i(-\tau(0), 0)$, implying $ex(0, uc_i(x_i)) \geq -\tau(0)$. Moreover, there is some i for whom $u_i(x_i) = u_i(-\tau(0), 0)$ and therefore $ex(0, uc_i(x_i)) = -\tau(0)$. As a consequence, one has $\min_i ex(0, uc_i(x_i)) = -\tau(0)$.
(2) Min Egalitarian-Equivalence: For every $i \in N$, let x_i^* be such that $u_i(x_i^*) = u_i(x_i)$ and $c_i^* - s_m \ell_i^* = ex(s_m, uc_i(x_i))$. In other words, x_i^* minimizes $c - s_m \ell$ under the constraint $u_i(c, \ell) = u_i(x_i)$. By incentive compatibility, $c_i^* \geq s_i \ell_i^* - \tau(s_i \ell_i^*)$, so that

$$ex(s_m, uc_i(x_i)) \geq s_i \ell_i^* - \tau(s_i \ell_i^*) - s_m \ell_i^*.$$

For every agent i, $s_i \geq s_m$, so that, as $q - \tau(q)$ is non-decreasing,

$$s_i \ell_i^* - \tau(s_i \ell_i^*) - s_m \ell_i^* \geq s_m \ell_i^* - \tau(s_m \ell_i^*) - s_m \ell_i^* = -\tau(s_m \ell_i^*).$$

Therefore, $ex(s_m, uc_i(x_i)) \geq -\tau(s_m \ell_i^*)$ and, as obviously

$$-\tau(s_m \ell_i^*) \geq \min_{\ell \in [0,1]} -\tau(s_m \ell),$$

one has

$$ex(s_m, uc_i(x_i)) \geq \min_{\ell \in [0,1]} -\tau(s_m \ell).$$

By saturation, the graph of $q - \tau(q)$ coincides over $[0, s_m]$ with the envelope curve of the indifference curves of individuals with $s_i = s_m$. Therefore there is j in this subpopulation such that

$$\min_{\ell \in [0,1]} -\tau(s_m \ell) = ex(s_m, uc_j(x_j)) = s_m \ell_j^* - \tau(s_m \ell_j^*) - s_m \ell_j^* = -\tau(s_m \ell_j^*).$$

In conclusion,

$$\min_{i \in N} ex(s_m, uc_i(x_i)) = \min_{\ell \in [0,1]} -\tau(s_m \ell) = - \max_{q \in [0, s_m]} \tau(q).$$

(3) Wage Egalitarian-Equivalence: The argument mimics the previous point. For every $i \in N$, let x_i^* and $\tilde{s}_i$ be such that $u_i(x_i^*) = u_i(x_i) = u_i(B(\tilde{s}_i, 0))$ and $x_i^* \in B(\tilde{s}_i, 0)$. In other words, $\tilde{s}_i$ minimizes c/ℓ under the constraint $u_i(c, \ell) = u_i(x_i)$. Since $\tau(0) < 0$, necessarily $\tilde{s}_i > 0$ and $\ell_i^* > 0$. By incentive compatibility, $c_i^* \geq s_i \ell_i^* - \tau(s_i \ell_i^*)$, so that

$$\tilde{s}_i \geq \frac{s_i \ell_i^* - \tau(s_i \ell_i^*)}{\ell_i^*}.$$

For every agent i, $s_i \geq s_m$, so that, as $q - \tau(q)$ is non-decreasing,

$$\frac{s_i \ell_i^* - \tau(s_i \ell_i^*)}{\ell_i^*} \geq \frac{s_m \ell_i^* - \tau(s_m \ell_i^*)}{\ell_i^*} = s_m \left[1 - \frac{\tau(s_m \ell_i^*)}{s_m \ell_i^*} \right].$$

Therefore,

$$\tilde{s}_i \geq s_m \min_{\ell \in (0,1]} \left[1 - \frac{\tau(s_m \ell)}{s_m \ell} \right].$$

By saturation, the graph of $q - \tau(q)$ coincides over $[0, s_m]$ with the envelope curve of the indifference curves of individuals with $s_i = s_m$. Therefore there is j in this subpopulation such that

$$\tilde{s}_j = \frac{s_m \ell_j^* - \tau(s_m \ell_j^*)}{\ell_j^*} = s_m \left[1 - \frac{\tau(s_m \ell_j^*)}{s_m \ell_j^*} \right] = s_m \min_{\ell \in (0,1]} \left[1 - \frac{\tau(s_m \ell)}{s_m \ell} \right].$$

One then has

$$\min_{i \in N} \tilde{s}_i = s_m \min_{\ell \in (0,1]} \left[1 - \frac{\tau(s_m \ell)}{s_m \ell} \right] = s_m \left[1 - \max_{q \in (0, s_m]} \frac{\tau(q)}{q} \right],$$

which concludes the proof. ∎

This proposition does not say anything about cases of equality (e.g., $\tau(0) = \hat{\tau}(0)$, for Zero Egalitarian-Equivalence), because what happens to better-off individuals then determines social preferences, according to the leximin criterion. It is therefore not exactly true that these criteria focus exclusively on the unskilled in all cases.

Let us now turn to Conditional Equality, with an arbitrary reference $\tilde{u}$. The comparison of taxes proceeds again by determining what category of agents are the worst-off in each tax. For every $q \in [s_m, s_M]$, let $s^-(q) = \max_{i:s_i \leq q} s_i$ and $s^+(q) = \min_{i:s_i \geq q} s_i$. Note that for every $i \in N$, $s^-(s_i) = s^+(s_i) = s_i$.

The next proposition (due to Fleurbaey and Maniquet 2007) can be introduced by looking at Figs 5.4 and 5.5. In Fig. 5.4(a), dealing with space (c, ℓ), one sees an allocation with lump-sum transfers, in which two budgets are equivalent for $\tilde{u}$. Figure 5.4(b) reproduces the same figure in (c, q) space. Each skill level then corresponds to an horizontal expansion or reduction of the initial figure.

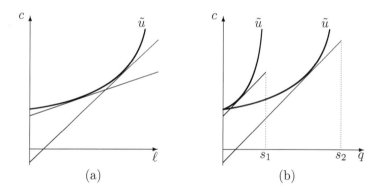

Figure 5.4: Conditional Equality with lump-sum transfers

The condition stated in the next proposition, for the comparison of taxes, is illustrated in Fig. 5.5. It consists in looking at the budget curve $q - \tau(q)$ (not represented in the figure), and seeking the highest indifference curve for $\tilde{u}$ (or upper contour set $\widetilde{uc}(x)$) so that the budget sets constructed in Fig. 5.4(b) are all below the curve $q - \tau(q)$. The thick kinked curve in Fig. 5.5 is the lowest non-decreasing curve which covers these various budget sets. One therefore seeks the highest $\widetilde{uc}(x)$ so that this kinked curve is everywhere below $q - \tau(q)$. Figure 5.5 also shows how this thick curve relates to the graph of a particular function, namely, $c = q + ex(q, \widetilde{uc}(x))$: All budgets have their extreme North-East point in this graph.

Proposition 5.3 *Let $\tau, \hat{\tau}$ be two saturated taxes. τ is preferred to $\hat{\tau}$ by Conditional Equality with reference $\tilde{u}$ if there is x such that for all $q \in [0, s_m]$*

$$\tau(q) \leq -ex(s_m, \widetilde{uc}(x)),$$

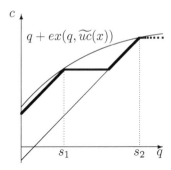

Figure 5.5: Conditional Equality and income tax

and for all $q \in [s_m, s_M]$

$$\tau(q) \le \min \left\{ q - s^-(q) - ex(s^-(q), \widetilde{uc}(x)), -ex(s^+(q), \widetilde{uc}(x)) \right\},$$

while, for the same x, this is not true for $\hat{\tau}$.

Proof. Let τ be a saturated tax and take $\bar{q} \ge s_m$ for which there is a subpopulation of agents i such that $s_i = \bar{q}$. Conditional Equality evaluates the situation of such an agent i by $\tilde{u} \left(B\left(s_i, \hat{t}_i\right) \right)$, where $\hat{t}_i$ is defined by $u_i(x_i) = u_i(B(s_i, \hat{t}_i))$. This means that $\hat{t}_i = ex(\bar{q}, uc_i(x_i))$, so that the worst-off agent in this subpopulation is the agent with the lowest $ex(\bar{q}, uc_i(x_i))$. For this agent,

$$ex(\bar{q}, uc_i(x_i)) = ex(\bar{q}, \bigcup_{j:s_j=\bar{q}} uc_j(x_j)).$$

The tax is saturated, so that

$$\bigcup_{j:s_j=\bar{q}} uc_j(x_j) = \{ x \in X \mid c \ge \bar{q}\ell - \tau(\bar{q}\ell) \}.$$

As a consequence,

$$\min_{i:s_i=\bar{q}} ex(\bar{q}, uc_i(x_i)) = ex(\bar{q}, \bigcup_{j:s_j=\bar{q}} uc_j(x_j)) = \min_{q \le \bar{q}} (-\tau(q)).$$

Now, one computes

$$\min_{i:s_i=\bar{q}} \tilde{u} \left(B\left(\bar{q}, ex(\bar{q}, uc_i(x_i))\right) \right) = \tilde{u} \left(B\left(\bar{q}, \min_{i:s_i=y} ex(\bar{q}, uc_i(x_i))\right) \right)$$

$$= \tilde{u} \left(B\left(\bar{q}, \min_{q \le \bar{q}} (-\tau(q))\right) \right).$$

Let $\hat{q} \ge s_m$ and $x \in X$ be such that

$$\min_{i \in N} \tilde{u} \left(B\left(s_i, ex(s_i, uc_i(x_i))\right) \right) = \min_{i:s_i=\hat{q}} \tilde{u} \left(B\left(\hat{q}, ex(\hat{q}, uc_i(x_i))\right) \right) = \tilde{u}(x).$$

This means that $\min_{q \leq \hat{q}} (-\tau(q)) = ex(\hat{q}, \widetilde{uc}(x))$, or equivalently

$$\max_{q \leq \hat{q}} \tau(q) = -ex(\hat{q}, \widetilde{uc}(x)),$$

while for all $q' \neq \hat{q}$ such that $q' = s_i$ for some $i \in N$, $\min_{q \leq q'} (-\tau(q)) \geq ex(q', \widetilde{uc}(x))$, or equivalently

$$\max_{q \leq q'} \tau(q) \leq -ex(q', \widetilde{uc}(x)).$$

This implies in particular that for all $q \in [0, s_m]$

$$\tau(q) \leq -ex(s_m, \widetilde{uc}(x)).$$

Now take q such that $s^-(q) < q < s^+(q)$. The above implies that

$$\tau(q) \leq \max_{a \leq s^+(q)} \tau(a) \leq -ex(s^+(q), \widetilde{uc}(x)).$$

In addition, by saturation $q - \tau(q)$ is non-decreasing, so that one has $q - \tau(q) \geq s^-(q) - \tau(s^-(q))$, implying

$$\tau(q) \leq q - s^-(q) + \tau(s^-(q)) \leq q - s^-(q) - ex(s^-(q), \widetilde{uc}(x)).$$

If a tax $\hat{\tau}$, with associated allocation x'_N, does not satisfy these conditions with respect to the same x, then either there is q such that

$$\hat{\tau}(q) > -ex(s^+(q), \widetilde{uc}(x)),$$

which, as $q \leq s^+(q)$, implies

$$\max_{a \leq s^+(q)} \hat{\tau}(a) > -ex(s^+(q), \widetilde{uc}(x)),$$

or there is q such that

$$\hat{\tau}(q) > q - s^-(q) - ex(s^-(q), \widetilde{uc}(x)),$$

which, as $\hat{\tau}(q) \leq q - s^-(q) + \hat{\tau}(s^-(q))$, implies

$$\hat{\tau}(s^-(q)) > -ex(s^-(q), \widetilde{uc}(x)).$$

In any of these two possibilities, necessarily there is $i \in N$ such that $\max_{q \leq s_i} \hat{\tau}(q) > -ex(s_i, \widetilde{uc}(x))$, implying that

$$\min_{i \in N} \tilde{u} \left(B \left(s_i, ex(s_i, uc_i(x'_i)) \right) \right) < \tilde{u}(x) = \min_{i \in N} \tilde{u} \left(B \left(s_i, ex(s_i, uc_i(x_i)) \right) \right),$$

and therefore that τ is preferred to $\hat{\tau}$. ∎

When there is a continuum of values of s_i, the condition stated in the proposition simplifies into

$$\tau(q) \leq -ex(\max\{s_m, q\}, \widetilde{uc}(x)).$$

The function $f(q) = -ex(\max\{s_m, q\}, \widetilde{uc}(x))$ has an interesting shape. It is continuous, constant over $[0, s_m]$ and then non-decreasing. It is also convex, because an expenditure function is concave in prices. One can therefore consider this function as an interesting upper bound for a progressive income tax.

It is useful to examine a few illustrative examples of this function, in relation to salient examples of reference $\tilde{u}$.

(1) If $\tilde{u}$ is extremely averse to work, then for all $q \leq \max_{i \in N} s_i$,

$$ex(\max\{s_m, q\}, \widetilde{uc}(x)) = ex(0, \widetilde{uc}(x)),$$

i.e., the function is constant, and the criterion then boils down to minimizing $\max_{q \leq s_M} \tau(q)$. This obviously points toward laissez-faire ($\tau \equiv 0$), which is the optimal policy in this case.

(2) If $\tilde{u}$ is indifferent to ℓ (flat indifference curves), then there is $\tilde{t}$ such that

$$ex(\max\{s_m, q\}, \widetilde{uc}(x)) = \tilde{t} - \max\{s_m, q\},$$

and the opposite of this, as a tax function, gives a constant subsidy for all earnings below s_m, and taxes the earnings above s_m at 100%. This is the maximal rate for saturated taxes, so that what happens for $q > s_m$ will never be determining in this case. Therefore, a tax τ will be preferred to another tax $\hat{\tau}$ if there is $\tilde{t}$ such that for all $q \leq s_m$, $\tau(q) \leq \tilde{t} - s_m$ while there is $q \leq s_m$ such that $\hat{\tau}(q) > \tilde{t} - s_m$. This is equivalent to the condition $\max_{q \leq s_m} \tau(q) < \max_{q \leq s_m} \hat{\tau}(q)$, which is identical to the condition stated for Min Egalitarian-Equivalence.

(3) If the indifference curve for $\tilde{u}(x)$ is piecewise linear, with a slope $s > s_m$ on the left of a certain ℓ and $s' > s$ on the right of ℓ, then $-ex(\max\{s_m, q\}, \widetilde{uc}(x))$ is also piecewise linear, with a slope ℓ for $q \in (s, s')$. This is because, for $s < q < s'$, there is $\tilde{t}$ such that

$$ex(q, \widetilde{uc}(x)) = \tilde{t} - q\ell.$$

(4) A special case of this is when there is a special ℓ^* such that indifference curves for $\tilde{u}$ are flat on the left of ℓ^* and extremely steep on the right. Recall from Section 4.5 that the first-best allocation in this case has budget lines crossing at the vertical of ℓ^* (as advocated by Kolm 2004b). For this particular $\tilde{u}$, one has

$$ex(\max\{s_m, q\}, \widetilde{uc}(x)) = \tilde{t} - \max\{s_m, q\}\ell^*,$$

which corresponds to a tax function giving a fixed subsidy to all earnings below s_m, and taxing all earnings above s_m at the fixed rate ℓ^*.

It is worth insisting on the fact that, like Min Egalitarian-Equivalence, Conditional Equality for any $\tilde{u}$ always compares $\tau(q)$ to a constant for $q \leq s_m$, and therefore always pushes toward a zero marginal tax rate for earnings below s_m. It can actually be shown that, under reasonable conditions, the optimal tax will have this feature for these two criteria.[11] This can be viewed as a good illustration of the combination of liberal reward, which pushes toward zero marginal tax

---

[11]See Fleurbaey and Maniquet (2007).

(same lump-sum transfer for all agents with identical skill), and compensation, which gives priority to the worst-off, i.e., the unskilled in this context.

With the same methodology, one shows that Envied Intensity also provides a rather simple criterion. It focuses, for saturated taxes, on the expression

$$\sum_{i \in N} ex\left(s_i, \{x \in X \mid c \geq s_m \ell - \tau(s_m \ell)\}\right).$$

For a tax function τ such that the marginal tax rate is non-negative over $[0, s_m]$, this expression is simply equal to

$$[s_m - \tau(s_m)] n - \sum_{i \in N} s_i,$$

which implies that this criterion will seek to minimize $\tau(s_m)$ for this class of tax functions. It can be shown that, for this criterion as well as for Wage Egalitarian-Equivalence,[12] the optimal tax will have a non-positive marginal tax rate, on average, over $[0, s_m]$, or, in other words, that one will have $\tau(s_m) \leq \tau(0)$. This can be understood as being particularly favorable to the working poor.

5.6   *Unearned income

This section offers only a few insights into a wide topic. Individual wealth comes from two sources, bequests and savings. It appears reasonable not to hold individuals responsible for the bequest they receive, and it is interesting to examine what conclusions would follow from holding them responsible for their saving choices.

Let us introduce two periods. In period 1 agent i works ℓ_i, consumes c_i and saves z_i. In period 2, agent i does not work, receives a bequest[13] b_i and consumes d_i. At the end of period 2 she leaves a bequest h_i, with an amount actually received by her descendants (after tax) equal to k_i. Her utility function is $u_i(c_i, d_i, k_i, \ell_i)$. Let $x_i = (c_i, d_i, k_i, \ell_i)$. An economy is now described as $e = (s_N, b_N, u_N)$. Agent i is not responsible for (s_i, b_i) but is responsible for u_i.

There is a fixed interest rate r. If redistribution is made only through lump-sum transfers t_i (in period 2), agent i's budget is

$$B(s_i, b_i, t_i) = \{(c, d, k, \ell) \mid (1 + r)c + d + k \leq (1 + r)s_i \ell + b_i + t_i\}.$$

A tax policy is now made of three tax functions: τ_e on earnings of the period, τ_s on interests (paid or received), τ_b on bequest received. Agent i's

---

[12] See Fleurbaey and Maniquet (2006) for the analysis of Wage Egalitarian-Equivalence.

[13] The assumption that bequests are received in period 2 can be considered more realistic for an ageing society in which most people inherit after the age of fifty. It implies that those who expect a large bequest will be among the big borrowers rather than the big savers. This has consequences over the evaluation of taxes on interest income. The alternative assumption that bequests are received in period 1 would also deserve to be studied. The changes to be made to the analysis of this section are rather straightforward and are omitted here.

budget constraint is then

$$\begin{cases} c_i + z_i = s_i \ell_i - \tau_e(s_i \ell_i) \\ d_i + h_i = (1 + r)z_i - \tau_s(rz_i) + b_i - \tau_b(b_i) \\ k_i = h_i - \tau_b(h_i). \end{cases}$$

For each of these taxes, i.e., for $\alpha = e, s, b$, we assume that $a - \tau_\alpha(a)$ is non-decreasing and $\tau_\alpha(0) \leq 0$.

The analysis of social ordering functions from the previous sections can be extended to this setting. Conditional Equality assesses individual situations in terms of

$$\tilde{u}\left(B(s_i, b_i, \tilde{t}_i)\right),$$

where $\tilde{t}_i$ is solution to $u_i(x_i) = u_i\left(B(s_i, b_i, \tilde{t}_i)\right)$. Liberal reward axioms would now take account of b_i as an additional circumstance characteristics, and would limit requirements of equal treatment to agents with identical (s_i, b_i). But this is a minor change.

Zero Egalitarian-Equivalence refers to $\tilde{t}_i$, solution to

$$u_i(x_i) = u_i\left(B(0, 0, \tilde{t}_i)\right),$$

assuming that the reference value for the bequest is, as for the skill level, zero. Similarly, Min Egalitarian-Equivalence could compute $\tilde{t}_i$ as the solution to

$$u_i(x_i) = u_i(B(\min_{j \in N} s_j, \min_{j \in N} b_j, \tilde{t}_i)).$$

The case of Wage Egalitarian-Equivalence is more problematic. An axiom of *Laissez-Faire for Uniform Circumstances* should presumably replace *Laissez-Faire for Uniform Skills*, and would advocate laissez-faire when all skills *and all bequests* are equal. This axiom is satisfied, for instance, by a variant of Wage Egalitarian-Equivalence which evaluates agent i's situation by $\tilde{s}_i$ such that

$$u_i(x_i) = u_i(B(\tilde{s}_i, \min_{j \in N} b_j, 0)).$$

This social ordering function does not satisfy *Separability* and Proposition 5.1 is no longer valid.

The evaluation of policies can be done with the same methodology as above, determining who are the worst-off in the population according to the relevant criterion. In order to take account of incentives over bequest, it is convenient to consider the situation when this population is made of overlapping generations, every individual having a child, and to focus on stationary allocations.

For every Egalitarian-Equivalence criterion, the worst-off under any given tax policy are – assuming sufficient diversity of preferences in the population – among the agents with lowest wage rate $s_m = \min_{i \in N} s_i$ and lowest bequest $b_m = \min_{i \in N} b_i$. If one considers each tax separately from the others, these criteria may therefore advocate minimizing $\tau_b(b_m)$, but one must take account of a possible impact on b_m via an incentive effect. The true objective is to maximize $b_m - \tau_b(b_m)$. As far as the other taxes are concerned, Zero Egalitarian-Equivalence will advocate minimizing $\tau_e(0)$, i.e., maximizing the minimum income, and minimizing $\max_{z \leq -\tau_e(0)} \tau_s(rz)$. Min Egalitarian-Equivalence will advocate minimizing $\max_{q \leq s_m} \tau_e(q)$ as well as $\max_{z \leq q^* - \tau_e(q^*)} \tau_s(rz)$ for $q^* \in \arg\max_{q \leq s_m} \tau_e(q)$. The conclusions obtained in the previous sections about the tax on earnings are not altered, and it is not surprising to see that the interest tax should be minimized on low savings. It is worth stressing that, even though individuals are held responsible for their saving decisions, this does not entail, even in the absence of bequests, that the optimal tax on interest income should be null. Indeed, if total tax receipts can be increased by taxing interests on large savings, this may help improve the subsidies paid to the worst-off.

When the three taxes are jointly evaluated, trade-offs between these tax minimizations appear. For instance, if $b_m = 0$ a tax policy is better for Zero Egalitarian-Equivalence if it has a lower value for the expression

$$(1 + r)\,\tau_e(0) + \tau_b(0) + \max_{(z,h) \in Q} [\tau_s(rz) + \tau_b(h)],$$

where Q is the set of pairs (z, h) satisfying:

$$\begin{cases} z \leq -\tau_e(0) \\ h \leq (1 + r)\,z - \tau_s(rz) - \tau_b(0). \end{cases}$$

Let us briefly explain how this result is obtained. The worst-off individual has the lowest $\tilde{t}_i$ solution to $u_i(x_i) = u_i\left(B(0, 0, \tilde{t}_i)\right)$. For a saturated tax this will be computed as the lowest lump-sum transfer $\tilde{t} = (1 + r)\,c + d + k$ compatible with the budget constraint

$$\begin{cases} c + z = -\tau_e(0) \\ d + h = (1 + r)z_i - \tau_s(rz_i) - \tau_b(0) \\ k = h - \tau_b(h). \end{cases}$$

One computes $(1 + r)c + d + k = -(1 + r)\tau_e(0) - \tau_b(0) - \tau_s(rz) - \tau_b(h)$. The above criterion is then obtained by minimizing this expression over the permissible (z, h).

5.7   Skills and quality of life

We have assumed until now that individuals are sensitive to the quantity of work but not to the type of work they do. It is well known, however, that jobs corresponding to higher skills are generally more pleasant and are tied with many material and symbolic advantages. From this perspective, it is questionable to hold individuals responsible for their preferences over leisure and consumption. Those who only have access to unpleasant jobs will naturally be more averse to work and should not be held responsible for this.

The various criteria proposed above are not affected in the same way by this observation. Zero Egalitarian-Equivalence is immune to this problem, since by asking individuals to consider an equivalent situation with a zero wage rate (i.e., typically, with no work) we automatically take account of the unpleasantness of their job. An individual with a less pleasant job will naturally ask less income in the situation of no work, in order to reach an equivalent situation, and therefore will be considered worse-off than another with the same earnings and the same quantity of labor but a more pleasant job.

Min Egalitarian-Equivalence would now ask individuals to consider working with the lowest wage rate in a typical unskilled job. This implies that those who currently work in pleasant jobs will ask for a greater lump-sum transfer in order to accept the change, and will be considered better-off than before. However, among the unskilled, if one assumes that their jobs are similar, or at least that they all have access to the same kind of jobs, one can consider that they are responsible for the differences in their preferences, and since they are ascertained to be the worst-off even more than before, the policy conclusions about income tax will not be altered. One should still maximize the smallest subsidy that they receive. A similar argument applies to Wage Egalitarian-Equivalence.

The case of Conditional Equality is more complex, but the qualitative orientation of the change is clear. This criterion would, after taking account of this issue, put greater emphasis on the unskilled, and would therefore tend to come closer to Min Egalitarian-Equivalence.

There are also some skilled jobs (e.g., artists) which do not pay more than unskilled jobs. The individuals engaged in such activities will typically not be amongst the worst-off for the above criteria because they prefer their activities to a typical unskilled job, but they may benefit from the tax policies which support low incomes, just like other skilled individuals who work part time in better paid jobs.

The issue of unemployment can be dealt with here. To be unemployed is like being deprived of one's skills, and is even worse because the status of unemployed is very hard to bear for most people. Insofar as unemployment is observable (by a declaration of availability to work and observable search actions), it is possible to give the unemployed a special treatment. In particular, their allowance can be greater than the minimum income in order to compensate for the unpleasantness of their situation. The same can be said about those who suffer from disabilities which can be medically ascertained.[14]

5.8   Education and skills

The previous section addressed a possible objection to the idea that individuals are responsible for their preferences. Symmetrically, the assumption that individuals are *not* responsible for their skills may appear questionable to those who consider that education choices made by young adults should be viewed as responsible decisions.

It is, however, hard to consider that the unskilled have chosen to remain unskilled in spite of having full access to high education. Most of them have

---

[14] Further analysis of the issues of this section can be found in Fleurbaey (2006b).

met serious obstacles due to personal or social limitations and difficulties of integration in the school system. Moreover, the decision to drop out is made at
an early age when people cannot be seriously held responsible, and is not comparable to responsible choices of specialization made later on at the university
by young adults. A reasonable stance would therefore be to hold people responsible for their level of skill beyond a certain threshold, but not below. More
precisely, there would be two skill characteristics. One, for which individuals
would not be held responsible, would decide whether the individual has access
to high education or not. The other, for which the individuals would be held
responsible, would decide which level of wage rate the individual would have
conditionally on having access to high education. For those who do not have
access to high education, this variable is obviously unobservable, but informational difficulties should worry us only at the stage of policy evaluation, not at
the stage of defining social criteria.

This modification of the framework does not substantially affect the
Egalitarian-Equivalence criteria which will still give priority to the unskilled
and make similar evaluations of tax policies in terms of minimum income or
smallest subsidy. Conditional Equality would change its evaluation of the situation of high-skilled agents, and would advocate submitting all of them to the
same lump-sum tax, in the first-best context. In the context of income taxation,
it would be more favorable to the high-skilled, without modifying its evaluation
of the situation of low earnings. It would push toward a zero marginal tax rate
for high incomes. This is interesting because there has been some controversy in
optimal tax theory about the robustness of the result that the marginal tax rate
should decline to zero for very high incomes.[15] We see that the liberal reward
principle embodied in Conditional Equality can yield a more radical conclusion
of this sort since it concerns all incomes of higher education, not just the greatest
incomes.

5.9   Conclusion

This chapter has shown that the analysis of redistribution in complex populations which are heterogeneous in multiple characteristics and partly responsible
for them is not out of reach. On the contrary, it is possible to reach simple and
intuitive conclusions. In virtue of the compensation principle, the focus should
be put on low incomes, especially earnings up to the lowest wage. In virtue
of liberal reward, it is enough to look at the budget set delineated by the tax
policy. In particular, one can ignore utility levels, even with criteria which satisfy the Pareto principle and therefore respect individual preferences. Moreover,
the liberal reward principle pushes in the direction of low marginal tax for low
incomes, which is well in line with the idea that there is no reason to interfere
with labor choices made by the worst-off. Of course, the same could be said
about labor choices of the better-off, but, in the context of income taxation, the

---

[15] See in particular Diamond (1998).

compensation principle advocates taxing them in order to increase the subsidies granted to the unskilled.

This analysis questions the thesis that "real freedom for all" (the title of Van Parijs' 1995 book) necessarily implies focusing on the payment of a large basic income, and ignoring what happens to disposable income for positive levels of earnings. It is also possible, however, to argue in favor of a maximal basic income on the basis of the above analysis, if one adopts the criterion of Zero Egalitarian-Equivalence. Moreover, an additional argument in favor of choosing this criterion rather than Min or Wage Egalitarian-Equivalence will be provided in Chapter 10.

It is hoped that this chapter will encourage researchers to refine the analysis in the many directions which can be explored. Two issues, in particular, appear especially interesting and will not be examined here. First, gender and household issues, in relation to time use and task sharing at home would enrich the analysis in order to take account of unpaid labor jointly with paid labor. As mentioned above, this could help, among other things, to refine the analysis of responsibility for preferences over paid labor and income. Second, integrating the health system, which becomes more and more resource consuming in developed economies, with the redistribution system would also make it possible to refine the analysis of individual availability for work, and to examine the contribution of health care delivery and health care funding to redistribution in general. Finally, what has been said about unearned income, job quality and education is only introductory and a full-fledged analysis is yet to be done.

Chapter 6

Risk, insurance and option luck

6.1 Introduction

One of the intuitively challenging features of theories of equal opportunities is that, when individuals take risks and are especially unlucky, it seems harsh to consider that they should bear the full consequences of their behavior. The penalty may be out of proportion with the fault. Consider a motorbiker who wants to have a taste of the wind in his hair for a while and has an accident just at this moment, putting him in a coma and in need of a very costly operation that would not have been necessary had he worn a helmet. In a sense he can be held responsible for his fate, because the cost is directly due to his decision not to wear a helmet. But one feels a reluctance to let him bear the full cost, which may be death in this case if he cannot afford the operation.

There may be several factors in our reluctance to let responsibility play its full role here. One is that the victim is really below a threshold of decent life, and one could argue in favor of guaranteeing everyone a minimum threshold of subsistence independently of past responsible decisions that may have caused the situation. Another element, which will be the topic of this chapter, is that the motorbiker has been *unlucky*. His decision was not to have a cranial traumatism, but only not to wear the helmet for a while. With a reasonable, indeed a minimum, amount of luck, nothing bad would have happened. Several authors (e.g., Arneson, Cohen, Roemer) in the field of responsibility-sensitive egalitarianism are attracted by the idea that individuals should be held responsible only for what really lies under their control. Now, nobody controls one's luck and that might be the paradigmatic example of something that is not controlled. "Luck-egalitarianism" has even become the catchword for responsibility-sensitive egalitarianism in a part of the literature, with the idea that all circumstances (i.e., non-responsibility characteristics) in general can be brought under the heading of luck.

If, in this perspective, it is decided that no individual is ever responsible for being lucky or unlucky, one must deduce that individuals should never bear the consequences of risky decisions, such as low-stake gambling. Some authors, such as Le Grand (1991), do accept this conclusion and consider that individuals should be fully insured and should only bear the consequences of their decisions over the expected value of their well-being. For instance, if the smokers have a lower expected value of well-being as a result of smoking, the unlucky among them who develop related diseases should be helped in order to reach the average well-being of all smokers, while the lucky would pay the corresponding taxes.

Other authors do not take this line of reasoning, because it amounts to imposing full insurance to all individuals in all (insurable) cases. All those undertaking a risky activity would pay a special tax that would fund the indemnity paid to the unlucky among them, so that *ex post* they all end up with the same well-being. Applied to smoking or mountaineering, this does not sound unreasonable. Applied to low-stake gambling, however, this seems equivalent to a prohibition. Dworkin, for instance, argues that "if winners were made to share their winnings with losers, then no one would gamble, as individuals, and the kind of life preferred by both those who in the end win and those who lose would be unavailable" (2000, p. 75). He proposes to distinguish between option luck, i.e., "accepting an isolated risk he or she should have anticipated and might have declined" (p. 73) and brute luck, i.e., risks "that are not in that sense deliberate gambles" (ibid.). He immediately acknowledges that this distinction may be a matter of degree and may be hard to apply in concrete cases. But he cites the example of sick smokers as individuals who may be considered as (responsible) victims of an unsuccessful gamble.

In this chapter we will examine this difficult issue in light of the conceptual apparatus developed in the previous chapters. I will defend the principle that individuals should never be held responsible for being lucky or unlucky, and as such the notion of option luck is prima facie unacceptable. But applying the Conditional Equality and Egalitarian-Equivalence criteria to problems of allocation under risk will provide a rationale for policies which are sometimes similar to policies based on the notion of option luck. This will allow us to see how the intuition underlying the notion of option luck can be reinterpreted in terms of liberal reward.

Dworkin's concept of option luck plays a key role in the development of his idea of a hypothetical insurance market that can help in calibrating the transfers between unequally talented individuals. The allocation criteria analyzed here will enable us to critically examine the performance of insurance markets in general, and to show that Dworkin's hypothetical market is highly problematic not only because it is hypothetical, but also because insurance markets suffer from deep flaws which have not been highlighted by economic theory so far.

6.2 The luck factor

The general framework in which risk will be discussed here is one in which there are several possible states of the world, and only one of them is the true state. Individuals do not know the true state and must make many decisions in this state of ignorance, but this ignorance is reduced over time and this has consequences for their well-being. For instance, depending on whether the coin falls on heads or tails some may win and others lose. In general individuals may have different beliefs about the likelihood of the various states of nature. They may even be unable to form coherent subjective probabilities about the states. They may also fail to have rational decision criteria under risk. Our problem here is to construct criteria for the evaluation of social situations involving risk, and such criteria should not depend on assuming too much about individual rationality. Three guiding principles will help us here. The first one is discussed in this section and the other two in the next sections.

The first principle is that individuals should not be held responsible for the "luck factor" which affects their life, i.e., simply, for being lucky or unlucky given the prospects they have or choose. This point may be defended in relation to various conceptions of responsibility. We can focus here on the main options defended in the field of responsibility-sensitive egalitarianism. One is the view that individuals should be held responsible only for what lies within their control. According to this view, since it is obvious that individuals do not control their luck factor, it really makes no sense to hold them responsible for it, as it has already been explained in the introduction. One can hold gamblers responsible for gambling, but not for winning or losing, unless they cheat and manipulate the outcome.[1]

An alternative view is that individuals should be held responsible for their goals and ambitions (at the exception of those which they do not identify with and which they consider as compulsions). Dworkin, in particular, defends the notion of option luck in terms of preference for a more or less risky lifestyle. The gamblers must be allowed to live the life they want just as those who like chocolate should be allowed to have it. The problem is that typically nobody has a preference for being unlucky. One can like gambling but few like losing, and it is therefore hard to defend the idea that we must condone the preferences of the losers for their unlucky lifestyle. They actually have no such preference. Again, it makes no sense to hold people responsible for their luck factor in this second conception of responsibility. They may be held responsible for their taste for risk, but not for their (nonexistent) taste for bad luck. It is true that the possibility of bad luck is part and parcel of a risky life, and the great value of a risky life for some people may force public authorities, at the end of the day, to allow some risky activities, as we will see below. But that does not mean that they should incorporate the luck factor into the responsibility characteristics of

---

[1] Arneson (1997b, p. 239) acknowledges that, strictly speaking, gamblers cannot be said to win or lose through their own fault or voluntary choice. He argues that they can nonetheless be said to have had equal opportunities "in the morally relevant sense." This statement sounds like a policy prescription more than a revision of the theory of responsibility.

individuals in the evaluation of social situations. The idea that people should be held responsible for their luck is, in this context, confusing policy conclusions with conceptual distinctions.

A Dworkinian would probably argue here that by choosing to gamble, an individual chooses the possibility of losing and must accept this (unpleasant) part of the package when it happens to be realized. But the idea that the choice of a lottery implies the choice of its consequences is just obviously wrong, unless it is understood as a policy conclusion. A gambler likes and chooses to gamble, which includes the possibility of losing, but he does not like or choose to lose. A gamble is not like a package with a determined content over which one has full information. The gambler makes a choice with imperfect information about the outcome. The change in his subjective probability of the true state of nature from a fraction of one (*ex ante*) to one (*ex post*) is much more like brute luck than like something that is chosen.[2] Moreover, it appears more compelling to cater to individual informed preferences than to *ex ante* ignorant preferences: When the *ex post* loser disagrees with the *ex ante* gambler (his former self), the former's informed view should naturally have priority over the latter's ignorant view. This point is developed in Section 6.4.

6.3   Comprehensive well-being

The second principle that will help us here is that the notion of well-being which serves to measure individual advantage should be comprehensive. Dworkin's defense of the risky lifestyle of those who like it must be taken seriously, and here is a way to do this.

Consider that individuals live a certain number of periods, with information about the true state of nature being progressively disclosed. A riskier life means that in early periods of life the span of possible outcomes is greater, and this prospect may have a significant impact on individual preference satisfaction and level of well-being. More risk in early life may enhance the well-being of the risk lover and dampen that of the risk-averse person. Even a risk-averse individual may like the side advantages of risky activities. One can be risk averse but nonetheless love mountaineering because of the beautiful views. By taking account of the direct impact of risk (and side effects of risky activities) on satisfaction, independently of what the outcome turns out to be, it is possible to make sense of the importance of letting people take risks if they wish.[3]

This does not mean that we should consider lifetime well-being as the simple addition of well-being levels at all periods of life. The way in which lifetime well-being depends on the sequence of life events may be more complicated. Moreover, the time sequence is not really the important feature here. What

---

[2] This argument is nicely developed in Fried (2003): "[From *ex ante* to *ex post*] what has changed is not the possibility of a particular outcome, but its probability... That change of probabilities is, I think, best understood as a species of brute luck: the product of events (changes in the external world, in available information about the external world, etc.) for which the individual in question cannot be held responsible." (p.152)

[3] This idea was suggested by Deschamps and Gevers (1979).

matters here is rather that preferences over more or less risky lifestyles can find an expression through the impact of risk on well-being.[4] There must be a place to record the fact that the individual has taken a risk and that this influences the relevant measure of her well-being. Considering the sequence of time periods is the most natural anchor to do this.

A difficulty here comes from the fact that individual subjective appreciations of risk may be flawed in many ways. Some individuals may have less information than is available to other people, they may be incompetent at thinking in terms of probabilities, they may have inconsistent attitudes about risky prospects, they may be myopic about the bad consequences that may unfold, and so on. Nevertheless, we may be interested in recording the impact on well-being of living with certain prospects, *as the individuals themselves view such prospects*. For instance, those who like taking risks may be completely irrational about this, but their (irrational) preference being satisfied or not has an impact on their well-being over their life. This can be explained with an analogy. How should we evaluate the situation of an individual who wants to consume a certain kind of food and is completely mistaken about the health impact of this food? We will not record a nonexistent health impact but we should record the impact of this mistaken belief on the individual's satisfaction, because this satisfaction is real. Now, whether this illusory satisfaction has a positive or negative impact on overall well-being is a matter of appreciation which can ultimately be decided by the concerned individuals' preferences over illusions. Such preferences are about the following kind of question. How do you rank: (1) a life in which you are wrongly confident you have healthy food; (2) a life in which you wrongly think your food is unhealthy; (3) a life in which you rightly think your food is unhealthy; (4) a life in which you rightly think your food is healthy? Presumably the last option is the best, but how to rank the other options depends on how much weight one puts on being healthy, being right, and being happy. Similarly, the little boy who dreams of becoming a football star may later turn sour about such illusions or cherish his happy youth.

6.4 An *ex post* evaluation

The third principle that plays a key role here is that social evaluation will be made from an *ex post* perspective. The *ex post* perspective differs from the *ex ante* perspective in the following way. The latter looks at individual well-being as it can be computed *ex ante* (for instance in terms of expected utilities) and then performs a social aggregation of the distribution of *ex ante* levels of well-being in order to evaluate the social situation. In contrast, the *ex post* approach looks at the *ex post* distribution of well-being, once all uncertainty is resolved.

---

[4]Gordon-Solmon (2005) claims that when risk is constitutive of certain valuable activities (such as risky sports or loving relations), certain elements of risk (e.g., the risk of grieving if the loved one dies) cannot be removed without devaluing these activities themselves. If this is true (which may be debated), then this is an example, different from risk-loving, of risk having a positive effect on well-being.

In case there are different possible *ex post* distributions depending on the true state of nature, then one performs an evaluation of this as a social lottery, for instance by computing the expected value of a social welfare function. But no such computation is needed when, as will be assumed here, all states of nature deliver the same *ex post* distribution of well-being. For instance, we may know for sure that there will be one winner and $n-1$ losers (in a population of n identical individuals), and the state of nature will only determine who is the winner without affecting the statistical distribution of individual outcomes. When there is no *ex ante* uncertainty about the *ex post* distribution of well-being and personal characteristics, from the standpoint of social evaluation there is no uncertainty at all.

Nonetheless, it should be stressed that the *ex post* approach need not ignore the effect of risk on individual well-being, since with a comprehensive notion of well-being one can record such effect. Similarly, the sense of agency that individuals may enjoy can also be part of the *ex post* picture. The example of gambling among n identical individuals is convenient for illustrating this point. We know that there will be one winner and $n-1$ losers. If individual well-being depends only on the *ex post* gain, then any inequality-averse criterion will declare the outcome of gambling worse than the pre-gambling distribution (which is egalitarian by the assumption that the individuals are *ex ante* identical). Therefore the *ex post* approach, in this case, favors a ban on gambling. But imagine that *ex post* well-being depends not only on the *ex post* gain, but also on *ex ante* satisfaction and on basic freedoms such as the freedom to organize games. Then a ban on gambling would improve the *ex post* distribution of gains but could very well worsen the *ex post* distribution of well-being if individuals miss the enjoyment of games and the corresponding freedom. The *ex post* approach would then reject such a ban.

In other words, taking the *ex post* point of view does not imply ignoring individuals' *ex ante* life and sense of agency, it simply consists in looking at their *ex ante* life with the benefit of hindsight about the *ex post* distribution of luck. The *ex post* perspective takes account of more information than the *ex ante* perspective. This, in itself, does not suffice to prove that it is superior but it is a key point. Indeed, the reason why the *ex post* approach is better than the *ex ante* approach is that it seeks to satisfy individuals' *informed* preferences rather than just their *ex ante ignorant* preferences.[5] In the gambling example, it is possible that *ex ante* everybody is happy to participate in the game. But such preferences are less informed than the *ex post* preferences based on full knowledge of the outcome of the game. Individual *ex post* preferences are superior because they incorporate more information about the true state of nature. It is therefore better to cater to individual *ex post* preferences than to *ex ante* preferences.

There is a bit of a paradox in the ability of the *ex post* approach to serve

---

[5] This turns on its head the argument (nicely developed in Williams 2004, for instance) that the *ex ante* approach takes account more fully of individual preferences – namely, registering risk aversion – than an *ex post* approach that supposedly only looks at final bundles. To the contrary, the *ex post* approach takes account of everything (including the *ex ante* enjoyment or fear of risk) and caters to informed preferences which are superior to ignorant preferences.

individual *ex post* preferences while nobody at the time of the evaluation, including the evaluator, knows what the true state of nature is. The trick here is simply that even when no individual agent knows his future fate, it is possible for the evaluator (as well as everybody else) to know the *ex post* distribution of well-being for sure. In the gambling example, nobody knows who wins, but it is already known that there will be one winner only. This information is sufficient for an impartial social evaluation which does not care who wins and is solely interested in the distribution of well-being.[6]

Most of the economic literature on risk and insurance adopts the *ex ante* perspective. This is probably based on the mistaken view that when the evaluator has the same information about the state of nature as the population, she cannot do better than cater to individual *ex ante* preferences. As we have seen, she can do better because, when she knows the distribution of *ex post* preferences and situations, she has all the relevant data for a fully informed evaluation. Welfare economists do consider that when individuals have mistaken beliefs, the evaluation should be based on correct information whenever possible. For instance, if consumers overestimate the quality of a product, their well-being when they buy it is not as great as they think. The same kind of correction should be performed in the case of risk,[7] and this is what the *ex post* approach does.

The *ex ante* viewpoint is also sometimes defended on the grounds that it enables the evaluator to take account of fairness in lotteries.[8] But there is no difficulty for the *ex post* viewpoint to incorporate a concern for fairness. If an indivisible prize must be given to one individual among n potential recipients, the final distribution can be deemed better by the *ex post* approach if it has a fair label attached to it. If a lottery is the best way to obtain this label, so be it. Most of our intuitive attraction toward fair lotteries has to do with non-discrimination in the selection process, and has nothing to do with lotteries as such or with the distribution of *ex ante* utilities.[9] But recall that a concern for the distribution of *ex ante* utilities can also be incorporated in the *ex post* approach with a comprehensive measure of well-being.

---

[6] When, contrary to our assumptions, there is uncertainty about the *ex post* distribution, the analysis is a little more complex but the bulk of the argument still holds true, because it is still possible for the evaluator to rank *some* social situations on the basis of the final distribution, and this seriously constrains his evaluations. See Fleurbaey (2006a) for the analysis of this more general case.

[7] For instance, if the world is deterministic, all probabilistic beliefs are wrong. But even when there are objective probabilities, there is, at the end of history, only one true state of nature, so that "correct" beliefs contain less information than *ex post* outcomes.

[8] This is Diamond's (1967) famous critique of utilitarianism.

[9] As argued in Broome (1984).

6.5   Two criteria

Equipped with these guiding principles, let us see how one can apply the concepts of Conditional Equality and Egalitarian-Equivalence in the current context. The *ex post* approach, under the assumption that there is no uncertainty about the *ex post* distribution, allows us to analyze the issue as if we knew the true state of nature. This simplifies some formulations, saving us the trouble of reasoning in terms of statistical distribution and enabling us to reason in terms of individual well-being as we have become accustomed to in the previous chapters.

One can compute individual well-being in the true state of nature as a function of responsibility characteristics (including possibly risky actions or risky dispositions), circumstance characteristics, including the luck factor, and resources. Note that resources available in the various states of nature, not just the true state, can matter because, as argued above, *ex ante* prospects may affect *ex post* well-being, and such prospects depend on resources that would have been made available in other states of nature. Note also that the circumstance characteristics can incorporate dispositions to react in different ways to different states of nature. For instance, pale skin may be a handicap in sunny weather but not in cloudy weather. Similarly, responsibility characteristics may determine changes of attitudes depending on states of nature. Even though the individual is not responsible for being in one state of nature rather than another, he may be responsible for how he reacts to various states of nature.

We can now define the two criteria that are the focus of this section.

Conditional Equality: Define a reference value of responsibility characteristics and give priority (according to the leximin criterion) to individuals who, with their current resources, circumstances including luck, and this reference value of responsibility characteristics, would be the worst-off.

This definition is essentially identical to that of Section 2.6.[10] In order to see what implications this criterion has in the current context, let us examine what happens when equality among all individuals, as measured by this criterion, is achieved. In order to make the analysis clearer, it is convenient to decompose redistributive policy into *ex ante* transfers designed to compensate for circumstance characteristics that are known *ex ante*, and specific *ex post* transfers for the compensation of luck.

We assume here that the reference responsibility characteristics are those of the most cautious individuals, because this is the relevant configuration for a discussion of option luck. Let us first examine the case in which, in absence of *ex post* transfers, these cautious individuals are already fully insured by their own

---

[10]When *ex ante* prospects matter to the computation of *ex post* well-being, well-being depends on resources available in the various states of nature, as it has just been explained. Resources are then multidimensional and this affects the definition of Conditional Equality if one wants this criterion to respect people's evaluation of *ex ante* prospects. This complication is dealt with in the next section.

private initiative.[11] In this context, full equality among them is achieved and Conditional Equality does not advocate any *ex post* transfer in this category. Now, since other individuals are evaluated by how well-off they would be if they had the cautious characteristics, it appears that they do not need any *ex post* transfer as well, and the best policy is then, as far as *ex post* transfers are concerned, a laissez-faire policy. No compensation *ex post* is made for the bad luck of those who undertake risky activities that the cautious individuals avoid.

This sounds like option luck, but before discussing option luck, let us examine what happens when the cautious do need *ex post* transfers because their private actions do not fully insure them. In this case, the cautious individuals will receive *ex post* transfers which will fully insure them if equality is achieved. Those who have more risky dispositions or behavior will obtain the same transfers, even if typically such transfers will fail to fully insure them. In other words, they will have to bear the extra risk that they take. Again, this seems quite in line with the idea of letting individuals bear the consequences of option luck. We therefore obtain here a consistent notion of option luck, without making the sloppy assumption that individuals must be held responsible for being lucky or unlucky, and without adopting an *ex ante* viewpoint in the evaluation. Even if individuals are not held responsible for their luck, they may be required to bear the consequences of the extra risk they take because their situation is evaluated by reference to what they would obtain with a more cautious behavior. The idea of option luck, in a nutshell, need not be interpreted in terms of incorporating luck into the responsibility sphere, which appears questionable, but can be redefined in terms of liberal reward as embodied in Conditional Equality.

Let us now turn to Egalitarian-Equivalence.

Egalitarian-Equivalence: Define a reference kind of circumstances including luck, and give priority (leximin) to individuals whose current level of well-being would be obtained with the least resources if their circumstances were of the reference kind (and their responsibility characteristics unchanged).

Take an individual with his current level of *ex post* well-being. He could have the same well-being with a reference kind of circumstances and a reference level of luck, but with a different quantity of resources. We want to evaluate his situation by this "equivalent" quantity of resources.[12]

One can get an idea of the implications of the Egalitarian-Equivalence criterion by looking at a situation in which full equality, according to it, is achieved. The compensation principle, fully satisfied by this criterion, implies that individuals with the same responsibility characteristics will obtain the same level of

---

[11] The most cautious individuals need not be extremely risk averse. Sometimes, being mildly risk averse suffices to take full insurance. (This is the case with actuarially fair insurance contracts against loss of replaceable wealth.)

[12] Again, a difficulty here is that resources are multidimensional because even when there is only one good like money, there is one quantity for each state of nature. As a consequence, one must not only choose reference circumstances and luck but also a certain kind of equivalent resources. The most natural, and simplest, option consists in taking a certain (i.e., riskless) quantity as the kind of resources considered for the computation.

well-being. This means that all categories of individuals will be fully insured, with a level of well-being that depends on their responsibility characteristics. This produces a situation similar to that advocated by Le Grand (1991), as recalled in the introduction. Every category of individuals will bear the average consequences (approximately) of their risky behavior but not the consequences of their personal luck.

A Dworkinian purist could object that the risk-lovers are prevented from living the kind of life they like. But there are two categories of risk-lovers to distinguish. The ordinary risk-lovers like risk *ex ante* and regret their folly once they discover that they are unlucky. For these, the evaluator should not feel compelled to respect their *ex ante* preferences since they are based on ignorance of their bad luck. But there can be super risk-lovers who, even when they lose, are still happy *ex post* to have played the game. This happens when the thrill provided by risk is so great that it compensates the disappointment of losing. Such individuals have preferences over resources which are then decreasing: They would not want to receive more resources in bad states of nature because this would reduce the thrill. This corresponds to preferences with satiation, which have been studied in Section 3.7, and it is indeed possible, in this case, for the Egalitarian-Equivalence criterion to leave the satiated individuals with less resources than others, which means here that the super risk-lovers are allowed to live their dangerous life.[13]

Let us illustrate the concepts introduced here with a simple example. In order to avoid the use of mathematical functions (representing utility), let us measure well-being in monetary terms, as in Examples 1.1, 1.2 and 1.4.

Example 6.1 *Assume that individuals receive a bequest and decide to invest it or not. The return on this investment is random and equals either +100% or −100%. Well-being equals their final wealth. Individuals can be submitted to transfers ex ante, i.e., before the investment decision, and possibly ex post as well, after the return on investment is known:*

$$well\text{-}being \;=\; ex\ post\ transfer\;+$$

$$(bequest \pm ex\ ante\ transfer) \times \begin{cases} 1 & \textit{if doesn't invest} \\ 2 & \textit{if invests and lucky} \\ 0 & \textit{if invests and unlucky.} \end{cases}$$

In this example, people's circumstances consist in luck and a quantity of bequest. Their investment decision is their responsibility characteristic. To fix ideas, let us consider a population composed of the following proportions. Sixty percent of the population (the "poor") receive no bequest while forty percent (the "rich") receive a bequest of $1,000,000 each. Observe that the poor have no bequest to invest, but if an *ex ante* transfer is made to them they can invest if they wish. Assume that in each of these two categories, half do not invest (the "cautious") and half do invest (the "entrepreneurs"). The cautious simply

---

[13]As explained in the previous section, it is also possible for considerations of freedom to make it disastrous to insure people against their will.

keep their bequest as it is, while the entrepreneurs invest it and either double it
if they are lucky, or lose it if they are unlucky. Assume that one fifth only of the
entrepreneurs are unlucky (the average rate of return is then 60%). It is possible
to make transfers *ex post* depending on luck. The profile of the population is
summarized in Table 6.1.

Table 6.1: Composition of the population

	cautious	lucky entrepreneurs	unlucky entrepreneurs
poor	30%	24%	6%
rich	20%	16%	4%

The obvious policy, as far as *ex ante* transfers are concerned, is to equalize
initial endowments by redistributing bequests. Everyone then obtains $400,000.
The cautious keep it safe while the entrepreneurs invest it and either obtain
$800,000 or lose everything. The average wealth *ex post*, among entrepreneurs,
is $640,000. Let us now look at *ex post* transfers.

Conditional Equality does not make any redistribution *ex post* when the
reference type is cautious. The idea is that the entrepreneurs could all obtain
$400,000 like the cautious, independently of their luck, and therefore there is
no need to redistribute among them. The final distribution then has half of the
population (the cautious) with $400,000, forty percent with $800,000 and ten
percent with $0.

Egalitarian-Equivalence refers to a reference level of bequest and a reference
rate of return (which corresponds to a reference level of luck) in order to compute
an equivalent *ex ante* transfer[14] in the following manner:

$$\text{actual well-being} \quad = \quad (\text{reference bequest} \pm \text{equivalent transfer})$$
$$\times \begin{cases} 1 \text{ if doesn't invest} \\ \text{reference return if invests.} \end{cases}$$

The optimal allocation is such that the equivalent transfer is the same for all
individuals. When average return (60%) is taken as the reference, Egalitarian-
Equivalence does not redistribute *ex post* between the investors and the cautious,
but equalizes the gains among the former, leaving each of them with $640,000
while the cautious end up with $400,000. This result does not depend on the ref-
erence bequest that is chosen since the reference bequest only adds or subtracts
a constant in the computation of the equivalent transfer.[15]

One complication has been ignored in this example and throughout this section. It has been assumed that risky actions (such as investing, in the above
example) are fixed and put into the responsibility sphere. But this is questionable when such actions are influenced by personal circumstances and when taxes

---

[14]The equivalent *ex post* transfer is at zero in this computation. Alternative ways of computing equivalent transfers are possible, they yield similar results.

[15]With maximal luck as the reference, a transfer from the cautious to the entrepreneurs
would be made in order to offer the latter the maximal rate of return *ex post*, no matter whether
they are lucky or unlucky. The cautious would all have $346,667 and the entrepreneurs would
all have $693,333.

and transfers can depend on such actions and can therefore directly influence them as well. It is then more sensible to hold individuals responsible for their risky dispositions but to incorporate their actions into the category of external "resources" (or, if one prefers, "functionings"), as we have done for instance with labor in Chapters 4 and 5. This is analyzed in the next section, where it is shown, with the help of some formalism, that the bulk of the above analysis remains valid.

6.6   *Risky actions and incentives

It is convenient to deal with an example. Let us imagine that individual i's utility, *ex post*, depends on three things: the level of consumption $c_i \in \mathbb{R}_+$, an enjoyable but dangerous activity $s_i \in \mathbb{R}_+$ (e.g., smoking, skiing, surfing, sky-diving, storm-chasing,...), and health $h_i \in [0,1]$ which can be adversely affected by the risky activity. Final utility is thus defined as $u_i(c_i, s_i, h_i)$.

The danger associated with s_i is a stochastic level of pre-treatment health $\theta_i \in [0,1]$ determined by a cumulative distribution function $F_i(\theta_i \mid s_i) : [0,1] \rightarrow [0,1]$. As this expression shows, the distribution of θ_i depends on s_i, since the more one practices the dangerous activity, the more likely it is that one will suffer a bad shock. The distribution is also specific to the individual, since different persons may be unequally vulnerable. We may call the function F_i itself the "vulnerability" of i, and the value of $F_i(\theta_i \mid s_i)$, which lies between 0 and 1, his "luck."

When the level θ_i is known *ex post*, the individual still has some leeway as regards his final health. There is a budget constraint, and in particular the medical cost of obtaining health h_i starting from level θ_i is a function $p(h_i, \theta_i) : [0,1]^2 \rightarrow \mathbb{R}_+$ such that $p(h, \theta) = 0$ whenever $h \leq \theta$. There is also a transfer policy which submits i to a transfer $t(w_i, s_i, h_i, \theta_i) \in \mathbb{R}$ as a function of his wealth $w_i \in \mathbb{R}_+$, his behavior and his health situation. This transfer function can encapsulate a wealth transfer, a tax on the risky activity, a reimbursement of medical expenditures. The *ex post* program for i is thus:

$$\max_{c_i, h_i} u_i(c_i, s_i, h_i)$$
$$\text{s.t. } c_i + s_i + p(h_i, \theta_i) = w_i + t(w_i, s_i, h_i, \theta_i).$$

Let $\bar{u}_i(t(.), s_i, \theta_i, w_i)$ denote the indirect function which is equal to this maximum. We will assume that $\bar{u}_i$ is increasing in θ_i, which means that $t(.)$ is not overly generous toward those who suffer bad luck.

Ex ante, the problem for i is to choose the level of s_i so as, for instance, to maximize expected utility:

$$\max_{s_i} \int_0^1 \bar{u}_i(t(.), s_i, \theta_i, w_i) dF_i(\theta_i \mid s_i).$$

Let $s(t(.), F_i, w_i, u_i)$ denote the chosen level of s_i.

In this example, it makes little sense to hold i responsible for s_i, since s_i is directly influenced by the transfer policy but also by i's vulnerability F_i. As in the previous chapters, we will hold the individual responsible only for u_i.[16]

The method for the computation of Conditional Equality and Egalitarian-Equivalence is to define an *ex post* function in which the circumstance and responsibility factors appear explicitly. Let $F_i^{-1}(. \mid s_i)$ denote the inverse of $F_i(. \mid s_i)$. One can define:

$$v(t(.), F_i, \lambda_i, w_i, u_i) = \bar{u}_i \left(t(.), s(t(.), F_i, w_i, u_i), F_i^{-1}(\lambda_i \mid s(t(.), F_i, w_i, u_i)), w_i \right).$$

The indirect function v tells us the *ex post* utility level of an individual facing policy $t(.)$, endowed with circumstances F_i, w_i and luck λ_i, and with utility function u_i. Such an individual would choose $s_i = s(t(.), F_i, w_i, u_i)$ *ex ante*, endure the shock $\theta_i = F_i^{-1}(\lambda_i \mid s_i)$ *ex post*, and therefore end up with utility level $\bar{u}_i(t(.), s_i, \theta_i, w_i)$. We will assume here that v is always increasing in $t(.)$ when $t(.)$ is a constant function (i.e., a lump-sum transfer).[17]

A naive application of the Conditional Equality idea would simply evaluate i's situation by computing

$$v(t(.), F_i, \lambda_i, w_i, \tilde{u}),$$

where $\tilde{u}$ is a reference utility function. The trouble here is that the expressions $v(t(.), F_i, \lambda_i, w_i, u_i)$ and $v(t(.), F_i, \lambda_i, w_i, \tilde{u})$ may disagree about how to rank different transfer policies $t(.)$. Relying on the latter may therefore lead us to advocate Pareto-inefficient policies.

The solution to this problem, as we have already seen in the previous chapter, is to compute a hypothetical transfer before substituting $\tilde{u}$ to u_i in the function. Let $\hat{t}_i$ denote a constant function (i.e., a lump-sum transfer) satisfying the equation

$$u_i(c_i, s_i, h_i) = v(\hat{t}_i, F_i, \lambda_i, w_i, u_i).$$

Since, by assumption, for all utility functions u_i the indirect function v is monotonically increasing in $\hat{t}_i$, this eliminates the conflict between u_i and $\tilde{u}$ over the ranking of policies. One can then evaluate individual situations, for Conditional Equality, by computing:

$$v(\hat{t}_i, F_i, \lambda_i, w_i, \tilde{u}).$$

The comparison of different policies is then made by applying the maximin or leximin criterion to the vector $\left(v(\hat{t}_i, F_i, \lambda_i, w_i, \tilde{u}) \right)_{i \in N}$.

---

[16] In this example one could also easily put w_i in the responsibility sphere, if one considered that inequalities in wealth are legitimate. We will not do so here, but the modifications to what is presented in this section would be straightforward.

[17] In general this is not necessarily true for low levels of λ_i, because with a greater wealth the agent may be induced to take more risk, ending up with a lower utility in case of bad luck. When this happens the analysis of this section has to be modified (lump-sum transfers should be replaced by something else in the computation of equivalent transfers).

The Egalitarian-Equivalence approach fixes a reference level of luck, $\tilde{\lambda}$, as well as a reference vulnerability $\tilde{F}$ and reference wealth $\tilde{w}$, and computes an equivalent lump-sum transfer $\tilde{t}_i$ solution to the equation:

$$u_i(c_i, s_i, h_i) = v(\tilde{t}_i, \tilde{F}, \tilde{\lambda}, \tilde{w}, u_i).$$

It then applies the maximin or leximin criterion to the vector $(\tilde{t}_i)_{i \in N}$.

In order to illustrate the difference between the two solutions, we may note the following fact: If i and j are such that $F_i = F_j$, $w_i = w_j$, $u_i(.) = u_j(.)$ and $\lambda_i > \lambda_j$, then necessarily $\tilde{t}_i > \tilde{t}_j$. (This is because $s_i = s_j$, so that, recalling that $\bar{u}_i$ is increasing in θ_i, necessarily $u_i(c_i, s_i, h_i) > u_j(c_j, s_j, h_j)$, implying that $v(\tilde{t}_i, \tilde{F}, \tilde{\lambda}, \tilde{w}, u_i) > v(\tilde{t}_j, \tilde{F}, \tilde{\lambda}, \tilde{w}, u_i)$.) This fact means that, as was already noted in the previous section, bad luck always entails a greater degree of priority, everything else equal, for Egalitarian-Equivalence.

This need not be the case for Conditional Equality. If i and j are as described above (they are *ex ante* identical and i is more lucky than j), one may nonetheless have the reverse ranking:

$$v(\hat{t}_i, F_i, \lambda_i, w_i, \tilde{u}) < v(\hat{t}_j, F_j, \lambda_j, w_j, \tilde{u}).$$

This reversal can occur when a generous insurance policy is implemented through t. Then it may be that, even though $u_i(c_i, s_i, h_i) > u_j(c_j, s_j, h_j)$, one has $\hat{t}_i < \hat{t}_j$ because the compensation of bad luck received by j is equivalent to receiving a greater lump-sum transfer. And if $\tilde{u}$ represents a more cautious type of preferences, $v(\hat{t}, F, \lambda, w, \tilde{u})$ is less sensitive to λ and more sensitive to $\hat{t}$ than $v(\hat{t}, F, \lambda, w, u_i)$. This shows, once again, that Conditional Equality is typically less generous than Egalitarian-Equivalence as far as the compensation of bad luck is concerned, at least when the reference preferences are the most risk averse of the population.

6.7   *The intrinsic failure of insurance markets

Insurance markets are known for being particularly vulnerable to market failures due to adverse selection and moral hazard. Here we will show that they suffer from a deeper problem.

In a nutshell, the problem is that in absence of market failures, an insurance market generates an allocation that is *ex ante* Pareto-efficient, and that such an allocation is unlikely to be a social welfare optimum. This means that, as far as insurance markets are concerned, the second welfare theorem – according to which any efficient allocation can be obtained by a competitive equilibrium after appropriate transfers – remains formally true for *ex ante* efficient allocations but no longer implies that any social welfare optimum can be obtained by competitive insurance markets operating after suitable *ex ante* transfers. In other words, the second welfare theorem is no longer a relevant "welfare" result in the context of insurance.

Let us consider a simple one-period exchange economy in which $x_{is} \in \mathbb{R}^{\ell}_{+}$ is the vector of consumption goods consumed by $i \in N$ in state $s \in S$ (where

S is assumed to be finite). Let $x_i = (x_{is})_{s \in S}$ and $x_N = (x_i)_{i \in N}$. Agent i has an initial endowment $\omega_i \in \mathbb{R}_+^\ell$. In state s, he is submitted to a luck factor λ_{is} which affects his endowment (changed into $\omega_i + \lambda_{is}$) and a luck factor λ'_{is} which directly alters his satisfaction. In the market, he faces prices $p_s \in \mathbb{R}_{++}^\ell$. When insurance markets are open which allow agents to transfer resources from one state to the other, the vectors p_s operate as prices for contingent commodities and the budget constraint can be simply written as

$$\sum_{s \in S} p_s x_{is} \le \sum_{s \in S} p_s (\omega_i + \lambda_{is}).$$

Agent i has an expected utility function

$$U_i(x_i) = \sum_{s \in S} \pi_{is} u_i(x_{is}, \lambda'_{is}),$$

where $\pi_i = (\pi_{is})_{s \in S}$ is the vector of subjective probabilities and u_i is the Bernoulli utility function which depends not only on consumption but also on the luck factor λ'_{is}.

An allocation x_N is feasible if for all $s \in N$,

$$\sum_{i \in N} x_{is} = \sum_{i \in N} (\omega_i + \lambda_{is}).$$

It is *ex ante* Pareto-efficient if there is no other feasible allocation x'_N such that $U_i(x'_i) \ge U_i(x_i)$ for all $i \in N$, with at least one strict inequality.

An allocation x_N is a Walrasian equilibrium if it is feasible and if there is a price vector $p = (p_s)_{s \in S}$ such that for all $i \in N$, x_i maximizes U_i under the budget constraint. The first welfare theorem applies here when for all $i \in N$, u_i is locally non-satiated[18] in x_{is} for all λ'_{is}: *every Walrasian equilibrium is ex ante Pareto-efficient.* (Indeed, $\pi_i > 0$, so that, when u_i is locally non-satiated in x_{is} for every s, U_i is locally non-satiated in x_i and the standard proof of this theorem works.)

A corollary of this first welfare theorem is that, if for all $i \in N$, u_i is locally non-satiated and concave in x_{is} for all λ'_{is}, then, *for every Walrasian equilibrium x_N^* there is $(\alpha_i)_{i \in N} \in \mathbb{R}_+^n$ such that x_N^* maximizes $\sum_{i \in N} \alpha_i U_i(x_i)$ over the set of feasible allocations.*[19]

Now consider two agents i and j who are "ex ante identical" in x_N^* under the price vector p, i.e., such that $u_i = u_j$, $\pi_i = \pi_j$, $\omega_i = \omega_j$, and for some permutation σ over the set S, for all $s \in S$, $\pi_{i\sigma(s)} = \pi_{is}$, $p_{\sigma(s)} = p_s$, $\lambda_{is} = \lambda_{j\sigma(s)}$

---

[18]i.e., for every x_{is}, every neighborhood of x_{is}, there is x'_{is} in this neighborhood such that $u_i(x'_{is}, \lambda'_{is}) > u_i(x_{is}, \lambda'_{is})$.

[19]This is because U_i is then concave for all $i \in N$, implying that the set of feasible utilities $\{(U_i(x_i))_{i \in N} \mid x_N \text{ is feasible}\}$ is convex. The first welfare theorem can be understood as saying that there is no intersection between this set and the other convex set $\left\{ (U_i(x_i))_{i \in N} \mid (U_i(x_i))_{i \in N} > (U_i(x_i^*))_{i \in N} \right\}$. The separating hyperplane theorem then implies that there is $(\alpha_i)_{i \in N} \in \mathbb{R}_+^n$ such that $(U_i(x_i^*))_{i \in N}$ maximizes $\sum_{i \in N} \alpha_i U_i$ over the set of feasible utilities.

and $\lambda'_{is} = \lambda'_{j\sigma(s)}$. In other words, they have identical characteristics and, up to a permutation of states s, they face exactly the same luck factors. This definition of *ex ante* identical agents is a little restrictive and one could enlarge it at the cost of cumbersome notations (for instance, state s for i might be equivalent to two states s', s'' for j), but this will suffice for our purposes. Since these two agents are identical *ex ante* and face the same prospects, necessarily $U_i(x_i^*) = U_j(x_j^*)$.

Moreover, the set

$$\left\{ (U_i(x_i), U_j(x_j)) \mid x_i + x_j = x_i^* + x_j^* \right\}$$

is symmetric with respect to the $45°$ line, so that $\left(U_i(x_i^*), U_j(x_j^*) \right)$ maximizes $U_i + U_j$ in this set. Equivalently, (x_i^*, x_j^*) maximizes $U_i(x_i) + U_j(x_j)$ under the constraint $x_i + x_j = x_i^* + x_j^*$. Note that, since $\pi_i = \pi_j$,

$$
\begin{aligned}
U_i(x_i) + U_j(x_j) &= \sum_{s \in S} \pi_{is} u_i(x_{is}, \lambda'_{is}) + \sum_{s \in S} \pi_{js} u_j(x_{js}, \lambda'_{js}) \\
&= \sum_{s \in S} \pi_{is} \left[u_i(x_{is}, \lambda'_{is}) + u_j(x_{js}, \lambda'_{js}) \right],
\end{aligned}
$$

and recall that $x_i + x_j = x_i^* + x_j^*$ means that for all $s \in S$, $x_{is} + x_{js} = x_{is}^* + x_{js}^*$.

Therefore, necessarily for all $s \in S$ such that $\pi_{is} > 0$, (x_{is}^*, x_{js}^*) maximizes $u_i(x_{is}, \lambda'_{is}) + u_j(x_{js}, \lambda'_{js})$ under the constraint $x_{is} + x_{js} = x_{is}^* + x_{js}^*$. By extension to more than two agents, we have then proved the following result:

Proposition 6.1 *Assume that for all $i \in N$, u_i is locally non-satiated and concave in x_{is} for all λ'_{is}. For every Walrasian equilibrium x_N^*, every subgroup $G \subseteq N$ of agents who are ex ante identical, and for every $s \in S$, $x_{Gs}^* = (x_{is}^*)_{i \in G}$ maximizes $\sum_{i \in G} u_i(x_{is}, \lambda'_{is})$ under the constraint $\sum_{i \in G} x_{is} = \sum_{i \in G} x_{is}^*$.*

In a nutshell, *ex ante* identical agents are treated in a utilitarian way, their sum of utilities being maximized whatever the state of nature.[20] Let us now examine how this can be assessed from the standpoint of social welfare. The disturbing feature of this result is that agents who are *ex ante* identical may be different *ex post*, because in a particular state s they may be hit differently by their own luck factors.

Let us assume for a moment that well-being, in the true state s, is measured by the function $u_i(x_{is}, \lambda'_{is})$. This means that *ex ante* prospects, as appreciated by the agent through $U_i(x_i)$, are not considered relevant. In this perspective, the compensation principle advocates equalizing the agents' well-being *ex post* when they are *ex ante* identical, since they differ only with respect to the luck factors for which they are not responsible.

---

[20] Dworkin (2002) objects to this description of the result that this is not necessarily utilitarian, because a utilitarian planner might retain a different measurement of utility. The point of the result, as it should be obvious, is that insurance markets share some qualitative and, possibly, quantitative, features with utilitarianism.

Let us first examine two agents whose endowments only are hit differently: $\lambda_{is} \neq \lambda_{js}$, $\lambda'_{is} = \lambda'_{js}$. One immediately sees that maximizing $\sum_{i \in G} u_i(x_{is}, \lambda'_{is})$ under the constraint $\sum_{i \in G} x_{is} = \sum_{i \in G} x^*_{is}$ will induce $u_i(x_{is}, \lambda'_{is}) = u_j(x_{js}, \lambda'_{js})$ as a possible solution, and as the only solution if utility functions are strictly concave. This is satisfactory at the bar of the compensation principle. Since it is obvious that appropriate lump-sum transfers made *ex ante* can adequately compensate for differences in initial endowments, one then sees that, when luck only affects endowments, insurance markets can correctly deal with the compensation of luck factors *ex post*.

Things are much less favorable when luck also affects utility directly: $\lambda'_{is} \neq \lambda'_{js}$. Then, typically, maximizing $\sum_{i \in G} u_i(x_{is}, \lambda'_{is})$ under the constraint $\sum_{i \in G} x_{is} = \sum_{i \in G} x^*_{is}$ will induce $u_i(x_{is}, \lambda'_{is}) > u_j(x_{js}, \lambda'_{js})$ when λ'_{is} entails a greater marginal utility than λ'_{js} with respect to x_{is}. It is well known since Arrow (1971) and Sen (1973) that the utilitarian approach is not well equipped to correct handicaps that lower utility levels without increasing marginal utility. The fact that maximizing expected utility induces strange properties of insurance demand for shocks affecting utility, since agents may demand insurance against the non-occurrence of damage, has long been recognized in insurance theory.[21] We find again an illustration of this problem here. The compensation principle will not be satisfied, and transfers between i and j will go to the agent with greater *marginal* utility even if he is also the agent with greater *level* of utility. Therefore, we reach here the conclusion that insurance markets should not be trusted in order to deal with luck factors which affect utility directly and not only endowments. Insurance markets against fire and theft (of replaceable objects!) are fine, but they should not be relied upon in order to deal with accidents, for instance.

We have been dealing here with a simple exchange economy. But recall from Section 4.2 that a difference in productive skills can be viewed essentially as a difference in the disutility of earning a certain level of pre-tax income. Therefore, with little change it can be shown that insurance markets cannot be used in order to compensate for luck factors which affect productivity.

The condemnation of insurance markets relies here on the compensation principle, and at this point one may wonder whether relying on Conditional Equality, which leans toward liberal reward more than toward compensation, would yield different conclusions. But Conditional Equality still makes transfers in favor of the unlucky when their bad luck lowers utility undoubtedly (i.e., including for the reference utility function), whereas the utilitarian criterion can make transfers in the reverse direction. In other words, the utilitarian criterion totally abandons the compensation ideal whereas Conditional Equality does retain it to some extent.

Moreover, the principle of liberal reward itself is not well served by insurance markets. In fact, even the more basic principle of impartiality, which is contained in the compensation principle as well as the liberal reward principle since both imply that identical agents should obtain equivalent resources, is violated by

---

[21] See Cook and Graham (1977), Schlesinger (1984).

insurance markets. Take two individuals who are *ex post* identical, in the sense that they have the same endowment $\omega_i + \lambda_{is}$ and the same utility function $u_i(., \lambda'_{is})$ in the true state s. From the *ex post* perspective it appears obvious that they should receive the same resources, or at least equivalent bundles of resources. Both Conditional Equality and Egalitarian-Equivalence do treat such agents identically, of course, since they are identical in their responsibility and circumstance characteristics. But this is not the case with the insurance market, because these agents may have different situations in other states of nature, and this may have led them to make different arrangements for the true state s. From the *ex post* standpoint, it appears utterly questionable to refer to counterfactual states (that do not correspond to any reality since the true state is s) in order to give different resources to identical agents. This is, nonetheless, what insurance markets do. In conclusion, the deep flaw of insurance markets does not come from any connection with liberal reward but from their connection with the *ex ante* perspective.

The above reasoning can be intuitively summarized as follows. Insurance markets, when they are *ex ante* efficient and when the set of feasible utilities is convex, maximize a weighted sum of utilities $\sum_{i \in N} \alpha_i U_i$. Therefore, in the true state of nature s, the same sum $\sum_{i \in N} \alpha_i u_i$ is maximized. Since the market is an impartial procedure, agents who are identical *ex ante* will have the same weight α_i, which entails that in the true state s the sum of their utilities is maximized, *even if they are ex post unequal in their luck*. This is a strong violation of the compensation principle. Conversely, agents who are not identical *ex ante* may have different weights α_i, *even if they are identical ex post*, which entails a violation of impartiality *ex post*.

Here one can ask whether these negative conclusions are alleviated if one assumes that agents are more prudent, in particular if their decision criterion is the maximin instead of expected utility. Proposition 6.1 is indeed substantially modified under this alternative behavioral assumption. Let us first imagine that utilities are transformed by a concave function: φ, so that one now has

$$U_i(x_i) = \sum_{s \in S} \pi_s \varphi(u_i(x_{is}, \lambda'_{is})).$$

Proposition 6.1 is then modified so that for every $s \in S$, x^*_{Gs} maximizes

$$\sum_{i \in G} \varphi(u_i(x_{is}, \lambda'_{is})).$$

When φ becomes more and more concave, the ranking obtained by this formula converges toward the leximin ranking. Therefore, in this case, for agents who are *ex ante* identical, the Walrasian equilibrium correctly gives priority to the worst-off in every state of nature.

Unfortunately, this does not mean that the compensation principle, or even impartiality, is satisfied when agents are maximinners. This is because the subsets of *ex ante* identical agents are typically strict subsets of the subsets of agents with identical u_i, and overlap with the subsets of *ex post* identical agents.

The Walrasian equilibrium therefore gives priority to the worst-off agents in too small groups and fails to make adequate transfers between agents with identical u_i but different *ex ante* characteristics. In practical terms, this means that a policy that only consists of *ex ante* transfers has to be supplemented by *ex post* transfers in order to satisfy the compensation principle or *ex post* impartiality.

The fact that, no matter whether agents are expected utility maximizers or maximinners, an optimal social state cannot be achieved in general by simply performing *ex ante* lump-sum transfers and letting insurance markets freely operate means, as announced above, that *the second welfare theorem loses its ethical relevance for insurance markets*. The second welfare theorem holds for insurance markets only with respect to social criteria of the *ex ante* sort (including utilitarianism which, concerned with the sum of expected utilities, is at the same time an *ex ante* and an *ex post* criterion). Most of the economics of risk adopts the *ex ante* viewpoint in order to evaluate the performance of markets, and therefore fails to see the problem. Hammond (1981) warned about this difficulty but this author eventually adopted utilitarianism and thereby avoided the conflict between the *ex ante* and *ex post* viewpoints. If one adopts an *ex post* egalitarian approach, as defended here, insurance markets are seen as having a special flaw that ordinary markets do not have.

All this analysis would be modified if, recalling the principle that well-being should be a comprehensive notion, well-being in the true state s were computed as a function of *ex post* utility $u_i(x_{is}, \lambda'_{is})$ *and* of *ex ante* utility $U_i(x_i)$. Suppose, to take an extreme case, that only *ex ante* utility matters. In that particular case, insurance markets (in absence of market failures) are acceptable, after initial transfers have equalized the agents' endowments properly. In less extreme cases where both $u_i(x_{is}, \lambda'_{is})$ and $U_i(x_i)$ matter to *ex post* well-being, insurance markets will not be fully acceptable in general, but the operation of *ex post* transfers in order to enforce the compensation principle might have to be curbed in order to let the agents enjoy, to some extent, their *ex ante* prospects as they see them.[22] In practice, one can then expect that some amount of minimal compulsory insurance will have to be imposed, for instance against severe accidents, letting the agents free to buy extra insurance if they wish. A detailed study of optimal insurance policies, which would have to incorporate adverse selection and/or moral hazard issues as well in order to be realistic, will not be undertaken here.

In many ways this chapter is but an exploratory venture into a wide unknown territory. An axiomatic analysis of the solutions presented in the previous sections would be worthwhile, and a detailed examination of public policies in a realistic setting would certainly uncover many new issues.

---

[22] This does not only concern the super risk-lovers mentioned in Section 6.5, who gamble on property and are happy even when they lose. One can also think of agents who want to spend money when they are fit rather than if they are crippled by an accident, and are so unhappy to pay a strong tax for the disabled that, even after their own accident, they still regret not having had enough good time beforehand.

6.8   Dworkin's hypothetical insurance

Dworkin's faith in insurance markets (which is understandable in view of the fact that most economic analyses adopt the *ex ante* viewpoint) leads him to rely on such markets in order to calibrate the transfers between lucky and unlucky agents, even when such luck comes with the birth lottery of talents. Since individuals cannot buy insurance before they are born, he imagines a hypothetical insurance market in which, behind a veil of ignorance hiding their personal talents and handicaps, individuals could take an insurance plan. The net payments of insurance premiums and indemnities that would occur *ex post* after the operation of such a hypothetical market can, according to him, give us an idea of the taxes and transfers that a public authority should implement.

We have seen in the previous section that insurance markets, in ideal circumstances without market failures, produce at best allocations that are efficient *ex ante*, but fail to be satisfactory for any reasonable *ex post* social welfare criterion that obeys the compensation principle to some extent (like Conditional Equality or Egalitarian-Equivalence). Insurance markets do not correctly compensate the unlucky, except in the special case of bad luck involving only the loss of replaceable wealth. Damages to personal talents which affect either productive capacities or consumption capacities do not fall into this category and cannot be properly treated by insurance markets. This is because insurance markets are devoted to satisfying people's *ex ante* (ignorant) desires, whereas a good social criterion, as argued in Section 6.4, must adopt the *ex post* viewpoint which takes advantage of knowledge of the *ex post* distribution. Typically, *ex ante* individuals are too willing to sacrifice their situation in a state of nature in which they have low marginal utility, because they hope to enjoy resources better in states of nature with greater marginal utility. We then obtain allocations which look like the allocations one would obtain with a classical utilitarian approach, i.e., individuals with equal marginal utility at the same levels of resources eventually get the same amount of resources, which is fine – this compensates for losses in replaceable property – while those with lower marginal utility get less of the resources than the others, which is much less fine. Indeed, when their low marginal utility is due to the fact that they have been unlucky and suffer from a loss of ability to enjoy resources, this dramatically violates the compensation principle which would require the reverse direction of transfers between these people.

The *ex ante* viewpoint is satisfied with insurance markets because it only seeks to satisfy individual *ex ante* preferences, which such markets serve well. For the *ex post* viewpoint, the perspective is quite different since the individuals who will end up in the bad situation appear just to be ignorantly acting against their own interests, and there is no reason to blindly condone their *ex ante* decisions.

Once it is understood that insurance markets are not trustworthy in the case of risk to personal talents, it immediately appears that Dworkin's idea to rely on such markets for the case of the birth lottery is wrongheaded. The fact that this will entail policies which have more to do with utilitarianism than with equality of resources has already been extensively shown by Roemer (1985, 2002a),[23] in results which are generalized in the analysis of the previous section. This utilitarian flavor of hypothetical insurance is not only bad in terms of the compensation principle, but also for the liberal reward principle. This is because transfers organized according to hypothetical insurance are sensitive to individual risk aversion. Recall that a basic consequence of liberal reward, exhibited in solutions like Conditional Equality and Egalitarian-Equivalence, is that transfers depend only on individual ordinal preferences, not on utility functions. In contrast, with hypothetical insurance, transfers for differential talent will depend on individual risk aversion over the birth lottery, even when the aim is to make transfers after the birth lottery has operated and *ex ante* risk aversion has become irrelevant. Advocates of hypothetical insurance would reply that the fair situation obtained in the hypothetical market is useful as a reference for devising just transfers. But since we have established that insurance markets do not produce a fair situation in the case of talents, this argument cannot be taken on board.

Dworkin (2000, 2002) has suggested that if agents buy insurance not in order to maximize expected utility but only in order to avoid catastrophes, the "utilitarian" consequences of insurance markets would be alleviated. In the previous section we have seen that the failure of insurance markets to satisfy compensation persists, albeit to a lesser extent, when agents are maximinners, because equality between *ex ante* identical individuals will be sought, but not always between individuals with identical responsibility characteristics as would be requested by the compensation principle. However, this problem is allevi- ated when agents with identical preferences are all *ex ante* identical. This is precisely a characteristic of the hypothetical insurance market when it is applied to the birth lottery (but not necessarily when it is applied to other contexts such as unemployment), since by assumption individuals are given equal initial en- dowments in this market, and face identical prospects with respect to talents. Assuming that individuals are maximinners therefore is sufficient to ensure that the hypothetical insurance applied to the birth lottery satisfies *Equal Well-Being for Equal Responsibility*.

The outlook is also improved for the liberal reward principle in this case. When all individuals are maximinners, hypothetical insurance treats individuals with the same ordinal preferences as identical agents, because utility functions do not matter in this case in order to determine individual demand for insurance. Moreover, independently of individual behavior rules, when all talents are the same, the insurance market collapses and the equal endowments in this market transform into equal resources after birth. *Equal Treatment for Uniform Cir- cumstances* is therefore satisfied. In the case when utility functions and talents are independently distributed, the allocation that results from the hypothetical insurance is rather nice. It puts all individuals with identical preferences in equivalent situations (assuming this is feasible with the available resources) and gives to each subgroup with identical preferences the same amount of resources

---

[23] See also Moreno-Ternero and Roemer (2007).

per capita.[24]

Assuming that individuals are extremely risk averse therefore provides a way to make the hypothetical insurance look more attractive. Since this assumption is, however, empirically and prudentially questionable, in view of the fact that the maximin criterion is too cautious a decision rule, hypothetical insurance does not find its salvation along this route.

There remains, however, a glimpse of hope for the advocate of insurance markets. We have seen in the previous section that, if well-being is measured *ex post* but takes account of periods in which individuals live with uncertain prospects, then it may be good for well-being to go some way in the direction of respecting individuals' *ex ante* decisions. In other words, people make uninformed decisions *ex ante* but these are their decisions and forcing them to do otherwise appears bad to them, at least until uncertainty is resolved. Therefore, it may be that in practice insurance markets, possibly with some safeguards, are not always a bad solution, even as far as personal talents are concerned.

These considerations do not appear promising for the hypothetical insurance. They are valid only when people do make decisions and live with these decisions for some time, so that their *ex post* well-being is strongly influenced by their perception of their *ex ante* prospects. In the hypothetical insurance market, in contrast, people operate under a veil of ignorance and make hypothetical decisions. It is as if they were souls taking insurance before being incarnated in particular bodies with special talents. Because actual people do not live before being born (as far as we know, and as far as it seems relevant for the purpose of social evaluation), there is no sense in which one could say that their current post-birth well-being is influenced by their enjoyment of having made good insurance decisions before being born. Therefore there is no hope to save the hypothetical insurance market by invoking a conception of well-being that incorporates *ex ante* utility. Ex-ante utility is not enjoyed by people in this case, in any reasonable sense.

Dworkin's general approach to the theory of equality of resources is very inspiring and deserves much praise, but we are now in a position to describe where and how it goes astray. He starts with the idea of the no-envy criterion, which we have seen to be a good starting point for defining equality in a multidimensional context. Dworkin aptly sees that personal talents should be counted among resources to be submitted to the envy test if compensation of personal handicaps by external transfers is to be envisaged. And he correctly notes that the envy test is likely to fail in the sense that envy-free allocations may not exist. He then argues that, applied to the context of uncertainty, the correct viewpoint for the evaluation of personal bundles is the *ex ante* viewpoint, because this is how one can take account of people's desires about more or less risky lifestyles. The envy test in the *ex ante* context is easily satisfied by operating an insurance market with equal initial endowments. Now, adopting the *ex ante* viewpoint is his main mistake here. As we have seen, it is indeed

---

[24]This situation corresponds to a solution introduced in Section 2.7 (Average Egalitarian-Equivalence).

important to take account of people's wishes about lifestyles, but the correct viewpoint for social evaluation is the *ex post* viewpoint.

The next point in Dworkin's reasoning is that, since the envy test does not work well with personal talents but (allegedly) works well with insurance markets, the situation would be perfect if individuals had the opportunity to insure against personal handicaps before being born. They have no such opportunity in practice, but one can imagine what they would do if they had it. Hence the idea of the hypothetical insurance. He then extends this idea to all situations in which an insurance market does not exist and a tax and transfer policy is needed. The wrong premise in this step is that insurance markets work well as compensatory devices, which is related to the mistake of adopting the *ex ante* viewpoint. Moreover, as we have just seen, insurance markets work especially badly for personal talents and when *ex ante* utility does not matter in the computation of *ex post* well-being, and these are precisely two features of the hypothetical insurance.

The alternative route that Dworkin should have explored consists in analyzing the envy test, distinguishing the compensation principle and the liberal reward principle that it encapsulates, and seeking criteria which satisfy these principles in a sufficiently moderate way so that optimal allocations can always be found. Conditional Equality and Egalitarian-Equivalence, for instance, are much more faithful to Dworkin's initial vision than the hypothetical insurance market.

6.9 Conclusion

The three guiding principles in this chapter have been that individuals should not be held responsible for their luck, that *ex ante* prospects may also matter *ex post*, in the evaluation of a life, and that social evaluation should adopt the *ex post* viewpoint. They make the idea of option luck quite suspect, but we have seen that Conditional Equality provides a rather natural way to define and apply it in a consistent way. The gamblers may be required to bear the consequences of their gambles, not because their being lucky or unlucky should be amalgamated with their decision to gamble in their responsibility characteristics, not because from the *ex ante* viewpoint a gamble looks like a package that includes the possibility of losing, but because they could have avoided gambling and what they would then have obtained may serve as a reference in the evaluation of their situation. Even with Egalitarian-Equivalence, which typically advocates full insurance of bad luck, it is possible to leave room for uninsured risky activities if this corresponds to lifestyles the enjoyment of which is essential to well-being.

The *ex post* viewpoint, however, makes it legitimate for social policies not to condone each and every *ex ante* wish that people may have. In particular, insurance markets which leave it to individuals to decide *ex ante* how much coverage they want operate well (in absence of market failures) only in the case of damage to replaceable property and cannot be safely relied upon in other cases. This appears to radically undermine Dworkin's idea that hypothetical insurance markets can give us a rough idea of the optimal tax and transfer policies in many contexts, especially the case of unequal personal talents. The criteria of Conditional Equality and Egalitarian-Equivalence studied in this chapter appear definitely superior, even according to the general principles set out by Dworkin himself, such as the idea that the allocation must be "endowment insensitive" (compensation principle) and "ambition sensitive" (liberal reward). The hypothetical insurance market does not compensate bad luck properly, as it has been explained in detail in this chapter. It does not satisfy the liberal reward principle either, since individuals with identical endowments and luck may end up with very different transfers if their hypothetical insurance decisions are different.

A particular form of risk which has not been explicitly studied here is when one's view of life, one's preferences and ambitions happen to change and one regrets one's past way of life. Should people be left to bear the consequences of such changes, on the grounds that they are responsible for their preferences no matter how they evolve, or can we imagine policies that provide a second chance? Practical discussions around the theme of responsibility and equality of opportunities often touch the issue of enabling people to have a fresh start. This is the topic of the next chapter.

Chapter 7

Fresh starts

7.1 Introduction

This chapter is about regret.[1] When people regret their past decisions, should they be compelled to bear the consequences just as if they were still happy about them? "Is someone entitled to a fresh stock of resources when he rejects his former life and wants a fresh start? Suppose he is a profligate who has wasted his initial endowment and now finds himself with less than he needs to provide even for basic needs in later life." (Dworkin 2000, p. 109).

There are at least two kinds of regret. One kind is linked to learning. When information increases, one may regret past decisions which were based on erroneous beliefs. The previous chapter has somehow covered this kind of regret, since one can view the difference between *ex ante* prospects and *ex post* outcomes as a difference in information about the true state of nature. But there are specific features to forms of learning which affect preferences over lifetime consumptions and activities, and it is worth making a specific analysis of such phenomena. A second kind of regret can be depicted in terms of genuine changes in preferences. It is hard to be sure that there exist changes in preferences that cannot ultimately be interpreted in terms of learning, but we will not examine this issue here and, in some contexts, it may at any rate be convenient to analyze the situation in terms of change in preferences rather than in terms of change in information. A possible difference between learning and changes in preferences is that learning is an accumulative process so that later beliefs are naturally considered superior to earlier beliefs. For pure preference changes this is less obvious, and giving priority to the later preferences requires a justification.

To the above question about whether individuals should be held responsible for regretted past choices, a literal interpretation of theories of equal opportunity would answer in the affirmative, but this may seem unforgiving. After all, one can argue that changes of preferences or personalities amount to a succession of different selves, and it is not clear that our current self should be held responsible

---

[1] This chapter is based on Fleurbaey (2005).

for all the decisions of past selves. We would not hold individuals responsible for the decisions of other responsible individuals, unless they have manipulated them, and, although different selves are not different persons, they may have sufficient separation so that a similar kind of consideration applies – moreover, later selves cannot be suspected of having manipulated earlier selves.

It is actually possible to formulate modified theories of equality of resources or opportunities in such a way that "every morning is a fresh start." For a modified theory of equality of resources, one would then require that people's current situations be compatible with what their *current* (as opposed to past) ambitions and life goals would yield out of equal resources over their life span. For a theory of equality of opportunity, the corresponding requirement would be that people should enjoy situations that would have arisen from equal opportunities had they always acted according to their *current* mind-set. Obviously, the implementation of such modified theories raises delicate incentive problems (all the profligates would pretend they regret their past behavior in order to obtain additional resources), but it is nonetheless interesting to examine whether this could be a sensible social objective. Dworkin (2002) rejects such a modification of the theory of equality of resources not because of incentive constraints but because of "fatal problems of unfairness." According to him, this "seems an almost literal case of allowing people to eat cake and have it too. Why should the spendthrift be rewarded for hard work and frugality he never practiced, out of taxes raised from those who have in fact worked hard and been frugal?" (n. 8, p. 113).

This ethical intuition can be challenged. It is just an intuition without serious argument backing it, and one can defend another moral standard, which endorses the principle of "forgiving" past mistakes and welcoming changes of mind, accepting the implication that the cost of such mistakes or changes has to be shared among the whole community. In particular, it will be argued below that the ideal of freedom contains the idea of fresh starts, and therefore pushes in the direction of forgiveness. In the free society that endorses this alternative view, everyone's current situation should ideally be permanently compatible with the application of one's current preferences over an equal share of resources, independently of one's past behavior. Because of incentive constraints, this fully egalitarian ideal is not generally feasible, but it may be considered useful as an ethical objective. Section 7.2 below will bear on this ethical problem.

It is, however, quite important to check that the incentive constraints do not make this an idle issue. After all, it might be that incentive-compatible fresh starts boil down to nothing, so that the forgiving ethic might have the same practical consequences as the unforgiving theories of equality. We might end up telling the repentant spendthrift: "Sorry, we would like to help you, but if we give you additional resources, all spendthrifts will apply for a fresh start, and everyone except the most frugal would become a spendthrift in the first place." This would be equivalent, not in motivation but in consequences, to saying: "Sorry, but it would be unfair to help you at the expense of the prudent." The fact that Dworkin himself mixes a discussion of fairness with the "feasibility" issue of eating a cake without destroying it suggests that the separation between feasibility concerns and fairness concerns is indeed rather obscure in this context. As a matter of fact, the incentive issue in such a case is far from obvious, and the actual shape of "incentive-compatible" fresh starts is hard to figure out. This is the second topic addressed in this chapter, in Sections 7.3–7.5. It will be shown that, actually, even when disincentives are taken into account it is possible to provide substantial help to the regretful "spendthrifts." As a consequence, the ethical quarrel between forgiving and unforgiving attitudes is very relevant to practical issues of social policy.

7.2 Freedom and forgiveness

Before embarking on such a project, the choice of terminology should be discussed. Dworkin uses the value-laden words of "hard work," "spendthrift" and I describe the approach proposed here under the banner of "forgiveness." But the issue at hand really has nothing to do with a moral evaluation of people's choices and changes of preferences. It may be picturesque to think of the problem as dealing with the conversion of sinners into saints. But even when we are absolutely neutral about people's choices (for instance, their specialized training in philosophy or gardening), it is unforgiving to deny them any help when they change their preferences, regret their past choices, and want to modify their life-style (e.g., go back to school to study gardening or philosophy, respectively). That is the point of this chapter. The use of the word "forgiveness" simply refers to the opposite of "unforgiving," and does not involve any evaluation of the worth, moral or otherwise, of the lifestyles being regretted or adopted. Moreover, it does not imply that the redistributive policies discussed below require or force the population to forgive in their heart any past sin of anybody. The idea is not to force the virtuous to forgive the sinners for their wrongdoing and give them money on top of that. The idea is simply to set up redistributive institutions so as to give more possibilities to those who change their preferences.

Another possible misunderstanding that the word "forgiveness" may create is due to the fact that in ordinary life it is most often used when there is harm or damage, that is, when those who forgive have suffered directly from the culprit's behavior. Here nothing like that is at stake, and the scope of forgiveness in this paper is limited to the consequences of past decisions on the decision-maker himself. If those decisions have also hurt other people, then some kind of compensation or repair should presumably be enforced in favor of the victims, but this is out of the scope of this chapter. Attention will be restricted here to cases in which there are no externalities in personal decisions. The only nuisance entailed by changes of mind and mistakes will then lie in the taxes levied so as to finance the fresh starts. It would certainly be quite interesting to extend the analysis to cases of harm or tort. For instance, when someone imposes a great financial loss on others, should he be condemned to repay even if this means that he will work like a slave for the remainder of his life? Or should there be some pooling of the cost of such offenses in order to give the offender a second chance in life? These hard issues are ignored here.

The scope of forgiveness is also limited to cases when there is regret about past choices, not simply changes of preferences. For instance, someone who formerly disliked olive oil and now likes it a lot need not have any regret about his past consumptions, and it would be strange to imagine institutions trying to compensate for such changes in preferences.

Even though an external moral evaluation of preferences and choices is absent from this analysis, it may matter that individuals themselves consider their new preferences to be superior to their former preferences. The new preferences may be cognitively superior, when people come to discover new perspectives of life, or morally superior, when people adopt new values that override their old ones. When individuals consider their new preferences to be inferior to their old preferences, for instance because they have gone through a process of addiction, it is much more questionable to cater to the new preferences. We will focus here on those cases in which individuals consider their new preferences to be the relevant ones for the evaluation of their situation, and this is why we will refer to current preferences without making a normative judgment on the relative worth of old versus new preferences.

Let us now go to the heart of the matter and examine why the ethical intuition that goes against fresh starts is questionable. Consider two kinds of games. In the first game, all the chips are distributed equally at the beginning, and players may gain or lose chips according to some rules. In the second game, only two thirds of the chips are distributed, and one third serves as a stock which is distributed to players who have lost all their chips in order to give them a second chance. Nobody would claim that the second game is less fair than the first one. One may certainly argue that once all players have agreed to play by the rules of the first game, those who lose their chips cannot complain and ask for a redistribution of chips. It would then be unfair to break the rules and redistribute. But this is no argument in favor of the rules of the first game, when the question is to choose the rules of the game. The question addressed in this chapter is, in some sense, whether society should look like the first game or the second game (whether society should look like a competitive game at all is another issue that is ignored for the moment). The apparent appeal of Dworkin's objection that it would be unfair to tax the frugal may involve a category mistake, i.e., a confusion between choosing rules (just institutions) and playing by the rules. One may defend the plausible claim that a society like the second game is not less fair and is even better, which is not to be confused with the implausible claim that in the best society the rules may be violated in order to help some people. Rejecting the latter claim does not provide an objection against the former.

Now, how can fresh start institutions be ethically defended as bringing about a superior situation? The argument put forth here is that they provide more freedom. Consider an individual who has been living a particular kind of life and suddenly decides that she would like to change. Let us add that she regrets the consequences of what she has done so far, and would like to overturn them. If there was no feasibility constraint, she could wipe out everything, erase the past and start over again. Let us now introduce the constraint that the past cannot be altered and that there is only one life to be lived, but retaining a full freedom to change the future as one wishes. What would our character do in such a setting? She would wipe out the current consequences of her past follies, and start living a new life-style. Now, because the past cannot be modified, she may take account of this in her future behavior, because the past appears as a kind of handicap in her global evaluation of her life. For instance, if she has had a profligate record, she can immediately create savings that she failed to make in the past, but she cannot alter the quantity and kind of consumption made in the past, and she may for instance want to adjust her future consumption in order to compensate for some features of past consumption (e.g., she may have traveled a lot, and therefore need not travel any more in the future).

The reasonable point I am trying to extract from this wild fantasizing is that, in absence of feasibility constraints and in particular in absence of any cost to others, people would certainly want to enjoy the possibility of fresh starts and nobody would complain that they have it. There is no deep moral duty to bear the consequences of one's choices till the end. Therefore, the obligation to bear such consequences, to the extent to which it is imposed, is a limitation of freedom, and a regrettable one. This is a key point.

An easy objection to this reasoning is that removing feasibility constraints puts us in an irrelevant context to discuss such matters. Of course, actual feasibility constraints, scarcity and the resulting conflict of interests between individuals profoundly change the outlook of morality and of social justice. They form an essential part of what makes social justice an issue at all. But it is, I think, a mistake to believe that removing constraints produces irrelevant insights. On the contrary, it may be a good way to see in what direction one should try to go. Obsessed with constraints, we lose sight of the objective. The unforgiving moral intuition that makes some say that the frugal ought not to be taxed for the spendthrifts may just be due to a "sour grapes" effect. Because it looks difficult to help the spendthrifts (it looks like having one's cake and eating it too), we may end up thinking that it is not desirable anyway. This is mistaken. In absence of any cost to others, it would always be a good thing to help the spendthrifts because it would give them more freedom. A simple proof that there is no deep moral duty to bear the consequences of one's choices is that there are real-life situations in which it is feasible to wipe out the consequences of one's past choices without bothering others, and that for such cases no one questions such a freedom. If I buy a painting and after some time come to dislike it, who objects if I resell it and replace it with another one that I now prefer? Yet by doing this I escape the consequences of my initial choice. Imagine a variant of the story in which the only way to change the painting is by exchanging it with my neighbor. If my neighbor is happy to swap our paintings, again nobody objects. If my neighbor would rather keep his, then one can start arguing that I should bear the consequences of my choice. But the only reason is the cost to my neighbor. No intrinsic value of commitment to one's choices appears in this story.

Another objection is that such a freedom to change the future would remove the freedom to make firm commitments. I think one could argue that a commitment is precisely a reduction in freedom, a voluntary enslavement. It is true, however, that there may be trade-offs between immediate freedom and future freedom or welfare, so that commitments are sometimes very useful, especially in strategic contexts. To burn one's boats may be the only way to win the war. Commitments are also useful against future selves when current preferences are deemed better than future preferences (Ulysses and the sirens). Therefore it would probably be excessive to declare that a full freedom to change the future is preferable in all respects. But my claim is more limited than that. I am concerned with people who regret their past decisions and would like, with good reasons, to overturn their consequences. Such a bad configuration never occurs in the examples where commitment has a positive value. Therefore the commitment objection does not impugn the thesis that in absence of any cost to others, helping the regretful spendthrifts would increase freedom unambiguously.

When there is a cost to others, because subsidies to spendthrifts must be financed by taxes from the frugal, the increase in freedom is no longer unambiguous because the freedom of the frugal is then reduced. But this should then be a matter of weighting priorities, comparing well-being or degrees of freedom across people. There should not be a principled opposition to it.

This point deserves some emphasis. Suppose it is agreed that, as argued above, in absence of any cost to others there is no duty to bear the consequences of one's past decisions. What happens when there is a cost to others, that is when any help devoted to alleviating the consequences of one's past decisions must be drawn from the others' wealth? Can one defend the view that this cost creates a duty to bear the consequences, derived from a duty not to bother others? This is extremely implausible. Suppose the cost to others, in an imaginary counterfactual sequence, vanishes to zero. At the limit, there is no duty. At what threshold does the duty disappear? It would be very hard to defend the claim that the duty arises as soon as the cost to others is positive, no matter how small. Now, if there is no absolute duty not to bother others, it is then a matter of comparing the situation of people and weighting their conflicting interests. The regretful would benefit from help, the others would rather keep their wealth. Let us compare their situations in order to decide who should be given priority. This is the most reasonable way to address this issue.

Let us indeed figure out how the increase in freedom that a "fresh-start" fund would provide to the regretful should be weighted against the decrease in freedom imposed on the rest of the population by the corresponding tax. In an egalitarian approach this boils down to determining who are the least free in the worst case for them, namely, the regretful in absence of fund or the others after tax. Forcing people to bear the consequences of their choices may certainly be a very serious reduction of freedom when it means that they may have to live a substantial part of their life in poverty or close to poverty. In absence of any fund for fresh starts, the situation of the regretful spendthrifts obviously appears worse than the situation of the prudent. This holds true even when one makes the comparison in terms of freedom. Because by squandering her resources, the spendthrift has squandered her freedom as well. This strongly suggests that the absence of a fund for fresh starts is a more serious reduction of freedom than any small tax which would be set up to finance such a fund. Of course, the size of the fresh-start program (the amount of subsidy granted for fresh start, the tax paid by others) has to be adapted to the comparison of the relative situations of those who benefit from it and those who finance it. If the program is too small, the regretful spendthrifts are still the worst-off. If the program is too ambitious, the prudent may become the worst-off or start to behave like spendthrifts. The rest of the chapter will provide more material about this. An additional consideration is that *ex ante* no one knows who will experience a change in preferences, so that even those whose preferences remain firm do benefit from the assurance that in case of regret some help would be available. A society which sets up such a fund can then be depicted as giving more freedom than a society based on an unforgiving conception of equality of opportunities. There is more freedom for everyone when every individual knows he has to pay a tax when things go well and he gets a second chance when things go badly, than in a society in which things go slightly better when they go well, but get terrible otherwise.

This line of argument can be generalized. Shiffrin (2004) gives an interesting list of examples of widespread social customs in which the costs of personal decisions are collectively shared, and she also argues in favor of such "accommodation" practices in terms of freedom, on the grounds that they widen the range of possible lifestyles. In short, subsidizing a costly way of life which will be, presumably, adopted by a minority makes it accessible to everyone, whereas otherwise it might be totally out of reach.

Carter (2005) objects that a really free society would provide the possibility to take an insurance against changes in preferences, and those who fail to insure and then endure a change have no claim to a fresh start. The next section will show that in fact such a policy is not feasible, and the question is to determine which of the two feasible policies (laissez-faire or tax-funded fresh starts) grants more freedom. But even if such a "voluntary-insurance" policy were feasible, recall that the analysis of the previous chapter has cast serious doubts on the virtue of insurance markets for taking care of shocks on preferences. From the *ex post* point of view, those who fail to insure themselves and are later hit by bad luck are just ignorantly acting against their own interests, and there is little value, even in terms of freedom, in sanctifying their folly.

7.3 Fresh start policies: an outline

Even if fresh starts are desirable, one may fear that they are not feasible because individuals may wish to fake regret if this is in their interest. In fact in many cases it is possible to set up policies of this kind. In order to see intuitively how fresh starts can be organized even under incentive constraints, we will focus in this section on a simple example.

Consider a population of individuals who live two periods. They receive an endowment in period 1 and they can save part of it for period 2. For simplicity we assume that the real interest rate is null. The population is made of two equally sized subgroups of individuals in the first period, the prudent and the spendthrifts. The latter think only of the first period and save nothing. The former always want to have equal consumption in the two periods and evaluate a stream of consumptions by the smallest value at any given period over their lifetime. Therefore, when the interest rate is null, they dutifully save half of their endowment for the next period.

In the second period, imagine that none of the prudent has any regret, while some of the spendthrifts convert into a prudent mood, albeit too late. How do the regretful spendthrifts view their situation? Given that they have nothing left, they are, with their new preferences, in a similar situation as a prudent who would have had no endowment at all. This is how we will evaluate individual situations here, in order to focus on freedom while taking account of regret. More precisely, individual well-being will be measured by the "equivalent endowment" that would give individuals the same satisfaction as when they evaluate their whole life with the second-period preferences, under the assumption that this equivalent endowment would have been managed with the second-period preferences. In other words, consider an individual who examines his whole life with his second-period preferences. If his second-period preferences had prevailed in the first period as well, he could have obtained his current level of satisfaction with a certain amount of endowment in a society without any redistribution or state intervention. This hypothetical amount is the equivalent endowment.

For individuals who do not endure a change of preferences and are not submitted to any constraint or transfer in their saving decision, this is just their actual endowment and this resource evaluation has an intuitive meaning in terms of freedom since the size of the budget set is proportional to the endowment.[2] For individuals who regret their situation because of a change in preferences, this measure typically records their regret by yielding a value of the equivalent endowment that is below their actual endowment.

In our special example, the laissez-faire situation is such that the equivalent endowment of all the non-regretful (prudent and spendthrifts alike) is their actual endowment, while it is equal to zero for the regretful spendthrifts. Let us seek to obtain a situation in which the equivalent endowments of all are equal. In order to do this, we must make a transfer in favor of the regretful spendthrifts, during the second period. Since this will attract all spendthrifts independently of whether they are truly regretful or not, this means that the transfer is really taking place from all the prudent to all the spendthrifts. In fact, in this particular example, the non-regretful spendthrifts do not care about

---

[2] One could object that an individual who is forced to pick the point he would spontaneously choose in his budget set would not have this constraint registered by this measure. Therefore this appears to be a poor measure of freedom in general and may seem too close to a measure of satisfaction. But it is interesting for interpersonal comparisons, because in cases when budget sets all have a reasonable shape, this measure does make a sensible evaluation of the amount of freedom enjoyed by different individuals, while taking account of their preferences, i.e., the value of freedom in their eyes.

their consumption in the second period and could be requested not to apply for the fresh start, without violating incentive constraints. But we assume here that they will all apply anyway, as is the case in more realistic settings, when their preferences lead them to care also about their consumption in the second period. We can now see why Carter's (2005) proposal to set up a voluntary insurance for the spendthrifts would not be feasible. Since regret is not observable, all those who have taken an insurance would apply for the indemnity in the second period. When all insured customers claim the indemnity, the insurance breaks down – unless the premium is raised to the level of the indemnity, which also destroys the insurance.

Assume the average per capita value of the endowment is E. Consider the situation in which the spendthrifts are compelled to save one fifth of it in the first period and obtain a subsidy of the same amount in the second period, financed by a tax on the prudent. Since prudent and spendthrifts come in equal numbers, this means that each prudent pays one fifth of E as a tax. His equivalent endowment, equal to his actual endowment, is then $.8E$ and he consumes half of it at each period. For the nonregretful spendthrifts, their equivalent endowment corresponds to the amount of their consumption in the first period, since they would reach the same satisfaction with consuming this in the first period and nothing in the second period. This is also equal to $.8E$ since in this situation they are forced to save $.2E$. What about the regretful spendthrifts? They consume $.8E$ in the first period and $.4E$ (i.e., $.2E$ of savings and $.2E$ of subsidy) in the second period. For prudent preferences which focus on the smallest amount of consumption, this provides the same satisfaction as the consumption stream of the prudent in this allocation. Therefore the equivalent endowment of the regretful spendthrifts is also $.8E$. All individuals, therefore, have the same equivalent endowment in this particular allocation.

This example displays the most relevant features of an incentive-compatible fresh start policy which applies the maximin criterion to equivalent endowments, and the next section will generalize this analysis. First, all spendthrifts end up with the same consumption stream, because it is impossible to separate the regretful from the others. As a consequence, the proportion of regretful among the spendthrifts does not matter at all for the optimal policy, provided this proportion is strictly positive. Second, the policy does not only consist in a subsidy paid in the second period, but also in a constraint in the first period. The spendthrifts pay something like a social security tax in the first period, which is meant to force them to save a minimum. The purpose of this tax is not to fund the subsidy of the second period, since this is funded by the tax on the prudent, but to reduce the amount of the subsidy that has to be given to spendthrifts in the second period in order to alleviate their regret. In this particular example, if they were not forced to save, the prudent would have to pay them a subsidy equal to one third of E, and this would be, in absence of savings, the consumption of the spendthrifts in the second period. Equivalent endowments would then be equalized between the regretful spendthrifts and the prudent at a level of $2/3$ of E, while the non-regretful spendthrifts would enjoy an equivalent endowment of E. This situation is less satisfactory than the previous one, in terms of the smallest equivalent endowment observed in the population.

It may seem paradoxical that a policy meant to increase the freedom to change one's mind combines constraints with subsidies, but on reflection there is nothing surprising about this. The forced saving is meant to prevent the agents from committing to consume little in the next period. They can still consume little if they wish, since there is no forced consumption here. But they are prevented from committing to do so. The constraint is there in order to allow for a greater array of choices in the future, and this is valuable in view of the possible different preferences they may adopt later on. The idea, broadly speaking, is to preserve future opportunities.

A third typical feature is that the total amount of resources consumed by the different subpopulations is unequal, with the spendthrifts consuming more over their lifetime than the prudent. One can often hear the "deserving poor" complaining that others who are less deserving actually get more help in spite of the fact that such resources would be better used by the more deserving. We find a possible justification for such apparently unfair pattern here. The additional resources spent on the problematic people take account of the fact that they are among the worst-off anyway. The more "deserving" people do not need as much help because indeed they take care of themselves in a better way. Evaluating people's situations by the amount of resources they actually consume is not the proper metric of well-being. One has to take account of how individuals evaluate a lifetime with regretful or non-regretful preferences. Notice that in the above allocation the non-regretful spendthrifts are not better-off than the others, because they suffer from the constraint imposed on them by the social security tax. It is true that in absence of this constraint, they would be better-off than the others, as explained above, but even then this might be considered an admissible cost to pay in order to alleviate the plight of the regretful who cannot, due to incentive constraints, be separated from them.

Other features of this particular example are not general, as will be shown in the next section. First, it is not generally possible to equalize all the equivalent endowments, when there are more than two types of preferences in the population. A more typical situation is such that individuals with intermediate preferences (between the prudent and the most myopic of the population), who are rather happy to save the amount that social security imposes on them, and to pocket the subsidy on top of that without actually enduring regret about their middle-of-the-ground preferences, are better-off than other agents. Even the most prudent can end up being better-off than the spendthrifts. Another unusual feature in the above example is that the social security tax paid by the spendthrifts is exactly equal to the tax paid by the prudent. In a more typical situation, the former is actually greater than the latter.

7.4 *Savings and moans

The model is a simple generalization of the example of the previous section. The population is $N = \{1, ..., n\}$, every agent i consumes $x_i = (x_{i1}, x_{i2}) \in \mathbb{R}^2_+$, and has a utility function u_i defined over $\mathbb{R}^2_+$, which is assumed to be continuous, increasing in each argument and quasi-concave. Given the possibility of a change in preferences, we distinguish the utility function of the first period, $u_{i1}(x_i)$, from that of the second period, $u_{i2}(x_i)$. Note that for both utility functions the argument is the two-period bundle x_i. An agent i is said to have steady preferences when $u_{i1} = u_{i2}$.

An allocation $x = (x_i)_{i \in N}$ is feasible if (assuming a zero interest rate)

$$\sum_{i \in N} (x_{i1} + x_{i2}) \leq \Omega,$$

for a given $\Omega > 0$. It is incentive-compatible if for all $i, j \in N$,

$$u_{i1}(x_i) \geq u_{i1}(x_j).$$

This condition of incentive-compatibility is motivated by the following scenario. The transfers coming in the second period are correctly forecast by the agents, and they act in the first period as if their preferences were to remain valid in the second period (nobody forecasts that his preferences will change – the possibility of lifting this assumption will be discussed below). Since, in the second period, all preferences over x_{i2} are the same (i.e., more is better), it is impossible to distinguish agents and therefore all agents with the same initial preferences will have the same consumption, independently of whether their second-period preferences are different or not.

The "equivalent endowment" for agent i consuming x_i is computed as follows:

$$e_i(x_i) = \min \{q_1 + q_2 \mid u_{i2}(q_1, q_2) \geq u_{i2}(x_i)\}.$$

If i was given the possibility to maximize $u_{i2}(x_i')$ under the budget constraint $x_{i1}' + x_{i2}' \leq e_i(x_i)$, he would indeed obtain utility $u_{i2}(x_i)$. Figure 7.1 illustrates how this is computed for an agent whose preferences change. In the figure the initial preferences are described by a continuous indifference curve, while the new preferences are depicted by a dotted curve.

We assume throughout that the profile $(u_{i2})_{i \in N}$ contains only functions that already appear in the profile $(u_{i1})_{i \in N}$. We assume moreover that any pair of utility functions satisfies the single-crossing condition. Under this assumption, all preferences can unambiguously be ranked in terms of time preference. More precisely: v is more impatient than u if for all $q, q' \in \mathbb{R}^2_+$,

$$u(q) = u(q') \text{ and } q_1 > q_1' \Rightarrow v(q) > v(q').$$

It is assumed that in the profile under consideration, there is a "prudent" kind of preferences with no time preference: for all $x, x' \in \mathbb{R}_+$

$$u_i(x, x') = u_i(x', x).$$

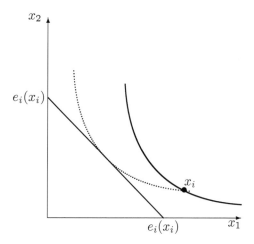

Figure 7.1: Equivalent endowment

This kind of preferences is moreover assumed to lie at an extreme end of the spectrum, so that there is no type of preference with a bias toward the future. At the other end of the spectrum, the preferences in the profile with the greatest degree of preference for the present will simply be called "the most impatient." The terms "prudent" and "impatient" are chosen for their intuitive simplicity but this does not involve a value judgment. It may be that the impatient are simply those who like consuming at a young age whereas the prudent have different views about quality of life.

We are now ready for the main result of this section.

Proposition 7.1 *Consider a profile such that for any i such that $u_{i1} \neq u_{i2}$, u_{i1} is more impatient than u_{i2}, and in which there is (at least) an agent i_m such that $u_{i_m 1} = u_{i_m 2}$ is of the most impatient type, and an agent i_{mp} such that $u_{i_{mp}1}$ is of the most impatient type while $u_{i_{mp}2}$ is of the prudent type. Then, a feasible and incentive-compatible allocation x_N which maximizes $\min_{i \in N} e_i(x_i)$ is such that:*
(i) $e_{i_m}(x_{i_m}) = e_{i_{mp}}(x_{i_{mp}}) = \min_{i \in N} e_i(x_i)$;
(ii) if j is more impatient than i, then $x_{j1} + x_{j2} \geq x_{i1} + x_{i2}$;
(iii) if i, j have steady preferences, j is more impatient than i, and the best bundle q for j under the constraint $q_1 + q_2 \leq x_{i_m 1} + x_{i_m 2}$ is such that $q_1 \leq x_{i_m 1}$, then $e_j(x_j) \geq e_i(x_i)$.

Proof. The proof relies on the following lemma which, interestingly, does not involve the single-crossing assumption.[3]

---

[3] This lemma is reminiscent of the classic optimal taxation result that the second-best allocation is on the production frontier (see, e.g., Mirrlees 1986).

Lemma 7.1 *If x_N is an incentive-compatible allocation such that*

$$\sum_{i \in N} (x_{i1} + x_{i2}) < \Omega,$$

there is another incentive-compatible allocation x'_N such that

$$\sum_{i \in N} (x_{i1} + x_{i2}) < \sum_{i \in N} (x'_{i1} + x'_{i2}) \leq \Omega$$

and for all $i \in N$, $u_{i1}(x'_i) > u_{i1}(x_i)$.

Proof of the Lemma. (The proof is inspired by the "perturbation lemma" in Alkan et al. (1991), p. 1029.) We first assume that $u_{i1}(.)$ is piecewise linear in x_{i2}, with a right derivative denoted $\partial u_{i1}/\partial x_{i2}^+$. This implies that, for $\varepsilon > 0$ small enough,

$$u_{i1}(x'_{i1}, x'_{i2} + \varepsilon) = u_{i1}(x'_i) + \varepsilon \frac{\partial u_{i1}}{\partial x_{i2}^+}(x'_i).$$

Define the $n \times n$ matrix (a_{ij}) by

$$a_{ij} = \begin{cases} \dfrac{\partial u_{i1}}{\partial x_{i2}^+}(x_j) & \text{for } (i,j) \text{ s.t. } u_{i1}(x_j) = u_{i1}(x_i), \\ 0 & \text{otherwise.} \end{cases}$$

One has $a_{ii} > 0$ for all $i \in N$. Let $\pi \in \Pi_N$ be a permutation which maximizes $\prod_{i \in N} a_{i\pi(i)}$. Necessarily $a_{i\pi(i)} > 0$ for all $i \in N$, implying that $a_{i\pi(i)} = \partial u_{i1}/\partial x_{i2}^+(x_{\pi(i)})$ and $u_{i1}(x_{\pi(i)}) = u_{i1}(x_i)$ for all $i \in N$.

Moreover, π maximizes $\sum_{i \in N} \ln a_{i\pi(i)}$, so that by Proposition 2.1 there exists a vector $\varepsilon_N \in \mathbb{R}_{++}$ such that for all $i, j \in N$,

$$\ln \varepsilon_i + \ln a_{i\pi(i)} \geq \ln \varepsilon_j + \ln a_{i\pi(j)}.$$

In other words, for all $i, j \in N$ such that $u_{i1}(x_{\pi(j)}) = u_{i1}(x_i)$,

$$\varepsilon_i \frac{\partial u_{i1}}{\partial x_{i2}^+}(x_{\pi(i)}) \geq \varepsilon_j \frac{\partial u_{i1}}{\partial x_{i2}^+}(x_{\pi(j)}).$$

Note that ε_N can be multiplied by a positive real number without altering this property.

We now prove that for ε_N small enough the allocation x'_N defined by $x'_i = x_{\pi(i)} + (0, \varepsilon_i)$ is incentive compatible. For ε_N small enough one has

$$u_{i1}(x_{\pi(i)1}, x_{\pi(i)2} + \varepsilon_i) = u_{i1}(x_{\pi(i)}) + \varepsilon_i \frac{\partial u_{i1}}{\partial x_{i2}^+}(x_{\pi(i)})$$

$$= u_{i1}(x_i) + \varepsilon_i \frac{\partial u_{i1}}{\partial x_{i2}^+}(x_{\pi(i)}).$$

If $u_{i1}(x_{\pi(j)}) = u_{i1}(x_i)$, one has

$$u_{i1}(x_i) + \varepsilon_i \frac{\partial u_{i1}}{\partial x_{i2}^+}(x_{\pi(i)}) \;=\; u_{i1}(x_{\pi(j)}) + \varepsilon_i \frac{\partial u_{i1}}{\partial x_{i2}^+}(x_{\pi(i)}) \geq$$

$$u_{i1}(x_{\pi(j)}) + \varepsilon_j \frac{\partial u_{i1}}{\partial x_{i2}^+}(x_{\pi(j)}) \;=\; u_{i1}(x_{\pi(j)1}, x_{\pi(j)2} + \varepsilon_j),$$

which implies that

$$u_{i1}(x_{\pi(i)1}, x_{\pi(i)2} + \varepsilon_i) \geq u_{i1}(x_{\pi(j)1}, x_{\pi(j)2} + \varepsilon_j).$$

If $u_{i1}(x_{\pi(j)}) \neq u_{i1}(x_i)$, necessarily $u_{i1}(x_{\pi(j)}) < u_{i1}(x_i)$ by incentive compatibility, so that

$$u_{i1}(x_i) + \varepsilon_i \frac{\partial u_{i1}}{\partial x_{i2}^+}(x_{\pi(i)}) \geq u_{i1}(x_{\pi(j)}) + \varepsilon_j \frac{\partial u_{i1}}{\partial x_{i2}^+}(x_{\pi(j)})$$

is true for ε_N small enough.

It remains to prove that for all $i \in N$, $u_{i1}(x_i') > u_{i1}(x_i)$. This holds for ε_N small enough, due to the fact noted above that for all $i \in N$,

$$u_{i1}(x_{\pi(i)1}, x_{\pi(i)2} + \varepsilon_i) = u_{i1}(x_i) + \varepsilon_i \frac{\partial u_{i1}}{\partial x_{i2}^+}(x_{\pi(i)}).$$

This completes the proof for the piecewise linear case. The proof for the general case follows from the fact that every continuous increasing function can be uniformly approximated by a piecewise linear function.

Proof of the Proposition. Only ordinal preferences matter. Let the T types of preferences in the profile $(u_{i1})_{i \in N}$ be ordered so that t is more impatient than $t + 1$. Then $t = 1$ is the most impatient and $t = T$ is the prudent type. Preferences of type t will be denoted R_t, P_t, I_t. An individual whose preferences are of type t initially will be assigned type t.

We restrict attention to allocations such that $x_i = x_j$ for all i, j of the same type. This is no loss of generality because for every allocation failing to obey this condition there is a Pareto equivalent allocation that does, is also incentive-compatible, and does not use more resources (just give all individuals of a type the bundle which uses the least resources among those observed in this group at the initial allocation – for the optimal allocation that maximizes $\min_{i \in N} e_i(x_i)$ all bundles for a type must consume the same amount of resources, otherwise, by Lemma 7.1 one could construct a better allocation). Therefore we can reason with types instead of individuals: let x^t denote the bundle of type t individuals, and $uc_t(x^t) = \{q \in \mathbb{R}_+^2 \mid q R_t x^t\}$.

Let x_N be an allocation maximizing $\min_{t=1,\dots,T} e_t(x^t)$. By single-crossing and incentive-compatibility, for all $t < T$, $x_1^t \geq x_1^{t+1}$. This implies in particular that for all $t' \geq t > 1$, $x^t R_{t'} x^1$. Single-crossing also implies that for all $t' \geq t \geq t''$, all q,

$$uc_t(q) \subseteq uc_{t'}(q) \cup uc_{t''}(q).$$

In particular, for all $t' \geq t > 1$,

$$uc_{t'}(x^1) \subseteq uc_1(x^1) \cup uc_T(x^1).$$

Since $x^t R_{t'} x^1$, one has $uc_{t'}(x^t) \subseteq uc_{t'}(x^1)$ and therefore, for all $t' \geq t > 1$,

$$uc_{t'}(x^t) \subseteq uc_1(x^1) \cup uc_T(x^1).$$

As a consequence, and relying on the assumption that there are agents (e.g., i_m) for whom the equivalent endowment is equal to $e_1(x^1)$ and agents (e.g., i_{mp}) for whom it is equal to $e_T(x^1)$, one has

$$\min_{t=1,\dots,T} e_t(x^t) = \min\left\{e_1(x^1), e_T(x^1)\right\}.$$

To prove (i), it remains to show that $e_1(x^1) = e_T(x^1)$.

Suppose $e_1(x^1) < e_T(x^1)$. This implies that x^1 is distorted to the left (excess saving) for R_1. One can move x^1 down the indifference curve of I_1, leaving the other bundles unchanged, so as to obtain a new incentive-compatible allocation with less total consumption and an unchanged $\min_{t=1,\dots,T} e_t(x^t) = e_1(x^1)$. By Lemma 7.1, one can then construct another feasible incentive-compatible allocation with greater $e_t(x^t)$ for all t; this contradicts the optimality of allocation x_N.

Suppose $e_1(x^1) > e_T(x^1)$. This implies that x^1 is distorted to the right (insufficient saving) for R_T. One can move x^1 and all $x^t = x^1$ up the indifference curve of I_T, leaving the other bundles unchanged, so as to obtain a new incentive-compatible allocation with less total consumption and an unchanged $\min_{t=1,\dots,T} e_t(x^t) = e_T(x^1)$. Again, this contradicts the optimality of allocation x_N. This achieves the proof of (i).

We will now show that for all $t < T$, $x^{t+1} I_{t+1} x^t$. Assume that, on the contrary, there is $t < T$ such that $x^{t+1} P_{t+1} x^t$. Pick the greatest t satisfying this property. Then, by single-crossing and incentive-compatibility, for all $t' \geq t+1$, all $t'' \leq t$, $x^{t'} P_{t'} x^{t''}$. Different cases have to considered.

(1) If $t = T - 1$, then there exists $\delta \in \mathbb{R}^2_{++}$ such that $x_T - \delta$ can replace x_T and the allocation is still incentive-compatible.

(2) If $t < T - 1$ and $x^{t+1} P_{t+1} x^{t+2}$, then by single-crossing $x^{t+1} P_{t+1} x^{t'}$ for all $t' \neq t+1$ and again x_{t+1} can be decreased by some $\delta \in \mathbb{R}^2_{++}$.

(3) If $t < T-1$ and $x^{t+1} I_{t+1} x^{t+2}$, then $x^{t+1} = x^{t+2}$ because otherwise, by single-crossing $x^{t+2} P_{t+2} x^{t+1}$, contradicting the assumption that t was the greatest satisfying this property. Consider the subgroup consuming x^{t+1}. This may include other types $t' > t+2$, and by the same reasoning, if $x^{t+2} I_{t+2} x^{t+3}$ then $x^{t+2} = x^{t+3}$, and so on. Therefore they all strictly prefer x^{t+1} to all other bundles, and their bundle can be decreased by some $\delta \in \mathbb{R}^2_{++}$.

In all three cases, one can reduce total consumption and still obtain an incentive-compatible allocation x'_N. Note that $x'^1 = x^1$, implying that $\min_{t=1,\dots,T} e_t(x'^t) = \min_{t=1,\dots,T} e_t(x^t)$. This contradicts the optimality of x_N.

Assume there is $t < T$ such that $x_1^t + x_2^t < x_1^{t+1} + x_2^{t+1}$. Let x'_N be a new allocation identical to x_N except that $x'^{t+1} = x^t$. By the above fact, $x^{t+1} I_{t+1} x^t$, so that x'_N is incentive-compatible. The value of $\min_{t=1,\ldots,T} e_t(x^t)$ is not affected since no type is affected. Total consumption in x'_N is less than in x_N, which contradicts the optimality of x_N. This proves (ii).

Consider a type t such that the best bundle q for R_t under the constraint $q_1 + q_2 \leq x_1^1 + x_2^1$ is such that $q_1 \leq x_1^1$. If $x^t = x^1$, then x^t is not distorted to the left for R_t. Consider the case $x^t \neq x^1$ and assume that x^t is distorted to the left for R_t. Without loss of generality, assume that $x^{t-1} \neq x^t$ (if not, take the smallest t^* such that $x^{t^*} = x^t$ and replace t with t^* – if x^t is distorted to the left for R_t so is it for R_{t^*}). Since $x_1^t + x_2^t \leq x_1^{t-1} + x_2^{t-1}$ and $x_1^t \leq x_1^{t-1}$, necessarily x^{t-1} is distorted to the right for R_t (recall that $x^t I_t x^{t-1}$). Let q be a point such that $q I_t x^t$ and $e_t(x^t) = q_1 + q_2$. Let x'_N be a new allocation identical to x_N except that $x'^t = q$. This allocation is incentive-compatible. One has $x_1^t + x_2^t > q_1 + q_2$, so that total consumption is less in x'_N than in x_N. This contradicts the optimality of x_N. As a conclusion, x^t is not distorted to the left for R_t.

From this, from single-crossing and from the fact that $x^{t+1} I_{t+1} x^t$, one deduces that $e_{t+1}(x^{t+1}) \leq e_t(x^t)$. This proves (iii). ∎

This proposition confirms the observations of the previous section about how paradoxical a fresh start policy looks. The impatient agents are among the worst-off in terms of the relevant evaluation (equivalent endowments), but they are the best-off in terms of total consumption of resources. Point (iii), moreover, states that even in terms of equivalent endowments, it is good to be impatient up to some degree: The agents who would spontaneously save as much as required by the policy are better-off, the less prudent they are. This is due to the incentive constraints, which, under the particular objective prevailing here, make more prudent agents indifferent between their bundle and the bundle consumed by the next less prudent agent, and to the fact that distortions operate in the sense of reducing such agents' savings. One then has the configuration illustrated in Fig. 7.2.

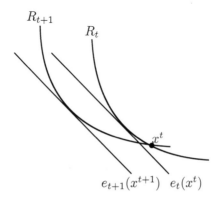

Figure 7.2: Equivalent endowment for two successive types

Figure 7.3 illustrates the budget set of a typical optimal second-best allocation (with a great number of agents so that the kinks of the envelope curve of indifference curves disappear), as compared to the laissez-faire budget set which is delimited by a straight line of slope -1 under the assumption of zero interest rate. The prudent, as usual for extreme agents in second-best contexts, are not distorted. The most impatient, on the contrary, are distorted even when there is no bunching at the cusp of the budget set, and this is because of the particular way in which their well-being is computed.

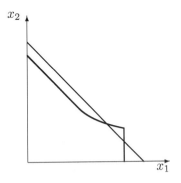

Figure 7.3: Laisser-faire vs. second-best policy

There are other contexts in which the best policy has a different outlook. In particular, it can be shown that the transfers in favor of the impatient are no longer possible when preferences can change in all directions, as well as when the agents' savings are not observed.[4] In both cases, only the "protective" part of the policy (i.e., forced savings) remains operative. When preferences can change in all directions, one has to forbid excessive consumption and excessive saving, so as to reduce future regret in the two ways. When savings are not observable, one can still force the agents to save a minimum (by taxing them), but it is no longer possible to tax the savers in order to fund a subsidy for the non savers, so that the prudent are then not affected by this policy (the tax is repaid in the second period to all agents).

On the contrary, a more favorable context occurs when it is possible to distinguish between the regretful and the non-regretful in the second period. This is still, however, different from the pure first-best context because the policy is still constrained in the first period by ignorance of who will eventually come to regret their decision.[5] In this case, all agents with the same *ex ante* preferences must consume the same amount in the first period. It is only in the second period that their consumptions can differ. Figure 7.4 shows a typical configuration, for the simple case of a population consisting of half prudent, one fourth steady impatient, and one fourth regretful impatient. The bundles

---

[4]See Fleurbaey (2005), Th. 2 and 3.

[5]In the pure first-best context, one could simply assign to every agent the bundle that will be optimal for his future preferences, and there would be no deadweight loss at all.

of the impatient are determined by seeking the point which has a slope of -1 on the average indifference curve computed by taking the vertical average of the two indifference curves of regretful and non-regretful impatient. This is the point where the total consumption of the impatient (regretful and non-regretful) is the smallest. The "protective" part of the policy is still operative, and the impatient are induced to make excess savings, because the point of slope -1 on the average curve corresponds to a point of steeper slope on the impatient indifference curve. Then, in the second period, the "transfer" part of the policy applies only to the regretful, who receive a subsidy so that they end up in a situation that is equivalent in their eyes to that of the prudent. When there are more than one impatient type, the same kind of computation is performed, and a nice feature of this situation, which contrasts with the case studied above, is that equality of equivalent endowments across all agents can always be obtained.

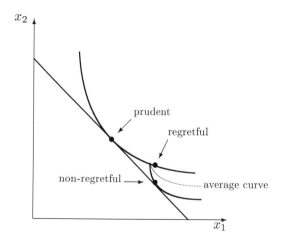

Figure 7.4: The case of verifiable regret

It has been assumed so far that the agents do not anticipate that their preferences could change. Now imagine they do. If the utility functions u_{i1}, u_{i2} can be used as Bernoulli functions, one can consider that in period 1 the agent would choose x_i so as to maximize

$$\sum_{j \in N} \pi_{ij} u_{j1}(x_i),$$

where π_{ij} is i's subjective probability that $u_{i2} = u_{j1}$. This defines *ex ante* preferences which are just a mixture of the prudent and impatient preferences. If one defines $v_{i1} = \sum_{j \in N} \pi_{ij} u_{j1}$ and $v_{i2} = u_{i2}$, the above analysis, applied to v_{i1}, v_{i2}, provides a direct treatment of this case as well.

7.5 Education, earnings, savings

Let us briefly summarize the insights on fresh start policies obtained in the last two sections, trying to formulate them in general terms, forgetting the special issue of savings that served to give a concrete framework to the previous sections. The main feature of fresh start policies is that they combine constraints, meant to protect from potential regret, and transfers, meant to help the regretful. When the regretful can be separated from the non-regretful, the transfer part of the policy is greatly enhanced, although the protective part remains operative. When the regretful cannot be separated and transfers benefit the non-regretful as well, the balance between constraints and transfers is tilted toward constraints, but transfers are still important and the imprudent typically obtain more resources than the prudent, although it is essential to remember that they are, in the relevant measure of well-being, among the worst-off. When changes of preferences can occur in all directions, or when individual personal initiatives that go beyond the protection imposed by the policy are not observable, the transfer part of the policy vanishes and only the protective part remains useful. The key questions to ask, then, when considering a context of possible changes in preferences, are: (1) what are the directions of changes (one way or multiple ways)? (2) can the regretful be separated from the others? (3) can individual precautions be observed and be a basis for transfers?

With these general ideas, we can consider a richer framework where individuals make decisions over their life regarding education (how much time to spend at school), earnings (how much to work) and intertemporal allocation of consumption (how much to borrow and to save).

If one takes it as a main insight of this chapter that fresh start policies do not only give money to the imprudent but also impose constraints on initial decisions, one can see that the constraints that are commonplace in this kind of context can be viewed in a new light. For instance, requirements of minimal education are usually depicted as inspired by externalities (over productivity and the quality of social relations) and perfectionist principles (education is a basic dimension of human development and underlies many functionings) or paternalism (people are myopic). Now we see that forcing some people to take more education than they spontaneously would is also a protection against their potential future regret and provides them with more freedom to change their views about the value of education. It is important to distinguish this kind of protection from a paternalistic protection against myopia and time-inconsistent preferences.[6] When individuals are fully rational and do not suffer from any myopia, paternalistic justifications for compulsory education are weakened, whereas

---

[6] Myopia is sometimes modelled like a change in preferences, with the presumption that later preferences are superior to earlier preferences (see, e.g., Feldstein 1985). Models with quasi-hyperbolic discounting (Laibson 1997) have a similar feature, with a "correct" discount factor over future periods and a distorted factor for trade-offs between present and future periods. Therefore, formally, the analysis of this chapter can be applied to the problem of myopia, with the twist that not all spendthrifts are myopic, since some of them do not change their preferences.

the rationale for protection against possible future regret remains unscathed because even fully rational individuals may undergo preference changes.

Similarly, social security contributions for the payment of future pensions can also be viewed under a new light, as we have already seen.[7] In addition, the limitations on borrowing, which are usually perceived negatively as due to imperfections of the credit market, can now also be positively appreciated in terms of protection against future regret over intertemporal allocation of consumption. As far as earnings are concerned, things are slightly more complex. The equivalent of social security contributions or borrowing constraints, in the case of labor, would be a minimum requirement of labor, and this appears out of question in a free society.[8] But in fact, constraints can be replaced by incentives and there is no substantial difference, in the simple and abstract models analyzed in the previous two sections, between a minimum requirement and a subsidy scheme which makes it strongly attractive to comply with the requirement. In other words, a minimum requirement of labor is unthinkable, but a good substitute for it is a strong tax credit paid to the working poor. We have seen in Chapter 5 that such policies could be justified by some criteria like Wage Egalitarian-Equivalence or Envied Intensity. Here we find an additional rationale for such policies: they protect against potential future regret of not having earned enough money in the past.

Now, let us briefly ask the key questions about the three kinds of decision under consideration. For education, the direction of regret is probably one-way for most people, when it is about the length of education. People typically regret having stopped too early. But when, for a given level of education, various fields of specialization are considered, all directions seem a priori possible. This problem is however alleviated by the fact that the regretful can be separated from the non-regretful very easily when the transfer can be made in kind, in the form of subsidized training. Moreover, individual decisions about education can be traced rather easily, and it does not appear strange to give greater subsidies to lower levels of education. In summary, a combination of compulsory minimal education, greater subsidies for low levels, and subsidies for retraining programmes appears as the most likely kind of optimal policy in this case.

As far as labor is concerned, it is not clear what direction regret typically takes. One can regret to have worked too little (earning too little) or too much (e.g., having neglected one's children). The regretful cannot be separated from the non-regretful, and it is still debatable whether individual decisions of work-

---

[7] It is often said that myopia is the main justification for social security. In fact, the economic literature on social security and myopia (e.g., Feldstein 1985, Imrohoroglu et al. 2003) questions the efficacy of this policy. But it focuses on unfunded social security, which has many distortionary effects. Moreover, it relies on utilitarian welfare evaluations that do not give special priority to the plight of the worst-off, i.e., the myopic in absence of social security.

[8] Why are forced savings generally considered more acceptable than (paid) forced labor? This might be because forced savings incorporate the guarantee of consuming the savings in the future (if one lives long enough), whereas a norm of compulsory labor does not include a possibility of additional leisure in the future. The impossibility to implement compulsory labor in presence of unemployment is another obvious consideration.

ing time can be the basis of transfers, although some forms of tax credit nowadays do depend on working time specifically. Therefore, in view of the fact that a minimal requirement of labor is out of question, it is possible that some tax incentives to work a minimal amount of time, combined with constraints on maximal working time, would be the optimal policy in this case. A more general transfer scheme would not appear desirable in view of the multiple directions of regret in this case.

Savings have already been dealt with extensively (although borrowing was not considered in the previous sections). In this case the direction of regret is probably mostly one-way; the regretful cannot be identified, but saving decisions can form the basis of transfers. Therefore constraints on maximum borrowing and minimal saving are natural policies to introduce in this context. Transfers from high savers to low savers are less common, and when they exist (e.g., tax exemption of certain basic forms of savings) they are motivated by inequality of wealth between people rather than possible regret. They find here an additional justification.

7.6 Conclusion

In summary, the policy conclusions that emerge from the idea of fresh starts are not particularly eccentric, and often amount to providing additional justifications for compulsory requirements, tax incentives and transfer schemes that are already commonplace and are usually justified on other grounds. Contrary to Dworkin's argument against the idea of fresh starts, one sees that such policies do not allow people to have their cake and eat it, but they still differ from pure laissez-faire policies which leave the regretful to their plight.

The analysis has moreover revealed some subtle features of such policies, which are not a priori obvious. One is that transfers should be supplemented by constraints, which looks surprising when the motivation for such policies is formulated in reference to freedom. But the usual mistake is to view freedom from a pure *ex ante* point of view. The constraints that appear in the optimal policies discussed in this chapter do reduce *ex ante* freedom somewhat, although the accompanying transfers also increase it at the same time in some other parts of the set of options. But the constraints also contribute to making future changes of preferences less harmful, so that in terms of equivalent freedom evaluated *ex post*, the situation is much better. In other words, such constraints put people in a situation which is equivalent for them, *ex post*, to a much freer situation. Fresh starts increase freedom over a lifetime; they are not meant to increase initial freedom.

The second feature, a special distribution of resources and well-being, suggests an argument that can be offered as a consolation to the "deserving poor" who complain that the "undeserving" are getting more help than themselves. The argument is that the metric of resource transfers is not the correct one. Over their lifetime, the situation of the undeserving is still bleak and the additional help they receive does not make them better-off overall. They are, in the relevant measure of well-being, the worst-off. It is true, however, that some among the moderately imprudent who may also benefit from such policies may end up being the best-off both in terms of resources and in terms of the relevant measure of well-being. This fact can be justified by saying that this is an undesired consequence of feasibility and incentive-compatibility constraints, but a consequence which we should view as a necessary cost if we give priority to the plight of the worst-off.

Chapter 8

Utilitarian reward

8.1 Introduction

The previous chapters have focused on the liberal approach to reward, which is based on the intuitive idea that responsibility diminishes the need for transfers between individuals. This approach places responsibility-sensitive egalitarianism somewhere between full egalitarianism and libertarianism: (a) if individuals were not responsible for anything, equality of well-being[1] should be sought; (b) if they were fully responsible for their characteristics, no redistribution would need to take place. We have seen how these general ideas can be incorporated in precise social criteria such as Conditional Equality, Egalitarian-Equivalence, or Envied Intensity. In this chapter we turn to an alternative interpretation of responsibility which rejects assertion (b), and replaces it with the idea that if individuals were fully responsible for their characteristics, we should be indifferent to the distribution of well-being and only be interested in the sum total.

This idea is more remote from commonsense and from the philosophical literature, but it is defensible if one interprets the idea of responsibility as removing our concern with the inequalities in well-being. In welfare economics, this can be understood as meaning that the social welfare function can have a diminished aversion to inequality. The utilitarian criterion is famously known and criticized for being indifferent to the distribution of a given sum of well-being. But when responsibility vindicates such indifference, one can consider that the utilitarian approach recovers some ethical relevance.

The utilitarian principle of reward is very different from the liberal approach. It advocates making transfers from those who have responsibility characteristics inducing a low marginal utility to those with a high marginal utility. Individuals are then not only asked to bear the direct consequences of their responsibility characteristics, but also the indirect consequences due to the transfers that are triggered by their corresponding level of marginal utility. Such transfers can, but need not, be justified in terms of desert. One can indeed tell a story that

---

[1]Recall that "equality" here means "priority to the worst-off."

stigmatizes the poor transformers of resource into well-being (when they are responsible for being so) and praises those who deserve the resources because they will make good use of them. But such a "desert" coating of the transfer policy is not at all necessary. One can simply say that the transfers are made in order to increase the sum total, without any moral evaluation of the different levels of marginal utility. In other words, the utilitarian reward principle can still be neutral in terms of judgment and aim. But it obviously fails to satisfy neutrality as no-intervention which underlies the liberal reward principle.

In the following sections, we first examine (Section 8.2) how a social criterion can at the same time embody a concern for equality along dimensions for which individuals are not responsible, and a concern for the sum along responsibility dimensions. The literature offers two main criteria, and their difference can be analyzed in terms of the dilemma between compensation and reward (Section 8.3), which resurfaces again with the utilitarian reward principle in a slightly different form. Section 8.4 develops an axiomatic analysis of this dilemma and the two criteria, while Section 8.5 compares the operation of these criteria with the liberal criteria introduced in the previous chapters, and gives some indications about the allocations that are obtained in the main models studied above. In Section 8.6 we briefly examine Roemer's proposal for the measurement of responsibility, which is often presented and discussed jointly with the particular social welfare function he advocates. Section 8.7 examines alternative approaches to the reward problem, in particular one recently proposed by Arneson.

8.2   Two social orderings

As before, but with even more importance now, we assume that there is a well chosen notion of individual well-being that can serve for social evaluation. In the liberal approach this was already important, but we ended up using only ordinal features of this measure because the non-ordinal features could be disregarded when they belonged to the individuals' responsibility sphere. In the utilitarian approach summations will be performed, implying that the cardinal properties of this measure acquire a key significance even when, and especially when, people are responsible for them.

Consider a population of individuals with a variety of circumstance and responsibility characteristics. Each combination of characteristics is associated with a certain level of well-being. The population can be partitioned into circumstance classes (subgroups of individuals with identical circumstances) or into responsibility classes.

With the ordinary utilitarian criterion, we would simply compute the sum of well-being levels over the whole population. With the ordinary maximin criterion, we would simply compute the lowest value of well-being over the whole population. Now, imagine that we want to adopt the utilitarian criterion within circumstance classes, because within such classes inequalities are due to responsibility characteristics, and the maximin criterion within responsibility classes, because within such classes inequalities are due to circumstances. Since these two kinds of classes overlap, it is not obvious how to proceed.

Two simple options immediately come to mind. If one first computes the average well-being in each circumstance class, one can then apply the maximin or leximin criterion to such average figures. Symmetrically, if one first computes the minimum within each responsibility class, one can then apply the utilitarian criterion over such minimum numbers. This provides two social orderings which have been introduced respectively by Van de gaer (1993)[2] and Roemer (1993).

Min of Means: Give priority (according to the leximin criterion) to circumstance classes which are the worst-off in terms of average well-being.

Mean of Mins: Maximize the average well-being over the whole population that would be obtained if every individual's well-being were put at the minimum observed in her own responsibility class.

The Mean of Mins can also be refined in the direction of the leximin criterion, as discussed in Section 8.4.

Let us illustrate how these criteria work, with Example 1.1 from Section 1.3. Recall that

$$\text{well-being} = (\text{bequest} \pm \text{transfer}) \times \text{dedication}.$$

Suppose again that there are four types of individuals, coming in equal numbers, each type being characterized by a low (=1) or high (=3) bequest and a low (=1) or high (=3) level of dedication to personal well-being.

Consider a policy producing the distribution of well-being in Table 8.1.

Table 8.1: Example

	low dedication	high dedication
low bequest	0	12
high bequest	1	9

The Min of Means proceeds as follows. The low-bequest class has an average well-being of 6, while the high-bequest class has an average well-being of 5. The latter, in this case, is then given priority.

The Mean of Mins proceeds as follows. The worst-off in the low-dedication class has 0, while the worst-off in the high-dedication class has 9. The average value over these figures is 4.5 (the two classes have equal size). The priority is given, in this case, to the low-low class and the high-high class.

---

[2]In fact Van de gaer (1993) considered a more general criterion in which the maximin criterion is replaced by an inequality-averse additive social welfare function. Vallentyne (2002, 2007) proposes a formally similar approach in which individual opportunities are computed not in terms of average outcome per circumstance class, but in terms of individual expected outcome. Expected outcome is computed as the weighted average of possible individual outcomes, with weights defined as dispositions to end up at the different levels. This approach, describing individuals as semi-automata with exogenous random dispositions to choose, is hard to reconcile with standard theories of decision-making – it can however be applied to the rational model of utility-maximizing decisions, but then it simply evaluates an opportunity set by the maximum utility obtainable with it.

We will first compare these two criteria to those studied in the previous chapters before comparing one to the other in more detail. The information that matters is very different for the liberal criteria and for the utilitarian criteria. The latter, as already explained, need a precise cardinal and interpersonally comparable measure of well-being, whereas the former rely only on how individuals ordinally rank combinations of resources and circumstances. But, on the other hand, the liberal criteria need information about transfers, i.e., about the way in which the distribution of well-being is obtained by a specific allocation of resources, whereas the utilitarian approach does not care at all about how a distribution of well-being is generated and, as shown in the above computations, relies only on the distribution of well-being over the circumstance and responsibility classes. In this sense it is more welfarist than the liberal approach.

But the utilitarian criteria are not purely welfarist. Indeed, a purely welfarist criterion is only interested in the distribution of individual well-being, and is not concerned about how individual well-being relates to circumstances or responsibility characteristics. For instance, assuming that each box of the tables below represents a subgroup of equal size, a welfarist criterion would be indifferent between the distributions in Tables 8.2 and 8.3:

Table 8.2: A (2,2,6,6) distribution

	low dedication	high dedication
low bequest	2	6
high bequest	2	6

Table 8.3: Another (2,2,6,6) distribution

	low dedication	high dedication
low bequest	2	2
high bequest	6	6

In contrast, the two utilitarian criteria introduced above are sensitive to such a relation, and will definitely prefer the first distribution to the second.

8.3   Another compensation-reward dilemma

Let us now compare Min of Means and Mean of Mins. They actually use different kinds of information too. Min of Means computes the average well-being of circumstance classes, and therefore needs to know how the population is partitioned into such classes. But it does not need to measure responsibility characteristics and compare them across individuals, which can be viewed as a great advantage since responsibility characteristics may be thought to be typically harder to measure than circumstances.

In dual fashion, Mean of Mins computes the lowest level of well-being for each responsibility class, so that it does not need to know anything about circumstances. One could then imagine that the choice between the two criteria could be determined by whatever kind of information is more readily available.

But in fact such differences between the two criteria relate to different ethical options as well, and this is more interesting.

Let us first formulate a basic requirement embodying the compensation principle, for social orderings. In Chapter 3 we have seen how to extend allocation rules into orderings that rank all allocations in a fine-grained way, and, as was analyzed in Section 3.3, this adaptation can be made for axioms as well. In particular, instead of simply requiring any pair of two individuals with identical responsibility characteristics to have the same level of well-being, one can rewrite *Equal Well-Being for Equal Responsibility* as follows.

Equal Well-Being for Equal Responsibility: The social situation does not worsen if, in a change affecting only a pair of individuals with identical responsibility characteristics, the worse-off's well-being increases (although he remains the worse-off).

This is equivalent to applying the maximin criterion to each pair of individuals with identical responsibility characteristics. It is clear that the Mean of Mins criterion satisfies this condition, since the change cannot decrease the lowest level of well-being in the contemplated responsibility class, so that on average these lowest numbers cannot decrease. But Min of Means does not satisfy the requirement, because if the better-off among two individuals belongs to the worst circumstance class (in terms of average well-being), while the worse-off belongs to a better circumstance class, the change can decrease the average well-being of the worst circumstance class and therefore be judged as bad.

The Min of Means criterion satisfies, however, the above requirement when it is restricted to situations where the ranking of circumstance classes is uniform across responsibility characteristics. Such a uniformity means that, if one looks at the ranking of individual well-being in any responsibility class, one finds that individuals with various circumstances always come in the same order. Let us call this kind of situation a "class-ranked" situation. The Min of Means criterion satisfies *Equal Well-Being for Equal Responsibility* in all class-ranked situations.

Now let us turn to the utilitarian reward principle. Recall how the liberal reward principle was embodied in particular in conditions requiring equal transfers for individuals with identical circumstances. The utilitarian reward principle can also be reflected in a condition focusing on pairs of individuals with identical circumstances. But a straightforward requirement to apply the utilitarian criterion to any such pair would be problematic, because it would mean that if one considers two individuals with identical characteristics (both in circumstances and responsibility), it would be acceptable to make them unequal provided the sum of their well-being remains the same or increases. That is a blatant violation of the impartiality requirement to treat identical agents equally. It is better to restrict attention to situations in which for every subset of individuals with identical characteristics – which will be called a "characteristic class"[3] – all members of the subset have the same well-being, as normally

---

[3] A characteristic class is the intersection of a circumstance class and a responsibility class.

happens when individuals are submitted to an impartial treatment by social institutions. We will now restrict attention to such "impartial" situations.[4]

Utilitarianism for Equal Circumstances: The social situation does not worsen if, in a change affecting only two characteristic classes with the same circumstances but different responsibility characteristics, the sum of their well-being increases.

The Min of Means criterion obviously satisfies this requirement since the change contemplated in it increases the average well-being in the affected circumstance class. The Mean of Mins, in contrast, does not satisfy it because the group whose well-being is decreased in the change may be among the worst-off in their responsibility class, whereas the group whose well-being increases may not, so that the change is harmful for the average well-being of the worst-off of all responsibility classes. However, the Mean of Mins satisfies *Utilitarianism for Equal Circumstances* when it is restricted to class-ranked situations.

In conclusion, we see that the two requirements are satisfied by both criteria when one restricts attention to class-ranked situations, but divide the two criteria in general situations. Is it possible to find a new criterion satisfying both conditions in general? The answer is negative, and this reveals another compensation-reward conflict, which is formally similar to the conflict analyzed previously for the liberal reward principle. In order to understand this new conflict, consider a simple population as in Example 1.1 with four equally sized groups and examine the situations shown in Tables 8.4, 8.5 and 8.6, where we simply focus on the well-being outcomes, since this is sufficient information in the case at hand.[5]

<table>
<tr><td colspan="3">Table 8.4: Situation 1</td></tr>
<tr><td>beq.\ded.</td><td>1</td><td>3</td></tr>
<tr><td>1</td><td>$u = 2$</td><td>$u = 22$</td></tr>
<tr><td>3</td><td>$u = 10$</td><td>$u = 15$</td></tr>
</table>

<table>
<tr><td colspan="3">Table 8.5: Situation 2</td></tr>
<tr><td>beq.\ded.</td><td>1</td><td>3</td></tr>
<tr><td>1</td><td>$u = 3$</td><td>$u = 17$</td></tr>
<tr><td>3</td><td>$u = 6$</td><td>$u = 16$</td></tr>
</table>

<table>
<tr><td colspan="3">Table 8.6: Situation 3</td></tr>
<tr><td>beq.\ded.</td><td>1</td><td>3</td></tr>
<tr><td>1</td><td>$u = 1$</td><td>$u = 20$</td></tr>
<tr><td>3</td><td>$u = 9$</td><td>$u = 14$</td></tr>
</table>

Let us imagine that the story starts with Situation 1, and we make an equalizing move in each dedication class, yielding Situation 2. *Equal Well-Being for Equal Responsibility* tells us that this is an acceptable move. Then we impose a change on both bequest classes, which increases the total well-being in each

---

[4] As we have defined it, it seems that Min of Means actually satisfies the bad property described above. But we implicitly assumed in the definitions that we were dealing with impartial situations. If this were not the case, presumably the Min of Means criterion would have to be refined and would feature a preliminary application of the maximin criterion so as to focus on the worst-off in every characteristic class.

[5] The per capita amounts of resources consumed in these three situations are, respectively, 4 for Situation 1, 3 for Situation 2, and 10/3 for Situation 3.

class and produces Situation 3. By *Utilitarianism for Equal Circumstances*, this is again acceptable. Therefore, Situation 3 is, according to these judgments, at least as good as Situation 1. But this is unacceptable since everyone is worse-off in Situation 3 than in Situation 1. The Pareto principle cries out for the opposite judgment.

Observe that this example features situations that are not class-ranked. With class-ranked situations, the conflict vanishes, as witnessed by the fact that Min of Means and Mean of Mins both satisfy the two conditions in this restricted case. Actually, Min of Means and Mean of Mins coincide over class-ranked situations.[6] Since configurations with a uniformly worst circumstance class are often observed in applications, the practical implications of the differences between these two criteria, and of the conflict between compensation and utilitarian reward, should not be overstated. It is nonetheless instructive to see that we again have a conflict between the full-fledged compensation principle and the utilitarian reward principle, and that the two social orderings that have been introduced in this context divide on which principle should be given priority over the other.

The fact that Mean of Mins satisfies the compensation principle better than Min of Means does not, however, imply that it always looks more egalitarian. Consider the two policies shown in Tables 8.7 and 8.8, where again we only focus on the well-being outcomes.

Table 8.7: Policy A

beq.\ded.	1	3
1	$u = 1$	$u = 17$
3	$u = 14$	$u = 15$

Table 8.8: Policy B

beq.\ded.	1	3
1	$u = 0$	$u = 17$
3	$u = 14$	$u = 17$

The Min of Means criterion prefers policy A, whereas the Mean of Mins criterion prefers policy B which makes a transfer from the worst-off of the worst circumstance class to the best-off of the best circumstance class. This is because the latter is actually the worst-off in his responsibility class, so that if he has a greater marginal utility (i.e., he transforms resources into well-being more efficiently), such a transfer is good for social welfare.

Pursuing this kind of example, it is also worth noting that the utilitarian feature shared by the two criteria overrides compensation in some circumstances in a way which is reminiscent of the easiness with which classical utilitarianism sacrifices the poor transformers of resources into utility. In Example 1.1, the sacrifice policy shown in Table 8.9 takes a heavy tax on the worst-off individual in order to subsidize those with a high level of dedication. This produces a distribution of well-being which is considered better than that obtained with the pro-dedication policy (recalled in Table 8.10) by both criteria, even by Mean of Mins in spite of its greater connection with the compensation principle.

---

[6] This is true if one takes either the maximin or the leximin version for both criteria.

Table 8.9: Sacrifice policy

beq.\ded.	1	3
1	$t = -5$ $u = -4$	$t = +5$ $u = 18$
3	$t = -3$ $u = 0$	$t = +3$ $u = 18$

Table 8.10: Pro-dedication policy

beq.\ded.	1	3
1	$t = -1$ $u = 0$	$t = +3$ $u = 12$
3	$t = -3$ $u = 0$	$t = +1$ $u = 12$

8.4   *Axiomatic analysis

Since, as argued above, it is better to work with impartial situations, we describe a social situation by the level of well-being obtained for every combination of circumstance y and responsibility characteristics z rather than for every individual. Let p_{yz} (resp., p_y, p_z) denote the fraction of the population with characteristics (y, z) (resp., y, z), and $w(y, z)$ the level of well-being of individuals with characteristics (y, z) in a situation which will be simply denoted w. The distribution of y has a finite support Y, and the distribution of z has a finite support Z. We will restrict attention to situations so that $p_{yz} > 0$ for all $y \in Y$, $z \in Z$. Let $p_{z/y}$ be defined by $p_{z/y} = p_{yz}/p_y$.

A social ordering is a complete transitive binary relation R which ranks the situations w. The relevant domain of evaluation is $\mathcal{D} = \mathbb{R}^{Y \times Z}$, i.e., all functions w from $Y \times Z$ to $\mathbb{R}$ are admissible, while p is assumed to be fixed.

A class-ranked situation is such that for all $y, y' \in Y$, $z, z' \in Z$,

$$(w(y, z) - w(y', z)) \, (w(y, z') - w(y', z')) \geq 0.$$

Let $\mathcal{D}_{CR}$ denote this domain. We will also be interested in subcases of class-ranked situations. One is the "uniform-reward" case, defined by: for all $y \in Y$, $z, z' \in Z$, $w(y, z) = w(y, z')$. Let $\mathcal{D}_{UR}$ denote this domain, in which z does not ultimately (i.e., possibly after transfers) affect well-being. Another is the "one-class" case, defined by: for all $y, y' \in Y$, $z \in Z$, $w(y, z) = w(y', z)$. Let $\mathcal{D}_{OC}$ denote this domain in which, symmetrically to the previous one, y does not ultimately affect well-being.

The two social orderings are defined as follows, in the maximin version.

Min of Means ($R_{\min M}$): $\forall w, w' \in \mathcal{D}$, $w \, R_{\min M} \, w'$ if and only if

$$\min_{y \in Y} \sum_{z \in Z} p_{z/y} w(y, z) \geq \min_{y \in Y} \sum_{z \in Z} p_{z/y} w'(y, z).$$

Mean of Mins ($R_{M \min}$): $\forall w, w' \in \mathcal{D}$, $w \, R_{M \min} \, w'$ if and only if

$$\sum_{z \in Z} p_z \min_{y \in Y} w(y, z) \geq \sum_{z \in Z} p_z \min_{y \in Y} w'(y, z).$$

A leximin refinement of Min of Means is almost immediate. One has to be cautious when the circumstance classes do not all have the same size. Imagine a population with two circumstance classes and compare two situations in which the average level of well-being for the two classes is $(1, 2)$ in the first situation and $(2, 1)$ in the second. Which situation is better? Presumably, the better situation is the one in which the class with the smaller size is at the lower level of average well-being. More generally, for given values of the average levels of well-being of circumstance classes, the smaller the lower classes, the better. One must then rely on the weighted leximin criterion, which is defined as follows. Let $(x_i; \alpha_i)_{i \in I} \geq_{\text{lex}} (x'_i; \alpha_i)_{i \in I}$ mean that, after having rearranged i so that x_i increases with i, the step function f defined by $f(t) = x_i$ for $t \in (\sum_{j<i} \alpha_j, \sum_{j \leq i} \alpha_j]$ is identical to the function f' similarly constructed (with a rearrangement of i so that x'_i is increasing with i) or there is some $t_0 \leq \sum_{i \in I} \alpha_i$ such that $f > f'$ over $(0, t_0]$ (i.e., over this interval, f is nowhere below f' and somewhere above it). For instance,

$$((1; .3), (2; .5), (3; .2)) >_{\text{lex}} ((2; .3), (1; .5), (5; .2))$$

because the functions

$$f(t) = \begin{cases} 1 \text{ if } 0 < t \leq .3 \\ 2 \text{ if } .3 < t \leq .8 \\ 3 \text{ if } .8 < t \leq 1 \end{cases} \quad \text{and } f'(t) = \begin{cases} 1 \text{ if } 0 < t \leq .5 \\ 2 \text{ if } .5 < t \leq .8 \\ 5 \text{ if } .8 < t \leq 1 \end{cases}$$

are such that $f > f'$ over $(0, .8]$.

Leximin of Means ($R_{\text{lex}M}$): $\forall w, w' \in D$, $w \, R_{\text{lex}M} \, w'$ if and only if

$$\left(\sum_{z \in Z} p_{z/y} w(y, z); p_y \right)_{y \in Y} \geq_{\text{lex}} \left(\sum_{z \in Z} p_{z/y} w'(y, z); p_y \right)_{y \in Y} .$$

Refining Mean of Mins is less obvious and also requires a new piece of notation. Let $v(k, z; w)$ denote the value of the kth component of the $|Y|$-vector $(w(y, z))_{y \in Y}$ when it is rearranged by increasing order. Let $y(k, z; w)$ denote the corresponding y (when there are ties, the smallest group comes first). The following leximin version of Mean of Mins proceeds as follows. It first rearranges y classes, for each z, so that $v(k, z; w)$ is increasing in the index $k = 1, ..., |Y|$. Then it works exactly as Leximin of Means, by first looking at the average level of well-being for $k = 1$, then for $k = 2$, and so on.

Mean of Leximin ($R_{M\text{lex}}$): $\forall w, w' \in D$, $w \, R_{M\text{lex}} \, w'$ if and only if

$$\left(\sum_{z \in Z} \frac{p_{y(k,z;w)z}}{\sum_{s \in Z} p_{y(k,s;w)s}} v(k, z; w); \sum_{z \in Z} p_{y(k,z;w)z} \right)_{k=1,...,|Y|} \geq_{\text{lex}}$$

$$\left(\sum_{z \in Z} \frac{p_{y(k,z;w')z}}{\sum_{s \in Z} p_{y(k,s;w')s}} v(k, z; w'); \sum_{z \in Z} p_{y(k,z;w')z} \right)_{k=1,...,|Y|} .$$

So much for the social orderings. The basic axioms of compensation and utilitarian reward are as follows. (Note that in this framework liberal reward axioms cannot be formulated because the relevant information about resource transfers is missing.)

Equal Well-Being for Equal Responsibility: $\forall w, w' \in \mathcal{D}, \forall (y, y', z) \in Y \times$ $Y \times Z$, if $\forall (a, b) \in Y \times Z \setminus \{(y, z), (y', z)\}$, $w(a, b) = w'(a, b)$, then

$$[w'(y, z) > w(y, z) \geq w(y', z) > w'(y', z)] \Rightarrow w \, R \, w'.$$

Utilitarianism for Equal Circumstances: $\forall w, w' \in \mathcal{D}, \forall (y, z, z') \in Y \times Z \times$ Z, if $\forall (a, b) \in Y \times Z \setminus \{(y, z), (y, z')\}$, $w(a, b) = w'(a, b)$, then

$$p_{yz} w(y, z) + p_{yz'} w(y, z') > p_{yz} w'(y, z) + p_{yz'} w'(y, z') \Rightarrow w \, R \, w'.$$

We will be interested in restrictions of these axioms to the subdomains $\mathcal{D}_{UR}$ and $\mathcal{D}_{OC}$. In order to avoid any ambiguity, the full definitions for these restrictions are given here. Observe how the population unaffected by the change is defined. For instance, if a transfer is made from (y, z) to (y', z), other transfers have to be made simultaneously for other values of z so as to impact the whole y and y' classes uniformly if we deal with situations in $\mathcal{D}_{UR}$.

Equal Well-Being for Equal Responsibility over $\mathcal{D}_{UR}$: $\forall w, w' \in \mathcal{D}_{UR}$, $\forall (y, y', z) \in Y \times Y \times Z$, if $\forall a \in Y \setminus \{y, y'\}, \forall b \in Z, w(a, b) = w'(a, b)$, then

$$[w'(y, z) > w(y, z) \geq w(y', z) > w'(y', z)] \Rightarrow w \, R \, w'.$$

This restriction appears interesting for the following reason. Recall how, in the previous chapters, it was useful to examine whether a criterion satisfied at least *Equal Well-Being for Uniform Responsibility*, an axiom which examines situations such that the whole population has identical responsibility characteristics. Here the profile of characteristics of the population, depicted by $(p_{yz})_{y \in Y, z \in Z}$, is fixed. But a situation is very similar to a uniform responsibility situation when the z factor has no influence on well-being, and this is precisely what happens in $\mathcal{D}_{UR}$. Therefore, *Equal Well-Being for Equal Responsibility over $\mathcal{D}_{UR}$* can be viewed as the adaptation of *Equal Well-Being for Uniform Responsibility* in this setting.

The restriction to $\mathcal{D}_{OC}$ will be useful for the utilitarian reward axiom.

Utilitarianism for Equal Circumstances over $\mathcal{D}_{OC}$: $\forall w, w' \in \mathcal{D}_{OC}, \forall (y, z, z') \in Y \times Z \times Z$, if $\forall a \in Y, \forall b \in Z \setminus \{z, z'\}, w(a, b) = w'(a, b)$, then

$$p_z w(y, z) + p_{z'} w(y, z') > p_z w'(y, z) + p_{z'} w'(y, z') \Rightarrow w \, R \, w'.$$

This axiom can be viewed as an adaptation of an axiom of "Utilitarianism for Uniform Circumstances" to this setting. Over $\mathcal{D}_{OC}$, all circumstance classes have exactly the same fate, which is very much, in this somewhat welfarist perspective, like a situation in which the whole population has identical circumstances.

Let us finally briefly state the Weak Pareto axiom in this context.

Weak Pareto: $\forall w, w' \in \mathcal{D}$, if $\forall (y, z) \in Y \times Z$, $w(y, z) > w'(y, z)$, then $w \, P \, w'$.

We now have a first result which provides a characterization of the strict preference part of the criteria, in their maximin versions.

Proposition 8.1 *No social ordering satisfies* Equal Well-Being for Equal Responsibility, Utilitarianism for Equal Circumstances *and* Weak Pareto. *If R satisfies* Equal Well-Being for Equal Responsibility, Utilitarianism for Equal Circumstances over $\mathcal{D}_{OC}$ *and* Weak Pareto, *then for all $w, w' \in \mathcal{D}$, $w \, P_{M \min} \, w'$ implies $w \, P \, w'$. If R satisfies* Equal Well-Being for Equal Responsibility over $\mathcal{D}_{UR}$, Utilitarianism for Equal Circumstances *and* Weak Pareto, *then for all $w, w' \in \mathcal{D}$, $w \, P_{\min M} \, w'$ implies $w \, P \, w'$.*

Proof. (1) The impossibility has been proved in a special case in the previous section and this is easily extended to the general case by focusing on situations such that only four different values of $w(y, z)$ are observed.
(2) Let $w, w' \in \mathcal{D}$ be such that $w \, P_{M \min} \, w'$. By repeated application of *Equal Well-Being for Equal Responsibility* in each z class, one can find $w'' \in \mathcal{D}_{OC}$ such that $w'' \, R \, w'$ and

$$\sum_{z \in Z} p_z \min_{y \in Y} w''(y, z) < \sum_{z \in Z} p_z \min_{y \in Y} w(y, z).$$

By *Weak Pareto*, one can find $w''' \in \mathcal{D}_{OC}$ such that $w \, P \, w'''$ and

$$\sum_{z \in Z} p_z \min_{y \in Y} w'''(y, z) > \sum_{z \in Z} p_z \min_{y \in Y} w''(y, z).$$

Since $w'', w''' \in \mathcal{D}_{OC}$ the above inequality means that for all $y \in Y$,

$$\sum_{z \in Z} p_z w'''(y, z) > \sum_{z \in Z} p_z w''(y, z).$$

By a repeated application of *Utilitarianism for Equal Circumstances over $\mathcal{D}_{OC}$*, one easily obtains $w''' \, P \, w''$. By transitivity, therefore, $w \, P \, w'$.
(3) Let $w, w' \in \mathcal{D}$ be such that $w \, P_{\min M} \, w'$. By repeated application of *Utilitarianism for Equal Circumstances* within each y class, one can find $w'' \in \mathcal{D}_{UR}$ such that $w'' \, R \, w'$ and

$$\min_{y \in Y} \sum_{z \in Z} p_{z/y} w''(y, z) < \min_{y \in Y} \sum_{z \in Z} p_{z/y} w(y, z).$$

Similarly, one can find $w''' \in \mathcal{D}_{UR}$ such that $w \, R \, w'''$ and

$$\min_{y \in Y} \sum_{z \in Z} p_{z/y} w'''(y, z) > \min_{y \in Y} \sum_{z \in Z} p_{z/y} w''(y, z).$$

Since $w'', w''' \in \mathcal{D}_{UR}$ the above inequality means that for all $z \in Z$,

$$\min_{y \in Y} w'''(y, z) > \min_{y \in Y} w''(y, z).$$

By a repeated application of *Equal Well-Being for Equal Responsibility over* $\mathcal{D}_{UR}$, one can find $v \in \mathcal{D}_{UR}$ such that $v \, R \, w''$ and for all $y \in Y$, $z \in Z$,

$$\min_{y \in Y} w'''(y, z) > v(y, z).$$

By *Weak Pareto*, $w''' \, P \, v$. By transitivity, $w \, P \, w'$. $\blacksquare$

In empirical applications, one often finds a clear dominance between the opportunities of different circumstance classes. Therefore, it is interesting to examine what happens to the above result when the domain of R is restricted to $\mathcal{D}_{CR}$. As observed in the previous section, the incompatibility between *Equal Well-Being for Equal Responsibility*, *Utilitarianism for Equal Circumstances* and *Weak Pareto* disappears, the three axioms being satisfied on this domain by $R_{M\,\min}$ and $R_{\min M}$, which then coincide. Interestingly, however, the characterizations remain valid (with a minor change for the second one).

Proposition 8.2 *On the domain* $\mathcal{D}_{CR}$, *if R satisfies* Equal Well-Being for Equal Responsibility, Utilitarianism for Equal Circumstances over $\mathcal{D}_{OC}$ *and* Weak Pareto, *then for all $w, w' \in \mathcal{D}_{CR}$, $w \, P_{M\,\min} \, w'$ (or equivalently $w \, P_{\min M} \, w'$) implies $w \, P \, w'$. If R satisfies* Equal Well-Being for Equal Responsibility over $\mathcal{D}_{UR}$, Utilitarianism for Equal Circumstances, Utilitarianism for Equal Circumstances over $\mathcal{D}_{OC}$ *and* Weak Pareto, *then for all $w, w' \in \mathcal{D}_{CR}$, $w \, P_{M\,\min} \, w'$ (or equivalently $w \, P_{\min M} \, w'$) implies $w \, P \, w'$.*

Proof. (1) The previous proof remains valid.
(2) Let $w, w' \in \mathcal{D}_{CR}$ be such that $w \, P_{M\,\min} \, w'$. Construct $w'' \in \mathcal{D}_{CR}$ such that for all $(y, z) \in Y \times Z$, $w''(y, z) > w'(y, z)$, $w \, P_{M\,\min} \, w''$, and for all $y, y' \in Y$ such that $w'(y, .)$ dominates $w'(y', .)$, $\max_{z \in Z} w''(y', z) < \min_{z \in Z} w''(y, z)$. By Weak Pareto, $w'' P w'$. By *Utilitarianism for Equal Circumstances*, one can flatten each $w''(y, .)$ and slightly increase its average outcome, in order to construct $w''' \in \mathcal{D}_{UR}$ such that $w''' R w''$ and $w \, P_{M\,\min} \, w'''$. By repeated application of *Equal Well-Being for Equal Responsibility over* $\mathcal{D}_{UR}$, one can then pull down the upper classes and only slightly raise the lower class so as to construct $w^* \in \mathcal{D}_{OC} \cap \mathcal{D}_{UR}$ such that $w^* R w'''$ and $w \, P_{M\,\min} \, w^*$. By *Utilitarianism for Equal Circumstances over* $\mathcal{D}_{OC}$, one can find another $w^{**} \in \mathcal{D}_{OC}$ such that $w^{**} R w^*$ and for all $(y, z) \in Y \times Z$, $w^{**}(y, z) < w(y, z)$. By *Weak Pareto*, $w P w^{**}$. By transitivity, $w^{**} P w'$ and therefore $w P w'$.[7] $\blacksquare$

---

[7]Note that *Utilitarianism for Equal Circumstances over* $\mathcal{D}_{OC}$, which is not logically weaker than *Utilitarianism for Equal Circumstances* (because the latter only allows us to modify one $w(y, .)$ at a time), is necessary for the result to hold. Here is an example of social ordering satisfying the other axioms. For each w, evaluate it by $V(w)$, the greatest value of $\min_{y \in Y} \hat{w}(y, z)$ that can be obtained when $\hat{w} \in \mathcal{D}_{UR}$ (which implies that $\hat{w}(y, z)$ does not depend on z) is derived from w by a finite sequence of modifications of one $w(y, .)$ at a time such that for each of these modifications, the resulting function belongs to $\mathcal{D}_{CR}$ and the value of $\sum_{z \in Z} p_z w(y, z)$ for the y under consideration does not increase. The computation of $V(w)$ is complex in general (it depends on how close the functions $w(y, .)$ for different values of y are), but it is equal to $\min_{y \in Y} w(y, z)$ when $w \in \mathcal{D}_{UR}$, which implies that it satisfies *Equal Well-Being for Equal Responsibility over* $\mathcal{D}_{UR}$. And *Utilitarianism for Equal Circumstances* is satisfied because a modification of one $w(y, .)$ that keeps $\sum_{z \in Z} p_z w(y, z)$ unchanged does not alter $V(w)$.

The leximin versions of the social orderings can be characterized more easily in the special case when p_{yz} takes the same value for all $y \in Y$ and $z \in Z$.[8] For the rest of this section we make this assumption about $(p_{yz})_{y\in Y, z\in Z}$. We first need to supplement the Equal Well-Being axiom with a permutation proviso, as in Section 3.3.

Equal Well-Being for Equal Responsibility (incl. permutation): $\forall w$, $w' \in \mathcal{D}$, $\forall (y, y', z) \in Y \times Y \times Z$, if $\forall (a, b) \in Y \times Z \setminus \{(y, z), (y', z)\}$, $w(a, b) = w'(a, b)$, then

$$[w'(y, z) > w(y, z) \geq w(y', z) > w'(y', z)] \quad \Rightarrow \quad w\,R\,w',$$
$$[w'(y, z) = w(y', z) \text{ and } w'(y', z) = w(y, z)] \quad \Rightarrow \quad w\,I\,w'.$$

Notice that the permutation part of the axiom would be questionable if p_{yz} differed from $p_{y'z}$, because the permutation might then lift up a small group and pull down a large group. It is actually still questionable here, for a different reason. It implies indifference between the two situations in Tables 8.11 and 8.12, in a simple four-category example similar to the examples of the previous section.

Table 8.11: Situation 1

beq.\ded.	1	3
1	$u = 1$	$u = 10$
3	$u = 10$	$u = 1$

Table 8.12: Situation 2

beq.\ded.	1	3
1	$u = 1$	$u = 1$
3	$u = 10$	$u = 10$

Arguably, Situation 2 is worse than Situation 1 because the opportunities of poorly endowed agents are much lower. This objection would in effect be equally relevant in the context of Section 3.3 where we introduced a similar axiom involving a permutation clause, but in that section we relied only on the "uniform" version of the axiom, which is immune to the objection. Here as well, the above axiom can be restricted to $\mathcal{D}_{UR}$, and under this restriction the above criticism vanishes and the axiom becomes quite compelling.

A slightly stronger version of the Utilitarianism axiom is required here. The axiom below is stronger than *Utilitarianism for Equal Circumstances* because it involves a weak inequality. This is still totally faithful to the utilitarian reward principle. Note that the weights in the summation disappear thanks to the assumption of constant p_{yz}.

Strong Utilitarianism for Equal Circumstances: $\forall w, w' \in \mathcal{D}$, $\forall (y, z, z') \in Y \times Z \times Z$, if $\forall (a, b) \in Y \times Z \setminus \{(y, z), (y, z')\}$, $w(a, b) = w'(a, b)$, then

$$w(y, z) + w(y, z') \geq w'(y, z) + w'(y, z') \Rightarrow w\,R\,w'.$$

The restricted version of this axiom that will serve for the characterization of Mean of Leximins applies to $\mathcal{D}_{CR}$ instead of $\mathcal{D}_{OC}$.[9]

---

[8] When y and z are independently distributed, such a situation can always be obtained by splitting the y and z classes. At the limit, each (y, z) box may contain only one individual, so that $p_{yz} \equiv 1/n$, where n is the size of the population.

[9] As in the restriction to $\mathcal{D}_{OC}$, it allows for changes in several y classes at once.

Strong Utilitarianism for Equal Circumstances over $\mathcal{D}_{CR}$**:** $\forall w, w' \in \mathcal{D}_{CR}$, $\forall z, z' \in Z$,

$$[\forall y \in Y, \ w(y, z) + w(y, z') \geq w'(y, z) + w'(y, z')] \Rightarrow w \, R \, w'.$$

We also need to introduce the Strong Pareto axiom.

Strong Pareto: $\forall w, w' \in \mathcal{D}$, if $\forall (y, z) \in Y \times Z$, $w(y, z) \geq w'(y, z)$, then $w \, R \, w'$; if, in addition, $\exists (y, z) \in Y \times Z$ such that $w(y, z) > w'(y, z)$, then $w \, P \, w'$.

Proposition 8.3 *If R satisfies* Equal Well-Being for Equal Responsibility (incl. permutation), Strong Utilitarianism for Equal Circumstances over $\mathcal{D}_{CR}$ *and* Strong Pareto, *then for all $w, w' \in \mathcal{D}$, $w \, R \, w'$ if and only if $w \, R_{\text{Mlex}} \, w'$. If R satisfies* Equal Well-Being for Equal Responsibility (incl. permutation) *over* $\mathcal{D}_{UR}$, Strong Utilitarianism for Equal Circumstances *and* Strong Pareto, *then for all $w, w' \in \mathcal{D}$, $w \, R \, w'$ if and only if $w \, R_{\text{lexM}} \, w'$.*

Proof. (1) Let $w, w' \in \mathcal{D}$. By applying the permutation part of *Equal Well-Being for Equal Responsibility (incl. permutation)* in each z class, one can find $w'' \in \mathcal{D}_{CR}$ such that $w'' \, I \, w$, and $w''' \in \mathcal{D}_{CR}$ such that $w''' \, I \, w'$, with the same ranking of y classes in w'' and w'''.

By *Strong Utilitarianism for Equal Circumstances over $\mathcal{D}_{CR}$*, one can equalize well-being in each y class and obtain v, v' such that $v \, I \, w''$ and $v' \, I \, w'''$ and for all $y \in Y$,

$$v(y, z) = \frac{1}{|Z|} \sum_{z \in Z} w''(y, z) \ \text{and} \ v'(y, z) = \frac{1}{|Z|} \sum_{z \in Z} w'''(y, z).$$

If $(v(y, z))_{y \in Y}$ is a permutation of $(v'(y, z))_{y \in Y}$ (for any z), then this means that one has $w \, I_{\text{Mlex}} \, w'$. By *Equal Well-Being for Equal Responsibility (incl. permutation)*, $v \, I \, v'$ and then, by transitivity, $w \, I \, w'$.

If $w \, P_{\text{Mlex}} \, w'$ then (for any z)

$$(v(y, z))_{y \in Y} >_{\text{lex}} (v'(y, z))_{y \in Y}.$$

The rest of the proof is a straightforward application of the inequality reduction part of *Equal Well-Being for Equal Responsibility (incl. permutation)* and *Strong Pareto*, as in Hammond (1979, Th. 4).

(2) Let $w, w' \in \mathcal{D}$. By repeated application of *Strong Utilitarianism for Equal Circumstances*, one can equalize well-being within each y class and construct $w'', w''' \in \mathcal{D}_{UR}$ such that $w'' \, I \, w$ and $w''' \, I \, w'$.

If $(w''(y, z))_{y \in Y}$ is a permutation of $(w'''(y, z))_{y \in Y}$ (for any z), then this means that one has $w \, I_{\text{lexM}} \, w'$. By *Equal Well-Being for Equal Responsibility (incl. permutation) over $\mathcal{D}_{UR}$*, $w'' \, I \, w'''$ and then, by transitivity, $w \, I \, w'$.

If $w \, P_{\text{lexM}} \, w'$ then (for any z)

$$(w'''(y, z))_{y \in Y} >_{\text{lex}} (w''(y, z))_{y \in Y}.$$

The rest of the proof is again an application of the inequality reduction part of *Equal Well-Being for Equal Responsibility (incl. permutation) over* $\mathcal{D}_{UR}$ and *Strong Pareto.* ∎

The literature contains a few other characterizations of these social orderings[10] which rely on different considerations. In particular these characterizations derive utilitarian reward from assumptions about the measurability and comparability of well-being. Here we have instead dwelled on the main motivation for utilitarian reward, which is the principle of zero inequality aversion for inequalities due to responsibility characteristics.

8.5 Applications

In this section we compare the allocations obtained by application of the Min of Means and Mean of Mins criteria in the economic models of the previous chapters to the allocations obtained by the liberal criteria.

Example 1.1 provides a striking illustration of the difference since all the liberal-reward criteria advocate the natural policy (Table 1.3) in this example whereas the utilitarian-reward criteria prefer the Pro-Dedication policy (Table 8.10), or even the sacrifice policy (Table 8.9), to it. This kind of example is the topic of Subsection 8.5.2. Subsection 8.5.1 deals with cases like Example 1.4, where the difference between the two families of criteria is much smaller, because, for instance, any allocation equalizing well-being within every responsibility class (as required by compensation) and consuming the available amount of resources is optimal for Mean of Mins; this includes the Egalitarian-Equivalence allocations. The non-technical subsection 8.5.3 is about income taxation.

8.5.1 *The TU case

In the TU case one has $u_i = x_i + v(y_i, z_i)$. For simplicity fix $\Omega = 0$. A striking feature of this model is that the classical utilitarian criterion which seeks to maximize $\sum_{i \in N} u_i$ is indifferent between all allocations $x_N \in F(e)$. The Min of Means and Mean of Mins criteria will therefore also exhibit a large amount of indifference.

Let the various y and z classes be denoted $N_y = \{i \in N \mid y_i = y\}$ and $N_z = \{i \in N \mid z_i = z\}$, with $n_y = |N_y|$, $n_z = |N_z|$.

The average well-being of a y class is computed as

$$\frac{1}{n_y} \sum_{i \in N_y} u_i = \frac{1}{n_y} \sum_{i \in N_y} x_i + \frac{1}{n_y} \sum_{i \in N_y} v(y, z_i).$$

The Min of Means criterion will equalize this expression across y classes, implying that for all y,

$$\frac{1}{n_y} \sum_{i \in N_y} x_i = \bar{v}(e) - \frac{1}{n_y} \sum_{i \in N_y} v(y, z_i),$$

---

[10] See Ooghe et al. (2007), Ooghe and Lauwers (2005).

where $\bar{v}(e)$ is average well-being over the whole population. The criterion is indifferent about the distribution of $\sum_{i \in N_y} x_i$ within the y class. In particular, it is compatible in this case with Equal Treatment for Equal Circumstances, and one can then have, for all $i \in N$,

$$x_i = \bar{v}(e) - \frac{1}{n_{y_i}} \sum_{j \in N_{y_i}} v(y_i, z_j).$$

If y and z are statistically independent, then

$$\frac{1}{n_{y_i}} \sum_{j \in N_{y_i}} v(y_i, z_j) = \frac{1}{n} \sum_{j \in N} v(y_i, z_j).$$

In this particular case the above allocation coincides with the allocation selected by the Average Conditional Equality rule S_{ACE}.

Let us now examine Mean of Mins. In this model it recommends equalizing u_i within each z class, so that for every z class there is a value C_z such that for all $i \in N_z$, $u_i = C_z$. The total value of the allocation for this criterion is then:

$$\frac{1}{n} \sum_z n_z C_z = \bar{v}(e).$$

This value is independent of the allocation of resources across z classes. In other words, any efficient allocation which equalizes well-being within every z class is then optimal for Mean of Mins. Again this allows us to implement some degree of liberal reward, as with the egalitarian-equivalent allocation rules analyzed in Section 2.7.

The fact that marginal utility is always equal to one in this model eliminates the conflict between liberal and utilitarian reward, by making the latter largely indifferent about reward. We summarize these findings in the following proposition.

Proposition 8.4 *All egalitarian-equivalent allocations are optimal for $R_{M\,\min}$, and if y and z are statistically independent, then S_{ACE} selects a best allocation for $R_{\min M}$.*

Let us now briefly look at the second-best context studied in Section 3.5. In the case of observable circumstances and unobservable responsibility characteristics (all characteristics being fixed), we see that the incentive-compatibility constraint of submitting agents with identical y to the same transfer x imposes no deadweight loss for $R_{\min M}$, but does impose a loss on $R_{M\,\min}$ because inequalities within z classes will generally not be eliminated. The latter criterion then recommends an allocation such that every y class contain members who are the worst-off (in terms of well-being) in their own z class.

In the observable well-being case (transfers x are a function of $v(y, z)$), we have a striking result: In Example 3.3, the second-best optimal allocation is, for both criteria, the egalitarian allocation (which equalizes well-being), if we restrict attention to policies such that post-transfer well-being $x(v) + v$ is non-decreasing in pre-transfer well-being v.[11] This can be explained as follows. Under the above restriction, the low y class $(y = 1)$ necessarily has the lowest average well-being, and the high y class has the highest. Equality between them is achieved only when full equality of well-being is obtained. And no other allocation gives a greater average well-being to the low y class. This result can be extended to more general situations, but is not totally general. For instance, if there are two z classes, with values z and z', and $v(y,z) > v(y',z')$ for all $y, y' \in Y$, then a large indifference obtains and the criteria accept redistributions which deepen inequalities between z classes.

8.5.2 *The distribution case

The TU case alleviates two problematic features of the utilitarian approach, namely, its tendency to redistribute in favor of agents with high marginal utility (even if this is their responsibility) and its strong dependency on a cardinal measure of well-being. In the distribution case, these problems resurface because we have a more general function $u_i = u(x_i, y_i, z_i)$.

We only briefly examine the first-best context. The contrast between utilitarian and liberal reward is most striking when the well-being function is separable in (x_i, y_i):

$$u(x_i, y_i, z_i) = f(g(x_i, y_i), z_i),$$

where f is increasing in $g(x_i, y_i)$ for all values of z, and g is increasing in x_i for all values of y.

In this case, *all the allocation rules* studied in Chapter 2 equalize $g(x_i, y_i)$ across all agents whenever this is possible. When full equality is not possible, the Conditional Equality and Egalitarian-Equivalence criteria apply the leximin criterion to $g(x_i, y_i)$.

In contrast, the Min of Means applies the maximin (or leximin) criterion across y classes to

$$\frac{1}{n_y} \sum_{i \in N_y} f(g(x_i, y), z_i).$$

Maximizing this expression implies maximizing

$$f(g(x_i, y), z_i) + f(g(x_j, y), z_j)$$

for every pair $i, j \in N_y$. The goal is then no longer to equalize $g(x_i, y) = g(x_j, y)$, unless z has no impact on the derivative of f with respect to $g(x, y)$. It will then be optimal to have $g(x_i, y) > g(x_j, y)$, and therefore $x_i > x_j$, whenever z_i is better than z_j in terms of the derivative of f with respect to $g(x, y)$.

This observation is generalized in the following proposition. Let u_x denote $\partial u / \partial x$.

---

[11] This restriction is necessary for incentive compatibility if $v(y, z)$ is a potential that can be wasted or hidden by agents when this is in their interest.

Proposition 8.5 *If $u(x, y, z)$ is differentiable with respect to x and i, j are such that $y_i = y_j$ and for all $x \leq \Omega$,*

$$u_x(x, y_i, z_i) > u_x(x, y_j, z_j),$$

then in all (first-best) optimal allocations for $R_{\min M}$ and $R_{\text{lex}M}$ one has $x_i > x_j$ whenever $x_i + x_j > 0$.

Proof. $R_{\min M}$: Let x_N be an optimal allocation. If $x_i + x_j > 0$, not all of Ω is spent on other classes, and therefore

$$\frac{1}{n_{y_i}} \sum_{k \in N_{y_i}} u(x_k, y_i, z_k) = \min_y \frac{1}{n_y} \sum_{k \in N_y} u(x_k, y, z_k).$$

As a consequence, necessarily $x_{N_{y_i}}$ maximizes

$$\frac{1}{n_{y_i}} \sum_{k \in N_{y_i}} u(x'_k, y_i, z_k)$$

under the constraint that $\sum_{k \in N_{y_i}} x'_k = \sum_{k \in N_{y_i}} x_k$. And therefore, (x_i, x_j) maximizes $u(x'_i, y_i, z_i) + u(x'_j, y_j, z_j)$ under the constraint that $x'_i + x'_j = x_i + x_j$. The rest of the argument is immediate.

As an allocation that is optimal for the leximin version of a criterion has to be optimal for the maximin version, the result immediately extends to the leximin version of this ordering, $R_{\text{lex}M}$. ∎

This result does not hold for $R_{M \min}$, because even if $u_x(x, y_i, z_i) > u_x(x, y_j, z_j)$, one may nonetheless have $x_i = 0$ and $x_j > 0$, when $u_i > \min_{k \in N_{z_i}} u_k$ and $u_j = \min_{k \in N_{z_j}} u_k$. For $R_{M \min}$, the utilitarian reward operates only for the agents who are the worst-off in their z class. Nonetheless, the above result carries over to $R_{M \min}$ when $x_i > 0$ for all $i \in N$ in the optimal allocation.

8.5.3   Unequal skills and income taxation

In the model of Section 5.5, assuming that utility functions (the responsibility characteristic) and skill levels (the circumstance characteristic) are independently distributed, it is very simple to describe how the optimal policy for Min of Means and Mean of Mins is computed: For both criteria, this is the policy *which maximizes the average utility of the low-skilled agents.* This is because the low-skilled agents have the smallest budget set, under the incentive constraints. For Min of Means, this implies that they have the lowest average utility if the distribution of utility functions is the same in all skill classes. For Mean of Mins, in every subgroup with a given utility function, the worst-off is a low-skilled agent.

This conclusion is, from the point of view of compensation, rather satisfactory, since the low-skilled obtain priority, as with the Egalitarian-Equivalence social orderings studied in Chapter 5. From the standpoint of reward, however, the idea that the income tax should seek to maximize the average utility of a subgroup of agents is an idea which, although familiar to specialists of public economics, would certainly sound strange to the general public.[12]   It implies in particular that the optimal tax might change when some utility functions change, even when all ordinal preferences remain the same in the population. The possibility for features of the conversion of ordinal satisfaction into numerical utility to have a direct relevance to the design of the income tax appears far-fetched. This may be, precisely, because the liberal interpretation of responsibility is pervasive in our culture and commands a separation between social issues and the private sphere. Such a separation forbids any connection of this sort between institutions and personal psychology. Even the idea that one could sensibly measure and compare a numerical utility across individuals with different views of the good life is controversial.

Alternatively, some studies of the utilitarian reward approach to optimal taxation have considered the possibility of adopting an objective measure of well-being instead of subjective utility.[13]   This alley of research opens many possibilities. One possibility is to take an objective measure which is totally independent of individual preferences, such as disposable income. The problem with this line is that one may then obtain optimal taxes which are inefficient with respect to individual preferences. Another possibility, which avoids this problem, is to choose a measure of well-being which is a correct representation of individual preferences without being simply a measure of subjective utility.

8.6   A statistical measurement of responsibility

It has been highlighted in Section 8.3 that the Min of Means criterion requires measuring circumstances only, which may be an advantage over the Mean of Mins criterion if circumstances are easier to observe. Roemer (1993, 1998) has proposed a clever and attractive way to measure responsibility, which requires only the knowledge of the distribution of well-being for each circumstance class, and therefore makes it possible to apply the Mean of Mins criterion even when circumstances only are known or observable.

This measurement consists in examining the distribution of well-being[14] for each circumstance class separately. The "responsibility characteristic" of an individual is then measured by her relative position in the distribution of her own circumstance class. More precisely, it is measured by the value of the cumulative distribution function at her level of well-being in this distribution. That is, if, in her circumstance class, there are q percent of individuals at or below her level of well-being, then her responsibility is measured by the quantity

---

[12] This is emphasized in Kolm's (2004b) discussion of the theory of optimal taxation.

[13] See Schokkaert et al. (2004), Roemer et al. (2003).

[14] Roemer (1993, 1998) actually refers to the distribution of some observable "effort" variable rather than well-being. But later applications have tended to rely directly on the distribution of outcome (called well-being here), which makes sense if one considers that the relevant notion of effort refers to the production of well-being rather than to a kind of intrinsic effort exerted (with more or less efficiency) by the individual.

q. For instance, two individuals who are at the median level in their respective circumstance classes will be given the same responsibility number (fifty percent). Two individuals at the bottom, or at the top, of their respective circumstance classes will similarly be identified at the bar of responsibility. We will therefore refer to this measure as the "CDF" measure of responsibility.[15]

It is essential to understand that this particular way of measuring responsibility is not tied in any way to Roemer's favorite criterion, namely, the Mean of Mins. It is not even especially connected to utilitarian reward and can be applied in conjunction with criteria such as Egalitarian-Equivalence.[16] The CDF measure of responsibility can be interpreted in two ways. The first interpretation, suggested by Roemer's description of it, is that it actually captures the true notion of responsibility. A particular property of this measure, which mechanically follows from its construction from the CDF function, is that the distribution of responsibility numbers is the uniform distribution in each circumstance class. The fraction of individuals below number q is, by construction, equal to q itself. In particular, this means that the responsibility numbers are statistically independent of the circumstance characteristics. In this way, this measure excludes the possibility of a correlation between circumstance and responsibility. This can be viewed as a serious advantage on the grounds that it would be strange to hold individuals responsible for a variable that is correlated with their circumstances. Roemer takes the example of smoking behavior, which differs across social groups. Assuming that people are not held responsible for ending up in the blue collar group rather than the white collar group, it would be strange to hold the blue-collar workers responsible for smoking more, on average, than the white-collar workers. It appears more sensible to equate the median quantity of smoking in the two groups, e.g., three cigarettes a day for a blue-collar worker may be equivalent to two per day for a white-collar worker, and to compute this kind of equivalence for all levels.

The problem with this first interpretation is that it appears unwarranted just to posit that the CDF measure is the true measure of responsibility. It is of course always possible to make the political decision to hold individuals

---

[15]Hurley (2003, pp. 191–203) criticizes Roemer for saying that people of different circumstance classes but with the same CDF measure of responsibility are "equally responsible," because by assumption all people are equally responsible for how much effort they expend. According to her, Roemer confuses responsibility, which serves to identify circumstance classes (by checking what individuals are *not* responsible for), with deservingness, which the CDF approach really measures. Roemer does indeed mention desert as an interpretation of the CDF measure. But it seems that Hurley fails to see the difference between (1) the tautology that people are equally (and fully) responsible for their responsibility characteristics, and (2) the problem of measuring the responsibility characteristics (which the CDF measure is supposed to be helpful for).

[16]It may, however, appear somewhat problematic to rely on it in the context of the liberal approach to reward, for the following reason. The CDF measure requires ranking individuals in terms of well-being within each circumstance class, and therefore requires comparing well-being across individuals with different utility functions. Normally, liberal criteria do not need to make such comparisons. This advantage seems to be wasted if one tries to apply the CDF measure of responsibility before implementing such criteria. In effect, the liberal criteria ultimately discard the irrelevant information about interpersonal comparisons, so that, if the CDF measure does not distort the measurement of responsibility, this is not really a problem.

responsible for their relative positions in the distribution of well-being in their respective circumstance classes. But such a decision may not be immediately appealing. For instance, if the blue-collar workers smoke more, there probably is a mechanism which explains it. Such a mechanism may be such that some true underlying responsibility variables translate into relative positions in the distributions of well-being in a complex way. The interaction between the circumstance characteristics and the (true) responsibility characteristics in such a mechanism should presumably be studied before any conclusion is drawn over the link between responsibility and the CDF function.

This argument suggests an alternative interpretation of the CDF measure, namely, as an approximation or a short-cut that may or may not be acceptable depending on how well-being is determined by various individual characteristics. This interpretation raises an interesting issue. Considering that there is a function that relates individual well-being to circumstances and (true) responsibility characteristics, one can ask under what conditions the CDF measure is an acceptable proxy for true responsibility characteristics. Note that, within a given circumstance class, two individuals with identical (true) responsibility characteristics will necessarily have the same well-being, when they are submitted to impartial policies which treat identical individuals in the same way. Therefore the CDF measure will always correctly attribute the same responsibility level to them. What can happen with the CDF measure is only that some individuals with different (true) responsibility characteristics will be considered identical because they happen to have the same well-being.

This configuration cannot occur when there is a one-to-one relationship between the CDF measure and the true responsibility characteristics. In particular, when the (true) responsibility characteristic (1) is a one-dimensional parameter that (2) is identically distributed in every circumstance class, and (3) well-being is strictly monotonic with respect to this parameter, there is no loss of information in relying on the CDF measure instead of the true parameter.

Let us examine what happens when the conditions listed in the previous sentence are not satisfied. When the responsibility characteristics are not identically distributed in all circumstance classes, the CDF measure is generally biased. We have observed above that a correlation between circumstances and other characteristics makes it dubious to hold individuals responsible for these characteristics. But this observation is not absolutely compelling. Depending on how one defines responsibility, one need not be shaken by such correlations. For instance, if one decides to hold individuals responsible for their preferences, it is not clear why this should be undermined by the fact that some circumstance classes exhibit a greater fraction of members with, say, expensive tastes. It may also happen that, depending on their responsibility characteristics, individuals are exposed to different external influences for which they cannot be held responsible.[17] If we factor in these differential exposures in the definition of circumstance characteristics, there will automatically be a correlation with

---

[17] This idea is put forth, with an example of a targeted advertising campaign, by Hild and Voorhoeve (2004, p. 123).

responsibility characteristics.

When well-being is not monotonic with respect to the one-dimensional responsibility parameter, it is very easy to put individuals in the same responsibility class whereas they should actually be treated in a totally different way. Figure 8.1 illustrates this phenomenon. In the figure the two curves depict the relationship between well-being and a true responsibility parameter, for two different circumstance classes. Individuals at A and B have equal well-being and belong to the same circumstance class, but the former should be taxed while the latter should be helped, in view of their relative position in their respective responsibility classes. Amalgamating them in the same responsibility category is therefore undesirable when one wants to implement a criterion satisfying the compensation principle.

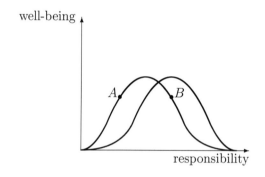

Figure 8.1: Non-monotonic relationship between responsibility and well-being

When responsibility characteristics are irreducibly multidimensional, the same problem can arise for similar reasons. Instead of giving a three-dimensional geometric example, let us take up again the smoking example. Imagine that people have different preferences about the trade-off between health and other goods, and also have different levels of concerns for their own appearance. For the sake of the example, imagine that we want to hold individuals responsible for both features of their preferences. One can safely assume that those who care less about their health tend to smoke more, other things being equal. Let us now also assume that, among blue-collar workers, those who care more about their appearance tend to smoke more, other things being equal, whereas the reverse is observed among white-collar workers. Consider two blue-collar workers, Adam and Bob, who smoke the same amount but for different reasons: Adam does not care about his health, Bob cares about his appearance. If both were white-collar workers, Adam would smoke more than Bob. It is therefore incorrect to put them in the same responsibility category if one wants to apply the compensation principle, because in their true responsibility classes, Adam may be relatively "well off" (his level of smoking is not so much due to being a blue-collar) and Bob relatively "badly off."

A final puzzle about the CDF measure of responsibility is that it makes responsibility characteristics endogenous to policy in principle, so that it may happen that some individuals are moved from "low effort" classes to "high effort" classes simply as a result of a change of policy. This direct influence of policy over responsibility characteristics is puzzling, as we have already noted in Section 3.4. It would be more appealing to discover an underlying exogenous disposition to react to external stimuli that would be the real responsibility characteristic. Hild and Voorhoeve (2004) also remark that Mean of Mins can violate the Pareto principle when responsibility characteristics are endogenous, a problem that does not affect Min of Means. To illustrate this point, consider the policies in Tables 8.13 and 8.14. In each box, n indicates the number of people in this category.

Table 8.13: Policy A

beq.\ded.	1	3
1	$n = 1$ $u = 1$	$n = 1$ $u = 3$
3	$n = 3$ $u = 3$	$n = 1$ $u = 3$

Table 8.14: Policy B

beq.\ded.	1	3
1	$n = 1$ $u = 1$	$n = 1$ $u = 2$
3	$n = 0$ $u = 1$	$n = 4$ $u = 2$

Policy B induces the high-bequest-low-dedication people to move to high dedication. We observe that every individual has an equal or lower well-being with policy B than with policy A. But Mean of Mins prefers policy B, as can be computed, since

$$4 \times \min\{1,3\} + 2 \times \min\{3,3\} < 1 \times \min\{1,1\} + 5 \times \min\{2,2\}.$$

8.7   Alternative approaches to reward

The liberal and the utilitarian conceptions of reward are prominent because they can be given straightforward rationales. The liberal approach associates responsibility with a disregard for consequences and with the absence of external intervention. The utilitarian approach associates responsibility with a disregard for inequalities, understood as the absence of aversion to inequalities.

Arneson (1999a, 2000a, 2001) has introduced a third approach to the reward problem, which is based on the idea that individuals should obtain the level of well-being that they deserve in view of their responsibility characteristics. This is a new approach because neither the liberal nor the utilitarian conceptions involve a direct notion of desert. In the liberal approach, one simply ignores the consequences of responsibility characteristics over well-being, as much as is compatible with efficiency concerns. In the utilitarian approach, one similarly disregards the relationship between responsibility and well-being and only focuses on a collective outcome, the sum of well-being levels over the relevant subpopulations.[18]

---

[18] Roemer (1998, e.g., p. 15) does refer to desert in relation to the CDF measure of responsibility, with the idea that individuals in the same responsibility class for the CDF measure are equally deserving. But, unlike Arneson, he does not rely on desert in order to allocate advantages across individuals who are *unequally* deserving.

Arneson proposes a version of prioritarianism which can be described as follows. The social value of giving a certain benefit to a given individual is the greater (1) the worse off this individual is; (2) the more he would benefit; (3) the more deserving he is. The degree of desert of an individual can depend on several things, such as his moral character and the features of her personality or her behavior for which she is morally responsible. In particular, at a low level of well-being, an individual is less deserving of receiving help if he is more responsible for being that low. Arneson's theory can perhaps be formalized as an additive social welfare function in which the priority assigned to individuals depends on their level of well-being and their degree of desert. For instance, one can obtain this by the formula

$$w(d_1)\varphi(u_1) + ... + w(d_n)\varphi(u_n),$$

where $w(d_i)$ is a weight that increases with the measure of desert d_i, and $\varphi(u_i)$ is a concave increasing function of well-being u_i. Less formally, the definition can be enshrined in the following way.

Desert-sensitive Prioritarianism: The priority assigned to an individual decreases with her level of well-being and increases with her deservingness and with her marginal well-being (i.e., rate of transformation of resources into well-being).

The problem at this stage is to make the measure of desert (and how desert affects priority) sufficiently precise so that concrete applications can be imagined. Arneson (2007) provides interesting indications about how a notion of desert could be defined in conformity with his idea that individuals should be held responsible only for what is under their control. Desert would depend on how conscientiously, given her circumstances, the individual seeks what is good and right, as she can see it from her perspective. With unfavorable circumstances, the individual might end up making efforts in a wrong direction, or making apparently little effort, but what counts for desert, in Arneson's view, is not how objectively good and right the individual's deeds are, but how hard she tries given her background and the prevailing circumstances. In that sense desert concerns how the individual nurtures a certain disposition to react to circumstances, rather than what she achieves.

Another difficulty of this approach is that the link between responsibility and consequences is very roundabout, because the spendthrift who wastes his wealth is less deserving of receiving help but not necessarily in the proportion that corresponds to the direct consequences of his behavior. This, however, can also be viewed as a decisive advantage precisely because the liberal and utilitarian approaches are both blind to *ex post* inequalities. In contrast, the desert approach makes it possible to think of apportioning *ex post* inequalities to deservingness. One may accept that the spendthrift deserves less than others, but disagree with the liberal approach that he can be left to his own predicament, and disagree with the utilitarian approach that he might even be liable for additional taxes because the resources he gets yield little well-being. The issue of the relevance of *ex post* inequalities will be taken up again in the last chapter.

Arneson (2007) actually suggests that well-being should ideally be proportional to desert. This is a little mysterious, since the optimal distribution of well-being should depend on how well-being can be produced and distributed. Suppose we cannot reach a group of people stranded in an island. Then the optimal distribution, given the feasibility constraints, is unlikely to be proportional. Perhaps Arneson means that when there is a fixed sum of well-being which can be freely redistributed across individuals, then proportionality should obtain. One can show that this requirement imposes a very specific form on the social criterion. It must be ordinally equivalent to the formula

$$d_1 \ln u_1 + \ldots + d_n \ln u_n.$$

Another interesting idea one finds in Arneson (2007) is that, if public policy has an influence on the distribution of desert,[19] one should be prioritarian about this distribution other things equal, i.e., seek to raise the level of desert of the least deserving among individuals with the same level of well-being. This gives us a doubly prioritarian view: on well-being and on desert. One must, however, note that prioritarianism over desert is not satisfied by the formula $d_1 \ln u_1 + \ldots + d_n \ln u_n$, which is linear in desert. This observation suggests that double prioritarianism is incompatible with the idea that well-being should be proportional to desert.

Yet another approach to reward is to adopt an agnostic attitude and to focus on the compensation principle without seeking a precise judgment on reward schemes. Hild and Voorhoeve (2004) have proposed to consider that a social situation is better than another in terms of opportunities when it features a distribution of well-being in every responsibility class which is better according to the leximin criterion.

Leximin Opportunities: A situation x is better than a situation x' if for every responsibility class, the distribution of well-being in this class is better in x than in x' according to the leximin criterion.

It is a partial criterion and this should not be surprising because it does not take sides on the reward issue. This criterion encapsulates the most one can say about how to rank social situations, on the sole basis of the compensation principle and the Pareto principle. It is therefore compatible with all criteria satisfying the compensation principle, such as Egalitarian-Equivalence and Mean of Mins, in the sense that whenever Leximin Opportunities prefers a situation, so do these other criteria. This criterion has no implication about reward.

---

[19]This can only be the case with a compatibilist notion of control, such that the individual can be considered in control of his desert level even though this is at the same time influenced by institutions and policies.

8.8 Conclusion

One of the main points of this book is to highlight the importance of reward principles in responsibility-sensitive egalitarianism. It seems that some of the early developments of the utilitarian branch of the literature did not really adopt the utilitarian approach to reward on its own merit. It is in particular interesting to note a substantial flexibility on this issue in Roemer's seminal work. Roemer (1993) actually first considers a criterion that bears a strong similarity with Conditional Equality, before settling for Mean of Mins for the reason that the latter looks like an average version of the former and considers all possible levels of responsibility whereas a criterion like Conditional Equality focuses only on one reference level.[20] Roemer (1998) still presents the averaging performed by Mean of Mins as a "compromise" approach which balances the interests of all responsibility classes. At several places[21] he considers the liberal reward rule that all individuals in the same circumstance class should receive the same resources (Equal Treatment for Equal Circumstances) as a reasonable constraint that might be imposed on the computation of equal opportunity policies. More recently, Roemer (2002b, p. 459) says that he has no strong preference between Mean of Mins, Min of Means and a criterion similar to Average Conditional Equality (a liberal solution defined in Section 2.7 which computes the average of the Conditional Equality allocations obtained with all possible reference values for the responsibility characteristics).

The contrast between the utilitarian approach and the liberal approach to reward has been analyzed in detail in this chapter. The fact that philosophical theories, especially those of Rawls and Dworkin (as well as Van Parijs), but also, presumably, those of Cohen and Sen, espouse the liberal approach certainly imposes on economists a duty to explore the implications of this reward principle. It used to be the case that resource allocation principles such as the laissez-faire or the no-envy condition had no direct expression in social welfare functions, so much so that, paradoxically enough, the economic theory of redistributive policies had little affinity for such resourcist principles. We now have a battery of social orderings which incorporate a concern for equality of resources and supplement the traditional family of welfarist functions. However, the utilitarian reward principle studied in this chapter must also be taken seriously due to its filiation with welfare economics. Let us hope that the issue of determining the respective validity of the various reward principles, including the alternative desert principle put forth by Arneson, will attract more attention in future philosophical debates.

---

[20] This reason is especially valid for the criterion Roemer considers. Conditional Equality computes, for *each* individual, the level of well-being that he would obtain with his *current resources* and circumstances and the reference responsibility characteristics. In contrast, the criterion which Roemer (1993, p. 160) initially considers maximizes the smallest well-being in the reference responsibility class, regardless of what happens in other classes. One may be afraid that this criterion would advocate siphoning off resources from all other responsibility classes, and Roemer introduces a constraint over admissible policies in order to avoid it. This problem does not occur with Conditional Equality.

[21] See Roemer (1998, pp. 10, 28, 74).

Chapter 9

Inequalities of opportunity and social mobility

9.1 Introduction

We have so far been dealing with the broad issue of defining a general social criterion encompassing all aspects of efficiency and equity. In many contexts it is useful to describe an imperfect situation not just in terms of how far it is from the ideal, but also in what ways it differs from it, for instance in terms of degrees of inefficiency or of inequality. It is standard in welfare economics to depict social welfare as made up of the combination of an index of average individual well-being with an index of inequalities in well-being. It is often useful to analyze whether a given evolution in social welfare comes from the former or from the latter index, or even from conflicting movements of the two indexes.

The first question addressed in this chapter is how this classical decomposition of social welfare into average well-being and inequalities can be adapted to the social orderings that incorporate a concern for personal responsibility and for opportunities. In other words, can one construct an index of inequalities of opportunity in a similar way as one does for indexes of inequalities in well-being or income? It is shown in Section 9.2 that this can indeed be done. The main idea is that, once a measure of individual situations which takes account of responsibility has been selected for the evaluation of social states of affairs, it can serve as an input in a related inequality index. For instance, Conditional Equality evaluates individual situations by the level of well-being that individuals would achieve counterfactually if their responsibility characteristics were at the reference value. The distribution of such hypothetical levels of well-being can be put in an inequality index, and one thereby obtains a measure of inequality that focuses on the features of individual situations that appear relevant from the standpoint of Conditional Equality. A similar procedure can be used with the other criteria which have been studied above.

Beside inequalities, social mobility is another feature of social situations which bears some obvious connection with opportunities. The literature on social mobility has initially focused on changes between generations, as if movement was good in itself. The idea that the situation is better if the children of the rich become poor while the children of the poor become rich can, however, be criticized on the grounds that, from an individualistic point of view, someone does not deserve to be favored or penalized just because of the status of his parents. Every child should be given the same opportunities, and that seems a better guideline for the study of social mobility than a pure preference for movement across generations. In Sections 9.3–9.5, we will examine how this idea can help us to construct appealing measures of social mobility. It will turn out that the conflict between compensation and reward, and the divide between liberal and utilitarian reward, provide interesting insights into the various possibilities in this field. Sections 9.6 and 9.7 focus on the difficulties induced by the fact that applied studies of inequalities and mobility typically fail to measure all the circumstance data and therefore bear the risk of attributing too much responsibility to individuals.

9.2   *Inequality indices

It may be useful to recall the classical decomposition of social welfare, due to Kolm (1968) and Atkinson (1970). For any social welfare function $W(u_1^*, ...u_n^*)$ which is continuous and increasing, one can define its "equal-equivalent" $E_W(u_1^*, ...u_n^*)$ by the formula

$$W(u_1^*, ...u_n^*) = W\left(E_W(u_1^*, ...u_n^*), ..., E_W(u_1^*, ...u_n^*)\right).$$

In other words, $E_W(u_1^*, ...u_n^*)$ is the per-capita level of well-being which would yield the same social welfare if there were perfect equality. For any inequality-averse social welfare function,

$$E_W(u_1^*, ...u_n^*) \leq \frac{1}{n}\sum_{i=1}^{n} u_i^*,$$

with a strict inequality when $(u_1^*, ...u_n^*)$ is not completely egalitarian. It is therefore possible to define a relative inequality index

$$I_W^r(u_1^*, ...u_n^*) = 1 - \frac{E_W(u_1^*, ...u_n^*)}{\frac{1}{n}\sum_{i=1}^{n} u_i^*},$$

and an absolute inequality index

$$I_W^a(u_1^*, ...u_n^*) = \frac{1}{n}\sum_{i=1}^{n} u_i^* - E_W(u_1^*, ...u_n^*),$$

which measure the loss in per capita well-being that one would accept if inequalities could be eliminated. With such indexes, social welfare can be decomposed as follows:

$$
\begin{aligned}
E_W(u_1^*, ... u_n^*) &= (\frac{1}{n} \sum_{i=1}^{n} u_i^*)(1 - I_W^r(u_1^*, ... u_n^*)) \\
&= \frac{1}{n} \sum_{i=1}^{n} u_i^* - I_W^a(u_1^*, ... u_n^*).
\end{aligned}
$$

The main idea here is to apply this methodology to a responsibility-sensitive definition of u_i^*.[1] We will focus here on the distribution case of the simple division model, and adapting these ideas to the other models is rather straightforward, although we will briefly discuss an example at the end of this section. In the division model, agent i's situation is described by $u_i = u(x_i, y_i, z_i)$, with the same notations as in Section 1.2.

For Conditional Equality, the relevant measure of individual situations is

$$
u(x_i, y_i, \tilde{z}),
$$

so that if one writes $u_i^* = u(x_i, y_i, \tilde{z})$, the above formulae can be directly applied. Two problems have to be addressed, though.

The first problem is to select the function W. In the previous chapters the leximin criterion has been advocated for the comparison of distributions $(u_1^*, ... u_n^*)$. This is not a continuous criterion, but if one considers the maximin instead, one observes that when

$$
W(u_1^*, ... u_n^*) = \min_{i \in N} u_i^*,
$$

one obtains $E_W = W$, and therefore

$$
\begin{aligned}
I_W^r(u_1^*, ... u_n^*) &= 1 - \frac{\min_{i \in N} u_i^*}{\frac{1}{n} \sum_{i=1}^{n} u_i^*}, \\
I_W^a(u_1^*, ... u_n^*) &= \frac{1}{n} \sum_{i=1}^{n} u_i^* - \min_{i \in N} u_i^*.
\end{aligned}
$$

These inequality indices are simple to apply. One may consider them a little unsatisfactory because they neglect the inequalities occurring at the various levels of the distribution, but any inequality index transforms an n-dimensional vector into a single number and therefore loses a lot of information about the distribution. However, in statistical applications, it may appear dangerous to give such a prominent role to an extreme value of the distribution which is often observed with low precision. Therefore, it would make sense to compute

---

[1] Devooght (2007) proposes an alternative approach. It consists in computing the distance between the actual and the ideal distribution of well-being $(u_i)_{i \in N}$ for the criterion under consideration. This approach cannot be related to a decomposition of social welfare and therefore cannot deduce the measure of inequalities directly from the social criterion. It can, however, be used to decompose inequalities in the actual distribution (which correspond to the distance between the actual distribution and the equal distribution) into two parts, "offensive" inequalities (distance between the actual and the ideal distribution) and "inoffensive" inequalities (distance between the ideal and the equal distribution).

inequality indexes related to the constant-elasticity-of-substitution (CES) social welfare function

$$W(u_1^*, ... u_n^*) = \left(\frac{1}{n} \sum_{i=1}^{n} (u_i^*)^{1-\varepsilon} \right)^{\frac{1}{1-\varepsilon}},$$

for various values of $\varepsilon > 0$, in order to get a more comprehensive view of the inequalities.

A second problem is that whereas the social ordering associated to $\min_{i \in N} u_i^*$ (or the leximin criterion) does not depend on the cardinal features of u, but only on how it ranks (x, y) bundles when $z = \tilde{z}$, the decomposition that is obtained does depend directly on it. This problem is more or less acute depending on the context, of course. There may be cases when $u(., ., .)$ is measured without any ambiguity. If one only knows the ordinal rankings and u is not well measured, there is a way out. It consists in picking a reference $\tilde{y}$ as well, and in defining u_i^* by the equation

$$u(u_i^*, \tilde{y}, \tilde{z}) = u(x_i, y_i, \tilde{z}).$$

In this fashion, u_i^* is measured in terms of resources. This measure is actually rather intuitive. It corresponds to the quantity of resources that would give the same hypothetical well-being if i had $y_i = \tilde{y}$. This is tantamount to computing the equivalent resources for Egalitarian-Equivalence, but restricted to the counterfactual case $z_i = \tilde{z}$. Since Conditional Equality satisfies the compensation principle under the restriction that $z_i = \tilde{z}$, this is rather coherent.

Let us now turn to Egalitarian-Equivalence. In view of the above, it appears straightforward to posit $u_i^* = \tilde{x}_i$, where $\tilde{x}_i$ is the equivalent resource defined by

$$u(\tilde{x}_i, \tilde{y}, z_i) = u_i.$$

If one had a good measure of well-being u and wanted to measure inequalities in terms of well-being rather than resources, one could pick a reference $\tilde{z}$ and define

$$u_i^* = u(\tilde{x}_i, \tilde{y}, \tilde{z}).$$

Observe the duality between Conditional Equality and Egalitarian-Equivalence, once again.

The utilitarian criteria are also amenable to inequality studies. The Min of Means lends itself easily to a measure of inequalities, by letting

$$u_i^* = \frac{1}{n_{y_i}} \sum_{j:y_j = y_i} u_j,$$

where n_{y_i} is the number of agents j such that $y_j = y_i$. Every individual situation is assessed by the average well-being of the corresponding circumstance class, and inequalities between these quantities are intuitively interpreted in terms of inequalities of opportunities.

The case of Mean of Mins is a little less obvious, because if one defines $u_i^* = \min_{j:z_j = z_i} u_j$, then the social welfare function corresponding to the Mean of

Mins is the inequality-neutral utilitarian social welfare function. The inequality indexes associated to this function are always null. But one actually has

$$\frac{1}{n}\sum_{i=1}^{n} u_i^* \leq \frac{1}{n}\sum_{i=1}^{n} u_i,$$

and one can therefore compute inequality indexes as follows:

$$
\begin{aligned}
I_W^r &= 1 - \frac{\frac{1}{n}\sum_{i=1}^{n} u_i^*}{\frac{1}{n}\sum_{i=1}^{n} u_i}, \\
I_W^a &= \frac{1}{n}\sum_{i=1}^{n} u_i - \frac{1}{n}\sum_{i=1}^{n} u_i^*.
\end{aligned}
$$

Such indexes measure the loss in average well-being that the Mean of Mins would accept in order to eliminate inequalities within each responsibility class. They are therefore the relevant indexes for this criterion.

These definitions are less different from the standard definitions of inequality indices than it seems. Indeed, let us focus e.g. on I_W^r, which can be rewritten as:

$$I_W^r = \sum_z \frac{\sum_{j:z_j=z} u(x_j, y_j, z)}{\sum_{i=1}^{n} u_i}\left[1 - \frac{\min_{j:z_j=z} u(x_j, y_j, z)}{\frac{1}{n_z}\sum_{j:z_j=z} u(x_j, y_j, z)}\right].$$

The expression between brackets is a standard inequality index for the z class, so that I_W^r appears to be a weighted[2] mean of inequalities within responsibility classes.[3]

The other criteria studied in the previous chapters could also be given associated inequality indexes, but we will restrict attention to these four main examples here.

Let us achieve this section by examining an example of application of the Egalitarian-Equivalence approach to the context of income distribution studied in Chapters 4 and 5. The theory is simple because one can apply inequality indexes to the equivalent transfers computed for the various Egalitarian-Equivalence criteria.[4] Here is an example of how, for Min Egalitarian-Equivalence,

---

[2] Moreno-Ternero (2007) also has a similar formula, but without weights.

[3] If one is uncomfortable with the maximin criterion in the definition of u_i^*, one can compute instead a CES equal-equivalent for each responsibility class,

$$u_i^* = \left(\frac{1}{n}\sum_{j:z_j=z_i} (u_j)^{1-\varepsilon} \right)^{\frac{1}{1-\varepsilon}},$$

and then proceed in the same way. Alternatively, Ruiz-Castillo (2003) and Villar (2005) propose the Theil index for the computation of inequalities within each responsibility class. Villar (p. 10) notes a difficulty with the Theil index in this context. It implies that social welfare is decreasing with respect to the utility of the individuals who are above the mean (of their responsibility class). This can be remedied by normalizing the index with $1/\ln n_z$, which however implies that inequalities matter less in larger responsibility classes.

[4] See Section 5.3 for the definitions.

one can relate individual values of equivalent transfers to more standard measures of income. Recall that Min Egalitarian-Equivalence evaluates individual situations by the equivalent transfer $\tilde{t}_i$ defined by $u_i(x_i) = u_i(B(s_m, \tilde{t}_i))$. We retain the same notations as in Chapters 4 and 5. If one approximates the representation of preferences by a CES function

$$u_i(c_i, \ell_i) = \left(a_i c_i^{\frac{\sigma-1}{\sigma}} + (1 - a_i) (1 - \ell_i)^{\frac{\sigma-1}{\sigma}} \right)^{\frac{\sigma}{\sigma-1}},$$

the parameter a_i will satisfy the equation

$$\frac{a_i}{1 - a_i} = \frac{1}{w_i} \left(\frac{c_i}{1 - \ell_i} \right)^{\frac{1}{\sigma}},$$

where w_i is the agent's *net* marginal wage rate. With standard algebraic computations using the expenditure function, one is then able to obtain $\tilde{t}_i$ from the formula:

$$\tilde{t}_i = \frac{f_i}{\left(\frac{c_i}{f_i} + \frac{w_i(1-\ell_i)}{f_i} \left(\frac{w_i}{s_m} \right)^{\sigma-1} \right)^{\frac{1}{\sigma-1}}} - s_m,$$

where $f_i = c_i + w_i (1 - \ell_i)$ can be read as the agent's full income (computed at his current net marginal wage rate). In the above formula this full income is divided by a correction term which is a weighted average of the distortion of prices between the prices at which the agent makes his choice, i.e., $(1, w_i)$, and the prices which serve for the computation of his equivalent budget, i.e., $(1, s_m)$. When the elasticity of substitution goes to zero, this formula simplifies into

$$\tilde{t}_i = c_i + s_m (1 - \ell_i) - s_m = c_i - s_m \ell_i.$$

The expression $c_i + s_m (1 - \ell_i)$ is a full income computed at the gross minimum wage rate s_m. Interestingly, this is very similar to how Nordhaus and Tobin (1973) computed full income in their estimation of standards of living.[5]

9.3   Social mobility and social welfare

Consider a society in which children with different origins end up, in their lives, in various social groups. Children with identical origin will be said to form "origin groups," while children with identical fates will form "final groups." These groups are assumed to be ranked by order of increasing social status.

The literature on social mobility very often refers to equality of opportunity. But there may be an ambiguity about the connection between social welfare, equality of opportunity and social mobility. The phrase "equality of opportunity" is perhaps too easily used in the literature on social mobility. For instance,

---

[5] This is also similar to Rawls' (1974) proposal to incorporate leisure into the index of primary goods by giving full-time leisure the same value as the full-time income of the unskilled, and measuring the value of one hour of leisure proportionally.

if one defines social welfare in terms of utilities of dynasties comprising parents and children, as in Markandya (1982), Atkinson (1983) or Dardanoni (1993), then one is naturally led to give different weights to the welfare of children with different origins, in order to give priority to those with poor parents. This asymmetric evaluation of the situation of children is in direct conflict with the general idea of equal opportunity, which is fundamentally impartial across children of all origins and would never consider giving lower opportunities to some children in order to punish them for their rich parents. Social welfare, from the perspective of equality of opportunity, should not be defined with respect to dynasties, but with respect to individuals facing different prospects or opportunity sets.

Another preliminary remark is that, if one wants to have a measure of social mobility which is consistent with a notion of social welfare, one must have a precise definition of social welfare first. Clearly, if social mobility is understood in terms of equality of opportunity, one should rely on a notion of social welfare that embodies basic principles of responsibility-sensitive egalitarianism. Therefore it seems that social orderings like those studied in this book are needed if one wants to develop a welfare-consistent measure of social mobility as equality of opportunity.

In this light, the studies of social mobility which focus exclusively on transition matrices must be taken with caution, as emphasized in Van de gaer et al. (2001). A transition matrix gives the probability that a child of origin i will end up in final group j, as in the following example with three social groups. In the matrix below, a child from origin group 1 has .6 probability of ending up in final group 1, .3 probability of ending up in final group 2, and so on.

$$\text{Origin groups} \quad \begin{array}{c} \text{Final groups} \\ \begin{pmatrix} .6 & .3 & .1 \\ .2 & .4 & .4 \\ .2 & .3 & .5 \end{pmatrix} \end{array}$$

Note that the matrix in itself does not provide any information about the inequalities of outcome between the various final groups. Since social welfare and inequalities in opportunities typically depend on the degree of inequality between various final groups, it appears necessary to analyze the distribution of well-being (however defined) before decomposing social welfare into a mobility component and other components. For instance, a perfectly immobile situation may have low inequalities in opportunities if inequalities between final groups are small. The mobility component may be ultimately reducible to features of the transition matrix, but one cannot make judgments about social welfare or even about inequality of opportunities simply by looking at transition matrices, when other features of the social situation may differ.

In this vein, a troubling observation is that mobility typically increases with inequalities within origin groups. Imagine a society where social stratification is depicted simply with three quantiles (upper, middle and lower). In situation A, children from lower origin end up in equal proportions at well-being levels 1, 2 and 3. The respective figures for children from middle (resp., upper) origin are 2, 3 and 4 (resp., 3, 4 and 5). The mobility matrix in terms of quantiles for this situation is

$$
\begin{pmatrix}
2/3 & 1/3 & 0 \\
1/3 & 1/3 & 1/3 \\
0 & 1/3 & 2/3
\end{pmatrix}.
$$

Now move to situation B, where the well-being figures are 0, 2, 4 (lower origin); 1, 3, 5 (middle); 2, 4, 6 (upper). The inequalities between origin groups have not changed but inequalities within them have increased. The mobility matrix is now

$$
\begin{pmatrix}
1/2 & 1/3 & 1/6 \\
1/3 & 1/3 & 1/3 \\
1/6 & 1/3 & 1/2
\end{pmatrix},
$$

which undoubtedly displays more mobility. By modifying this kind of example, one can find configurations in which a simultaneous increase in inequalities between and within origin groups yields an apparent increase in mobility, in spite of an obvious increase of inequalities of opportunities.

Relying on transition matrices is therefore not enough. But the distributions of well-being for the origin groups may not even provide enough information, if one wants to define social welfare with a criterion embodying the principle of liberal reward. This has already been explained in the previous chapter in some detail, but let us develop this point here, briefly, with respect to inequalities of opportunity. Consider a simple society in which well-being is equal for all individuals. If one simply looks at distributions of well-being, it appears that all individuals face the same prospects independently of their origin. Does this mean that equality is achieved? In the sense of compensation certainly, but it may be that equality across final groups is achieved by transferring resources between individuals with different responsibility characteristics in a way that blatantly violates the principle of liberal reward. Those whose responsibility characteristics yield more well-being appear in fact less well treated than those who are responsible for having less well-being before transfers. In conclusion, one sees that simply focusing on inequalities between distributions of well-being for different origin groups may miss an important dimension of inequalities, namely, the inequalities of treatment that individuals may be subjected to in connection with their responsibility characteristics.

9.4   *Social welfare decomposed

In Section 9.2 we have recalled how the measure of social welfare can be split into two terms, one of which reflects the loss in welfare due to inequality. Here we will show that it is sometimes possible to break this inequality term too, into a term reflecting inequality in final situations and a term reflecting imperfect mobility between initial and final situations. To do so, we will consider a situation in which it is possible to describe the social situation with the help of a bistochastic transition matrix (among other pieces of data). Bistochastic matrices are encountered in mobility studies which deal with origin and final groups described in quantiles. They are useful in order to isolate the pure mobility aspect of intergenerational movement, as opposed to "structural mobility," which refers to changes in the demographic importance of social groups from one generation to the next.[6]

Individuals are partitioned into n origin groups – to be interpreted as circumstance classes – of equal size, and in n final groups of equal size as well, defined on the basis of quantiles. The joint distribution of characteristics can then be described by a bistochastic matrix (p_{yq}) such that for all y, q, $\sum_s p_{sq} = \sum_s p_{ys} = 1$. The perfectly egalitarian matrix (e_{yq}) is defined by $e_{yq} = 1/n$ for all y, q. We simply assume here that origin defines circumstance classes. In contrast, final groups defined in terms of quantiles should not in general be identified with responsibility classes, because typically different origin groups have unequal access to different quantiles. (This is why the notation p_{yq} replaces p_{yz} here.)

Let us first take Min of Means, the measure advocated in Van de gaer et al. (2001), and examine how it can be decomposed so as to exhibit a mobility component. Let u_q denote the level of well-being in quantile q (final group). Social welfare, which depends not only on the matrix (p_{yq}) but also on the distribution of well-being (u_q), is defined as

$$W = \min_y \sum_{q=1}^n p_{yq} u_q.$$

This is also, as could be noted in the computations of Section 9.2, the lowest level of average well-being over the whole population that is needed in order to obtain this level of social welfare W if one can modify (p_{yq}) and (u_q) at will. In general one has $W \le \bar{u}$, where

$$\bar{u} = \frac{1}{n} \sum_{q=1}^n u_q.$$

Now let us compute the average level of well-being $\bar{u}^*$ that is needed in order to obtain social welfare W if one can modify (p_{yq}) and the norm of vector (u_q) but not its direction. Observe that with the egalitarian matrix (e_{yq}) instead of (p_{yq}), one has

$$\min_y \sum_{q=1}^n e_{yq} u_q = \bar{u},$$

so that, multiplying (u_q) by $W/\bar{u}$, one is able to obtain social welfare W with an average level of well-being $\bar{u}^* = W$. We already know that this is a lower bound, and therefore this is the value that we were seeking.

---

[6] As done, e.g., in Dardanoni (1993), one can also analyze pure mobility with simple stochastic matrices, if one only compares matrices with the same equilibrium distribution (the equilibrium distribution of population among groups is such that when the first generation is thus composed, the next generation, as produced by the matrix, is distributed in the same way). This, however, raises the issue of comparisons of situations out of equilibrium. It is therefore more straightforward to work with bistochastic matrices, for which the equilibrium distribution is uniform (each quantile has the same size) and is always achieved, by definition of the quantiles.

In summary, we have three average levels of well-being compatible with the same level of social welfare under different constraints: 1) $\bar{u}$ yields social welfare W with imperfect mobility (p_{yq}) and imperfect distribution (u_q); 2) $\bar{u}^*$ yields social welfare W with *perfect* mobility (e_{yq}) and the same distribution (proportionally) as in (u_q); 3) W yields social welfare W with *perfect* mobility (e_{yq}) and an *egalitarian* distribution.

Therefore one can write

$$W = \bar{u}\left(1 - I_w\right)\left(1 - I_m\right),$$

where

$$
\begin{aligned}
I_w &= 1 - \frac{W}{\bar{u}^*}, \\
I_m &= 1 - \frac{\bar{u}^*}{\bar{u}}.
\end{aligned}
$$

In other words, W can be decomposed into three terms. The first is, as usual, average well-being. The second, $(1 - I_w)$, measures the loss due to the suboptimality of (u_q) when individuals have equal access to all final groups.[7] In the case at hand $I_w \equiv 0$ because, from the standpoint of utilitarian reward, the distribution of (u_q) does not matter in the context of equal access. The third term, $(1 - I_m)$, measures the loss due to unequal access and I_m is an index of immobility. This is the mobility term that we were seeking. Note that, because the second term vanishes, this decomposition is in effect identical to the inequality decomposition proposed in Section 9.2.

A similar decomposition is readily obtained when a CES function replaces the maximin:

$$W = \left(\frac{1}{n}\sum_{y=1}^{n}\left(\sum_{q=1}^{n}p_{yq}u_q\right)^{1-\varepsilon}\right)^{\frac{1}{1-\varepsilon}},$$

since one then computes again $\bar{u}^* = W$.

The I_w index is no longer identically zero when one amends the utilitarian reward principle in order to endorse some aversion to inequality in final well-being. Consider the following variant of Min of Means:

$$W = \min_{y}\left(\sum_{q=1}^{n}p_{yq}\left(u_q\right)^{1-\gamma}\right)^{\frac{1}{1-\gamma}},$$

where $\gamma > 0$ measures the aversion to inequality of well-being within each circumstance class. With this formula, one then obtains

$$\bar{u}^* = W\,\frac{\bar{u}}{\left(\frac{1}{n}\sum_{q=1}^{n}\left(u_q\right)^{1-\gamma}\right)^{\frac{1}{1-\gamma}}},$$

---

[7]Note that $W/\bar{u}^*$ should not be read as a ratio involving a social welfare level, but as a ratio of average well-being levels, since W corresponds to the lowest level of average well-being needed in order to obtain the corresponding level of social welfare.

which is generally greater than W.[8]

Let us now turn to Mean of Mins, assuming that there is a function $g(y, z)$ mapping a responsibility variable z to a final group q for every y. For instance, with Roemer's statistical measure of responsibility, which was discussed in the previous chapter, one has $z \in [0, 1]$ and

$$g(y, z) = q \text{ such that } \sum_{t=1}^{q-1} p_{yt} < z \text{ and } \sum_{t=1}^{q} p_{yt} \geq z.$$

The social welfare function is now

$$W = \int_0^1 \min_y u_{g(y,z)} dz,$$

and again this is the value of average well-being which would be minimally needed in order to reach this level of social welfare.

In order to compute the same decomposition as above, we need to compute the level of social welfare obtained when equal access to all quantiles prevails in all circumstance classes. In this case it is natural to assume, as in Roemer's approach, that individuals at the same quantile also belong to the same responsibility class, so that one can simply write $z = q$. One therefore obtains

$$\frac{1}{n} \sum_{q=1}^{n} \min_y u_q = \bar{u}.$$

Here again the decomposition is identical to the inequality decomposition obtained in Section 9.2. The details can be omitted here.

The liberal criteria do not lend themselves as easily to such decompositions with a mobility term, because, unlike the utilitarian criteria, they do not just rely on information about the transition matrix and the level of well-being at each quantile. Nonetheless, it is also possible to perform this kind of decomposition if one is especially interested in the impact of the discrepancy between the transition matrix and the egalitarian matrix. Consider for instance the Egalitarian-Equivalence criterion. Recall that it is interested not directly in the distribution of well-being but in the distribution of $\tilde{x}_i$ defined by $u(\tilde{x}_i, \tilde{y}, z_i) = u_i$. The inequality decomposition compares the average value of $(\tilde{x}_i)$ in two cases yielding the same social welfare, namely, the current distribution $(\tilde{x}_1, ..., \tilde{x}_n)$ and the egalitarian distribution $(E_W(\tilde{x}_1, ..., \tilde{x}_n), ..., E_W(\tilde{x}_1, ..., \tilde{x}_n))$. One can introduce a third term by seeking a distribution $(\tilde{x}_1^*, ..., \tilde{x}_n^*)$ yielding the same social welfare with an egalitarian transition matrix. By definition of $E_W(\tilde{x}_1, ..., \tilde{x}_n)$, the corresponding average level $\bar{\tilde{x}}^*$ will be no less than $E_W(\tilde{x}_1, ..., \tilde{x}_n)$, and typically it will be less than the mean $\bar{\tilde{x}} = \frac{1}{n} \sum_i \tilde{x}_i$ because it is generally more equal than $(\tilde{x}_1, ..., \tilde{x}_n)$, in view of the fact that in order to make the transition matrix egalitarian, redistribution has to be made from the well-off circumstance classes to the less well-off.

---

[8] With this kind of social welfare function, a similar three-term decomposition formula is proposed in Martinez (2004).

One then obtains the decomposition:

$$E_W(\tilde{x}_1, ..., \tilde{x}_n) = \overline{\tilde{x}}(1 - I_w)(1 - I_m),$$

where

$$
\begin{aligned}
I_w &= 1 - \frac{E_W(\tilde{x}_1, ..., \tilde{x}_n)}{\overline{\tilde{x}}^*}, \\
I_m &= 1 - \frac{\overline{\tilde{x}}^*}{\overline{\overline{\tilde{x}}}}.
\end{aligned}
$$

A similar analysis is possible with Conditional Equality.

9.5   Opportunity dominance versus compensation

When examining the prospects of achievement for various origin groups, it is very tempting to declare that the clearest case of inequality of opportunity is when the achievements for one group are, for every value of the responsibility characteristics, nowhere below and somewhere above the achievements of the other group, as illustrated in Fig. 9.1. Let us say that in such a case, one "opportunity set" dominates the other.

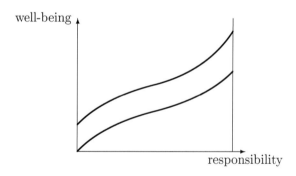

Figure 9.1: Opportunity set dominating another

In the studies that analyze opportunities in terms of distributions of achievements, this graphical configuration occurs when the distribution of well-being for one origin group "stochastically dominates" the prospects of another group.[9] Stochastic dominance simply means that the chance of achieving at least a certain level of outcome is at least as great (and sometimes greater), no matter what

---

[9]Rigorously speaking, stochastic dominance implies opportunity set dominance when (1) responsibility characteristics can be ordered on a line; (2) the distribution of responsibility characteristics is the same for all types; (3) well-being in each circumstance class is increasing in responsibility characteristics thus ordered. These assumptions are the same as those justifying Roemer's CDF measure of responsibility (Section 8.6).

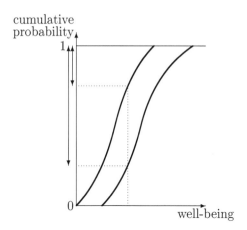

Figure 9.2: Stochastic dominance

level of outcome one considers. Figure 9.2, which depicts the cumulative distribution functions for two origin groups, illustrates how stochastic dominance is obtained by having the cumulative distribution function nowhere above (and somewhere below). The "chance of achieving at least a certain level of outcome" in each origin group is represented in the figure by the arrow-delimited line segments along the vertical axis. Figures 9.1 and 9.2 have been constructed with similar shapes so as to show how one can graphically interpret a cumulative distribution function as delineating an opportunity set, by permuting the axes and adopting Roemer's statistical definition of responsibility.

Following this line of reasoning, one can think of an egalitarian principle saying that the situation is improved when one reduces the gap between two opportunity sets (or distributions), while preserving dominance among the four sets under consideration, i.e., the two initial and the two final sets.[10] Figure 9.3 shows a typical configuration, where the dotted curves depict the final sets. Let us crystallize the definition of this principle.

Opportunity Dominance: Consider a social situation in which the opportunity set of a circumstance class dominates the opportunity set of another. It is improved if the dominating set shrinks and the dominated set expands, while remaining dominated.

This seems like a natural and uncontroversial principle, which, in particular, does not refer to any specific reward idea. It may therefore come as a surprise that, in effect, *Opportunity Dominance is incompatible with the compensation principle*. As a consequence, it is not satisfied by the compensation criteria such as Egalitarian-Equivalence or Mean of Mins, especially in their leximin

---

[10] A version of this principle, restricted to bistochastic transition matrices, is defended by Van de gaer et al. (2001) as *the* defining property of measures of immobility as inequality of opportunities.

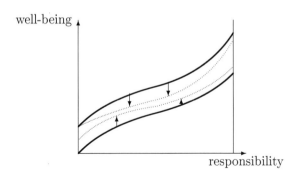

Figure 9.3: Opportunity Dominance

versions.[11]

In order to see this incompatibility, examine Fig. 9.4. It features the initial opportunity sets of four circumstance classes, denoted A, B, C and D. The dotted lines show possible modifications of the sets. It appears clearly that such modifications are considered good according to Opportunity Dominance, because they reduce inequalities between A and B, as well as between C and D, and bad according to the compensation principle because inequality is widened between the individuals with low responsibility characteristics from B and C, as well as between the individuals with high responsibility characteristics from A and D.

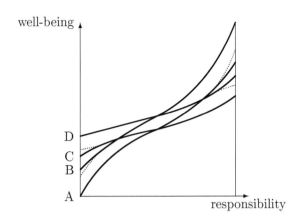

Figure 9.4: Opportunity Dominance vs. compensation

This incompatibility reveals that the incompatibilities between compensa-

---

[11] In the maximin versions, they satisfy the weak version of Opportunity Dominance saying that the final situation is at least as good as the initial situation.

tion and reward principles, which have been discussed previously with respect to liberal reward and utilitarian reward, may be rooted in a deeper incompatibility between the *"ex post"* approach that is embodied in the compensation principle and the *"ex ante"* approach which looks at the opportunities offered to individuals (as measured by the possible well-being levels achieved with given circumstances for the various values of responsibility characteristics).[12] The *ex post* approach focuses on inequalities within responsibility classes, whereas the *ex ante* approach is interested in inequalities between circumstance classes. Both kinds of inequalities may appear relevant, but the impossibility to embrace the two approaches at the same time forces one to give priority to one or the other.

The conflict disappears in class-ranked situations, i.e., when all opportunity sets can be ranked by the dominance relation.[13] Class-ranked situations, however, are common but far from universal. For instance, Lefranc et al. (2006, 2007) provide examples in which one cannot conclude about the stochastic dominance of distributions of income between various origin groups defined in terms of parent's occupation or in terms of income quantiles.

Moreover, even class-ranked situations do not eliminate the definitional differences between compensation criteria and other criteria. As a matter of fact, it seems that compensation criteria bear the risk of being too easily forgotten in studies of inequality of opportunities and social mobility, because the attraction of Opportunity Dominance pushes the analyst toward other criteria such as Min of Means, or studies of stochastic dominance of distributions.[14] The compensation criteria have been given equal importance in the previous sections of this chapter, and there is no reason to shun the compensation idea in inequality and social mobility studies more than in studies of full social welfare. Whenever possible, and especially when the situations under consideration are not class-ranked, the computation of the Min of Means should be supplemented with a computation of the Mean of Mins, and the study of stochastic dominance of distributions of outcome for circumstance classes should be supplemented with the study of stochastic dominance of distributions of outcome for responsibility classes.

---

[12]This does not mean that the incompatibility uncovered here logically implies the compensation-reward incompatibilities described earlier, because Opportunity Dominance is not a logically weaker condition than the reward axioms involved in those previous results.

[13]In the social mobility literature, this corresponds to "monotone" matrices.

[14]See, e.g., Van de gaer et al. (2001), Martinez (2004), Lefranc et al. (2006), Dardanoni et al. (2006), Bourguignon et al. (2007) and the related literature. However, Ruiz-Castillo (2003) and Villar (2005) adopt the ex post approach in the measurement of inequalities, and Peragine (2004b) makes a balanced treatment of the "types" approach and the "tranches" approach in the study of stochastic dominance (in his terminology, a type is a circumstance class, a tranche is a responsibility class).

9.6   The partial-circumstance problem

In *theory*, the compensation principle deserves as much attention as any kind of reward or *ex ante* principle (such as Opportunity Dominance). In *applied* studies of inequalities and social mobility, moreover, there is an additional reason to be cautious about adopting the *ex ante* approach. Indeed, such studies typically fail to register the whole set of circumstance parameters and therefore proceed as if the ignored circumstance parameters belonged to the responsibility sphere. This is quite problematic because it means that, with the *ex ante* approach, one will consider opportunity sets which do not contain true opportunities, but embody a mixture of circumstance inequalities and responsibility variations.[15]

In this context, Opportunity Dominance can contradict itself, in the following way. A change in the opportunity sets as measured with respect to a partial set of circumstances may be *good* according to Opportunity Dominance, whereas it would appear *bad* if one (correctly) measured opportunities with respect to the full set of circumstances. To illustrate this point, imagine that there are two circumstance characteristics, family background and personal ability, and that only the former is recorded. Suppose the (apparent) "opportunities" of children from poor families are dominated by those of children from rich families. A transfer from the untalented children from rich families to the talented children from poor families may thus be condoned by Opportunity Dominance, but turn out to be wrong according to the same principle if one observes that the (true) opportunities of the latter actually dominate the opportunities of the former.

In contrast, the compensation principle can never contradict itself in this way. An incomplete measurement of circumstances may entail a wrong definition of responsibility classes, but since the compensation principle always operates in the direction of reducing inequalities in well-being, it can never happen to increase such inequalities for a different definition of the circumstance and responsibility classes. Therefore, in applied studies where one is only able to record a subset of the circumstance parameters, it is safer to apply compensation criteria such as Egalitarian-Equivalence or Mean of Mins, rather than *ex ante* criteria such as Min of Means. This does not mean, of course, that errors are never made with criteria based on the compensation principle. The extent of the errors that are made with these various criteria is studied in more detail in the next section.

The study of errors due to a partial recording of circumstances is rather complex in general, but it is easy to see what happens when equality of opportunity is fully achieved for various definitions of circumstances. As noted in Roemer (2004), if the true circumstance classes face exactly the same opportunities, in the sense that for any responsibility characteristics, one achieves the same well-being independently of one's circumstances, then it has to be the case

---

[15] A related issue, which will not be studied here, is to examine what happens to the optimal policy when the responsibility cut is modified. Cappelen and Tungodden (2006b) observe that if one reduces the responsibility sphere by requalifying some responsibility characteristics as circumstance characteristics, inequalities may appear to *decrease*, not increase, if there is a negative correlation between the initial circumstance characteristics and the new ones.

that, for a definition of circumstance classes based on a subset of the circumstance parameters, there also is equality of opportunities. Indeed, individuals with the same characteristics other than the recorded circumstance parameters will necessarily have the same well-being because, in particular, they have the same responsibility characteristics. This reasoning is also valid when one defines responsibility classes, for both cases (i.e., the correct and the wrong measurement), in the statistical way: If the conditional distributions computed with respect to a set of circumstance parameters are exactly the same, then the conditional distributions with respect to a subset of these parameters also have to be identical. In conclusion, equality of opportunity, as defined in applied studies that typically fail to record the full set of circumstances, is a necessary but not sufficient condition for equality of opportunities with respect to the true set of circumstances.[16]

9.7   *More on the partial-circumstance problem

We restrict attention here to the case in which the set of recorded circumstance parameters is a strict subset of the true set of circumstance parameters. This implies that recorded circumstance classes form a coarser partition of the population than the true circumstance classes: Each recorded circumstance class contains several true circumstance classes. Let $y = (y^*, y^{**})$, where y^* denotes the recorded circumstance parameters, and y^{**} the rest. The set of y (resp., y^*, y^{**}) classes is denoted Y (resp., Y^*, Y^{**}). The size of the y (resp., y^*) class is denoted n_y (resp., n_{y^*}). The total population has size n.

Let I be a replication-invariant, decomposable inequality index defined on positive real vectors. Replication invariance means that for any real vector x, $I(x, ..., x) = I(x)$. Decomposability means that for any vectors x, x', $I(x, x')$ depends only on $I(x)$, $I(x')$, and on the dimensions and means of x and x'. By calling I an inequality index, we mean that I is a continuous and symmetric function satisfying $I(q, ..., q) = 0$ for all $q \in \mathbb{R}_{++}$, and $I(Bx) \leq I(x)$ for every bistochastic matrix. For instance, the CES function W mentioned in Section 9.2 yields the Kolm-Atkinson inequality index which satisfies these properties:

$$I(x) = 1 - \frac{\left(\frac{1}{n}\sum_i x_i^{1-\varepsilon}\right)^{\frac{1}{1-\varepsilon}}}{\frac{1}{n}\sum_i x_i}.$$

It is shown in Shorrocks (1984, Th. 2) that any inequality index satisfying the above properties (including decomposability) is ordinally equivalent to an

---

[16]Roemer (2004) suggests that, actually, applied studies consider circumstances which are not strict subsets of the true sets of circumstance parameters that one might want to record. Specifically, he claims that individual preferences which are influenced by family background are implicitly recorded as circumstantial, when origin is defined by parental income, education or occupation, whereas one might want to hold individuals responsible for their preferences even in such a case, as is argued for instance by Dworkin. When the true and the recorded sets of circumstance parameters overlap in this way, then equality of opportunity in observed opportunity sets is neither a necessary nor a sufficient condition for equality of opportunity in the true sense.

additively separable index J such that for all vectors $x_1, ..., x_m$:

$$J(x_1, ..., x_m) = J(\bar{x}_1, ..., \bar{x}_m) + \sum_{k=1}^{m} J(x_k),$$

where $\bar{x}_k$ is a vector of the same dimension as x_k, in which every component is equal to the mean of x_k.

Consider the Min of Means first. Let $\bar{u}_y$ denote the average well-being in the y class, and $\bar{u}_{y^*}$ the average well-being in the y^* class. An additively separable inequality index based on the Min of Means criterion can be written in this way:

$$I\left(\bar{u}_{y_1}, ..., \bar{u}_{y_n}\right) = I\left(\bar{u}_{y_1^*}, ..., \bar{u}_{y_n^*}\right) + \sum_{y^* \in Y^*} I\left((\bar{u}_{y_i})_{i:y_i^*=y^*}\right).$$

This formula makes clear that recording y^* classes instead of y classes produces an underestimation of the level of inequalities. Concerning evaluations of changes in inequalities, it appears that a necessary and sufficient condition for the observed $I\left(\bar{u}_{y_1^*}, ..., \bar{u}_{y_n^*}\right)$ to change in the same fashion as the truly relevant $I\left(\bar{u}_{y_1}, ..., \bar{u}_{y_n}\right)$ is that, on average, inequalities measured by $I\left((\bar{u}_{y_i})_{i:y_i^*=y^*}\right)$ for each recorded class y^* remain constant.

To illustrate the meaning of this condition, imagine one computed an inequality index on the average incomes per origin group defined in terms of parental income. Would a reduction of this index over time imply that inequalities of opportunities have decreased? According to the above formula, this depends on the inequalities, within each origin group, which are due to differences in other circumstance parameters such as talent. Imagine that the inequalities related to talent have increased. Then it may be that observed inequalities between observed origin groups have decreased while inequalities between (true) circumstance classes formed by origin and talent have actually increased.

When the inequality index I is decomposable but not additively separable, the description of the error term is more complex, but the main qualitative insight remains valid. Consider for instance the Kolm–Atkinson index, recalled above. For this index one computes:

$$[1 - I(\bar{u}_{y_1}, ..., \bar{u}_{y_n})]^{1-\varepsilon} = [1 - I(\bar{u}_{y_1^*}, ..., \bar{u}_{y_n^*})]^{1-\varepsilon}$$
$$+ \sum_{y^* \in Y^*} \frac{n_{y^*}\bar{u}_{y^*}}{n\bar{u}} \left[1 - I\left((\bar{u}_{y_i})_{i:y_i^*=y^*}\right)\right]^{1-\varepsilon}.$$

The error term is again a (weighted) sum of inequality terms for each y^* class, and therefore the qualitative conclusion obtained above about the conditions under which $I(\bar{u}_{y_1}, ..., \bar{u}_{y_n})$ and $I(\bar{u}_{y_1^*}, ..., \bar{u}_{y_n^*})$ move in the same direction still holds.

Let us compare these results with the possible errors that would be made with the associated compensation criterion, namely, the Mean of Mins. The

Mean of Mins is interested in inequalities within responsibility classes, and the partial recording of circumstance parameters means that the recorded partition of *responsibility* classes is *finer* than the true partition. However, this occurs only when all y^{**} parameters are observed and are (wrongly) used in the identification of responsibility classes. In the case when Roemer's statistical definition is applied, the situation is different because there will simply be a mismeasurement of responsibility and a reduction in the number of circumstances classes among which inequality is computed for every value of the responsibility measure. We will concentrate on this case which is probably more relevant to applied studies.

Let F_y and F_{y^*} denote the cumulative distribution functions for classes y and y^*, respectively. One has:

$$F_{y^*} = \sum_{y^{**} \in Y^{**}} \frac{n_{(y^*,y^{**})}}{n_{y^*}} F_{(y^*,y^{**})}.$$

When Mean of Mins is defined in a generalized way, i.e., with the min operator replaced by the equal-equivalent of a social welfare function W, the corresponding relative inequality index reads:

$$I_W^r = 1 - \frac{\int_0^1 E_W \left(F_{y_1}^{-1}(q), ..., F_{y_n}^{-1}(q) \right) dq}{\bar{u}}.$$

In this expression, for each y, the term $F_y^{-1}(q)$ appears n_y times, in order to take account of the size of each y class.

As shown in Section 9.2, the above formula can be written as an average over inequality indexes:

$$I_W^r = \int_0^1 \frac{\bar{u}(q)}{\bar{u}} \left[1 - \frac{E_W \left(F_{y_1}^{-1}(q), ..., F_{y_n}^{-1}(q) \right)}{\bar{u}(q)} \right] dq,$$

where $\bar{u}(q)$ is the average well-being for the q responsibility class:

$$\bar{u}(q) = \frac{1}{n} \sum_{i=1}^n F_{y_i}^{-1}(q).$$

A key difference with the analysis related to the Min of Means is that F_{y^*} is a mean of some F_y, but the inequality index depends on the inverses of such functions. Nonetheless, one necessarily has

$$F_{y^*}^{-1}(q) = \sum_{y^{**} \in Y^{**}} \alpha_{(y^*,y^{**})}(q) F_{(y^*,y^{**})}^{-1}(q),$$

for some suitably chosen weight functions $\alpha_y(q)$ such that for all y^*, all q, $\sum_{y^{**} \in Y^{**}} \alpha_{(y^*,y^{**})}(q) = 1$. This is because one has, for all q:

$$\min_{y^{**}} F_{(y^*,y^{**})}(q) \leq F_{y^*}(q) \leq \max_{y^{**}} F_{(y^*,y^{**})}(q),$$

which implies, since these functions are non-decreasing:

$$\min_{y^{**}} F^{-1}_{(y^*,y^{**})}(q) \leq F^{-1}_{y^*}(q) \leq \max_{y^{**}} F^{-1}_{(y^*,y^{**})}(q).$$

As a consequence, one is back to a seemingly similar situation as with the Min of Means, namely, one is computing inequalities over averages of the relevant well-being values instead of these values directly. Two differences appear, though. First, the average values over which inequalities are (wrongly) computed are weighted in a way that reflects not simply the demographic importance of y classes, but some features of the cumulative distribution functions. Second, the errors, like the inequality indexes, are averaged over the various q classes. More research is needed to quantitatively compare the error made with Min of Means and with Mean of Mins.

9.8   Conclusion

As we have seen in this chapter, social welfare can be decomposed into a component of inequality and a component of average outcome, in which the two components involve a responsibility-sensitive measure of well-being. It is even possible to break social welfare into three terms, by splitting the inequality component into a mobility (or opportunity) component and a component reflecting imperfections in the final distribution of well-being.

Two main messages emerge. First, if one wants to make sensible evaluations of social mobility and inequalities of opportunities, information about transition matrices is not enough and must be supplemented at least with information about levels of outcomes and, if one endorses the liberal approach, with information about resource transfers as well. Studies of conditional distributions per origin class do incorporate information about levels of outcomes, and we have shown that information about resources is not out of reach in some applications such as income distribution, even under the sophisticated assumption that individuals are fully responsible not for their level of work but only for their consumption-leisure preferences.

Second, one must resist the attraction of *ex ante* criteria and be careful about attributing opportunities to individuals when these opportunities are not really accessible to them, because one is only able to record a subset of the circumstantial parameters. This issue provides an additional argument in favor of compensation criteria.

Chapter 10

Responsibility, freedom and social justice

10.1 Introduction

The goal of the first chapters was primarily to analyze the distributive *implications* of holding individuals partly responsible for their own fate. The difference between liberal and utilitarian reward, and the conflicts between reward principles and the compensation principle, could be presented independently of how one decided to draw the boundary between responsibility and circumstances and of how one wanted to justify the role of responsibility in social justice.

This chapter addresses these protracted issues, not because it is logically indispensable to do so in any treatise on responsibility-sensitive egalitarianism, but because they are indeed pressing questions and the way they are answered strongly determines how appealing responsibility-sensitive egalitarianism can be for various sorts of egalitarians. This chapter is especially written for two kinds of egalitarians. First, there are the skeptics who doubt that responsibility should be given so much importance, and who believe that egalitarianism is primarily about a basic sort of social equality and a certain kind of social relations among citizens. Their concern should be taken seriously, and will find substantial support here. However, one must disagree with the contention that egalitarianism is not about distribution and is primarily about social relations. It is not hard to see that even the quality of social relations can ultimately be described as a distribution of a certain good among citizens.[1] Being treated as an equal or being subordinated, being respected or humiliated, being listened to or ignored, being welcomed or ostracized, being loved or hated, all of these are things that happen to individuals, they are not just holistic features of the social compact. Egalitarianism is not just about distributing material resources, but it is definitely and solely about distributing goods, including the goods that go with social relations. Such goods are not as simple to create and transfer

---

[1] This thesis is eloquently defended by Barclay (2007).

245

as material goods, but they ultimately affect individuals and the analysis of social situations should always be couched in terms of distributions of individual situations. It will be explained in this chapter how social relations can be incorporated into the analytical apparatus proposed in this book.[2] If we grant this point, it remains to see what role the concept of responsibility can be given in ethical evaluations. One may be rightly afraid that responsibility could serve to justify inequalities of indefinite extent and this chapter will address this worry.

This chapter is also written for a second kind of egalitarians, namely, the convinced who find it unquestionable that equality can only be about opportunities. In this book they have seen that there were different ways of unraveling the concept of opportunities in the design of distributive policies, connected to different reward principles and different articulations of reward and compensation. The idea that "people should bear the consequences of their choices" is not as simple as it seems. If they take this point, an important purpose of the book will have already been achieved. In addition, this chapter will develop the argument that the most attractive justification of responsibility in the context of the normative evaluation of social situations refers to the promotion of freedom and autonomy and, because of this orientation, requires a very cautious reward scheme. A comprehensive egalitarian theory of justice is, definitely, not just about equalizing opportunities, but also about providing adequate opportunities and putting opportunities in their proper place in the general distribution of goods among citizens.

The chapter is structured as follows. Section 10.2 examines how to draw the line between responsibility and circumstances and rejects the popular thesis that individuals should be held responsible for what lies in their control. In particular, the idea that social evaluation should import its definition of the responsibility sphere from the theory of moral responsibility is criticized as leading the theories of justice into a metaphysical dead end. But the alternative approach which assigns responsibility to individuals for their preferences is also found to be wanting, Dworkin's arguments in its favor appearing particularly insufficient.

Sections 10.3 and 10.4 then introduce two arguments in favor of the preference approach. The first argument (Section 10.3) is that freedom and autonomy are important values which make it important to let individuals choose and direct their lives and have their preferences satisfied. This makes responsibility derivative to the fact of individuals exercising their freedom. The second ar-

---

[2] The analysis of this book has been very limited about this issue because we have focused on simple frameworks in which resources and welfare is all that counts in the description of individual situations. Many authors – in particular Young (1990), Anderson (1999), Phillips (1999), Scheffler (2003), Armstrong (2006) – have criticized the liberal egalitarian literature for neglecting social relations and picturing social life as a simple matter of individual circumstances, resources, and choice. Here this choice of focus on resources and welfare was not meant to suggest that social relations are less important than private consumption, because evidence to the contrary is manifest in everyday life. But there was already quite a mouthful to be said on the issue of resource distribution, and the available concepts of economic analysis are more easily applied to this issue than to social relations. This is unfortunate and future research should urgently invest more in the latter topic.

gument (Section 10.4), inspired by Rawls (1982), is that it is inappropriate to compare different individuals' levels of satisfaction over their lives when their judgments are based on different conceptions of a good life. This also implies a certain kind of preference liability because it means that one should not try to compensate the influence of individual conceptions of the good life over satisfaction.

Sections 10.5 and 10.6 explore the implications of such considerations for the definition of the responsibility sphere (Section 10.5) and for the choice of a reward principle (Section 10.6). The latter section warns against uncompromising applications of the liberal and utilitarian reward principles. Some moderate version of the liberal reward principle is however defended, especially with respect to preference liability.

Sections 10.7 and 10.8 outline a theory of equality which takes account of these various points, and is tentatively dubbed "equality of autonomy." Section 10.7 shows how the Egalitarian-Equivalence family of criteria fits rather well into the approach proposed here, because it gives priority to the compensation principle while holding individuals responsible for their satisfaction levels. Additional considerations about freedom and the reward scheme make it possible to be more precise about how to select a particular member of the Egalitarian-Equivalence family. Section 10.8 summarizes the main features of the "equal autonomy" approach and compares it to the main theories of responsibility-sensitive egalitarianism. It also examines how the evaluation of social relations can be accommodated in this approach.

10.2 The responsibility cut

What should individuals be held responsible for? There are two main answers to this question in the egalitarian literature. One is that individuals should be held responsible only for what lies within their control. The other is that individuals should be held responsible for their preferences and the choices that follow from them.[3] I will argue here that the former approach leads theories of justice into a metaphysical dead end, while the latter has been inadequately defended by Dworkin.

Some preliminary remarks will help characterize these two approaches and show how they avoid basic objections. First, for both approaches, it makes sense to assign responsibility for choices only when individuals are put in equal conditions of choice. When an individual has less opportunities than another, he cannot be held fully responsible for his choice insofar as his choice is more constrained and is thereby influenced by his relative lack of opportunities. In practice it is often impossible to offer exactly the same opportunities or opportunities of the same relevant quality to all, so there will always be individuals with less favorable conditions. This is especially problematic for the control

---

[3]As already mentioned earlier, the first view has been defended by Arneson, Cohen and Roemer, while the second view can be traced to Rawls, Dworkin and Van Parijs.

approach to responsibility. For this approach, the only way to bypass this difficulty is to find out basic responsibility characteristics such that individuals have full and equal access to the same span of such characteristics, while inequalities of opportunities are fully depicted as differences in circumstances. Roemer's CDF measure of responsibility can be viewed as one pragmatic way, among others, to do this, because it identifies the percentile in the distribution of one's circumstance class as the responsibility characteristic which individuals fully and equally control. For the preference approach, the solution is simpler and consists in holding individuals responsible for their preferences only, and not directly for the choices that follow from them, as we have done in Chapters 4 and 5. In those chapters, individuals had irreducibly different budget sets due to their different skills, and were not held directly responsible for their choice of labor. Responsibility for preferences was nonetheless a powerful guide for the evaluation of redistributive policies.

A second point, relating to the control conception of responsibility, is that individuals may be unequally endowed with choice-making abilities, so that it is important to factor in these parameters when assessing their degree of control. For instance, an individual cannot be said to be in full control of his saving choices if he does not master the computation of compound interest. Therefore, this must be reckoned with when his situation is compared to that of others with better competence at intertemporal management. In other words, the notion of control that is relevant here is a demanding notion of *genuine* control. On the other hand, the notion of control covers more than competent and clear-minded choice, because there are cases of absent-minded choice where one can still consider that the individual was in full control (of his absent-mindedness).

Similar considerations apply to the preference conception of responsibility. Bad choice-making competence may make actual choices fail to adequately reflect individual preferences. Absent-minded choice, however, also typically fails to reflect preferences so that there may be a divide on this point between the control and the preference views.[4] A related point about the preference approach to responsibility is that, just as control must be genuine control, preferences must be genuine preferences. This is meant to exclude immediate preferences, impulses and cravings that do not correspond to the deeper inclinations of the individual. This criterion of authenticity, perhaps, also excludes adaptive preferences when they can be described as the result of some kind of conditioning process. Adaptive preferences are often invoked as an objection against the preference approach to responsibility, because one may think of situations where the individual really comes to identify with his adaptive preferences. Consider for instance the woman who comes to identify with the social role that is traditionally assigned to her gender and in particular develops inclinations for spending

---

[4]One way to reconcile them is by describing absent-minded choice as reflecting higher-order preferences about the time and resources devoted to making decisions of the first order. Specifically, if the individual has preferences that lead him not to devote much attention to certain decisions, then these decisions, even if they fail to reflect his preferences over the matter, still reflect his preferences over life in a broader way, when these decisions are examined not only for what they are but also for how they are made.

substantial time caring for her relatives.[5] As a consequence she invests less in her career and in other kinds of personal accomplishments. Insofar as she identifies strongly with this kind of preferences, it seems that the preference approach will attribute her full responsibility in this case. As a consequence this approach may appear dangerously prone to condoning social customs that distort opportunities, in comparison with the control approach which is more sensitive to the formation of preferences. But one sees that it all depends on how one defines authentic preferences. If the social conditioning that instills preferences of this kind is unmasked and shown to render such preferences inauthentic – if this woman can, even only counterfactually, put herself in a different mind-set and imagine what she would have liked to do in a more gender-equal society – it seems possible to make the preference approach at least partly immune to this objection.

There are additional arguments suggesting that the gap between the two views is narrower than it seems. First, the preference approach is often related to a broader approach, for which people should be held responsible for any kind of characteristics – not just preferences – or deeds which they endorse and identify with.[6] Endorsing is not controlling, but is connected to the idea of control in a counterfactual way. Endorsing some of one's characteristics means that if one were in control, one would choose them as they are, at least in some relevant context. Therefore, there is a sense in which this approach is closely connected to a notion of control.

Symmetrically, think of how to define a notion of genuine choice fitting the control approach. This essentially amounts to elaborating a doctrine on the vexed issue of free will. As it is well known, this issue opposes the compatibilists, who think that free will can exist in a deterministic world, to the incompatibilists, among whom the hard determinists completely deny the existence of free will whereas others (called "libertarians," without any connection to political philosophy) think that a non causally determined free will exists. If one adopts a compatibilist notion of free will for the egalitarian theory of justice,[7] one comes very close to a preference approach to responsibility, because

---

[5] Sen (1985, p. 21) famously introduced a similar example which came to be referred to as the "tamed housewife."

[6] Lake (2001), for instance, opposes the "affirmation" approach to the "control" approach of responsibility. Mason (2006) similarly refers to "responsiveness to reason".

[7] It is worth noting that the notion of genuine choice that is needed for a theory of justice based on the control approach to responsibility will serve a specific purpose, namely, delineating the personal characteristics that will not be compensated in redistributive policies of any sort. This need not be the same as the notion that would serve to attribute moral praise or blame, for instance, unless one wants to apportion the distribution of well-being to the distribution of moral status. It is possible, in particular, to adopt a compatibilist notion of free will for social policies and an incompatibilist notion for moral evaluation. One would then say that, in some cases, individuals can legitimately live with the bad consequences of their choices even though, at some deeper level, they may not be blamed for them. The opposite possibility – an incompatibilist approach in social justice, a compatibilist approach in morality – cannot be excluded either. One would then say that, in some cases, individuals are morally blamable for their choices but should not endure any social loss because at a deeper level they are not in control.

genuine control is then typically defined in terms of choices reflecting authentic preferences or asserting one's personality and responsiveness to reasons.[8] The control approach can then come very close to the preference approach.

There remains, however, an irreducible difference because the control approach, even in its compatibilist construal, assigns responsibility only for things that have been chosen in a certain array of options, or are retained although other options would be available. In contrast, the preference approach is happy to hold an individual responsible for her authentic preferences even if these preferences have not been chosen in any sense and cannot be changed costlessly. These two approaches can therefore yield very different conclusions in cases when individuals suffer disadvantages due to preferences which are deemed authentic by the preference approach but which are not under actual control. In the example of the woman who likes the social role of a carer, one can think of cases in which such preferences are authentic even though they are the product of external influences. Another example features a man who is educated in an ascetic religion imposing a miserable way of life. His preferences may be perfectly authentic, if he comes to embrace this religion in full conscience, but he cannot be said to have been in control of his poor achievements, because of the influence of his education.[9]

After these lengthy preliminaries, let us turn to an assessment of the control approach. It is popular and appears closer to a certain commonsense theory of moral responsibility. Its attraction comes from the charitable ring that it has when it objects to letting individuals suffer disadvantages which they have not brought upon themselves. This good feature, however, also makes this approach hostage to the free-will problem. How do we define genuine choice and how do we know when a particular choice is genuine?

The defenders of the control approach, facing this difficulty, simply defer either to intuition and ordinary morality, or to the specialized debate on free will.[10] The most comfortable attitude, for them, consists in saying that whatever is the correct theory of free will and moral responsibility should be used as an ingredient in the control-based theory of responsibility-sensitive egalitarianism, and that all practical difficulties in observing and measuring the relevant data

---

[8] Arneson (2003) cites Dworkin's theory as a compatibilist approach to moral responsibility. Recent compatibilist accounts of free will can be found in Wallace (1994), Fischer and Ravizza (1998).

[9] Considering a similar example, Scanlon (1986, p. 117) develops arguments similar to Dworkin's: "the idea that these [religious] burdens are grounds for such compensation (a form of bad luck) is incompatible with regarding them as matters of belief and conviction which one values and adheres to because one thinks them right." Interestingly, Roemer (1998, p. 20) sides with Scanlon on this kind of example, even though he otherwise defends the control approach. He would only consider the situation unfair if the man's beliefs were "due to circumstances which made penury seem unavoidable." Other kinds of causal factors (e.g., family tradition) are not apparently problematic for him.

[10] Cohen (1989, p. 934) famously writes that "we may indeed be up to our necks in the free will problem, but that is just tough luck. It is not a reason for not following the argument where it goes." Roemer (1998), in contrast, considers that every society can make a political decision about what constitutes a circumstance. Ramsay (2004) notes that this contradicts the theory that people should only be held responsible for what *really* lies within their control.

should be tackled so as to best approximate the desired just state of affairs. The comfort of this attitude is fragile, for three reasons.

First, practical difficulties can be overwhelming here. The practical difficulty of ascertaining the presence of free will may ultimately make it almost necessary to equalize outcomes rather than opportunities, if one considers that there is a greater injustice in holding an individual liable for a disadvantage that he does not control than in compensating an individual for a disadvantage that is under his control. This practical consideration is compounded by semi-theoretical issues having to do with the prevailing culture. Some form of hard determinism has gained considerable intellectual ground in modern culture.[11] Therefore, whenever a causal explanation is provided for a particular individual disadvantage, it is, in this cultural environment, hard to defend the idea that the situation is fair and that no correction needs to be made. Observing that determining the degree of each individual's responsibility is impossible not only for state agencies, but also for close relatives and even for the individuals themselves, Arneson (1997a) offers a compelling rebuttal of the project of distinguishing the undeserving from the deserving among the poor, and urges us "to forgo the attempt to make the treatment of individuals responsive to desert a major consideration in social welfare policy directed toward poverty relief." (p. 350) But denying any substantive role to responsibility in policy issues may appear to renege on the initial motivation that launched the luck egalitarian movement.[12]

The second reason is related to the previous one, insofar as the scientific approach that rules over social sciences is a token of the general determinist culture. We have seen in Section 3.4 that the control approach to responsibility does not fit well in the models of rational choice that are common in economics, since these models describe individual decisions as a mechanical optimization exercise with a given objective (preferences, utility function) and a given set of options (budget set). It is transparent in this kind of modelling that "genuine choice" is an elusive notion. By looking at Roemer's models, for instance, one sees that individual responsibility, as assessed by the CDF measure, is ultimately determined by fixed preference parameters, so that the individuals are in fact held responsible for such parameters and not for any kind of genuine choice (unless one assumes that these parameters themselves have been genuinely chosen outside the model). This cannot be otherwise, because by construction such models are deterministic – what has been done in this book is of course not different.[13] When translating a control-based theory of justice into economic models that are essential tools in the analysis of public policy, one therefore

---

[11] See, e.g., Scanlon (1988), Scheffler (1992). According to Greene and Cohen (2004), the development of neurosciences, by unveiling the mechanics of the mind, will increasingly challenge the naive libertarian beliefs of "folk psychology" and will spread hard determinism.

[12] As Phillips (2006, p. 19) writes, "it is difficult to expand equality of opportunity in ways that satisfactorily address the constraining effects of social circumstance, gender socialisation, cultural convictions and so on, without undermining the idea of people as responsible agents."

[13] Determinism in this sense encompasses random processes. Introducing random error terms in the decisions, as in the discrete choice models, would not change the outlook of the problem, since random errors do not represent genuine choice any better than fixed parameters.

faces a dilemma. Either the notion of free will prevailing in the theory of justice is libertarian, in which case it is impossible to introduce it in the models, or it is compatibilist, in which case it will be hard to swallow because the models will describe such "genuine" choice as a mechanical procedure determined by given desires and constraints and, in particular, influenced by public policy.

The third reason is that metaphysics is given a dangerous role here. The purists say that there simply is a true theory of moral responsibility, and that its dependence on metaphysical issues makes its discovery and application difficult but should not deter us from exploring its ramifications. This attitude, however, undermines the whole project of constructing a theory of justice. Just as it is problematic for a theory of social justice to rely on a special view of the good life, it is questionable to make it depend so dramatically on a metaphysical issue like free will. The justice of social arrangements should be assessed in a way that is not only compatible with the variety of moral conceptions that prevail in society, but also with the variety of metaphysical conceptions that similarly coexist and will remain with us for a long time. It should be possible for compatibilists and incompatibilists to live together and recognize their society as just, in a similar fashion as for theists and atheists.

A more pessimistic view on this issue is that the metaphysics of responsibility is so intimately connected to our conceptions of the good life and of the nature of human life, that it might be as illusory to seek a consensual theory of justice as to seek a consensual view of the good life.[14] The hard determinists and the believers in free will might never be able to agree on how to view one's personal action in the world and, relatedly, on how to allocate blame, praise and taxpayers' money. It is probably reasonable indeed to abandon overambitious hopes of neutrality. Such considerations, however, should not bar us from seeking consensual principles of justice that could, even if some disagreements remain over other principles, usefully shape the basic institutions of society. One goal of this chapter is to seek elements of a theory of responsibility which, even if – and because – they do not resolve all of the controversial issues, can be consensual and useful for applications.

In addition, one can argue that it is also a matter of justice to recognize metaphysical disagreements as reasonable disagreements and to adopt social institutions which do not offend certain views. As a consequence, it would be not only politically hopeless, but even unfair and disrespectful, to set up institutions which would openly implement a theory of justice based on a particular notion of free will and responsibility. In other words, there is an internal contradiction in theories of justice which adhere to the principle of equal respect for human beings and propose to rely on notions which, no matter how they are defined, ultimately insult the deep views of those who disagree with the particular definition that is adopted.

Should this criticism lead us to adopt the preference approach right away? This approach, insofar as it is similar to a compatibilist theory of genuine choice, is vulnerable to the same hard determinist objections. How can we let individ-

---

[14] This pessimistic view is suggested by Scheffler (1992) and Arneson (2008).

uals suffer disadvantages due to preferences which may be authentic in some sense but are nonetheless largely the product of social circumstances?

Dworkin's (2000, pp. 287–298) defense of the preference approach against this control-oriented and incompatibilist threat does not appear very successful.[15] Dworkin appeals to the fact that when people endorse their preferences and would not take a pill to change them in order to be more easily satisfied, it would be "bizarre" for them to consider their preferences a piece of bad luck. But this endorsement approach seems to expand responsibility too much. Are we relieved from fighting the disadvantages that women endure whenever they would refuse to take a pill in order to change their sex? One can endorse one's particular characteristic and be fully satisfied to have it, while consistently regretting that some disadvantages stick to it.[16] As argued in Cohen (1989), one can identify with one's expensive tastes and nonetheless regret that they are "expensive" in the prevailing conditions. A second argument Dworkin uses is that our ordinary morality ascribes responsibility for people's preferences. But ordinary morality is not a reliable guide to complex issues, and the task of normative theories is certainly not to blindly condone the mood of the times. Moreover, one could probably argue that ordinary morality leans toward the control approach – in its incompatibilist brand – rather than the preference approach.[17]

All in all, the foundations of the concept of responsibility used by luck-egalitarians turn out to be fragile. The control approach goes into a practical and metaphysical dead end, while the preference approach avoids this problem at the cost of appearing somewhat counterintuitive and possibly harsh toward some badly-off individuals because it expands the responsibility sphere too much.

10.3 Responsibility or freedom

The conclusion that emerges from the above is that egalitarians would be better off abandoning or at least putting aside the concept of responsibility as they use it, i.e., as a *moral justification* for disadvantages and inequalities suffered by some members of society. Barry (2005) eloquently warns against the moralistic and conservative abuses of the concept of responsibility that serve to justify welfare reforms which hurt the worst-off fraction of the population.[18] Nonetheless, he still believes in an ideal theory of moral responsibility and equality of opportunities. But, as we have seen, any version of such a theory is vulnerable

---

[15] See in particular the detailed critical analyses in Matravers (2002a,b).

[16] This reveals a limitation of the envy test, as noted in Clayton and Williams (1999). Even if there is no envy, it may be that the set of options is less favorable to some preferences. We will see how to address this problem below.

[17] Greene and Cohen (2004) describe "folk psychology" as involving a libertarian – hence incompatibilist – conception of free will, and argue that it underlies common moral intuitions about responsibility.

[18] See also Callinicos (2000), Armstrong (2006). The main target of these three authors is New Labour. Arneson (1997a) criticizes the conservative attacks on welfare in America.

to the same kind of accusation of involving easy excuses for inequalities[19] or of offending certain conceptions of life prevailing in the society. Egalitarians must look in a different direction in order to define fairness in a way that could ultimately become consensual. In this section it is proposed to take freedom as a fundamental value for a different justification of responsibility. An additional justification is introduced in the next section.

One way of describing the divide here is to oppose conceptions which seek a pre-institutional notion of responsibility on which to ground inequalities, to conceptions for which responsibility is the consequence or the expression of, not the rationale for, the assignment of roles and liabilities in institutions of social interactions and redistribution.[20] According to the latter view, responsibility is not something which justifies disadvantages, but something which is assumed by individuals when they accept liabilities, and which is justified by independent fairness principles.

The preference conception to responsibility may pertain to the "institutional" approach or to the "pre-institutional" approach depending on how it is elaborated and defended. When Rawls (1982) argues that autonomous moral agents must, by definition, assume responsibility for their goals in life, and that desires are not in themselves reasons for redistribution, one can understand this, as advocated by Scheffler (2003), as a description of basic fairness principles of social interaction, from which a certain assignment of liabilities follow. But one can also interpret it as related to a pre-institutional notion of responsibility as endorsement and identity, as in Dworkin's theory.

The institutional approach is not, in contrast with the pre-institutional approach, vulnerable to incompatibilist scruples. When independent fairness principles of interaction justify certain assignments of liabilities, it does not matter whether this ends up making some individuals suffer disadvantages for which they are not in control, because the reason for this assignment has an independent justification. But this line of defense critically depends on the strength of the fairness principles which ground the assignment. The weakness of the institutional approach is that it is often presented without a precise description of the principles which may play such a foundational role. For instance, Rawls' theory, in Scheffler's (2003) interpretation, defines fair shares not in terms of compensation for unchosen disadvantages, but in terms of "a distributive scheme that makes it possible for free and equal citizens to pursue their diverse conceptions of the good within a framework that embodies an ideal of reciprocity and mutual respect" (p. 28). Such principles of free and equal citizenship, neutrality with respect to conceptions of the good, reciprocity and mutual respect may appear too basic and too vague to justify any particular allocation of resources and responsibilities. One could defend the claim that, from Nozick's libertarian

---

[19] Moreover, many authors such as Anderson (1999), Gomberg (2007), Phillips (1999), Scheffler (2005) accuse luck egalitarianism of excessive moralizing as well. Eyal (2007) illustrates this moralistic tendency by arguing that agents should suffer disadvantages caused by their responsible deeds only when these are morally bad, while disadvantages generated by good actions should be compensated.

[20] See, e.g., Ripstein (1999), Fingarette (2004).

utopia to radical welfare egalitarianism, most modern theories of justice respect such principles. Certainly, one needs to be more specific in order to be able to determine specific assignments of responsibility.

Two particular principles justifying responsibility assignments will be defended here. The first one, which is the topic of this section, is a basic principle of freedom and autonomy: Individuals must have and exercise freedom. More precisely, the ideal of freedom implies that people must enjoy certain basic liberties and a basic autonomy, and, beyond that, practice the activity of choice as much as desired and possible. What is proposed here is, therefore, a two-tier formula. First, the principle of freedom acts as a constraint in order to make sure that a minimum level of autonomy is attained by individuals, with a minimum variety and quality of options offered to them, and with a minimum level of decision-making competence. Second, beyond this constraint it is considered to be a matter of preference whether one should have a larger menu or not, and whether additional training and counseling should be offered in order to enhance competence. In this understanding, the activity of choice is no more mysterious and metaphysical than other ordinary activities like writing, and for all such activities there may be degrees in the quality with which the activity is practiced and in how it reflects the agent's true goals.

Because freedom must be extensive and not just residual, one sees that this line of thought is bound to entail a large scope for responsibility in just social arrangements. At the same time, recognizing the importance of freedom does not require making egalitarian justice a matter of freedom or opportunities only. As argued in Arneson (1998, 1999a), it would be pointless to promote and equalize opportunities if a better distribution of achievements could be obtained otherwise (possibly counting among achievements a suitable dimension of freedom). The fact that freedom is important does not mean that it is all that counts, and it is especially clear that this is not all that counts for most people's subjective preferences. As a consequence, we will be able to argue in Section 10.5 that, in contrast with standard luck egalitarianism, the principle of freedom does not force us to accept inequalities of any kind or size. In this way, this approach removes one of the main worries of the critiques of luck egalitarianism.

Another advantage of making assignments of liabilities rely on freedom rather than (a pre-institutional notion of) responsibility is that it replaces the backward-looking, punitive and moralizing justification of disadvantages that is pervasive in luck egalitarianism with a forward-looking,[21] enhancing and non-moralistic approach. The idea that individuals can be left in their predicament when they are faulty totally disappears from the picture and is replaced with the objective of providing enough scope for free choice to individuals with all kinds of goals.

Dropping the notion of "fault" is not just meant to cater to the charitable feelings of egalitarian do-gooders. The basic principles which govern the organization of society, in particular its system of redistribution and social assistance,

---

[21]Goodin (1998) insists on the opposition between backward-looking and forward-looking conceptions of responsibility.

do not only serve the arithmetic purpose of achieving a better distribution of advantages, but also the symbolic purpose of expressing mutual feelings of solidarity and respect.[22] An equal opportunity society in which individuals can sometimes suffer serious disadvantages without raising any concern from their fellow citizens, who look upon them with some contempt and with full confidence that those feckless losers are "faulty," seems to look more like a variant of the Brave New World than like an egalitarian utopia. In contrast, a society in which the relevant question is not "Are you responsible for what happened to you?" but "Does this correspond to your choice of a life?" would normally exhale a much more pleasant and solidaristic atmosphere. In this way, one sees that fairness principles are not just a matter of distribution but can also contribute, in a similar way as public goods, to enhancing the quality of social relations and thereby the well-being of all.

Consider the example of the "serial squanderer," which is often taken by luck egalitarians as the proof that one cannot deny moral responsibility some role in the allocation of resources. This person repeatedly wastes the help extended to him. Surely, the luck egalitarians say, at some point he must be held responsible and denied further help on this ground. From the perspective of freedom, the treatment of such a case is nonetheless very different. The relevant question is then: Is this kind of life a good option for his preferences, and does repeated help best enhance life in this perspective? It may be that some forms of help are inefficient, as suggested by the mere repetition of similar events. Certainly, being abandoned to a life of pure destitution is not a good option to offer people, and neither is a life of luxury at taxpayers' expense. A simple repetition of a moderate level of help could be good, actually, for preferences enjoying a life of leisure and dependency on public help. Such preferences are rare in societies which give value to reciprocity and educate their children away from such preferences. But it may be unavoidable that a tiny proportion of the population develops such preferences, even in such societies. Affluent societies can afford accommodating such preferences,[23] even if this lifestyle is shocking for some of their members who would rather not subsidize it. But this is not different from public health insurance covering abortion costs. As a matter of fact, there are (not necessarily affluent) societies in which certain kinds of beggars are accepted and even revered. From the perspective of such cultures, the condemnation of dependency in luck egalitarians' writings seems culturally and morally idiosyncratic, and therefore somewhat illiberal.

Let us further explore the implications of the freedom perspective. First, there is a close link between freedom and preference satisfaction, which connects the freedom principle to efficiency concerns. Recent theoretical work on freedom of choice has emphasized the distinction between objective measures of freedom (such as counting the options) and subjective valuations of options and sets. Controversies have developed about whether freedom should be understood in

---

[22] As argued by Wolff (1998, p. 104), "there is more to a society of equals than a just scheme of distribution of material goods. There may also be goods that depend on the attitude people have toward each other."

[23] See Shiffrin (2004).

a purely objective way or whether the value of freedom for those who enjoy it contributes to determining the quantity of freedom.[24] Such distinctions and controversies, however, are of little relevance to the normative question of what follows from the desire to promote people's freedom. In this normative kind of questioning, it is clear that one should enhance freedom only when it has value, and that promising to give people what they want should normally follow from the idea of giving them freedom. Since we have already raised the issue of pointless opportunities, let us focus here on the latter point.

In normal conditions the activity of choice provides people with what they want. There may, however, be practical impediments to this activity, in which case preference satisfaction is still in line with the principle of freedom because the latter implies that it is better when people get what they *would* choose if the obstacles to free choice were removed. For instance, when individuals are caught in a prisoner's dilemma which prevents them from reaching an outcome which is more desirable for all of them, it would enhance their freedom if a communication and commitment device was offered to them which made this option accessible. In this perspective, one sees that the Pareto principle, which has occupied an important place in the analysis of this book, can be derived from an ideal of freedom, not just from a concern for efficiency.[25]

By imposing a basic list of liberties which cannot be waived, we however admit a potential conflict between certain concrete forms of freedom (not subordinating oneself to another's will, being able to participate in social interactions and collective decisions) and people's possible desires to live lives of submission and destitution. But this can be described as a conflict between different kinds of freedom. Imposing the basic list amounts to curtailing a general freedom to live all kinds of lives in order to promote certain kinds of lives in which particular forms of freedom are enjoyed throughout.

Another important implication of the principle of freedom is that individuals must be adequately prepared and equipped in order to exercise their freedom in a skillful way. Freedom is not just a matter of having many and good options, it is also a matter of how competent the moral agent is. A just society therefore has the duty to train the population and provide it with relevant information

---

[24]See, e.g., Carter (1999), Sen (1990, 1992), Arneson (1998).

[25]When preference satisfaction and freedom appear to clash, one can typically reframe the problem in terms of whether one should go with the choice that is actually made under imperfect conditions or with the hypothetical choice that would be made under better conditions. The prisoner's dilemma provides this kind of example. One description of the example is that the inefficient outcome of a prisoner's dilemma game is the true result of individual freedom, whereas the efficient outcome which could be obtained by forcing agents to cooperate would be better for preference satisfaction but less good in terms of freedom. But this description is less convincing than the previous one because, if offered the choice, the players would opt for the efficient outcome. It is the lack of communication and commitment in the prisoner's dilemma which impairs their freedom, not the other way around. Another kind of example is when the cost of screening the options or defining one's preferences makes it better for the decision-maker not to be offered too much choice. In this case preference satisfaction goes for obtaining the best of all possible options without having to carry out much choosing work. Again, this would be the result of free choice if the agent could not only choose among the options but also choose the process by which he obtains the final option.

so that the exercise of freedom can be more than whimsical picking and can develop into an artful way of life.[26]

10.4 Preference liability versus welfarism

In view of the close link between freedom and preference satisfaction, one might wonder in what ways this approach differs from a standard welfarist view which gives substantial freedom (and thereby responsibility) to people in order to promote their well-being, without any independent and non-instrumental concern for freedom or responsibility. If one makes abstraction of the requirement of a basic level of freedom and autonomy that is imposed independently of people's preferences for freedom, and focuses on the second stage of the principle of freedom, what is proposed here is not opposed to welfarism but can be described as a development of welfarism toward a more precise and concrete view. Welfarism is a comfortable doctrine in part because it is so abstract that it commits its advocates to very little. But it should be possible to develop a concrete and detailed version of it which explains the way in which freedom implies assigning liabilities to people for their choices. Once we decide to grant individuals certain freedoms and the ensuing liabilities, what does this imply for redistribution and the organization of social duties? Even a welfarist theory should, at some point, try to answer this kind of question.

But welfarism, if understood as seeking to promote *subjective* well-being and compare it across individuals, is not a viable approach, even when one disregards the usual objections to it that are based on pre-institutional notions of responsibility (such as the "expensive tastes" and the "adaptive preferences" objections). This observation will provide us with a second reason, in addition to the freedom principle, for assigning a certain liability to individuals.

There are two main varieties of welfarism which must be distinguished and discussed separately here. A first variety, which finds its inspiration in Bentham's utilitarianism, seeks to promote subjective feelings of happiness. This view is not appealing simply because happiness is not the only thing that matters in life for most people, even though it does matter a lot for many of them, and it is quite astonishing that such a reductionist conception of human goals can have had such a hold on the history of thought.[27] One can retain happiness as a valuable functioning – in Sen's (1992) terminology – among others, but

---

[26] This has deep consequences about the issue of the formation of conceptions of the good life, an important area in which freedom has to operate as much as possible. Certain liberal views of the subject consider that individuals should be left alone as far as their conceptions of the good life are concerned. But the assumption that individuals are magically self-equipped to handle these delicate matters is just as unrealistic as Hobbes' assumption that men simply sprung up from earth like mushrooms. In fact, the members of society need substantial help in order to go about forming and revising their views about morality and the good life. Turning a blind eye to how families, religious authorities and TV channels operate the basic and less basic training work in this field is ignoring one of the most important tasks of social institutions, and one can doubt that the institutions listed above generally perform this task in a satisfactory way.

[27] A recent and entertaining defense of this conception can be found in Layard (2005).

there is no reason to believe that it is the only valuable functioning, especially if one wants to cater to people's preferences over their lives. A more interesting variety of welfarism seeks to promote a more intellectual notion of satisfaction, i.e., to make people's lives go as they wish in a deep sense. This approach is quite attractive, but it has one drawback. In order to make use of this notion of welfare in the context of distributive justice, one must be able to evaluate the success of lives with some common measure which transcends the different views and goals which different individuals may adopt. This is a chimeric idea, as Rawls (1971, 1982) has forcefully argued. Even if one devised a sensible measure of this kind, it would be outrageous to seek to apply it in order to decide who is better off or worse off in society. If Ann considers that, given her conception of life, her life is much better than Bob's, it would be insulting to tell her that in terms of some overall measure of success her achievements are lower. In contrast, there would be nothing problematic about telling her that she is worse off according to some measure of resources or opportunities.

This argument must be distinguished from the questionable idea that an index of satisfaction cannot sensibly be constructed. Economists have long been wary of interpersonal comparisons of welfare, but their preventions were sometimes inspired by an extreme kind of behaviorism. As regards happiness as a feeling, it is clear that a measure is perfectly conceivable, and neurosciences are likely to provide a good biological index of happiness in the near future. As far as satisfaction – as a judgment rather than a feeling – is concerned, things are more complex. But after all people are able to say if they are more or less "satisfied" with their life, and in spite of all the problems with comparing such utterances, one might be able to use a sophisticated variant of this kind of data for the construction of an index. No matter how the index is built, the argument that is made here is against *using* any index of that sort for evaluative purposes. This is because different views of the good life are incommensurable and cannot be overwritten by an overarching index. The diversity of views of the good life precludes any reference to a shared higher-order ordering. Such an ordering would enable us to say that, given a certain objective situation, an individual in this situation would have greater well-being with a certain conception of the good life than with another conception. This is incompatible with the idea that conceptions of the good life are ultimate criteria in and of themselves, and that they are not interchangeable ingredients in a higher-order utility function to be maximized.

We end up with the idea that we should not try, for the sake of social justice, to compare people's situations in terms of a comparable index of satisfaction. This implies that individuals will have to be held responsible for their level of satisfaction. Indeed, consider two individuals who have the same ordinal preferences over the various dimensions of life[28] and have lives that they consider to

---

[28] In fact not all dimensions of life are relevant for distributive justice. One should restrict attention to personal situations and ignore features of the environment that do not directly affect the individual. In the previous chapters we have always been dealing with self-centered preferences for this reason, ignoring people's preferences over the state of the rest of the world. The boundary between personal and non personal dimensions is hard to delineate but this

be equally valuable. They may nonetheless have different levels of satisfaction (e.g., one may be more ambitious than the other), but comparing their lives in terms of personal satisfaction would contradict their common judgment that their lives are equally good. If no better judgment is available, we should concur with them that their lives are equally good, and ignore the difference in satisfaction, since comparing the levels of satisfaction naively does not correspond to a better judgment over their lives but to mingling inconsistent ambitions.[29] Now, ignoring the satisfaction levels in this way amounts to holding individuals responsible for them.

As this explanation makes clear, ignoring satisfaction levels does not mean that individual preferences should be disregarded altogether, but simply that the non purely ordinal part of "utility functions," i.e., the personal indexes which measure satisfaction according to people's own views, should be left in the responsibility sphere. We therefore obtain an additional channel, besides freedom, by which responsibility gets an important place in the definition of fairness. Moreover, disregarding a characteristic is the hallmark of liberal reward, so that we not only have a responsibility assignment here, but also the adoption of a precise reward principle with respect to it. Barring the use of an overall index of well-being will actually make it impossible to use the principle of utilitarian reward in connection with any kind of responsibility assignment in this context, since utilitarian reward requires a summable index of well-being.

In summary, responsibility being abandoned as a pre-institutional notion that would serve to justify advantages and disadvantages, it can still be an important part of a theory of justice, as an assignment of liabilities induced by two basic principles. One principle is that levels of satisfaction, as distinct from ordinal preference orderings, should be disregarded in the evaluation of social situations, which means that individuals should be held responsible (in the sense of liberal reward) for their "utility functions." The other principle is that people should be given substantial freedom over the conduct of their lives.

10.5   The responsibility sphere

The sphere of responsibility induced by these two principles can be described quite precisely: It will coincide with individual preferences and utility functions. Responsibility for one's utility function has already been explained, so that we can focus here on preferences. When people make choices, even if we want to

---

issue will not be explored further here.

[29] One could object to this reasoning by suggesting to take satisfaction as a functioning among others. But this is a very special functioning. For a given utility function, once all other dimensions of life are given, the satisfaction level is determined. This is not a functioning that can be changed independently of the others. Relatedly, this is not a functioning over which one can have preferences. To be satisfied with one's life is not a dimension of one's life along other independent dimensions. Only metapreferences can sensibly rank lives *cum* preferences and satisfaction. We ignore metapreferences here, since relying on such preferences in order to rank people's situations would directly violate a basic principle of neutrality over conceptions of the good life.

respect their choices we cannot hold them directly responsible for their choices when their menus differ, because, as explained above, their choices are then unequally constrained. Respecting their freedom of choice is expressed by holding them responsible for their preferences and only for their preferences (at least directly). Their preferences define how they would choose in different menus, and this what we want to respect if freedom of choice is to have any sense.

Are we falling back to the preference approach to responsibility? A key issue for the pre-institutional approach to responsibility for preferences is the authenticity of preferences. A serious difficulty in this respect is that "preferences are necessarily in large part imprinted in persons from their environment,"[30] as noted by Roemer (1996, p. 271) who concludes that authentic preferences can never be identified. This problem appears in a quite different light in the perspective of freedom. Providing people with freedom does imply respecting people's true preferences rather than cravings and whimsical fancies, and relying on the best information that is available if their information is imperfect, but it does not involve seeking ideal preferences that would be formed in an unrealistic ideal process of formation. Therefore, people will be held responsible for preferences which are in general close to their immediate preferences, so that, in many cases, their actual choices will be considered worthy of respect.

In particular, the fact that preferences are socially conditioned is not, in itself, a problem at all for this approach because the principle of freedom is about freedom for actual people, not for ideal people who would be formed in a very different way. Nonetheless, certain kinds of conditioning do raise a concern, not because they involve causal influence as such, but because they involve a direct violation of freedom, or because they operate to the service of others' unfair advantages. An obvious example of the former kind is engineered conditioning, when certain illegitimate authorities inculcate certain preferences in people's minds in order to serve a precise purpose. Whether this purpose is good or bad does not necessarily matter in this case, because the main problem lies in the illegitimacy of the process itself. Such illegitimacy can be traced to the principle of freedom itself, which forbids exerting certain kinds of influence over fellow citizens.[31] Similarly, one can easily condemn social norms which attribute an inferior symbolic status to certain citizens (e.g., women) and tend to shape individual preferences so as to make the targeted people accept and even seek inferior social roles.

More diffuse kinds of conditioning can be problematic in indirect ways. For instance, a society in which women are more attracted toward professions of care than men, because, for instance, they observe more women of the previous generation in these professions, does not raise a concern if professions of care are not disadvantaged and are not less prestigious than other professions. But if such professions are disadvantaged, then this social conditioning is problematic

---

[30] Phillips (2004) and Gomberg (2007) also emphasize that individual preferences are always strongly influenced by the social context.

[31] It is considered perfectly appropriate for parents and teachers to try to inculcate children with preferences for a life embodying certain moral values. Even then, not all forms of influence are acceptable.

because it operates to the unfair advantage of men. What is problematic is not the conditioning process in itself, if one considers – which is debatable – that there is nothing intrinsically wrong with mimetism, provided it is accompanied by proper education enabling individuals to think about the reasons involved. The practical conclusion in this case, then, should not be that there is something wrong about these preferences, or about the way in which they are formed. What is problematic in this case is the unfair advantage that attaches to certain jobs.

This point deserves some explanation. It is connected to the general meaning of holding people responsible for their preferences. In the literature it is often implicitly assumed that responsibility for one's preferences implies a liability to bear the direct (market) costs of the induced choices. This triggers feminist criticisms since, in this perspective, holding women responsible for their preferences for less well paid activities – when such preferences are not the result of sexist conditioning – implies that one can accept the ensuing gender inequalities. But we have seen in the previous chapters, in particular Chapters 4 and 5 dealing with consumption-leisure choices, that responsibility for preferences does not imply that any kind of budget set is acceptable, since, for instance, the optimal policy might seek to maximize either the minimal income or the working poor's income. In the perspective of freedom, especially, it is important to provide people with valuable menus of options. Mason (2006, p. 175) takes the example of a committed pacifist who lives in a region where most of the jobs are in the weapons industry. According to Dworkin's conception of responsibility, insofar as this pacifist endorses his own views he should be held responsible for the resulting lack of career opportunities. Mason concurs with Cohen (2004) in noting that the more reflectively an individual adheres to his own preferences, the more costly it would be for him to adjust his preferences to the environment, so that endorsing one's preferences in this sort of case seems to provide a reason against responsibility, not in favor of it. The freedom-based perspective that is proposed here suggests yet another conclusion: What is problematic in the situation is not that the pacifist cannot easily change his preferences, but simply that he faces a bad menu according to his own preferences.

A similar reasoning applies to gender issues. In a patriarchal society, sexist norms push women toward subordinate activities and condone wage inequalities between men and women, even for equivalent jobs. Let us assume away any such phenomenon, which is obviously undesirable, and focus on a non sexist society. In such a society, it may nonetheless happen that women are attracted by less lucrative activities. Is it acceptable to hold them responsible for it? Even when women are not influenced by oppressive norms, the fact that they develop preferences which push them toward less rewarding activities can be considered problematic in the approach that is developed here, if we find a way to describe the menu they face as less valuable for themselves than it is for men's typical preferences. Can we find such a way, when we posit, as we do here, that preferences over the good life are incommensurable? Such incommensurability prevents us from comparing satisfaction levels, but not from comparing the value of menus. The egalitarian-equivalent approach, in particular, provides a simple way of doing this, and this will be explained in Section 10.7.

10.6   Ex-post inequalities matter

When the sphere of responsibility is defined – in our case, preferences and utility functions – it remains to examine how the compensation and reward principles can be applied in the design of redistributive policies. The compensation principle remains unscathed by the above discussion about replacing a pre-institutional notion of responsibility with a freedom-based notion. But its justification is now a little more specific. The point of compensation is no longer to neutralize the influence of factors for which individuals are not responsible, because with the freedom perspective we have abandoned the view of life as a kind of competition in which the playing field must be levelled. Compensation remains desirable simply in order to achieve equality wherever this is not hampered by freedom and responsibility considerations. Therefore, adopting the freedom perspective does not question the idea that one should seek to reduce inequalities between individuals with identical utility functions. Such individuals would normally make the same choices and obtain the same utility when offered the same menu of options, and should indeed ideally end up with situations that they judge equivalent according to their own preferences. When this is not possible, this equality condition is simply replaced with a priority requisite in favor of the worse-off, as we have seen in detail in the previous chapters (e.g., Chapter 3). These equality and priority versions of the requirement are familiar expressions of the compensation principle, in the case when individuals are held responsible for their preferences and utility functions only.

Recalling that we actually want to apply the liberal reward principle to utility functions, i.e., to disregard them and focus only on the ordinal part of people's preferences, we can reformulate this requirement in a way that refers only to preferences: *Individuals with the same ordinal preferences should end up with situations that they judge equivalent according to their own preferences.* This implies an extension of the previous requirement, since it is now applied not only to people with the same utility functions, but also to people with identical preferences, whether or not their utility functions are the same. This particular formulation of the compensation principle incorporates the liberal reward principle applied to utility functions, since it implies in particular that two individual with identical preferences but different utility functions should ideally end up with equivalent options, even if this provides them with unequal levels of satisfaction – which occurs, for instance, if one of them is more ambitious than the other in terms of absolute or relative success.

Let us now turn to the reward principle. Beyond the case of utility functions, for which liberal reward is warranted, the question of reward is less simple. When freedom, rather than a pre-institutional notion of responsibility, is the basis for the assignment of liabilities, both the principle of liberal reward and the principle of utilitarian reward lose part of their attraction. Their common drawback, in this perspective, is that they consider inequalities to be permissible without limitation whenever they can be attributed to responsibility character-istics. Under liberal reward, laissez-faire is fine when individuals are responsible, independently of the technology which determines the rate of reward to effort. If this rate is very high, inequalities can be staggering. Under utilitarian re-ward, a greater sum of well-being always constitutes a social improvement when individuals are responsible, even if inequalities are tremendously increased in order to bring about the increase in the total.

This is not satisfactory when the motivation for the assignment of liabili-ties is to provide people with freedom, because freedom is valuable when the menu of options is itself valuable, not just when it has many items. When social arrangements permit more inequalities, the menu of options offered to individuals may perhaps contain more diverse options as a result, but it also contains more options of bad quality, and this is likely to trump the diversity consideration. Even the high options are then tainted by the fact that they involve social relations of smaller range and of lower quality. Being granted the additional option of living in incomparably better conditions than the others is not a real addition to one's freedom because this option actually has low (or even negative) value.

One can associate the standard luck-egalitarian approach with a kind of "forfeiture" view[32] according to which it is enough to give people access to good options, and if they fail to seize the opportunities and end up in dire straits no one can complain. Luck egalitarians have no principled objection to a society in which, on a background of equal opportunities, some end up in poverty or as the slaves of others. They would say that such a society can be just as egalitarian as another society in which *ex post* inequalities are much smaller and which guarantees to all equal status and participation in social life. From the perspective of freedom this view is not acceptable. A free life is better when it involves access to a diversity of good options, rather than to a mix of good and bad options, and a free society is one in which members are sufficiently equal so that they do not enter into relations of domination and subordination.

In order to defend this view of a free society, one must give an account of how to evaluate the array of options offered to people. On what basis can we reject certain bad options such as "destroying one's health without being of-fered help and advice," or "submitting oneself to the arbitrary will of another person?" It seems to me that the most promising account will combine some kind of perfectionism at a basic level with the respect of individual preferences at a higher level. This is what the two-tier principle of freedom introduced in Section 10.3 was meant to encapsulate. Perfectionism (or, simply, objectivism) intervenes here because there are certain basic freedoms which cannot be op-tional and which should be imposed on individuals whether they like them or not, because otherwise we are no longer dealing with a society of free and au-

---

[32]Cf. Scanlon (1988), Voorhoeve (2005, 2007). Although Scanlon rejects the forfeiture view, he does end up defending a view which is not very different and allows individuals to suffer serious disadvantages when it is considered that enough has been done in order to put them in good conditions of choice. The quality of the options themselves, as distinguished from the conditions in which choice is made, is largely ignored in his view.

tonomous agents. This is similar to Rawls' first principle of equal basic liberties, or Anderson's unconditional notion of democratic equality. Arneson's "objective list" approach to the measurement of well-being and Nussbaum's list of basic capabilities have similar implications.[33] The precise list of basic liberties is certainly a matter of controversy and I will not try to draw such a list here. Some would like to limit the list to basic human rights, while one should probably extend it to certain socioeconomic conditions. In particular, a guarantee of being offered a subsistence level of resources, and even more, i.e., a level of resources and a form of help enabling one to come back to an autonomous life[34] if one wishes so, seems warranted. A perfectionist list of liberties is also needed in order to prevent practices satisfying the anti-social preferences of those (who may be a majority of the population) who like dominant positions and are too ready to abuse others while in such positions.[35] Beyond what is required in the basic list, one can let people's preferences decide whether a menu of options is valuable or not. As we have seen with the example of gender inequalities (and will be explained in greater detail in the next section), different preferences may value the same set of options in different ways, and one should try not only to offer options which are valuable to people, but, out of egalitarian concern, to offer sets which are similarly valuable for the prevailing preferences in the population.

It may be that, for certain options, most preferences consider them to be bad and unacceptable, in which case it is not difficult to decide that they are not worth including in the package. The articulation between the basic list of freedoms and the preference-catering menu will be more or less smooth depending on the consensus, among prevailing preferences, on the exclusion of certain bad options. If everybody agrees that there is no value in putting "being a slave," or even "having a slave," in the menu, this will be excluded whether or not this is part of the basic list.

What does this imply for the reward principle? We have already seen that the utilitarian principle is in fact excluded by the fact that interpersonal comparisons of well-being are rejected and that it is impervious to *ex post* inequalities. One could amend the utilitarian principle in order to incorporate a concern for *ex post* inequalities, by introducing some inequality aversion about the distribution of well-being in circumstance classes. But the rejection of interpersonal comparisons of subjective well-being closes this alley as well.

The liberal reward principle, which is by force adopted with respect to levels of satisfaction, as we have seen, can still serve as a useful reference as far as

---

[33]See Rawls (1971), Anderson (1999), Arneson (2000b), Nussbaum (1993).

[34]The concept of self-reliance, as (mis)used in conservative parlance, is deceptive because, if one thinks a little about it, no one in a modern society is self-reliant. Even the super-rich would be totally lost without the workers who provide them with everything they need. The "autonomous life" referred to in the text is simply a life in which one's dependency on others involves exchanges rather than gifts. Another usual mistake is to believe that having a job is enough to be autonomous.

[35]The readers of reports on workplace relations, such as Ehrenreich (2001), should think that even the respect of basic forms of freedom and respect require extensive socioeconomic safeguards.

free choices are concerned, because it makes sense to try and interfere as little as possible with choice activities. But intervention is necessary when basic autonomy is at stake. Let us illustrate this point with the core example of income redistribution, which was the topic of Chapters 4 and 5. An important condition of liberal reward in those chapters was *Laissez-Faire for Uniform Skills*, which said that laissez-faire is the best policy when all individuals have the same level of skill. The laissez-faire, in fact, offers some bad options, because individuals who do not work enough may end up below the subsistence level.[36] From the perspective of freedom, what is the point of offering individuals the possibility to starve in idleness? It appears hard to defend the view that the presence of such options in the menu is warranted for the extension of freedom. In this perspective, on the contrary, it is arguable that no option below subsistence should be on the menu. What does this imply for the definition of a good menu? It is unlikely that freedom would be enhanced by forcing individuals to work some minimal amount of time (thereby obtaining earnings above subsistence), and therefore the best option is to guarantee a decent minimum income to all, independently of their work, in all the contexts where this is technically possible (if productivity is too low, this requirement is impossible to satisfy). At any rate, the requirement of Laissez-Faire for Uniform Skills should be dropped.

This does not mean that liberal reward, in this example, should be confined to ignoring the levels of satisfaction. In Sections 4.8 and 5.3, Zero Egalitarian-Equivalence was characterized with the help of a liberal reward condition saying that individuals who do not work should not be differentially treated as a function of their preferences (even if one could perfectly observe such preferences), and that they should all obtain the same income support. This condition remains quite attractive in the perspective of freedom, since it would be strange to seek to discriminate among such agents on the basis of their preferences. If we could give all agents the same set of options in terms of income and labor, those who do not work would automatically have the same disposable income, independently of their preferences. Since, as shown in Chapters 4 and 5, Zero Egalitarian-Equivalence is the criterion that is singled-out by the compensation principle and the above requirement of no-discrimination among non-working individuals, it appears that, from the perspective of freedom that is defended here, this is a better criterion than Min Egalitarian-Equivalence or Wage Egalitarian-Equivalence which satisfy Laissez-Faire for Uniform Skills (not to mention Conditional Equality, which is even more in the realm of liberal reward). The fact that, as we have seen in Section 5.4, this criterion ultimately advocates maximizing the minimum income, when applied in the context of income taxation with incentive constraints, is moreover very well in line with the concern that a good menu should not offer levels of income that are too low.

In conclusion, the approach to responsibility suggested here makes it possible and even desirable to retain the principle of liberal reward, insofar as minimal intervention about personal choices is an appealing ideal, but does so under

---

[36] This is the famous problem of surfers that worried Rawls (1974, 1988) from the opposite standpoint and led him to propose adding leisure to the index of primary goods in order to defend a laissez-faire attitude with respect to these people.

substantial limitations out of concern for the quality of options and the induced *ex post* inequalities.

The thesis that *ex post* inequalities matter and that egalitarians should be concerned not only with equality of opportunities but also with the egalitarian content of the opportunities themselves is compelling when one takes freedom as the leading principle for the definition of the scope of responsibility in social justice. But one can argue that even luck-egalitarians who rely on a pre-institutional notion of responsibility should be concerned, to some extent, with *ex post* inequalities.[37] Indeed, there is no reason why responsibility should trump any concern for the satisfaction of basic needs or for the absence of domination and oppression in society. It seems very easy to defend the principle that, no matter what, individuals who fall below a threshold should be offered help, and that certain inequalities of status and power should be banned. Human rights and the status of citizen, in particular, should not be for sale on the equal opportunity market. In other words, there are certain basic equalities that cannot be rendered contingent by the operation of personal responsibility.

10.7 Egalitarian-equivalence

So much for basic principles. Now let us see how this approach relates to the material provided in the previous chapters, in the elaboration of concrete criteria for social evaluation. We have already seen in the previous section that the compensation principle, understood as seeking to *give equivalent situations to individuals with identical preferences*, appears vindicated.

We have also seen that the liberal reward principle can be extended to preferences in general, i.e., turning into the principle that transfers should be as insensitive to changes in preferences as possible, under the constraint that the options offered on the menu are satisfactory. This precludes full laissez-faire policies even when individuals differ only in their preferences, because laissez-faire generally leaves it possible to end up below the subsistence threshold. And one may want to put more than a subsistence requirement in the constraint, because what really matters is not simply that people do not starve, but that they keep the means for a fruitful participation in social life. Moreover, in addition to requirements on resources, one may think of a requirement about the kind of relations and contracts in which people may engage, as it has been already explained in the previous section. But, under these acceptability constraints, the liberal reward principle remains appealing because it minimizes intervention

---

[37]This argument is developed in Fleurbaey (2001) and Dowding (2008). Several authors have argued in favor of an unconditional subsistence minimum, and also in favor of an unconditional ban on excessive inequalities entailing dominance relations between people. See, e.g., Anderson (1999), Phillips (1999), Armstrong (2006), Mason (2006). Jacobs (2004) incorporates a concern for "stakes fairness" within a conception of equal opportunities, rejecting winner-take-all situations. Gomberg (2007) argues that, even when opportunities are equal, it is fallacious to attribute inequalities to individual responsibility because they are always primarily due to social mechanisms.

and is therefore maximally neutral.[38]

In view of the analysis of the previous chapters, this combination of compensation and liberal reward should logically lead us to adopt a certain Egalitarian-Equivalence criterion, because such a criterion evaluates social arrangements on the basis of individual ordinal and non-comparable preferences over personal situations, which corresponds to liberal reward for utilities, but otherwise gives priority to the compensation principle. A new complication that appeared in this chapter is that the Egalitarian-Equivalence criterion would operate only under the constraint that individuals are given sufficient freedom, which involves a sufficient array and quality of choice – the options must be sufficiently good in terms of resources and of social relations – and a sufficient competence at making choices. We have already seen how this constraint could actually help select a particular member of the Egalitarian-Equivalence family, such as Zero Egalitarian-Equivalence in the simple setting of Chapters 4 and 5.

An issue which may be raised at this point is that an Egalitarian-Equivalence criterion simply records indifference curves and not the activity of choice itself, so that one may be afraid that such a criterion is a poor embodiment of the principle of freedom. Recall that the principle of freedom works as a two-tier formula such that, beyond a basic level of autonomy, it is considered to be a matter of preference whether one should have a larger menu or not, and whether additional training and counseling should be offered in order to enhance competence. The Egalitarian-Equivalence criterion operates at the second stage in order to respect people's preferences on these dimensions. Relying on preferences here is still compatible with the principle of freedom, by seeking to provide living conditions, including the scope of choice-making activities, which reflect what people would choose if they could. This implies of course that a detailed description of social arrangements and personal activities is incorporated into the application of the criterion so that individual preferences over these dimensions can find their expression in this way. We are getting quite far from the simple models studied in the previous chapters, but there does not seem to be any serious conceptual obstacle to refining the theory in this direction.

Let us briefly imagine what an extended theory would look like. The requirement of basic freedom and autonomy requires institutions to provide individuals with basic human rights, with training and information, and with a budget set that does not require a minimum amount of work, that always offers resources above the subsistence level (without forcing to consume them), and that does not offer certain kinds of subordination contracts. Beyond that, in order to compare individual situations with the Egalitarian-Equivalence approach, a set of reference situations has to be defined, which will serve to compute an equivalent situation for every individual. Reference situations in this set must be easily comparable to each other and this is obtained by requiring that they dominate one another, in one or several dimensions, while being identical in

---

[38] One could also argue that minimizing intervention may be good in terms of efficiency, but this is not guaranteed, since minimizing distortions does not necessarily lead to greater efficiency, unless they are all removed. Since we exclude laisser-faire policies, distortions will typically remain in every acceptable menu of options.

the remaining dimensions. To illustrate, suppose that there are seven dimensions: consumption, work, health, social relations, happiness, education, and choice.[39] The latter represents the quantity of discretion that the individual enjoys in organizing her life. One example of a set of reference situations, which extends Zero Egalitarian-Equivalence, consists in fixing the last six dimensions at a certain level: zero work, good health, good social relations, moderately high level of happiness, college education, and the level of choice enjoyed by a typical middle class person nowadays. The members of the set then differ only in the consumption dimension. In order to evaluate an individual situation, one then tries to determine the level of consumption that this individual would consider equivalent to her current situation if the six other dimensions were put at the reference level. This is but an example. A more realistic set of reference situations could make the education and choice dimensions vary alongside the consumption dimension so as to represent a more realistic set of situations. In real life, low levels of income typically go with low levels of education and little scope for choice in one's life. It would be easier to determine equivalent situations in the reference set, for all individuals, if the reference set contained more realistic situations. Whether or not some other dimensions vary with consumption in the reference set, once equivalent situations are computed for every type of individual in society, one can then give priority to those with the worst equivalent situations.

When some individuals fall below the threshold of basic freedom and opportunity, they should normally receive priority over those who are above the threshold. It is not clear how to compare and prioritize the situations of the subpopulation of individuals who are below the threshold. Some perfectionist criterion is probably needed in this respect, since perfectionist considerations also determine the threshold level itself.

For individuals above the threshold, the concern for freedom is captured in this approach in two ways. First, the dimension of choice can be taken as one dimension of quality of life among others, as illustrated in the above example of a reference set. Second, the approach respects individual preferences and therefore seeks to provide individuals with the combination of life dimensions that they desire. On the other hand, this approach does not fetishize choice and opportunities, and puts the satisfaction of preferences above the provision of opportunities, except when the basic level of freedom and autonomy is at stake.

As explained, the Egalitarian-Equivalence approach can easily incorporate the quality of social relations as a dimension of life. The fact that consumption or income is suggested as a possible metric for the comparison of equivalent individual situations is not meant to suggest that money is trivially commensurable to any kind of social relation. Imagine an individual involved in a wonderful love relation. There might be no amount of money that he would accept in order to fall back to a relation of lesser quality. If the reference situation is of this more ordinary kind, then his equivalent income is infinite. This does not

---

[39] I should insist that this is just a simple illustration. Chapters 5–7 have already examined additional complex issues having to do with time and uncertainty.

imply, however, that lovers should be taxed more than loners, first because this is not an incentive-compatible policy and also because money transfers are not the most efficient response to inequalities in social relations. There are better adapted responses to such inequalities, such as the promotion of activities which foster social relations.

One common objection to this treatment of social relations is that certain kinds of relations are private issues which should be left out of social justice concerns. It seems a little odd, the objection goes, to compare happy or unhappy lovers to others at the bar of justice. This objection simply builds on the bourgeois tradition of seeing the family as a private entity. In reality, all social relations are *social*. The fact that great liberty should be left to individuals in the management of certain personal relations (as opposed to economic contracts, for which more regulation is generally accepted) is simply explained by the importance of feelings and spontaneity in such relations, not by the mistaken idea that being lucky or unlucky in such things does not make you really better off or worse off than others for a criterion of social justice.[40]

These various considerations go against the view that social justice can be completely defined as variations around the themes of social relations, social status, or citizenship. It is important to give basic rights of citizenship their due place, and it is correct to say that they should be protected even against the free play of personal choice and responsibility, but from such a line of reasoning one only gets basic kinds of social equality, not a full-fledged theory of equality. Equality in resources and in all the functionings and freedoms that matter to people cannot be totally subsumed under the umbrella of equal and democratic citizenship. One must avoid the two opposite pitfalls of neglecting either the basic right to social equality or the comprehensive array of dimensions that make life valuable to people. While the luck egalitarian literature can be suspected of being trapped in the former, many of its critiques seem lured by the latter.[41]

A noteworthy feature of the Egalitarian-Equivalence criterion is that it provides a way out of the indexing dilemma which is commonly thought to plague theories of justice. According to the received wisdom on the topic, an index of individual well-being which summarizes multiple dimensions of life (such as resources or functionings) must be either an index of satisfaction if it espouses individual preferences, or a uniform index that is independent of individual preferences. In the former case, one supposedly falls into welfarism, which is embraced by some authors but abhorred by others. In the latter case, one ends

---

[40] Nussbaum (1993) and Baker et al. (2005), for instance, put love in the dimensions of life that serve for the evaluation of individual situations.

[41] That includes Fleurbaey (1995b), who proposed to focus on "primary functionings" and to neglect the rest, which was supposed to belong to a private sphere of responsibility. The idea of implementing a notion of responsibility by disregarding a private sphere is correct in the sense that one always ultimately does so. For instance, the Zero Egalitarian-Equivalent criterion of Chapters 4 and 5 disregards the precise consumption-labor bundle consumed by individuals, which is a private matter, and only focuses on a certain equivalent income. But defining a theory of justice in terms of neglect of a private sphere is not very helpful when it comes to determining what the private sphere consists of. The risk is to leave too much in it and to obtain a theory focusing on a basic kind of social equality.

up with a perfectionist approach which imposes a special view of the good life on all individuals. The Egalitarian-Equivalence criterion shows that the first horn of the dilemma actually divides into two possibilities. An interpersonally comparable index of satisfaction, suitable for a welfarist approach, is indeed one way of respecting individual preferences over personal situations. But there is another possibility, exemplified by the concept of egalitarian-equivalence, which consists in using an index constructed with ordinal non-comparable preferences. This is neither welfarist nor perfectionist. It is not welfarist because it does not rely on interpersonally comparable information about satisfaction. It is obviously not perfectionist since it faithfully obeys people's preferences.[42]

Let us come back to gender issues and illustrate, as promised in Section 10.5, how an Egalitarian-Equivalence criterion can avoid sanctifying disadvantages following from women's orientation toward less lucrative jobs.[43] The Zero Egalitarian-Equivalence criterion is a relevant example here. Let us see how it ranks the situations of people with different job preferences. Suppose that all activities are equally accessible to everyone, and that different people take up different activities only because of their specific preferences. Consider Ann and Bob, who have the same consumption-leisure preferences over their most preferred activity, their second most preferred activity, and so on. But they rank activities in a different way, and this leads Ann to choose an activity with a lower wage than Bob's. If we ask each of them for the "counterfactual amount of transfer which, combined with a null wage rate, would make them as happy as in the current situation,"[44] necessarily Bob gives a greater answer than Ann, because he is happy to choose an activity with greater pay than Ann's. Therefore we see that, even if individuals are held responsible for their preferences, it is possible to say that the menu of activities and wages offered by the market is less advantageous for one kind of preferences than for another, and that Ann is worse off than Bob because of her preferences for less well paid activities. We took the Zero Egalitarian-Equivalence criterion as an example in order to fix ideas, but most other Egalitarian-Equivalence criteria (in particular the Wage and Min Egalitarian-Equivalence criteria) would have similarly concluded that Ann is worse-off than Bob. In conclusion, all individuals face the same menu in this situation, but this menu is deemed less favorable by the Egalitarian-Equivalence criterion for those who prefer the less well-paid activities. What is problematic here is not women's preferences as such, provided they are formed in an acceptable way. What is problematic is the differential value of the menu for people with different preferences, and the best policy response in this case must operate at the level of the menu itself.[45] One can even say that, absent sexist norms directed at women, the fact that women develop certain preferences

---

[42]More on this issue can be found in Fleurbaey (2007a,b).

[43]Among such activities one may include parental leaves which reduce earnings and pension rights.

[44]Cf. Section 5.2.

[45]This does not imply that all post-tax wages will be equal in all activities. Incentive constraints will typically obstruct full equality, but one can seek to maximize the value of the worst-off's situation under such constraints.

more than men is not relevant in itself. What is unfair is simply the fact that people with certain preferences face a less valuable menu. The men who would like to take a parental leave to raise their children are no less unfairly treated than women with the same preferences.[46]

10.8 Equality of autonomy

If we sought a simple label for the conception of justice that tentatively emerges from the above analysis, we could propose "equality of autonomy." The word "autonomy" is chosen here instead of "freedom" or "opportunity," because it is more likely to convey two important features of this conception. First, autonomy is, more transparently, something that depends not only on the quality of the menu but also on the quality of the agent. In luck egalitarianism, in contrast, the quality of the agent is not something that needs to be promoted per se, but is only a matter of compensation when it makes some options less accessible to some individuals than to others. Second, autonomy can be easily understood as something that has to be maintained, not something that can be legitimately forfeited. This is in direct contrast with the notion of opportunity which, by definition, can be forfeited without raising any concern. In particular, the basic list of liberties and what has been said in Chapter 7 about fresh starts fit quite well into the frame of equality of autonomy.

A risk with this label is that it suggests that autonomy defines a metric of interpersonal comparison that trumps individual preferences in all circumstances, which is definitely not the case, since, beyond the basic list of liberties, the extent of freedom that should be granted to people is supposed to depend on their own preferences over the kind of menu they would like to have. This should be understood as respecting autonomy in a comprehensive sense, i.e., respecting people's views also about the appropriate extent of the activity of choice in their life. Moreover, the egalitarian-equivalent approach serves to evaluate people's actual situation, i.e., their achievements, even if a full description of their situation contains the array of options from which they choose and the way in which they exercise the activity of choice. Equalizing autonomy is not equalizing opportunities. It is an outcome-oriented view, in which exercising choice and enjoying liberties are no more than important features of individual lives, among other achievements.

Autonomy, or freedom, has been discussed here in terms of individual choice for personal matters, but an important aspect of freedom is the possibility to take part in collective choices. There is therefore a democratic component of the theory which is a direct extension of the idea that individuals should exercise their freedom in all affairs relevant to them. This component concerns not only the political sphere but all social entities in which collective decisions have to be made, including the family and the firm. This question will not be developed

---

[46]Phillips (2004) argues that we should focus on inequalities across social groups and genders. In view of the individual diversity of preferences, focusing on group and gender inequalities should probably be viewed as useful only in a second-best approach.

further here, as it is essentially orthogonal to the issue of responsibility and would require lengthy developments.[47]

Equality of autonomy differs from resource egalitarian and luck egalitarian theories by giving a more prominent role to the notion of freedom and a derivative role only to responsibility. In this way it may appear to be closer to Rawls' theory of justice and to Sen's theory of capabilities than to other theories. Recall how one can read Rawls' theory as defining fair shares in terms of "a distributive scheme that makes it possible for free and equal citizens to pursue their diverse conceptions of the good within a framework that embodies an ideal of reciprocity and mutual respect" (Scheffler 2003, p. 28). Equality of autonomy also puts a good deal of weight on the notion of free and equal citizens, but appears to demand more than simply making it possible for them to pursue their goals in a context of reciprocity and respect. The principle of freedom requires institutions to help citizens attain a good level of competence, and to shape the options in a way that preserves their autonomy and preserves equality in social relations. We have seen, for instance, how this can translate into seeking to provide a high minimum income and to bar subordination contracts. In contrast, Rawls is willing to put starvation for the surfers on the menu, and is not very demanding about social relations in "private" associations.

The proximity with Sen's theory is more apparent but requires scrutiny. Sen defends equality of capabilities primarily in terms of freedom rather than responsibility, which suggests a similar orientation as the idea of equal autonomy. However, he does not seem to argue for any serious difference between capability sets and opportunity sets.[48] It is indeed possible to understand the word "freedom" in a way that is congruent with the notion of genuine choice prevailing in luck egalitarianism: when Sen proposes to define egalitarian justice in terms of capabilities rather than functionings, he explains that what is really important is not the actual level of achievement but the *access to* functionings. This notion of access may involve a pre-institutional notion of responsibility and be vulnerable to incompatibilist worries. For instance, Sen opposes fasting to starving as an illustration of the priority of access over achievement. In such an example, one may be worried that the fasting individual is actually influenced in a way that makes satisfactory nutrition genuinely out of reach for him. In contrast, the notion of freedom as it is used in the theory of equal autonomy refers to the ordinary activity of choice – the scope of which is defined by institutions – and to the chooser's education and information, as well as to the quality of the menu. In this approach one no longer asks whether the fasting individual has genuine nutritional opportunities. It is still worth asking whether the fasting individual is endowed with sufficient resources, proper social surroundings, education and information, but not whether these elements provide genuine op-

---

[47]For an exploration into this problem, see Brighouse and Fleurbaey (2005). In particular, it is shown there that the potential divergence between democratic decisions and just decisions is remedied by defining the fair shares of power in line with what justice requires, so that the exercise of collective autonomy spontaneously converges toward the just outcome.

[48]See in particular the exchange between Sen (1993) and Cohen (1993), and further developments on responsibility in Sen (1992, 1999).

portunities in a deep sense. To that extent the theory of equal autonomy is less demanding than an opportunity theory. In counterpart it becomes essential for the theory of equal autonomy to wonder whether endangering one's health without any concern on behalf of social institutions is a valuable life option to put on the menu. The policy conclusion that is likely to come out of this approach is that, while one should not forcefully feed people (out of respect for basic autonomy), the fasting individuals should be offered assistance of some kind if they endanger their health and autonomy. In contrast, the capability approach might be understood as implying that fasting to death is perfectly fine provided genuine opportunities are available.

The variant of Sen's theory which is defined in terms of "refined functionings," namely, functionings associated with the capability sets from which they are chosen, is more appealing because it makes it possible to record individual achievements and the way in which individuals value these achievements together with the other possibilities. Sen argues that refined functionings and capabilities are equivalent, on the ground that the chosen functionings are part of the capability set. This argument, however, ignores the clear informational difference between saying that "Jones has access to food" (a capability information) and saying that "Jones has access to food but fasts" (a refined functioning information). The capability approach will consider that Jones is well off, even though he may be close to dying, whereas the refined functioning approach permits a more comprehensive evaluation.[49]

Sen has not proposed a specific way to compare individual situations, beyond the general reference to the notion of capabilities or refined functionings. The egalitarian-equivalent approach proposed here can be seen as a concrete proposal for this purpose,[50] which enables us to take account of individual preferences over the various dimensions of functionings, including the activity of choice in their life.

The theory of equal autonomy shares features with other theories. It holds individuals responsible for their preferences, like Dworkin's theory of equality of resources (but rejects the *ex ante* approach epitomized in the hypothetical insurance and perhaps considers a wider set of life dimensions as the object of preferences). It advocates a high minimum income, like Van Parijs (but is not focused only on resources and is more demanding on social relations). It is an outcome-oriented approach, like Arneson's responsibility-catering prioritarianism, and the way in which individual situations are measured and compared might not be very different from possible applications of Arneson's objective-list definition of welfare (but it shuns all pre-institutional notions of responsibility and desert). It incorporates a concern for social relations as in Anderson's and

---

[49]More on this isse can be found in Fleurbaey (2006c).

[50]Sen (1985, 1992) has, however, made an interesting concrete suggestion of a partial ordering, in the form of the "intersection" approach which ranks an individual situation above another when it dominates it for all possible preference orderings, e.g., when it dominates in all dimensions. This method is unfortunately incompatible with the Pareto principle, as noted in Brun and Tungodden (2004). The egalitarian-equivalence approach satisfies the Pareto principle and is not an instance of the intersection approach.

Scheffler's approaches (but retains a distributive framework and an important place for the allocation of resources).[51]

10.9 Conclusion

In summary, the basic tenets of the proposed theory of equal autonomy are:

1. A basic freedom requirement: Individuals should be guaranteed not only equal status but also a basic bundle of freedoms and the basic means of autonomy, including guaranteed subsistence, training, and protection from subordination.

2. Priority to the worst-off via Egalitarian-Equivalence (for individuals above the basic freedom threshold), which implies the following features:

   (a) Compensation: Among individuals with identical preferences over the dimensions of life, priority is given to the worst-off as determined by these preferences.

   (b) Utility and preference liability: Utility (subjective satisfaction levels understood as individual judgments of life success) is full individual responsibility in the liberal sense – not happiness, which is one dimension of life – and liberal reward is also applied to preferences insofar as it is compatible with the compensation principle.

   (c) Respect of individual preferences over the dimensions of life, including the level of discretion and choice, and the quality of social relations.

The theory of equality of autonomy which has been articulated in this chapter remains vague on certain points, in particular the basic list of liberties which individuals should not be permitted to waive, and the definition of the set of reference situations that serves in the computation of the Egalitarian-Equivalence criterion. Working out these details, for which several reasonable options are likely to emerge, would require a richer analytical framework than the simple models that have been used in this book. In particular, it is important to think more about social relations than is usually the case in economic models. This is left for another occasion.

Even if the notion of moral responsibility which is the cornerstone of luck egalitarianism has been rejected here as ill-suited for the construction of a theory of distributive justice, we have seen that the concepts developed in this book are still useful in order to think about a notion of responsibility which plays a derivative role with respect to a more basic notion of freedom. This is because these concepts are really about liabilities, i.e., the fact of holding people responsible for certain characteristics, no matter how this assignment of

---

[51] See Dworkin (2000), Van Parijs (1995), Arneson (1999a,b, 2000a,b), Anderson (1999), Scheffler (2003, 2005).

responsibility is justified. In particular, the Egalitarian-Equivalence criterion appears as a promising concept for the comparison of situations across individuals with heterogenous and incommensurable views about the dimensions of life. This concept avoids the pitfalls usually thought to be associated with the construction of indexes of individual situations, and it also avoids the serious flaws of Dworkin's hypothetical insurance. It incorporates a good balance of compensation and liberal reward, and respects individual preferences.

This book was organized around two goals. The primary goal was to propose an analytical set-up for the analysis of the distributive implications of holding individuals partly responsible for their situation. This goal has essentially occupied the first nine chapters and would be accomplished if this book helped to clarify some debates about responsibility-sensitive egalitarianism. The last chapter served the secondary goal of making a particular contribution to the substance of the debate on "equality of what?" It is hoped that, even if the reader does not agree with the theory of equal autonomy put forth at the end, she will still find the concepts articulated in this book of some use for her own reflection on these difficult topics.

Bibliography

Ackerman B. 1980, *Social Justice in the Liberal State*, New Haven: Yale University Press.

Alkan A., G. Demange, D. Gale 1991, "Fair allocation of indivisible goods and criteria of justice", *Econometrica* 59: 1023–1040.

Anderson E. 1999, "What is the point of equality?", *Ethics* 109: 287–337.

Armstrong C. 2006, *Rethinking Equality. The Challenge of Equal Citizenship*, Manchester: Manchester University Press.

Arneson R.J. 1989, "Equality and equal opportunity for welfare", *Philosophical Studies* 56: 77–93.

Arneson R.J. 1990a, "Liberalism, distributive subjectivism, and equal opportunity for welfare", *Philosophy and Public Affairs* 19: 158–194.

Arneson 1990b, "Primary goods reconsidered", *Noûs* 24: 429–454.

Arneson R.J. 1997a, "Egalitarianism and the undeserving poor", *Journal of Political Philosophy* 5: 327–350.

Arneson R.J. 1997b, "Postcript 1995", in L. Pojman, R. Westmoreland (eds.), *Equality: Selected Readings*, Oxford: Oxford University Press.

Arneson R.J. 1998, "Real freedom and distributive justice", in J.F. Laslier, M. Fleurbaey, N. Gravel, A. Trannoy (eds.), *Freedom in Economics, New Perspectives in Normative Analysis*, London: Routledge.

Arneson R.J. 1999a, "Equality of opportunity for welfare defended and recanted", *Journal of Political Philosophy* 7: 488–497.

Arneson R.J. 1999b, "Human flourishing versus desire satisfaction", *Social Philosophy and Policy* 16: 113–142.

Arneson R.J. 2000a, "Luck egalitarianism and prioritarianism", *Ethics* 110: 339–349.

Arneson R.J. 2000b, "Welfare should be the currency of justice", *Canadian Journal of Philosophy* 30: 497–524.

Arneson R.J. 2001, "Luck and equality", *Proceedings of the Aristotelian Society Supplement* 75: 73–90.

Arneson R.J. 2003, "The Smart theory of moral responsibility and desert", in S. Olsaretti (ed.), *Desert and Justice*, Oxford: Oxford University Press.

Arneson R.J. 2007, "Desert and equality", in N. Holtug, K. Lippert-Rasmussen (eds.), *Egalitarianism. New Essays on the Nature and Value of Equality*, Oxford: Oxford University Press.

Arneson R.J. 2008, "Rawls, responsibility, and distributive justice", in M. Fleur-
baey, M. Salles, J. Weymark (eds.), *Justice, Political Liberalism, and Utilitarianism. Themes from Harsanyi and Rawls*, Cambridge: Cambridge University
Press.
Arnsperger C. 1994, "Envy-freeness and distributive justice", *Journal of Eco-
nomic Surveys* 8: 155–186.
Arrow K.J. 1963, *Social Choice and Individual Values*, New York: John Wiley.
Arrow K.J. 1971, "A utilitarian approach to the concept of equality in public
expenditures", *Quarterly Journal of Economics* 85: 409–415.
Arrow K.J. 1973, "Some ordinalist-utilitarian notes on Rawls's theory of jus-
tice", *Journal of Philosophy* 70: 245–263.
Atkinson A.B. 1970, "On the measurement of inequality", *Journal of Economic
Theory* 2: 244–263.
Atkinson A.B. 1983, *Social Justice and Public Policy*, Cambridge, MA: MIT
Press.
Atkinson A.B. 1995, *Public Economics in Action*, Oxford: Clarendon Press.
Baker J., K. Lynch, S. Cantillon, J. Walsh 2004, *Equality. From Theory to
Action*, Basingstoke: Palgrave Macmillan.
Barbera S., W. Bossert, P.K. Pattanaik 2004, "Ranking sets of objects", in
S. Barbera, P.J. Hammond, C. Seidl (eds.), *Handbook of Utility Theory*, vol. 2,
Dordrecht: Kluwer.
Barclay L. 2007, "Feminist distributive justice and the relevance of equal rela-
tions", in N. Holtug, K. Lippert-Rasmussen (eds.), *Egalitarianism. New Essays
on the Nature and Value of Equality*, Oxford: Oxford University Press.
Barry B. 1991, *Liberty and Justice: Essays in Political Theory*, vol. 2, Oxford:
Oxford University Press.
Barry B. 2005, *Why Social Justice Matters*, Cambridge: Polity Press.
Blackorby C., D. Donaldson 1988, "Cash versus kind, self-selection, and efficient
transfers", *American Economic Review* 78: 691–700.
Boadway, R., M. Keen 2000, "Redistribution", in A.B. Bourguignon, F. Bour-
guignon (eds.), *Handbook of Income Distribution*, vol. 1, Amsterdam: North-
Holland.
Boadway R., M. Marchand, P. Pestieau and M.M. Racionero 2002, "Optimal re-
distribution with heterogeneous preferences for leisure", *Journal of Public Eco-
nomic Theory* 4: 475–498.
Border K. 1985, *Fixed Point Theorems with Applications to Economics and
Game Theory*, Cambridge: Cambridge University Press.
Bossert W. 1995, "Redistribution mechanisms based on individual characteris-
tics", *Mathematical Social Sciences* 29: 1–17.
Bossert W., M. Fleurbaey 1996, "Redistribution and compensation", *Social
Choice and Welfare* 13: 343–355.
Bossert W., M. Fleurbaey, D. Van de gaer 1999, "Responsibility, talent, and
compensation: A second-best analysis", *Review of Economic Design* 4: 35–56.
Brighouse H., M. Fleurbaey 2005, "On the fair allocation of power", mimeo,
University of Pau.
Broome J. 1984, "Selecting people randomly", *Ethics* 1: 38–55.

Brun B.C., B. Tungodden 2004, "Non-welfarist theories of justice: Is the 'intersection approach' a solution to the indexing impasse?", *Social Choice and Welfare* 22: 49–60.

Callinicos A. 2000, *Equality*, Cambridge: Polity Press.

Cappelen A.W., B. Tungodden 2002, "Responsibility and reward", *FinanzArchiv* 59: 120–140.

Cappelen A.W., B. Tungodden 2003, "Reward and responsibility: How should we be affected when others change their effort?", *Politics, Philosophy & Economics* 2: 191–211.

Cappelen A.W., B. Tungodden 2006a, "A liberal egalitarian paradox", *Economics and Philosophy* 22: 393–408.

Cappelen A.W., B. Tungodden 2006b, "Relocating the responsibility cut: should more responsibility imply less redistribution?", *Politics, Philosophy and Economics* 5: 353–362.

Cappelen A.W., B. Tungodden 2007a, "Fairness and the proportionality principle", mimeo, Norwegian School of Economics.

Cappelen A.W., B. Tungodden 2007b, "Local autonomy and interregional equality", *Social Choice and Welfare* 28: 443–460.

Cappelen A.W., B. Tungodden 2007c, "Rewarding effort", *Economic Theory*, forthcoming.

Carter I. 1999, *A Measure of Freedom*, Oxford: Oxford University Press.

Carter I. 2005, "Equal opportunity and equal freedom: The fate of the destitute in left-libertarianism", mimeo, University of Pavia.

Champsaur P., G. Laroque 1981, "Fair allocations in large economies", *Journal of Economic Theory* 25: 269–282.

Clayton M., A. Williams 1999, "Egalitarian justice and interpersonal comparison", *European Journal of Political Research* 35: 445–464.

Cohen G.A. 1989, "On the currency of egalitarian justice", *Ethics* 99: 906–944.

Cohen G.A. 1993, "Equality of what? On welfare, goods, and capabilities", in M.C. Nussbaum and A.K. Sen (eds.), *The Quality of Life*, Oxford: Clarendon Press.

Cohen G.A. 2004, "Expensive tastes rides again", in J. Burley (ed.), *Dworkin and his Critics*, Oxford: Blackwell.

Cook P.J., Graham D.A. 1977, "The demand for insurance and protection: The case of irreplaceable commodities", *Quarterly Journal of Economics* 91: 143–156.

Daniel T.E. 1975, "A revised concept of distributional equity", *Journal of Economic Theory* 11: 94–109.

Dardanoni V. 1993, "Measuring social mobility", *Journal of Economic Theory* 61: 372–394.

Dardanoni V., G.S. Fields, J.E. Roemer, M.L. Sanchez Puerta 2006, "How demanding should equality of opportunity be, and how much have we achieved?" in G.S. Fields, D. Grusky and S. Morgan (eds.), *Mobility and Inequality: Frontiers of Research from Sociology and Economics*, Palo Alto: Stanford University Press.

Deschamps R., L. Gevers 1979, "Separability, risk-bearing, and social welfare judgments," in J.J. Laffont (ed.), *Aggregation and Revelation of Preferences*, Amsterdam: North-Holland.

De-Shalit A., J. Wolff 2007, *Disadvantage*, Oxford: Oxford University Press.

Devooght K. (2007), "To each the same and to each his own: A proposal to measure responsibility-sensitive income inequality", *Economica*, OnlineEarly Articles.

Diamantaras D., W. Thomson 1990, "A refinement and extension of the no-envy concept", *Economics Letters* 33: 217–222.

Diamond P.A. 1967, "Cardinal welfare, individualistic ethics, and interpersonal comparisons of utility: Comment", *Journal of Political Economy* 75: 765–766.

Diamond P.A. 1998, "Optimal income taxation: An example with a U-shaped pattern of optimal marginal tax rates", *American Economic Review* 88: 83–95.

Dowding K. 2008, "Luck and responsibility", in M. Matravers, L. Meyer (eds.), *Democracy, Equality and Justice*, London: Routledge.

Dworkin R. 1981a, "What is equality? Part 1: Equality of welfare", *Philosophy & Public Affairs* 10: 185–246.

Dworkin R. 1981b, "What is equality? Part 2: Equality of resources", *Philosophy & Public Affairs* 10: 283–345.

Dworkin R. 2000, *Sovereign Virtue. The Theory and Practice of Equality*, Cambridge, MA: Harvard University Press.

Dworkin R. 2002, "Sovereign Virtue revisited", *Ethics* 113: 106–143.

Ehrenreich B. 2001, *Nickel and Dimed. On (Not) Getting By in America*, New York: Henry Holt and Company.

Eyal N. 2007, "Egalitarian justice and innocent choice", *Journal of Ethics and Social Philosophy* 2: 1–18.

Feldman A., A. Kirman 1974, "Fairness and envy", *American Economic Review* 64(6): 995–1005.

Feldstein M. 1958, "The optimal level of social security benefits," *Quarterly Journal of Economics* 100: 303–320.

Fingarette H. 2004, *Mapping Responsibility. Explorations in Mind, Law, Myth, and Culture*, Chicago: Open Court.

Fischer J.M., M. Ravizza 1998, *Responsibility and Control: A Theory of Moral Responsibility*, Cambridge: Cambridge University Press.

Fleurbaey M. 1994, "On fair compensation", *Theory and Decision* 36: 277–307.

Fleurbaey M. 1995a, "Equality and responsibility", *European Economic Review* 39: 683–689.

Fleurbaey M. 1995b, "Equal opportunity or equal social outcome?", *Economics and Philosophy* 11: 25–56.

Fleurbaey M. 1995c, "The requisites of equal opportunity", in W.A. Barnett, H. Moulin, M. Salles, N.J. Schofield (eds.), *Social Choice, Welfare, and Ethics*, Cambridge: Cambridge University Press.

Fleurbaey M. 1995d, "Three solutions for the compensation problem", *Journal of Economic Theory* 65: 505–521.

Fleurbaey M. 2001, "Egalitarian opportunities", *Law and Philosophy* 20: 499–530.

Fleurbaey M. 2002, "Equality of resources revisited", *Ethics* 113: 82–105.

Fleurbaey M. 2005, "Freedom with forgiveness", *Politics, Philosophy and Economics* 4: 29–67.

Fleurbaey M. 2006a, "Assessing risky social situations", mimeo, Paris-Descartes University.

Fleurbaey M. 2006b, "Social welfare, priority to the worst-off and the dimensions of individual well-being", in F. Farina, E. Savaglio (eds.), *Inequality and Economic Integration*, London: Routledge.

Fleurbaey M. 2006c, "Capabilities, functionings and refined functionings", *Journal of Human Development* 7: 299–310.

Fleurbaey M. 2007a, "Social choice and just institutions: New perspectives", *Economics and Philosophy* 23: 15–43.

Fleurbaey M. 2007b, "Social choice and the indexing dilemma", *Social Choice and Welfare* 29: 633–648.

Fleurbaey M., F. Maniquet 1996, "Fair allocation with unequal production skills: The No-Envy approach to compensation", *Mathematical Social Sciences* 32: 71–93.

Fleurbaey M., F. Maniquet 1999, "Fair allocation with unequal production skills: The solidarity approach to compensation", *Social Choice and Welfare* 16: 569–583.

Fleurbaey M., F. Maniquet 2004, "Compensation and responsibility," forthcoming in K.J. Arrow, A.K. Sen, K. Suzumura (eds.), *Handbook of Social Choice and Welfare*, vol. 2, Amsterdam: North-Holland.

Fleurbaey M., F. Maniquet 2005, "Fair orderings with unequal production skills," *Social Choice and Welfare* 24: 93–128.

Fleurbaey M., F. Maniquet 2006, "Fair income tax", *Review of Economic Studies* 73: 55–83.

Fleurbaey M., F. Maniquet 2007, "Help the low-skilled or reward the hardworking. A study of fairness in optimal income taxation", *Journal of Public Economic Theory* 9: 467–500.

Fleurbaey M., F. Maniquet 2008, "Utilitarianism versus fairness in welfare economics," in M. Fleurbaey, M. Salles and J.A. Weymark (eds.), *Justice, Political Liberalism and Utilitarianism: Themes from Harsanyi and Rawls*, Cambridge: Cambridge University Press.

Fried B. 2003, "Ex ante/ex post", *Journal of Contemporary Legal Issues* 13: 123–160.

Gaertner W., Schwettmann L. 2007, "Equity, responsibility and the cultural dimension" *Economica* 74: 627–649.

Gale D. 1960, *The Theory of Linear Economic Models*, New York: McGraw-Hill.

Gaspart F. 1996, "A contribution to the theory of distributive justice", Ph.D. thesis, FUNDP, Namur.

Gaspart F. 1998, "Objective measures of well-being and the cooperative production problem", *Social Choice and Welfare* 15: 95–112.

Gomberg P. 2007, *How to Make Opportunity Equal: Race and Contributive Justice*, Oxford: Blackwell.

Goodin R.E. 1998, "Social welfare as a collective social responsibility", in D. Schmitz and R. E. Goodin (eds.), *Social Welfare and Individual Responsibility*, Cambridge: Cambridge University Press.

Gordon-Solmon K. 2005, "Luck, love, and extreme skiing. Why egalitarians shouldn't aim to neutralize luck", mimeo, University of Oxford.

Goux D., E. Maurin 2002, "On the evaluation of equality of opportunity for income: Axioms and evidence", mimeo, INSEE, Paris.

Greene J., J. Cohen 2004, "For the law, neuroscience changes nothing and everything", *Philosophical Transactions B, Royal Society* 359: 1775–1785.

Hammond P.J. 1979, "Equity in two-person situations", *Econometrica* 47: 1127–1136.

Hammond P.J. 1981, "Ex-ante and ex-post welfare optimality under uncertainty", *Economica* 48: 235–250.

Hild M., A. Voorhoeve 2004, "Equality of opportunity and opportunity dominance", *Economics and Philosophy* 20: 117–146.

Hurley S.L. 2003, *Justice, Luck, and Knowledge*, Cambridge, MA: Harvard University Press.

Imrohoroglu A., Imrohoroglu S., Joines D.H. 2003, "Time-inconsistent preferences and social security", *Quarterly Journal of Economics* 118: 745–784.

Iturbe-Ormaetxe I. 1997, "Redistribution and individual characteristics", *Review of Economic Design* 3: 45–55.

Iturbe-Ormaetxe I., J. Nieto 1996, "On fair allocations and monetary compensations", *Economic Theory* 7: 125–138.

Jacobs L.A. 2004, *Pursuing Equal Opportunities. The Theory and Practice of Egalitarian Justice*, Cambridge: Cambridge University Press.

Kolm S.C. 1968, "The optimal production of social justice", in H. Guitton, J. Margolis (eds.), *Economie Publique*, Paris: Ed. du CNRS.

Kolm S.C. 1972, *Justice et équité*, Paris: Ed. du CNRS. Rep. and transl. as *Justice and Equity*, Cambridge, MA: MIT Press, 1999.

Kolm S.C. 1996a, "The theory of justice", *Social Choice and Welfare* 13: 151–182.

Kolm S.C. 1996b, *Modern Theories of Justice*, Cambridge, MA: MIT Press.

Kolm S.C. 2004a, "Liberty and distribution: Macrojustice from social freedom", *Social Choice and Welfare* 22: 113–146.

Kolm S.C. 2004b, *Macrojustice. The Political Economy of Fairness*, New York: Cambridge University Press.

Kranich L. 1994, "Equal division, efficiency, and the sovereign supply of labor", *American Economic Review* 84(1): 178–189.

Laibson D. 1997, "Golden eggs and hyperbolic discounting", *Quarterly Journal of Economics* 112: 443–477.

Lake C. 2001, *Equality and Responsibility*, Oxford: Oxford University Press.

Layard R. 2005, *Happiness. Lessons from A New Science*, London: Penguin.

Lefranc A., N. Pistolesi, A. Trannoy 2006, "Equality of opportunity: Definitions and testable conditions, with an application to income in France", IDEP Working Paper #62.

Lefranc A., N. Pistolesi, A. Trannoy 2007, "Inégalité de milieu d'origine et destin salarial en France, 1977–1993", *Revue d'Economie Politique* 117: 91–118.

Le Grand J. 1991, *Equity and Choice*, London: HarperCollins Academic.

Lippert-Rasmussen K. 2001, "Egalitarianism, option luck, and responsibility", *Ethics* 111: 548–579.

Luttens R.I. and E. Ooghe 2007, "Is it fair to make work pay?", *Economica* 74: 599–626.

Maniquet F. 1998, "An equal-right solution to the compensation-responsibility dilemma", *Mathematical Social Sciences* 35: 185–202.

Maniquet F. 2004, "On the equivalence between welfarism and equality of opportunity", *Social Choice and Welfare* 23: 127–148.

Mariotti M. 2003, "Opportunities, chances in life and inequality", mimeo, University of London.

Markandya A. 1982, "Intergenerational exchange mobility and economic welfare", *European Economic Review* 17: 307–324.

Martinez M. 2004, "Une contribution à la mesure de la mobilité intergénérationnelle", Ph.D. thesis, EHESS Paris.

Maskin E. 1999, "Nash equilibrium and welfare optimality", *Review of Economic Studies* 66: 23–38.

Mason A. 2006, *Levelling the Playing Field. The Idea of Equal Opportunity and its Place in Egalitarian Thought*, Oxford: Oxford University Press.

Matravers M. 2002a, "Luck, responsibility, and 'the jumble of lotteries that constitutes human life", *Imprints* 6: 28–43.

Matravers M. 2002b, "Responsibility, luck, and the 'Equality of What?' debate", *Political Studies* 50: 558–572.

Mirrlees J. 1971, "An exploration in the theory of optimum income taxation", *Review of Economic Studies* 38: 175–208.

Mirrlees J. 1986, "The theory of optimal taxation", in K.J. Arrow, M.D. Intriligator (eds.), *Handbook of Mathematical Economics*, vol. 3, Amsterdam: North-Holland.

Moreno-Ternero J.D. 2007, "On the design of equal-opportunity policies", *Investigaciones Económicas* 31: 351–374.

Moreno-Ternero J.D., J.E. Roemer 2006, "Impartiality, priority, and solidarity in the theory of justice", *Econometrica* 74: 1419–1427.

Moreno-Ternero J.D., J.E. Roemer 2007, "The veil of ignorance violates priority", CORE Discussion Paper.

Moulin H. 1994, "La présence d'envie: comment s'en accommoder?", *Recherches Economiques de Louvain* 60: 63–72.

Moulin H., W. Thomson 1997, "Axiomatic analysis of resource allocation problems", in K.J. Arrow, A.K. Sen, K. Suzumura (eds.), *Social Choice Re-examined*, vol. 1, International Economic Association, New York: St. Martin's Press and London: Macmillan.

Nehring K., C. Puppe 1999, "On the multi-preference approach to evaluating opportunities", *Social Choice and Welfare* 16: 41–63.

Nordhaus W., J. Tobin 1973, "Is growth obsolete?", in *The Measurement of Economic and Social Performance, Studies in Income and Wealth*, NBER, vol. 38.

Nussbaum M.C. 1993, "Non-relative virtues: An Aristotelian approach", in M.C. Nussbaum, A.K. Sen (eds.), *The Quality of Life*, Oxford: Clarendon Press.

OECD 2005, "Alternative measures of well-being", DELSA/ELSA 10.

Ooghe E., L. Lauwers 2005, "Non-dictatorial extensive social choice", *Economic Theory* 25: 721–743.

Ooghe E., E. Schokkaert, D. Van de gaer 2007, "Equality of opportunity versus equality of opportunity sets", *Social Choice and Welfare* 28: 209–230.

Otsuka M. 2002, "Luck, insurance, and equality", *Ethics* 113: 40–54.

Parfit D. 1995, "Equality or priority", Lindley Lecture, Lawrence: University Press of Kansas.

Pazner E., D. Schmeidler 1974, "A difficulty in the concept of fairness", *Review of Economic Studies* 41: 441–443.

Pazner E., D. Schmeidler 1978a, "Egalitarian equivalent allocations: A new concept of economic equity", *Quarterly Journal of Economics* 92: 671–687.

Pazner E., D. Schmeidler 1978b, "Decentralization and income distribution in Socialist economies", *Economic Inquiry* 16: 257–264.

Peragine V. 1999, "The distribution and redistribution of opportunity", *Journal of Economic Surveys* 13: 37–69.

Peragine V. 2002, "Opportunity egalitarianism and income inequality", *Mathematical Social Sciences* 44: 45–64.

Peragine V. 2004a, "Measuring and implementing equality of opportunity for income", *Social Choice and Welfare* 22: 187–210.

Peragine V. 2004b, "Ranking income distributions according to equality of opportunity", *Journal of Economic Inequality* 2: 11–30.

Phillips A. 1999, *Which Equalities Matter?*, Cambridge: Polity Press.

Phillips A. 2004, "Defending equality of outcome", *Journal of Political Philosophy* 12: 1–19.

Phillips A. 2006, " 'Really' equal: Opportunities and autonomy", *Journal of Political Philosophy* 14: 18–32.

Piketty T. 1994, "Existence of fair allocations in economies with production", *Journal of Public Economics* 55: 391–405.

Ramsay M. 2004, "Equality and responsibility", *Imprints* 7: 269–296.

Rawls J. 1971, *A Theory of Justice*, Cambridge, MA: Harvard University Press.

Rawls J. 1974, "Reply to Alexander and Musgrave", *Quarterly Journal of Economics* 88: 633–655.

Rawls J. 1982, "Social unity and primary goods", in A.K. Sen, B. Williams (eds.), *Utilitarianism and Beyond*, Cambridge: Cambridge University Press.

Rawls J. 1988, "The priority of right and ideas of the good", *Philosophy & Public Affairs* 17: 251–276.

Rawls J. 1993, *Political Liberalism*, New York: Columbia University Press.

Rawls J. 2001, *Justice as Fairness. A Restatement*, Cambridge, MA: Harvard University Press.

Ripstein A. 1999, *Equality, Responsibility, and the Law*, Cambridge: Cambridge University Press.

Rochet J.C., L.A. Stole 2003, "The economics of multidimensional screening", in M. Dewatripont, L.P. Hansen, S.J. Turnovsky (eds.), *Advances in Economics and Econometrics. Theory and Applications, Eighth World Congress*, vol. 1, Cambridge: Cambridge University Press.

Roemer J.E. 1985, "Equality of talent", *Economics and Philosophy* 1: 151–187.

Roemer J.E. 1986, "Equality of resources implies equality of welfare", *Quarterly Journal of Economics* 101: 751–784.

Roemer J.E. 1993, "A pragmatic theory of responsibility for the egalitarian planner", *Philosophy & Public Affairs* 22: 146–166.

Roemer J.E. 1996, *Theories of Distributive Justice*, Cambridge, MA: Harvard University Press.

Roemer J.E. 1998, *Equality of Opportunity*, Cambridge, MA: Harvard University Press.

Roemer J.E. 2002a, "Egalitarianism against the veil of ignorance", *Journal of Philosophy* 99: 167–184.

Roemer J.E. 2002b, "Equality of opportunity: A progress report", *Social Choice and Welfare* 19: 455–471.

Roemer J.E. et al. 2003, "To what extent do fiscal regimes equalize opportunities for income acquisition among citizens?", *Journal of Public Economics* 87: 539–565.

Roemer J.E. 2004, "Equal opportunity and intergenerational mobility: Going beyond intergenerational income transition matrices", in Miles Corak (ed.), *Generational Income Mobility in North America and Europe*, Cambridge: Cambridge University Press.

Ruiz-Castillo J. 2003, "The measurement of inequality of opportunities", in J. Bishop and Y. Amiel (eds.), *Research in Economic Inequality* 9: 1–34.

Scanlon T. 1986, "Equality of resources and equality of welfare: A forced marriage?", *Ethics* 97: 111–118.

Scanlon T. 1988, "The significance of choice", in S. McMurrin (ed.), *The Tanner Lectures on Human Values*, vol. 8, Salt Lake City: University of Utah Press.

Scheffler S. 1992, "Responsibility, reactive attitudes, and liberalism in philosophy and politics", *Philosophy & Public Affairs* 21: 299–323.

Scheffler S. 2003, "What is egalitarianism?", *Philosophy & Public Affairs* 31: 5–39.

Scheffler S. 2005, "Choice, circumstance and the value of equality", *Politics, Philosophy and Economics* 4: 5–28.

Schokkaert E., K. Devooght 1998, "The empirical acceptance of compensation axioms", in J.F. Laslier, M. Fleurbaey, N. Gravel, A. Trannoy (eds.), *Freedom in economics. New perspectives in normative analysis*, London: Routledge.

Schokkaert E., K. Devooght 2003, "Responsibility-sensitive fair compensation in different cultures", *Social Choice and Welfare* 21: 207-242.

Schokkaert E., G. Dhaene, C. Van de Voorde 1998, "Risk adjustment and the trade-off between efficiency and risk selection: An application of the theory of fair compensation", *Health Economics* 7: 465–480.

Schokkaert, E., D. Van de gaer, F. Vandenbroucke, R. Luttens 2004, "Responsibility-sensitive egalitarianism and optimal linear income taxation", *Mathematical Social Sciences* 48: 151–182.

Schokkaert, E. and Van de Voorde, C. 2004, "Risk selection and the specification of the conventional risk adjustment formula", *Journal of Health Economics* 23: 1237–1259.

Schokkaert, E. and Van de Voorde, C. 2007, "Incentives for risk selection and omitted variables in the risk adjustment formula", *Annales d'Economie et Statistique* 82: 327–352.

Schlesinger H. 1984, "Optimal insurance for irreplaceable commodities", *Journal of Risk and Insurance* 51: 131–137.

Sen A.K. 1970, *Collective Choice and Social Welfare*, San Francisco: Holden-Day.

Sen A.K. 1973, *On Economic Inequality*, Oxford: Clarendon Press.

Sen A.K. 1985, *Commodities and Capabilities*, Amsterdam: North-Holland.

Sen A.K. 1988, "Freedom of choice: Concept and content", *European Economic Review* 32: 269–294.

Sen A.K. 1990, "Welfare, freedom, and social choice: A reply", *Recherches Economiques de Louvain* 56: 327–355.

Sen A.K. 1992, *Inequality Reexamined*, Oxford: Clarendon Press.

Sen A.K. 1993, "Capability and well-being", in M.C. Nussbaum and A.K. Sen (eds.), *The Quality of Life*, Oxford: Clarendon Press.

Sen A.K. 1999, *Development as Freedom*, New York: Alfred A. Knopf.

Shiffrin S.V. 2004, "Egalitarianism, choice-sensitivity, and accommodation", in R.J. Wallace, P. Pettit, S. Scheffler and M. Smith (eds.), *Reason and Value. Themes from the Moral Philosophy of Joseph Raz*, Oxford: Oxford University Press.

Shorrocks A.F. 1984, "Inequality decomposition by subgroups", *Econometrica* 52: 1369–1386.

Sprumont Y. 1997, "Balanced egalitarian redistribution of income", *Mathematical Social Sciences* 33: 185–202.

Stiglitz J.E. 1987, "Pareto efficient and optimal taxation and the New New Welfare Economics", in A.J. Auerbach, M. Feldstein (eds.), *Handbook of Public Economics*, Amsterdam: North-Holland.

Suzumura K. 1983, *Rational Choice, Collective Decisions, and Social Welfare*, Cambridge: Cambridge University Press.

Svensson L. G. 1983, "Large indivisibles: An analysis with respect to price equilibrium and fairness", *Econometrica* 51: 939–954.

Tadenuma K., W. Thomson 1995, "Refinements of the no-envy solution in economies with indivisible goods", *Theory and Decision* 39: 189–206.

Thomson W. 1988, "A study of choice correspondences in economies with a variable number of agents", *Journal of Economic Theory* 46: 237–254.

Thomson W. 1994, "Notions of equal, or equivalent, opportunities", *Social Choice and Welfare* 11: 137–156.

Tungodden B. 2005, "Responsibility and redistribution: The case of first best taxation", *Social Choice and Welfare* 24: 33–44.

Vallentyne P. 2002, "Brute luck, option luck, and equality of initial opportunities", *Ethics* 112: 529–587.

Vallentyne P. 2007, "Brute luck and responsibility", mimeo, University of Missouri-Columbia.

Valletta G. 2007, "A fair solution to the compensation problem", mimeo, CORE.

Van de gaer D. 1993, "Equality of opportunity and investment in human capital", Ph.D. thesis, K. U. Leuven.

Van de gaer D., M. Martinez, E. Schokkaert 2001, "Three meaning of intergenerational mobility", *Economica* 68: 519–538.

Vandenbroucke F. 2001, *Social Justice and Individual Ethics in an Open Society. Equality, Responsibility, and Incentives*, Berlin: Springer-Verlag.

Van der Veen R. 2004, "Basic income versus wage subsidies: Competing instruments in an optimal tax model with a maximin objective", *Economics and Philosophy* 20: 147–184.

Van Parijs P. 1990, "Equal endowments as undominated diversity", *Recherches Economiques de Louvain* 56: 327–355. ·

Van Parijs P. 1995, *Real Freedom for All*, Oxford: Oxford University Press.

Van Parijs P. 1997, "Social justice as real freedom for all: A reply to Arneson, Fleurbaey, Melnyk and Selznick", *The Good Society* 7(1): 42–48.

Varian H. 1974, "Equity, envy and efficiency", *Journal of Economic Theory* 9: 63–91.

Varian H. 1975, "Distributive justice, welfare economics, and the theory of fairness", *Philosophy & Public Affairs* 4: 223–247.

Villar A. 2005, "On the welfare evaluation of income and opportunity", *Contributions to Theoretical Economics* 5(1), Article 3.

Voorhoeve A. 2005, "Equal opportunity, equality, and responsibility", Ph.D. thesis, UCL, London.

Voorhoeve A. 2007, "Scanlon on substantive responsibility", *Journal of Political Philosophy*, forthcoming.

Wallace R.J. 1994, *Responsibility and the Moral Sentiments*, Cambridge, MA: Harvard University Press.

Williams A. 2004, "Equality, ambition and insurance", *Proceedings of the Aristotelian Society Supplement* 78: 131–150.

Wolff J. 1998, "Fairness, respect, and the egalitarian ethos", *Philosophy & Public Affairs* 27: 97–122.

Yaari M.E., M. Bar-Hillel 1984, "On dividing justly", *Social Choice and Welfare* 1: 1–24.

Young I.M. 1990, *Justice and the Politics of Difference*, Princeton: Princeton University Press.

Index